PROCESSING THE EXPERIENCE

STRATEGIES TO ENHANCE AND GENERALIZE LEARNING

Second Edition

John L. Luckner, Ed.D.
Reldan S. Nadler, Psy.D.

True North Leadership, Inc.
1235 Coast Village Road, Suite F, Montecito, CA 93108
805-565-9997 ❖ FAX 805-565-0043

KENDALL/HUNT PUBLISHING COMPANY
4050 Westmark Drive   Dubuque, Iowa 52002

To order additional copies of this or other Kendall/Hunt books, please call customer service at 800-228-0810, 319-589-3020, or fax us at 800-772-9165. We are open 7:00 a.m. to 6 p.m. central standard time, Monday through Friday.

BIOGRAPHIES

Dr. Luckner is a Professor in the Division of Special Education at the University of Northern Colorado. He has spent the past 20 summers working for Outward Bound and other adventure-based programs. Dr. Luckner's expertise is in the field of education. His current interests include developing and implementing experienced-based programs in schools as well as providing training for educators, corporations, and therapists. He lives in Greeley, Colorado with his wife, Sue and his daughter, Maya.

Dr. Nadler is a leadership consultant and licensed clinical psychologist. He is a principal in True North Leadership, Inc. a leadership development and change management firm. Since 1974, he has been creating training programs in experiential learning with various organizations from Outward Bound Schools to Fortune 100 companies. Dr. Nadler's expertise lies in bringing leading edge organizational and psychological concepts to his corporate training's. Currently, he is developing and implementing innovative programs for leaders in hospitals, families, and corporations. He lives in Santa Barbara, California with his wife Juli, son Dillon, and new baby daughter, McKensey.

CONTENTS

FOREWORD

Each of us are a product of our heritage, and our experiences. We can't change our history, but we can optimize each experience by adhering to the following guiding principles:

The experience is coming, get ready, envision your end result.

The experience is new, be open to it.

The experience is novel, embrace it.

The experience is unique, expect the best.

The experience is challenging, establish the skills and resources you need, encourage yourself.

The experience is a problem, reflect on it, identify what is already working.

The experience is complex, ask for help, solicit other viewpoints.

The experience is confusing, verbalize your feelings and thoughts.

The experience is overwhelming, stay with it, revisit your end again, take your next step.

The experience is frightening, breathe, focus, move forward.

The experience is fun, share it with others.

The experience elicits tense feelings, endure it and talk about it.

The experience puts you on the edge, normalize it and take a risk.

The experience is a failure, learn from it, what worked? what didn't work?

The experience is a success, examine and identify your success factors and write the new story.

The experience is exhilarating, celebrate it, internalize it, share the new story.

The experience is affirming, where else can you use it and teach others?

The experience is over, revisit it, recycle it, reuse it.

The experience is a metaphor for your life, make it meaningful!

ACKNOWLEDGMENTS

We would like to thank the many persons who have assisted us in the completion of this new text. First, we both would like to express gratitude to the 23 contributors, who gave of their time and expertise to help improve the breadth and depth of this book. Thanks for your dedication to the field and to learning. We also want to acknowledge Gregg Butterfield for his years of friendship, dialogue, and for helping us always see, and enjoy, the lighter side of life.

John would like to thank his wife, Sue for her love, friendship, unwavering commitment, and wisdom. His daughter, Maya for her insatiable curiosity, heart-warming smile and laugh, and playful disposition. You each provide a daily reminder of what is important and rewarding in life.

Relly would like to acknowledge his wife Juli for her continual support, patience, and encouragement. His son, Dillon for his inspiration, demonstration of the beauty of learning, and overall excitement, especially when he sees his picture in this book. To the Nadler and Brown family, Ann, Martin, Patricia, Nancy, Larry and Ivan, along with the Hayes family for their love, fun times, faith and strong support. To Terry Horsmon for his creativity, synergy, and partnership in generating some of these ideas. To Tiffany Lona for the many hours of support in putting this book together.

INTRODUCTION

"What is of greatest consequence in a person's life is not just the nature and extent of his or her experiences but what has been learned from them."

—N. Cousins

We are very fortunate. We have been good friends for more than 35 years—a time period that has seen us transition from *pre*-puberty to *pre*-maturely gray; from playing hide-n-go-seek in the neighborhood to playing peek-a-boo with each other's child. Throughout this time period, we have shared an incredible number of experiences together. We've also spent extensive hours processing those experiences—at least now we know enough to call it processing; when we were younger, we used to call it "figuring stuff out."

One thing that we recently "figured-out" is that it's an exciting time to be an experiential educator, trainer or therapist. It is an era of accelerating change, forcing each of us to grow and learn in many new ways. It is also a time period of great opportunity. The fields of education, psychology, and business are now becoming united in using experiential approaches to promote learning, change, and growth. Consequently, experiential learning is found in corporate-training rooms, educational classrooms, therapeutic-group rooms as well as in the community, parks and wilderness settings.

What is an experience? It is an event, training, activity, occurrence, adventure, experi-

ment, endeavor, lecture, outing, undertaking, project, seminar, quest, escapade, happening, or effort. The experience is nothing more than a reference point or marker in one's life. It can be overlooked, discounted, passed by, ignored, or forgotten. Then again, it can be the turning point, catalyst, energizer, enzyme, breakthrough, impetus, stimulus, incentive, or driving force for great changes and learning. The experience is just the experience. What we bring into it, take from it, leave there, reach for, and continue to use, are all up to us. The difference between a lackluster experience and a truly great experience is how we use it as a reference point in our life story. What sense does it make to us? What difference will it matter? How can we look it up or retrieve it when we really need it? Making experiences usable, relevant, far-reaching, and connected to other learning are the goals of this book. Educators, trainers, and therapists are the midwives of the learning experience. In the experience lies the heart beat and life potential. Our job is to help the seeds of experience develop into a rich and meaningful story that can inspire participants throughout the seasons of their lives.

This text is about learning. It is a celebration of all the work that dedicated educators, trainers, and therapists, have compiled over the decades to help each of us understand the importance of active involvement in the learning process—as well as concern for the total development of individuals—social, psychological, and intellectual. It is also an attempt to summarize our current understanding of how to promote and to expand learning. We draw from our personal experiences as lifelong learners, the literature from psychology, education, business, and organizational development, as well as the expertise of many professionals, whose lives have been significantly altered through their involvement in experiential learning, therapy and training.

Throughout this text, we use the term "learning" to describe the method by which we acquire skills, knowledge, values, attitudes, and emotions. It involves a relatively permanent change in behavior and/or in mental associations as a result of participation in an experience (Ormrod, 1990). It is our contention that learning is enhanced through active involvement in personally, meaningful experiences accompanied by processing for meaning, differences and for future use. While some processing takes place automatically as a result of the brain's ongoing search for meaningful patterns in experience, there is a great deal that we can do strategically to enhance and generalize learning (Caine & Caine, 1994).

In order for experiences to be more than incidental undertakings they must have meaning that enables us to think, feel, and behave in useful ways in the future (Knapp, 1990). As professional trainers, educators and therapists, we need to be able to structure experiences that maximize learning rather than allowing learning to be left to chance. The better that we understand the factors that influence learning and the processes that underlie it, the better we can design experiences that will benefit individuals, and continue to be reference-points and turning-points throughout their lives.

"Processing" (sometimes referred to as debriefing, reflecting, analyzing, or generalizing) facilitates the sorting and ordering of information. Processing promotes the consolidation and internalization of information by the learner in a way that is both meaningful and conceptually coherent. It is the pathway to understanding and application, rather than simply to memory. Processing is not just a stage in an experience. It does not occur at one, specific time, it happens before, during, and after the experience. Nor is it something that can be done in only one way. It is a matter of constantly co-constructing, co-creating, and editing the information so that individuals can internalize the meaning from the experience.

Because experiential approaches to learning, training and therapy require each of us to make numerous, instantaneous decisions based on new information as well as rely on our intuition and previous experiences, there will never be a recipe for processing that can be handed-down from one professional to the next. However, if we are knowledgeable, skilled, prepared, and able to focus on the needs of the individuals we work with and the objectives that they would like to achieve, we can become highly-skilled professionals.

We believe that this text is a valuable resource for all experiential educators, trainers and therapists. The information within is practical, and it can be used in a variety of settings. We divided the book into 6 primary parts. In the **Rationale** we define experiential learning and processing—this can be considered *the what* of the text. In the **Theory** sections, we provide support for using an experiential approach and processing—answering the question *why*. In the next three sections—**Effective Leadership Knowledge and Skills, Application and Practice,** and **Notes from Experts**

in the Field, we address the nuts and bolts issues of *how to process experiences* with attention to a wide array of populations, age groups, and settings. These sections will have the practitioner's tool kit bulging! The text ends with *reflections* from a couple of seasoned, experiential educators sharing their perceptions of **Current and Future Perspectives.** Then two appendices, an extensive **Reference and Resource List** and some **Reproducible Transperencies,** that you can use to integrate cognitive content into experiential learning.

In addition to the comprehensive and multi-dimensional information that is provided, we have been able to convince well-known leaders in the field to share their knowledge and perspectives. Consequently, we have included 7 case studies as well as responses to each case study from noted practitioners. All together, we have twenty-three

(23) guest contributors. There are also 12 Leadership topics written to use as teaching units along with 13 reproducible transparencies to help enhance your processing and presentations. To enhance the transference and generalization of learning experiences there are also 85 learning activities and retention strategies.

In summary, it is our belief that when we are knowledgeable and skilled at something, we are able to relax more, be more spontaneous, and have more fun doing what we are doing. The purpose of this text is to increase knowledge and skills. As a result, we hope it will permit us to better facilitate our own learning as well as the learning of the people with whom we work. We hope that you learn as much from reading and using this book as we have learned from writing it.

CONTRIBUTORS

Dene Berman, Ph.D., and Jennifer Davis-Berman, Ph.D., have Lifespan Counseling Associates, a multidisciplinary counseling practice, one component of which is the Wilderness Therapy Program. They are authors of *Wilderness Therapy: Foundations, Theory, and Research.* Dene is a psychologist and a Clinical Professor in the School of Professional Psychology at Wright State University. Jen is a social worker and an Associate Professor in the Department of Sociology, Anthropology and Social Work at the University of Dayton.

Christian Bisson is currently completing a Doctoral degree in pedagogy with emphasis in adventure education at the University of Northern Colorado. He has been involved in outdoor experiential education since 1986. He has worked with young offenders in a longer term wilderness therapy program, been a Chief Instructor for a residential outdoor education center on Vancouver Island, and instructed seasonally for the National Outdoor Leadership School (NOLS) since 1991.

Micheal Gass, Ph.D., is Professor in the Department of Kinesiology/School of Health and Human Services and Coordinator of Outdoor Education Program at the University of New Hampshire. He also is the Project Director of the Family Expedition Program and a Professional-in-Residence at the Marriage and Family Therapy Center. He frequently serves as a consultant for therapeutic and corporate organizations interested in systemic change. His address is NH Hall, 124 Main Street, UNH; Durnham, NH 03824. Phone (603) 862-2024. FAX (603) 862-0154. Email mgass@christa.unh.edu.

Jackie Gerstein, Ed.D., is a Licensed Professional Clinical Counselor and an Assistant Professor at Western New Mexico University (WNMU). Her areas of specialization include counseling and teaching others to counsel children, youth, and families. She is the author of *Experiential Family Counseling: A Practitioners Guide to Orientation, Warm-Ups, and Family Building Initiatives.* She can be contacted at WNMU, School of Education, PO Box 680, Silver City, NM 88062, (505)-538-6426.

Lee Gillis, Ph. D., is a licensed psychologist who has worked with Project Adventure's direct service therapeutic programs. He is also an associate professor of psychology at Georgia College and directs a master degree program in adventure therapy. Lee has worked with adolescents populations in adventure settings since 1975 in camps, schools, and treatments settings. He can be reached at Project Adventure, Inc. PBX 2447 Covinton, GA 30210 770-784-9310 or by email at Igillis@mail.gac.peachnet.edu or on the wide world web at http://advthe.gac.peachnet.edu

John Guarrine, M.Ed., is the director of the Sunrise Lake Outdoor Education Center (SLOEC). SLOEC specializes in providing outdoor experience for children of all abilities and all ages. Sunrise Lake facilities and programs are specifically designed to serve children with disabilities, ages three to twenty-one years. The center is an extension of the services provided by the Northwest Suburban Special Education Organization. John is also an instructor at the College of DuPage.

Juli Hayes, R.D., is a registered Dietician with eleven years of experience working with eating disorders. She has worked in both hospital and out patient clinic settings, served as a consultant to hospital eating disorder programs, and worked with the University of California at Santa Barbara eating disorder education program. She is currently in private practice in Santa Barbara, California where she lives with her husband Relly Nadler and son Dillon.

Terry Horsmon, M.B.A., is a principal in True North Leadership, Inc., and an expert in providing organizational change programs to businesses of all sizes. He specializes in strategic planning, corporate reorganization, and creation of customized leadership tools for change-driven organizations. Terry holds an M.B.A. from Harvard University Graduate School of Business, and A.B. from Amherst College, and was a Presidential Fellow at Yale University.

John Huie, Ph.D., served as Executive Director of North Carolina Outward Bound School 1977–1994. He began his career in adventure education in 1960's as an instructor and program director at the Minnesota Outward Bound School. He pioneered experiential outdoor programs at St. Mark's School of Texas, Queen University (Ontario), and Verde Valley School (Arizona) where he served as headmaster. John is Director Emeritus of the North Carolina Outward Bound School. He is Executive Director of the Environmental Leadership Center of Warren Wilson College, Ashville, NC, one of the country's most environmentally focused liberal arts colleges.

Richard Jenkins, M.Ed., has an extensive twenty-five years' background in the area of student personnel services. He currently serves as an advisor to campus organizations at the University of California, Santa Barbara. He enjoys consulting with students from diverse ethnic backgrounds and rich cultural traditions. He hold two masters degrees, one in Confluent Education and the other in Counseling and Guidance. This year he will continue to pursue his doctorate in the field of education.

Stephen Klett, M.A., is a founding partner and president of Peak Performance Associates, Inc., a leadership and team development firm utilizing experiential methodologies. Steve serves on the adjunct faculty of the Center of Creative Leadership, the U.S. government's Western Executive Development Center, and the management development programs of numerous Fortune 500 companies.

Jeff Nelson is the Program Director for the Minnesota program of the Voyageur Outward Bound School (VOBS). Previously, Jeff was the associate program director in charge of staffing. Prior to becoming involved in administration, Jeff instructed and course directed courses for youth-at-risk, adults in transition, young adolescents, semester students, and standard populations. Jeff can be reached at VOBS, P.O. Box 450, Ely, Minnesota 55731, (218) 365-5761.

Dennis Nord is a licensed psychologist and the Associate Director for Career Services at Counseling and Career Services, UCSB in Santa Barbara, CA. He has been leading retreats with

Debbie Connor and Steve Roberts of Teamworks and Camp Whitier. He can be reached at 805-893-4411 or by email zcapn@seaside.quad.ucsb.edu.

Craig Penner, M.A., M.F.C.C., is a licensed Marriage, Family, and Child Counselor in private practice in Santa Barbara, CA. In addition to psychotherapy, he works as a clinical supervisor, graduate school instructor, corporate consultant and adventure therapy facilitator. Craig draws on his orientation in Gestalt Therapy and Solution-Focused Therapy to enhance the opportunities for growth that come from experiential learning.

William J. Quinn, Ph.D., is an Associate Professor at Northeastern Illinois University in Chicago, where he teaches Adventure Education theory and skills in the undergraduate program. Bill is also the President of Cliffs and Cables, a challenge course construction, training and consulting organization. He is an avid outdoor trip leader and participant. He has taught for the Voyageur Outward Bound school in Minnesota, provided consultation to many organizations in the northern Illinois area and has delivered corporate team building programs at home and abroad.

Karl Rohnke recently finished 25 years as an employee for Project Adventure (PA), Inc. During that time period he served as President of the company for 11 years. Currently he is working part time for PA and part time for himself. He has published over ten books in the field of adventure education and looks forward to having more time to write.

Suzanne Rudolph, Ed.D., is a licensed Clinical Psychologist and Clinical Member of the American Association for Marriage and Family Therapy. She worked as an instructor for the Voyageur Outward Bound School for eight years. She currently has a private practice in Loveland and Greeley, Colorado.

John Ruffin is the president of The Synergy Group, an organization development consulting firm in Santa Barbara, CA, specializing in organizational systems and performance improvement. John has been an OD consultant for the past 18 years and has served a nationwide client base in both the private and public sectors. The Synergy Group provides consulting in strategy formulation, performance system development, training in decision making and problem solving, managing the dejobbed workplace, and conducts a considerable amount of teambuilding using adventure programming techniques. The Synergy Group may be contacted at 2069 Las Canoas Rd., Santa Barbara, CA 93105, or at 1 (800) 6-Synergy, or by FAX at (805) 898-3679.

Jim Stiehl, Ph.D., is the Coordinator of the University of Northern Colorado's (UNC) Outdoor Physical Education (OPE) program. He is also an instructor with the National Outdoor Leadership School (NOLS). Jim strives to enhance people's respect and responsbility toward themselves, others, and their surroundings. The undergraduate and graduate OPE programs at UNC prepare teachers and leaders to advance outdoor adventure experiences, especially in school settings.

Paul Suding is the program coordinator for True North Leadership, Inc. in Santa Barbara, California. He lives there with his wife, son and daughter. Besides his experience as a facilitator, Paul has had experiential learning of the best kind to help him with his contribution on addictions. At the date of publication, Paul has been in recovery, clean and sober, for over ten years and hopes that by facilitating ropes courses, he is "carrying this message to other alcoholics and addicts. . . ."

Tom Vache't is President of VisionWorks, which provides sales, marketing, and general management consulting. He has a diversity of sales and corporate management experience. In addition, his work in the development of corporate marketing materials he has won several prestigious awards. Tom resides in Moorpark, CA.

Wendy Webb, M.A., has a Masters Degree in Counseling Psychology. She works as an independent contractor in outdoor adventure programs combining her therapeutic skills with an extensive background in outdoor education. She currently resides in Big Bear Lake, California and can be reached at P. O. Box 414, Big Bear Lake, CA 92315 or at (909) 866-2657.

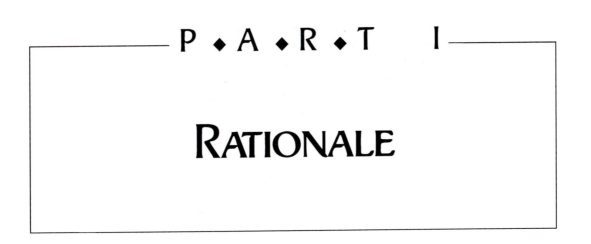

P ◆ A ◆ R ◆ T   I

RATIONALE

Experiential Learning—What Is It?
Processing—What Is It?
Why Process?

EXPERIENTIAL LEARNING— WHAT IS IT?

"We don't receive wisdom; we must discover it for ourselves after a journey that no one can take for us or spare us."

—*Marvel Proust*

Experiential learning is learning through doing. It is a process through which individuals construct knowledge, acquire skills, and enhance values from direct experience (Association of Experiential Education, 1995). Experiential learning occurs when individuals engage in some activity, reflect upon the activity critically, derive some useful insight from the analysis, and incorporate the result through a change in understanding and/or behavior. Experiential learning is based on the assumption that all knowing must begin with the individual's relationship to the topic. The effectiveness of experiential learning is derived from the maxim that, "nothing is more relevant to us than ourselves." One's own reactions to, observations about, and understanding of something are more important than someone else's opinion about it.

Experiential learning is a philosophical orientation toward teaching and learning which values and encourages linkages between concrete, educational activities and abstract lessons to maximize learning (Sakofs, 1986). What experiential learning does best is to instill a sense of ownership over what is learned. It adds to the interest and involvement of the participants, but most importantly it contributes significantly to the

transfer of learning. The ultimate result is that individuals accept responsibility for their own learning and behavior, rather than assigning that responsibility to someone else. Specific principles of experiential learning that have been adapted from the Association of Experiential Education, 1995; Kraft & Sakofs, 1985; and Weil & McGill, 1989 are presented in Table 1.

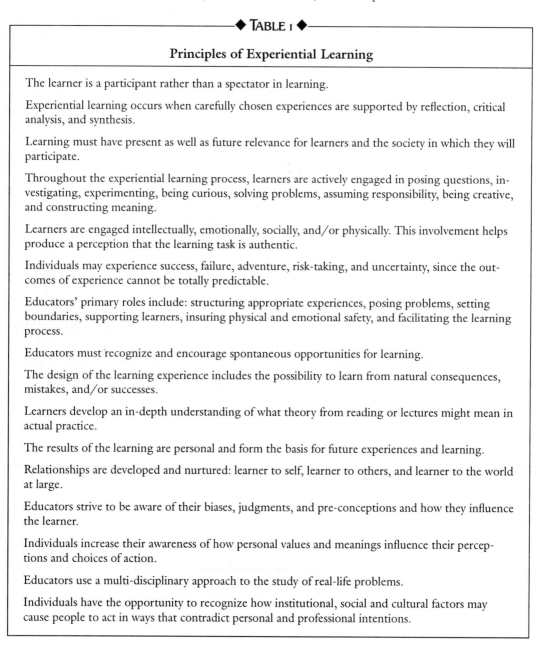

◆ TABLE 1 ◆

Principles of Experiential Learning

The learner is a participant rather than a spectator in learning.

Experiential learning occurs when carefully chosen experiences are supported by reflection, critical analysis, and synthesis.

Learning must have present as well as future relevance for learners and the society in which they will participate.

Throughout the experiential learning process, learners are actively engaged in posing questions, investigating, experimenting, being curious, solving problems, assuming responsibility, being creative, and constructing meaning.

Learners are engaged intellectually, emotionally, socially, and/or physically. This involvement helps produce a perception that the learning task is authentic.

Individuals may experience success, failure, adventure, risk-taking, and uncertainty, since the outcomes of experience cannot be totally predictable.

Educators' primary roles include: structuring appropriate experiences, posing problems, setting boundaries, supporting learners, insuring physical and emotional safety, and facilitating the learning process.

Educators must recognize and encourage spontaneous opportunities for learning.

The design of the learning experience includes the possibility to learn from natural consequences, mistakes, and/or successes.

Learners develop an in-depth understanding of what theory from reading or lectures might mean in actual practice.

The results of the learning are personal and form the basis for future experiences and learning.

Relationships are developed and nurtured: learner to self, learner to others, and learner to the world at large.

Educators strive to be aware of their biases, judgments, and pre-conceptions and how they influence the learner.

Individuals increase their awareness of how personal values and meanings influence their perceptions and choices of action.

Educators use a multi-disciplinary approach to the study of real-life problems.

Individuals have the opportunity to recognize how institutional, social and cultural factors may cause people to act in ways that contradict personal and professional intentions.

❖ EXPERIENTIAL LEARNING CYCLE

Experiential learning as an approach to education and therapy has grown in popularity over the past 20 years. In spite of its relative popularity, experiential learning remains a concept that is easier to experience than explain, and it encompasses many different viewpoints. These diverse perspectives cross a wide variety of disciplines and practices, which may include: traditional education, alternative education, career education, outdoor-adventure education, special education, therapy, social and cultural work, teambuilding and corporate training.

While experiential learning models vary from theorist to theorist (i.e., Dewey, 1938; Joplin, 1986; Kolb, 1984) it is generally agreed that there are four phases that comprise the experiential learning cycle (see Figure 1). The following are brief explanations for each of the phases. Although the stages of the model are presented in discrete terms, the interaction between them, and within them, is complex. A major challenge for educators and therapists who use experiential learning lies in the completion of the latter phases of the cycle. Often, the economics of time and the exhilaration of active involvement finds reflecting and generalizing relegated to brief blocks of time and a lack of closure. However, the implications of the model and the primary focus of this text is to stress the necessity for adequate planning and sufficient time for each step.

EXPERIENCING

Learning experiences are generated naturally in one's daily life, but they also can be arranged to provide opportunities for specific types of learning. Once specific learning objectives are identified, many types of activities and experiences can be selected to facilitate their achievement. The structured experience is the stage in which individuals participate in a specific activity. This is the data-generating part of an experience. If the process stops after this stage, all learning is left to chance, and instructors have not fulfilled their responsibilities for facilitating individuals' learning.

REFLECTING

Experience alone is insufficient to ensure that learning takes place. A need exists to integrate the new experience with past experiences through the process of reflection (Kolb, 1984). It is the reflection process which turns experience into experiential learning. People have experienced an activity and time needs to be allocated for individuals to look back and examine what they saw, felt, and thought about during the event. Reflection may be an introspective act in which the learner alone integrates the new experience with the old, or it may be a group process whereby sense is made of an experience by discussion.

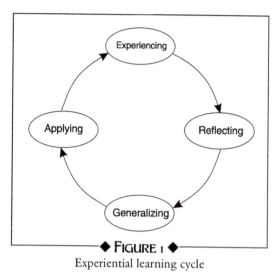

◆ FIGURE 1 ◆

Experiential learning cycle

GENERALIZING

If learning is to transfer from the structured experience to the other situations and settings, it is essential for individuals to be able to make inferences from this specific experience to everyday life. An essential aspect of experiential learning is the search for patterns. Patterns unite previously isolated incidents. This search for patterns is undertaken to explore whether emotions, thoughts, behaviors or observations occur with some regularity. When these emotions, thoughts, behaviors or observations are understood in one situation, this understanding can be generalized and applied to other situations. The meaningful question here is "So what?" Thus, the generalizations are to be made about "what tends to happen," not what specifically happened in this experience.

APPLYING

For experiential learning to be effective, it is necessary for individuals to use the learning that they acquired through participation in the structured experience and make an inferential leap to the outside world. Consequently, the key question of this stage is "Now What?" At this point, individuals are encouraged to plan ways to put into action the generalizations that they identified in the previous stage. The procedure of focusing attention from the structured experience to actual situations and settings in individuals' daily lives is what makes experiential learning practical and meaningful, and if it is overlooked or neglected, the learning is likely to be shallow and short-term.

EXPERIENCING

As indicated in the diagram of the experiential learning cycle (Figure 1) there is an arrow from "applying" to "experiencing." This indicates a belief that the application of learning becomes part of one's background knowledge for the next experience. In essence, the completion of these four steps brings us back to the beginning of the learning cycle which is then initiated by the next structured experience.

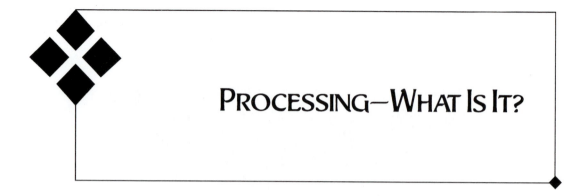

Processing—What Is It?

"Everything that happens to you is your teacher. The secret is to learn to sit at the feet of your own life and be taught by it."

—*Polly B. Berends*

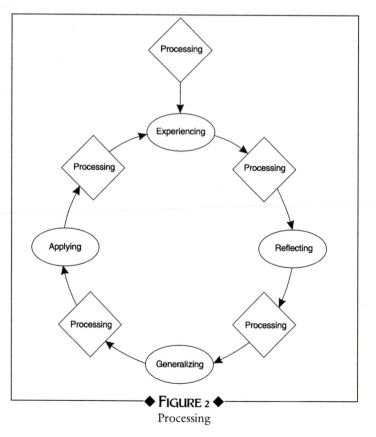

◆ **Figure 2** ◆
Processing

Our lives are comprised of billions of experiences. What is most important though is not just the quantity and quality of those experiences, but what we learn from each experience (Cousins, 1981). Processing is best viewed as an activity that is structured to encourage individuals to plan, reflect, describe, analyze, and communicate about experiences (Gass, 1993b; Knapp, 1990; Quinsland & Van Ginkel, 1984; Nadler & Luckner, 1992). As shown in Figure 2, processing can occur prior to, during, or after the experience. Processing activities can be used to: (a) help individuals focus or increase their awareness on issues prior to an event or to the entire experience; (b) facilitate awareness or promote change while an experience is occurring; (c) reflect, analyze, describe, or discuss an experience after it is completed; and/or (d) reinforce perceptions of change and promote integration in participants' lives after the experience is completed (Gass, 1993a).

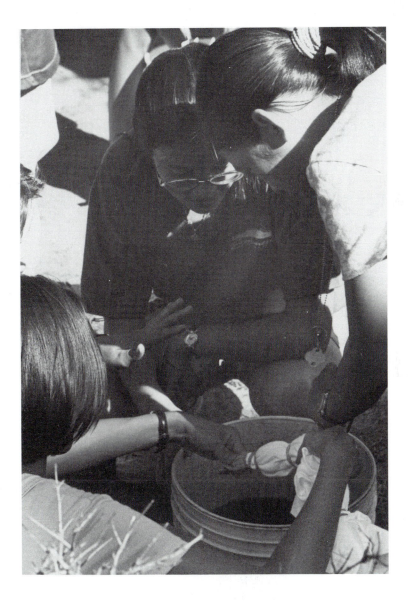

❖ WHY PROCESS?

"The belief that all genuine education comes about through experience does not mean that all experiences are genuinely or equally educative."

—*John Dewey*

In general, experiential educators and therapists agree that learning occurs through active extension and grounding of ideas and experiences in the external world, and through internal reflection about the attributes of the experiences and ideas (Kolb, 1984). Processing enhances the richness of the experience, so it stands out and apart, like the important lines of a page underlined with a yellow highlighter. These unique learnings then can be used again and generalized to other settings. When a new experience is processed, integrated, and internalized, individuals are able to grow, and as a result, they have more choices and influence in their lives.

Additional support for experiential learning and the essential role of processing for promoting learning and development can be found in four theories that have gathered considerable attention among educators and psychologists in recent years—brain research, active learning, constructivism, and narrative. A brief explanation of each theory and how it relates to processing the experience follows.

❖ Brain Research

Human beings are biologically driven to make sense of their world. While the primary function of the brain is health maintenance, recent brain research suggests that a critical function of the cognitive system is to search for patterns that can impose meaning on the input received in order to make sense of the chaos which surrounds us (Caine & Caine, 1994; Gruneberg & Morris, 1979). We do not input facts into a memory system as is done with a computer. Rather, learning is the process of constructing meaning—developing associated maps which continually evolve in response to experiences.

Learning represents the opening of new or enlarged neural pathways in the brain (Rose, 1989). The more powerful, significant or varied the experience or stimuli which initiated the learning, the stronger and more numerous are the synaptic connections, resulting in better understanding (Dozier, 1992). Our consciousness or reality is a model of the world that draws on the past—memory, the present—awareness and the future—extrapolation or anticipation of future events (Dozier, 1992).

Learning takes place when the brain sorts out patterns by using past experiences to help make sense out of the input that the brain receives. Recognition of patterns facilitates transfer of learning to new situations. Understanding concepts, behaviors, procedures, or skills result from perceiving relationships and linking what is being learned to the individual's past knowledge, current experience, and future needs and aspirations. Hart (1983) identified six major patterns to which the brain attempts to attach meaning:

1. Objects—dog, caterpillar, chairlift, desk, glacier, water fountain.
2. Actions—walking, running, swimming, hiking, working on a computer.
3. Procedures—getting dressed, showering, paddling a kayak, preparing a report.
4. Situations—taking a test, making a presentation, first-aid emergency.
5. Relationships—me/you, friend/enemy, supervisor/employee, sun/heat.
6. Systems—family, political, school, law, weather, organizations.

One of the most important lessons to derive from the brain research is that in a very important sense, all learning is experiential. Individuals are perceiving, patterning, and creating meanings, all the time in one way or another. We do not, however, automatically learn enough from our experiences. What matters is how each experience is used. Since, the brain is designed as a pattern detector, our primary function as facilitators of learning and development is to provide individuals with experiences that enable them to perceive "the patterns that connect" (Bateson 1980) while simultaneously allowing individuals to plan, reflect and generalize how and what they have learned, so they begin to take charge of learning and the development of personal meanings.

Learning is a natural, developmental process, the same as is breathing, eating, and sleeping, but like all processes, it can be either inhibited or enhanced. Caine and Caine (1994) suggest that educators, trainers and therapists who want to promote learning and development based on the principles of brain research should:

1. Design and orchestrate lifelike, enriching, and appropriate experiences for individuals. and
2. Ensure that individuals process experiences in such a way as to increase the extraction of personal meaning.

❖ ACTIVE LEARNING

Over the last decade the fields of education and cognitive psychology have produced a large and growing body of research that focuses on the teaching-learning processes (e.g., Harris & Pressley, 1991; Heron, 1989; Shuell, 1986). This research suggests that learning is not merely the acquisition of knowledge whereby information is delivered from teachers to their students, but rather learners create their own knowledge and understanding using the prior knowledge and experiences that they bring to the learning setting. As noted by Cross (1991) "Learning is not so much an additive process, with new learning simply piling up on top of existing knowledge, as it is an active, dynamic process in which the connections are constantly changing and the structure reformatted" (p.9).

For centuries, educators have relied upon the "transmission" model of teaching. Within the transmission model, educators deliver knowledge to students through lectures. This model of education may have been appropriate during our Agrarian age; however, as our society has transitioned to the Information age and the quantity of information appears to be doubling every 20 months (Beyer, 1987). The transmission model of teaching fails to prepare individuals for the future. As a result, there is a growing desire among educators to involve students more actively in learning projects and to assist them in becoming more self-regulated and autonomous learners who establish personal educational goals, employ learning strategies that are appropriate to task completion and manipulate learning environments to ensure success. This shift in perspective about the teaching/learning process requires educators to change how they define their roles as teachers. It means spending less time trying to be the "sage on the stage" and more time as the "guide on the side"—designing, supporting, and managing the learning environment and teaching process. Similar insight is surfacing in the corporate world where organizations are realizing that good ideas can't only come from the top, but also need to come from the frontline people, who are constantly interacting with customers, products, and services.

Professionals who are aware of the demands of our changing society and who want to prepare individuals who can meet these challenges are incorporating active learning strategies into their work. Active learning can be defined as learning in which individuals, by acting on objects and interacting with other people, ideas, and events, construct new understanding. Active learning derives from two basic assumptions: (1) that learning is by nature an active endeavor and (2) that different people learn in different ways. Active learning strategies help individuals connect what they are learning to their work and personal lives. Professionals who employ active learning are not giving students disembodied facts, figures, theories, and methodologies, but are sharing the practical ways that professionals go about working in their disciplines. Active learning strategies allow individuals to become self-directed, collaborative, and critically reflective; knowledge and skills that are essential to meaningful lives and careers. This transition in perspective currently is evident within many corporations who encourage employees to become better learners, so the corporation can function as a learning organization that is skilled at "creating, acquiring, and transferring knowledge and at modifying its behavior to reflect new knowledge and insights" (Garvin, 1993, p. 80).

Additional information about structuring learning environments that use active learning strategies are provided in the section entitled Educational Guiding Practices.

❖ CONSTRUCTIVISM

Constructivism is a theory of learning and change that is based on the premise that learning is a process whereby new meanings are created (constructed) by learners within the context of their current knowledge. Educators, trainers and therapists who support a constructivist perspective believe that knowledge is constructed in the process of reflection, inquiry, and action, by learners themselves. Efficient learning is predicated on individuals' active involvement in the learning process and opportunities for interactive communication among other learners (Fosnot, 1989).

Educators, trainers and therapists who adhere to a constructivist perspective contend that people are always trying to make sense of their own lives and the interactions they experience around them. The process of making sense of these interactions involves a never-ending search for and construction of personal meaning. Consequently, learning is not simply the taking in of new information as it exists externally; it is the natural, continuous construction and reconstruction of new, richer, connected, and more complex meanings by the learner.

One of the major tenets of constructivism is that individuals do not acquire knowledge from outside information given to them, but rather they learn by constructing new meanings from

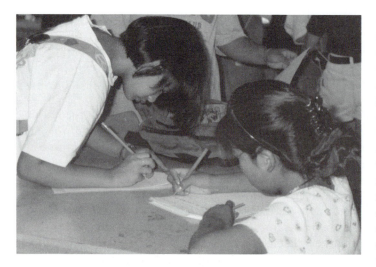

new and preceding experiences in a context of rich social interactions. Similarly, learning does not occur by transmission but by interpretation and interpretation is always influenced by prior knowledge. Individuals, in an attempt to make sense of new information and experiences, transform and organize the new information in relation to their own meaning-base. Consequently, learning is viewed as an organic process of invention, rather than a mechanical process of accumulation. As a result, constructivists view the learning process as analogous to impressionistic art rather than photography. Accordingly, educators, trainers and therapists who adhere to a constructivist perspective act as problem posers, coaches, and mediators. They help individuals put their own reasoning into words by raising questions and inviting them to share their opinions, solutions, reflections, and strategies with others. In addition, these constructivists encourage individuals to try to solve problems their own way and to observe and evaluate the results. They also ask probing questions or note aspects of the problem that will help individuals think about the problem in diverse ways.

Several principles of constructivism, adapted from Fosnot (1989) and Poplin (1988), which are especially applicable to the field of experiential education are found in Table 2.

❖ NARRATIVE

A story is a "telling or recounting of a string of events" (Scholes, 1982, p. 59). Social scientists such as Bruner (1985) who spoke of a narrative mode of thought and Sarbin (1986) who proposed story as a "root metaphor" for the study of human conduct, believe that the story helps individuals organize and understand new experiences and simultaneously provides a unit of meaning that stores and permits retrieval of experiences. As noted by Olson (1990), "Narrative structures provide a format into which experienced events can be cast in the attempt to make them comprehensible, memorable, and shareable" (p. 100–101). From this perspective, it is contended that we live storied lives; "human beings think, perceive, imagine, and make moral choices according to narrative structures" (Sarbin, 1986, p. 8).

Stories consist of events, characters, and settings that are gathered together into a plot in which significance and causality are given to the events, characters, and settings as they relate to the theme of the story. The plot configures the events into a whole, and the events are transformed from a series of independent happenings into meaningful happenings that contribute to the whole theme (Polkinghorne, 1988). In essence, stories become a way of capturing the com-

---

◆ TABLE 2 ◆

Principles of Constructivism

---

1. All people are learners, always actively searching for and constructing new meanings. Thus, they are always learning.

2. The process of learning is self-regulating and self-preserving.

3. Knowledge consists of past constructions.

4. The best predictor of what and how someone will learn is what they already know.

5. Learning often proceeds from whole to part to whole.

6. Errors promote growth and are critical to learning.

7. Meaningful learning occurs through reflection and resolution of cognitive conflict and thus serves to negate earlier, incomplete levels of understanding.

8. People learn best from experiences about which they are passionately interested and involved.

9. People learn best from people they trust.

10. The purpose of education is long-term knowledge that can be used flexibly and independently.

11. Teaching is a process of providing learners with experiences, activities, and prompts that enables them to make meaning through self-regulation.

12. Instructional goals change momentarily as learners gain knowledge and acquire new skills.

---

plexity, specificity, and interconnectedness of an experience and linking them into coherent, meaningful, unified themes.

Stories are not merely raw data from which to construct interpretations but products of an interpretive process that are shaped by the impulses of the author and by the requirements of narrative structure. The process of transforming experience into story is so much a part of our daily existence that we usually are not aware of its operation (Polkinghorne, 1988). Simultaneously, the stories we live by are not purely private inventions; rather, we build them from the information provided by experience, from the inventory of stories or prepackaged expectations, and ways of interpreting them supplied by our culture and from those significant individuals that we interact with in our lives (Chafe, 1990). With regard to experiential learning and therapy, the role of stories play an integral part in the following ways:

1. The story that is created from the experience determines the meaning given to the experience.
2. The stories determine the real effects, type and degree of transfer of the experience.
3. The stories select which aspects of the experience will be highlighted and then given expression.
4. The stories encompass the learning, and helps us store the information in our memory so that we can later generalize to other experiences.

As professionals seeking to promote learning and development, we can help individuals co-create their new stories that are developed as a result of their experiences as well as to help them re-create more positive perspectives of old stories. By helping them become aware of and articulate the narratives they have developed, this give richer meaning to their lives. Individuals are then able to examine and reflect on the themes they are using to organize their lives and to interpret their own actions and the actions of others. Additional information about how to process experiences using narratives is provided in the section on Effective Leaders Knowledge and Skills.

❖ SUMMARY

In summary, the challenges of living in our current world require each of us to (a) be able to effectively interact with others, (b) learn how to acquire information, (c) apply information; and (d) create new knowledge and information. These goals are best achieved in situations where individuals are supported and challenged to construct and apply meaning to experiences and activities which are relevant to their lives. In this section, experiential learning and the role of processing for facilitating learning and development has been substantiated from a variety of perspectives.

Because of the active and personal nature of experiential learning, each experience provides an avenue for thoughts, feelings, insights, metaphors, and behavior patterns to surface. These feelings, thoughts, and behaviors may continue to exist at an unconscious level if we do not take the time to reflect and articulate them. Processing is a developmental endeavor of discovering patterns and unique outcomes. It is a liberating and generating process that helps individuals construct a new reality or generate new meanings from their experiences. Our challenge as experiential educators, trainers and therapists is to help individuals become aware of their thoughts, feelings and behavior patterns and to promote the transfer and generalization of this new learning.

P ◆ A ◆ R ◆ T II

THEORY

❖ Promoting Change

"If I could wish for my life to be perfect, it would be tempting but I would decline, for life would no longer teach me anything."

—*Allyson Jones*

People develop and change over time as a result of their heredity, their environment, and the experiences that they have. As experiential educators and therapists we can further individuals' learning and development by establishing environments characterized by a state of dynamic tension (Doll, 1989). This state of dynamic tension is composed of two conditions: (1) a sense of safety and security, and (2) a sense of disequilibrium. Disequilibrium refers to an individual's awareness that a mismatch exists between old ways of thinking and new information. It is a state of internal conflict which comes from our innate drive to act and understand. Thus, providing motivation for individuals to integrate new knowledge or reshape existent perceptions. These qualitative and quantitative changes are referred to as the processes of accommodation and assimilation (Piaget, 1977).

As professionals, our greatest successes occur when we support, challenge, and help individuals internalize knowledge in a way that is

personally meaningful (Caine & Caine, 1994). Through involvement in experiences that are beyond one's comfort zone, individuals are forced to move into an area that feels uncomfortable and unfamiliar—the groan zone. By overcoming these anxious feelings and thoughts of self-doubt while simultaneously sampling success, individuals move from the groan zone to the growth zone. Figure 3, which has been adapted from Gerstein, (1990) attempts to represent how individuals involved in experiential education and/or therapy gain knowledge and skills. More specific information on the process of change is provided in the section entitled "Change Conditions."

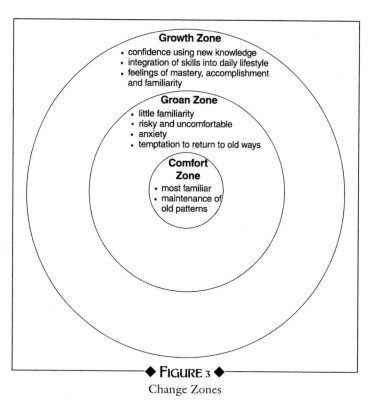

Growth Zone
- confidence using new knowledge
- integration of skills into daily lifestyle
- feelings of mastery, accomplishment and familiarity

Groan Zone
- little familiarity
- risky and uncomfortable
- anxiety
- temptation to return to old ways

Comfort Zone
- most familiar
- maintenance of old patterns

◆ FIGURE 3 ◆
Change Zones

GENERALIZATION AND TRANSFER

As previously indicated, one of the primary purposes of experiential learning is to assist individuals in developing insight, knowledge and skills that transfer to their lives when they complete a structured experience. Generalization of learning is the application of what individuals learned as a result of attending an educational or therapeutic program. Earlier in this text, we referred to this as the "so what" phase of the learning process. Transfer and generalization occur when the learning in one situation carries over to another. Individuals' real gain of participation in an experience is best measured by examining how much has been learned and whether or not it has been sustained and applied after the experience. Without such positive transfer, programs that use an experience-based approach have limited long-term value (Gass, 1993b).

The more individuals digest, synthesize, and assimilate what's happening to them, the more self-knowledge becomes available for learning and development. Increased awareness and understanding of feelings, thoughts, and behaviors provide people with a better chance of making changes in their lives, and in similar situations at work, school, and at home. The activities and events may be different, but the emotions, thoughts, and behavior patterns are not. Generalization and transfer can take place at the unconscious level. However, we can be more effective and increase the conscious aspects of the transfer of learning by considering several important factors:

1. Individuals must see the similarities between situations that happen during the experience and situations that have occurred in other aspects of life (e.g., resolving conflict verbally rather than stomping out or stuffing feelings).

2. Individuals who see that new knowledge or behaviors bring about beneficial results are more likely to be motivated to use this new learning (e.g., talking about fear, asking for support, sharing feelings).

3. It is helpful if individuals can identify opportunities to use new knowledge (e.g., planning to eat balanced meals and exercise to reduce stress). This is encouraged by realistically comparing a structured experience with specific past and possible future situations in their lives.

4. Meaningful learning promotes better transfer than rote learning.

5. The more thoroughly something is learned, the more likely it is to be transferred to a new situation.

6. Numerous and varied examples and opportunities for practice increase the extent to which knowledge and skills may be applied in new situations.

7. The probability of transfer decreases as the time interval between the original task and the transfer task increases.

The following figure attempts to illustrate the manner in which thoughts, feelings, and behaviors that occur during learning experiences likely exist in different settings. Processing helps individuals bring the circles closer together, and optimally they become interwoven so that the awareness and growth that occurs during the learning experience produces gains in other settings and situations. (See the "Learning Activities and Retention Strategies" section for additional information specific to transfer and generalization).

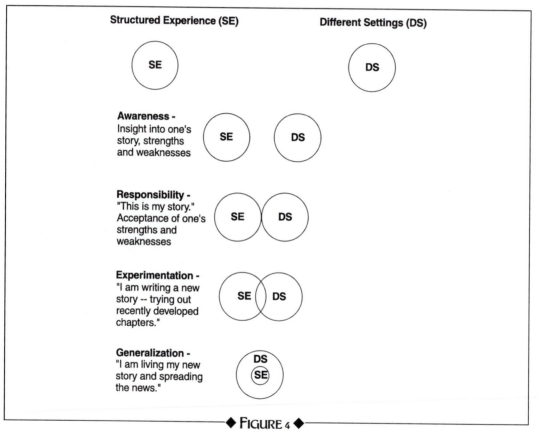

◆ FIGURE 4 ◆

Processing for generalization and transfer

CHANGE CONDITIONS

"Behold the turtle. He makes progress only when he sticks his neck out."
—*James Bryant Conant*

So how do people change? What positive internal and external factors affect change? Why is experiential-based learning, training and therapy such a powerful change agent? Primarily, the answers to these questions lie in the understanding of the role of disequilibrium, as described earlier. The state of disequilibrium creates an unorganized affect or ego-confusion wherein a quality of disorganization or dissonance predominates. The act of restructuring or reordering to re-gain balance (called equilibration) is where change in feelings, thoughts, attitudes, and behavior patterns occur. Ironically, it is in the process of getting lost, feeling anxious and/or uncomfortable, that individuals find direction and themselves. The process of change and conditions that enhance the state of disequilibrium are described below.

❖ DEFENSES

Carl Whitaker (1981) describes anxiety as the most primitive form of affect or feeling. People learn to develop defense mechanisms as an intrapersonal protection against their own anxiety. Some common defenses are: denial, blaming others, taking control, anger, aggressiveness, being overly-responsible, perfectionism, intellectualizing, charming others, and humor. These defenses protect individuals from feeling some of their deeper feelings, such as, fear, inadequacy, loneliness, hurt, rejection, embarrassment, and helplessness. Figure 5, which has been adapted from Wegscheider (1979), attempts to show how we protect those core feelings with specific, defensive behaviors.

When the wall of defenses is shaken, even momentarily, some deep feelings might be experienced more profoundly and become better integrated. The emotional arousal may be very intense at first. Without the normal defenses intact, disequilibrium becomes a driving force which increases emotional intensity. At these times, new ways of reacting and feeling can be tried

23

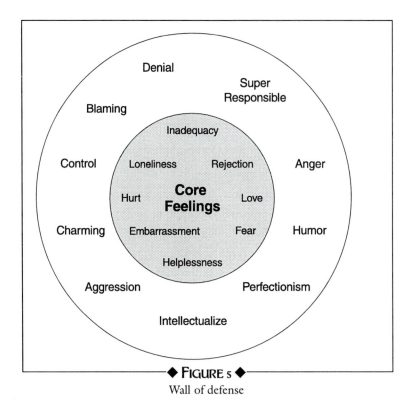

♦ FIGURE 5 ♦
Wall of defense

as means to reestablish equilibrium. Individuals can experience their feelings and deal with them in a unique way. This fresh experience can form the basis for new approaches to thinking, feeling, and acting.

Structured experiences that involve each of the following "change conditions" promote disequilibrium by lessening normal defense mechanisms. This process of disarmament forces people to search for new ways of relating, and it provides the foundation for having a meaningful experience.

❖ CHANGE CONDITIONS

These are conditions or states that people can be placed in order to accentuate disequilibrium, dissonance, disorder, frustration, or anxiety. Enhancing these feelings increases the need to order, restructure, or alter one's cognitive map of the world and of oneself in an effort to restore equilibrium. Ilya Prigogine (1984) calls this restructuring "order out of chaos." Each of these conditions may be overlapping or interdependent. Understanding these conditions and finding ways to create them can increase your ability to promote change.

1. *Hope*—This condition exists when individuals view the experience as a way to dissolve some of their problems, heal their wounds, or fulfill their needs. There is an expectation of a pos-

itive outcome or attainment of a new goal. You can enhance individuals' sense of hope by: (a) telling stories about what other people took away from the experience in the past; (b) asking participants to write down and share their goals; (c) talking about their goals and how there is real potential to attain them, and (d) helping participants break down their goals into smaller achievable steps, so that they can more readily reach their desired goals without being overwhelmed.

2. *Effort*—This condition entails taking physical, emotional, mental, and behavioral action. Risk-taking is encouraged. Every time one domain is activated, whether it is the cognitive, affective, or psychomotor, the other domains also become aroused. For example, the literature on running suggests that physical exercise also activates the emotions. In essence, there is a holistic connection that exists within our bodies.

Attention, concentration, and focusing are also aspects of effort. Another aspect of effort is surrender. It may take a lot of emotional effort to surrender to something, such as the situation or one's feelings. There are times that encouraging a surrender or giving up an unproductive pattern will entail a great deal of effort in order to generate a meaningful experience. Effort can be depicted by the clichés "Go for it!" or "You only know how far you can go by going too far." Additional ways that you can improve effort are by (a) encouraging all participants to talk and

share their thoughts and feelings, (b) appointing leaders or recorders for the day, (c) asking participants to experiment with new roles or behaviors, (d) pushing through resistance when people want to stop or quit, and (e) identifying a limit or "edge" and going one step beyond.

3. *Trust*—This condition connotes an assured reliance or confident dependence on others, one's self, the leader, and/or the experience. The more trust that exists; the easier it is to make an effort or endure the tension of being in disequilibrium. Learning to trust one's own abilities resulting in the increase in self-esteem is a fundamental outcome of experiential education. In the "Processing Activities" section, there is information on how to develop and enhance feelings of trust.

4. *Constructive Level of Anxiety*—This condition exists when individuals feel in trouble, ambivalence, confusion, dissonance, discomfort, frustration, or stress. You want to continue to assess the group and each individual to ensure that the anxiety level is constructive and safe. Humans feel vulnerable when there is anxiety. When this disorientation occurs, it is possible that something meaningful can seep in when the defense system is less intact. In the psychological literature, many authors call this "change condition" many terms. Alfred Ban-

dura calls it "emotional arousal"; Fritz Perls calls it "frustration"; and Ilya Prigogine calls it "chaos or fluxuatations." To change, old structures have to be dissipated, and new structures have to be built in their place. Anxiety causes people to leave the comfort zone, and try new behaviors to lessen the anxiety. You can enhance the constructive level of anxiety by (a) using handicaps (discussed in the section entitled Using Handicaps), (b) increasing the sense of the unknown, (c) increasing the perceptions of risk, (d) having participants experiment with new roles, and (e) doing activities differently or in novel ways.

5. *A Sense of the Unknown or Unpredictable*—This condition exists when individuals have a sense of awe or mystery regarding what they anticipate that they're going to experience. There's a limited time for rationalizing, defending, psyching-up or psyching-out. Individuals ask many questions when experiencing this ambiguity. When possible, answers should not be given, rather participants should be encouraged to experience and accept their feelings of uncertainty. As discussed in the section on "brain-based learning", human brains are designed to develop structures or make meaning. The more unknown, unfamiliar, and unpredictable the experience, the harder peo-

ple work to make sense of what is happening to them. The unpredictable keeps people off balance. They don't know what to set up barriers for, and as a result, they may experience something purely and naively. This sense of the unpredictable or unexpected compels individuals to live in the here and now.

The motivation to predict and control our environment and our behavior is very powerful and it's for this reason that the field of psychology emerged. When appropriate, you may harness this powerful change condition by (a) refraining from giving answers which let participants predict and control the future, (b) taking away watches from people if it is possible, (c) constantly changing rules or procedures so that participants live in the unexpected, (e) using handicaps, (f) increasing the constructive level of anxiety, and (g) enhancing the perception of risk.

6. *Perception of Risk*—This condition exists when individuals perceive the experience as either a physical, emotional, and/or behavioral risk or danger. It usually is a perceived risk and a participant may say something like "I feel I may die or get hurt." In most experiential programs, there is a large contrast between the perceived risk and actual risk. One of the major components of processing is to help the participants understand how their perceived risks are created and then transfer that learning to other perceived risks that exist in their lives.

Thompson (1981) stated, "Reactions to potentially stressful events depend on their meaning for the individual." She encourages people to assign meaning that will be most beneficial. You have many opportunities to use your processing skills to help participants integrate the learning and take responsibility for their perceptions. The perception of risk is engendered mostly by the activities. You can add to the perception of risk by (a) increasing the constructive level of anxiety, (b) increasing the sense of unknown and unpredictable by doing what is unexpected, and (c) developing behavior contracts for emotional and behavioral risks taken.

❖ SUMMARY

In summary, we have attempted to explain how to help people have meaningful learning and/or therapeutic experiences. We suggest that the more you can establish a supportive environment while simultaneously taking in consideration the six "change conditions" to create disequilibrium, the less individuals are able to use their defenses to arrest the growth process. Therefore, in an attempt to restore equilibration, participants reorder and restructure their cognitive, affective and behavioral maps. Consequently, they may be able to experience their core feelings in greater depth and come to feel better about themselves and the world that they live in.

EDGEWORK: CREATING BREAKTHROUGHS TO NEW TERRITORY

"If you want to succeed you should strike out on new paths rather than travel the worn paths of accepted success. "

—*John D. Rockefeller*

Disequilibrium, as mentioned earlier, is a major catalyst for change. This is true not only for individuals, but for systems and organizations, alike. Developments in physics and the natural sciences have led some recent organizational theorists to consider that disequilibrium might be a better strategy for survival in the corporate world than coherence and order (Kotter, 1996; Pascale, 1990; Wheatley, 1992). The thrust of this thinking is that the "creative tension" generated by internal differences and new points of view can widen an organization's options and abilities to change with the times. Smith (1984) writes that survival requires that organizations periodically "step out" of well-worn routines created and reinforced by past success.

In an effort to attenuate the disequilibrium, an individual or organization may experiment with a new "mind set", product, or action in order to experience success. It is in this brief moment or moments prior to a unique action or "breakthrough" that the ingredients for change are found. Here in these moments also resides information that will facilitate the transfer of learning from this success to other successes for the individual and the organization. This section will explore how to process the experience for these breakthroughs.

One of the cornerstones of experiential education and therapy is that we encourage people to try things that they wouldn't generally do on their own. In other words, they leave their safe, familiar, comfortable and predictable world for uncomfortable new territory. Like the pioneers and explorers who traveled to the "Old West" in search of fortune, we hope that the learning adventures of participants also will lead them to "gold." When they find the gold, we assume that they will locate additional treasures in their new territory. The assumption that the gold is the sole treasure to be gained from the journey is limiting. In actuality, it's the struggle of the journey between the known and unknown where the "gems" for future learning reside. Wheatley (1992) reinforces this when she writes, "Only by venturing into unknown do we enable new ideas to take shape, and those shapes are different for each voyager." (p. xii)

What is gained from the struggle can lead to learning that can be applied in the future. At the "edge" is where many explorers turned back because of the lack of water or food, battles with Native American Indians, or an inability to endure and tolerate the continual fears and apprehensions. Breaking through the edge into the realm of possibilities and the land of gold was thereby suppressed. It is at the edge of the breakthrough where processing the experience is most important. Figure 6 represents the journey between the two worlds, where individuals choose to either turn back or break through. Figure 7 attempts to show how personal growth or stretching previous risky and unknown experiences can be tamed and incorporated within the comfortable and safe zone, thus enhancing one's self-esteem.

So what happens at the edge? As people get closer to this unknown, new territory, their sense of disequilibrium increases and a sense of uncertainty exists. As mentioned earlier, the wall of defenses and habitual patterns become prominent in an effort to control the sense of disequilibrium. In addition, peoples' feelings intensify at the edge; they may be fearful, anxious, confused, excited, or feeling alone. Their physiological symptoms change, palms sweat, hearts race, respiration quickens, pupils dilate, posture stoops, faces become flush, and individuals may start pacing.

Also, the internal conversations we all have with ourselves gets louder, more frequent, and our self-limiting beliefs may surface, such as, "I can't do this"; "I won't"; "I'll fail"; "I'm stupid"; "I'll make a fool of myself"; "I must do it perfectly"; "Life is hard"; "The company has always done it this way"; "What will others think of me?"; or "There must be something wrong

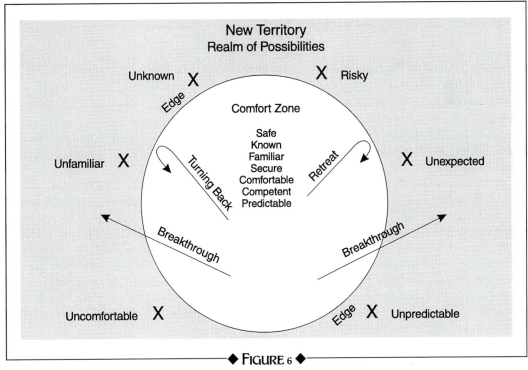

◆ FIGURE 6 ◆

Edgework: breaking through limits to new growth

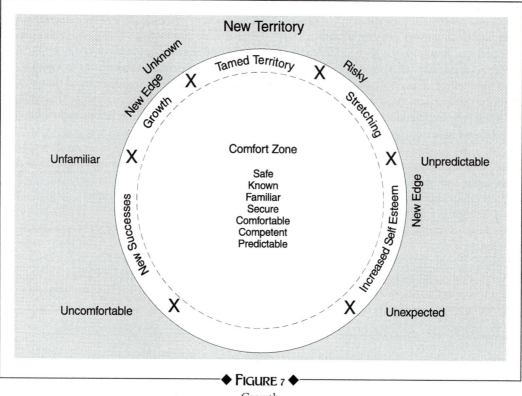

◆ FIGURE 7 ◆
Growth

with me." At the edge is also where feelings may be communicated via metaphors, such as "I feel like I'm about to be shot"; "I have a weight on my chest"; "I feel paralyzed"; "I feel dead inside"; or "It's like my heart is going to jump out of my body." All of these things happen in a split second at the edge, and individuals either break through and take the leap or turns back to their safe territory.

A wealth of valuable information is lost when we wait until everyone has completed a learning activity before asking individuals to reflect and process. Participants have experienced strong mental, emotional, and physiological changes; yet, by the time we make the time to discuss it with them, they have returned to equilibrium without developing a true awareness of what they recently experienced. As a result, future struggles at the edge are devoid of this knowledge, and they may simply react to these symptoms rather than act on, with, or in spite of them. The impact of repeating these same patterns without realizing it in the future may be poor business decisions, lost profits, inability to perform at the same level, relapse, low self-esteem, or attributing successes to luck or chance. In corporations, these repeated patterns are examples of "organizational learning disabilities" (Senge, 1990).

Some pioneers turned their wagons around and headed back East without realizing that they may have been only moments or miles away from gold or success. Similar missed opportunities have most likely happened to us and to participants as well. We can try to offset these

missed opportunities by doing "edgework" and processing for breakthroughs. In essence, we heighten the possibility of promoting change by using more of the experience as stimuli for growth and development.

❖ THE MOMENTS BEFORE SUCCESS

Learning takes place before doing, while doing, and after doing (Garvin, 1996). Typically, we process what happened after the doing or success, which we'll call S+1—the moments after the success. This is still very valuable and can be greatly enhanced when we explore what happened right at the edge while doing, or the moment or moments before the success—S-1. Usually these moments pass quickly without the awareness of individuals or the group and are generally lost for current and future learning. What we are advocating is putting this moment or moments at the edge **under a microscope** and examining the feelings, patterns, conversations, physiology, beliefs, support, and metaphors that encompass these moments. In effect, what we want to do is slow down or freeze the moments before the success or the retreat, so that individuals' thoughts, feelings, and actions that make up their strengths and/or weaknesses become conscious and both internally and externally communicated. We want to know what specifically happened at S-1 to allow for a successful leap, or what did the person do to retreat to safer territory? Herein, lies the golden nuggets to be treasured and used again and again when the experience is over, and new edges in other settings are approached.

In some circumstances, S-1 can be a split second, yet, in other activities, S-1 may last from a few minutes up to an hour. Some examples of the S-1 experiences include:

1. A manager expresses an idea that is counter to the new vision and obviously is not "walking the talk."
2. Walking across the "beam" on the ropes course, where the emotions are at their height. There may be a brief S+1 respite at the end of the beam before a new S-1 experience on the next event.
3. Being blindfolded in an activity for the first time will engender disequilibrium, tension, or anxiety.
4. The moments while the group is confused, frustrated, or anxious before figuring out how to solve a problem.
5. The moments on the perch before jumping for the trapeze bar while on the pamper pole exemplifies being on the edge with all its encompassing intensity.
6. You've talked about rock climbing and provided instruction in the area of climbing techniques and style. The frightened look in peoples' eyes as they look at the upcoming climb tells you that they are at S-1.
7. In your corporate group, the CEO just shot down someone's idea and there is an uncomfortable silence, before something is said again.

The experience and processing can be viewed in the following manner:

S-1	S	S+1
A. The edge	Success	A. Moments after the success
B. Freezing the moments before the success	or	B. Reflection about experience
C. Discovery of the success or retreat chemistry	Breakthrough	C. What can be taken away from the experience
D. Examining the components or ingredients		

Figure 8 is a graphic that identifies factors or components to look for when S-1 is put under the microscope.

❖ PROCESSING AT S-1

The following are thoughts and strategies that you can use to gather information about what happens the moment before a success or retreat. The learning **while doing** time frame yields rich data for generating new knowledge. There are two parts to consider: (a) what happened either to promote or inhibit a success—the ingredients or components existing at S-1; and (b) what can the individual bring to the edge to increase the likelihood of a success? We'll explore each of these major components.

First of all, using our levels of processing model, we want individuals and the group to be **aware** of what is happening at S-1. How do they personally sabotage their efforts or encourage their own successes? Next, in the **responsibility** level, we would like them to own these patterns, conversations, feelings, etc., and establish these as typical responses. At the **experimentation** level, participants will try new behaviors or strategies. When at the edge, they can utilize these

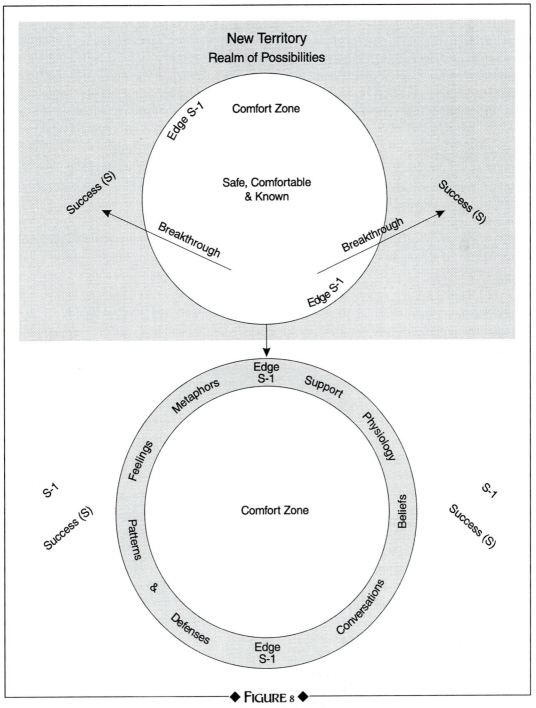

◆ FIGURE 8 ◆

Putting the edge under the microscope

new sources. And finally, with **generalization and transference,** participants can predict how they'll respond at new edges at home or work and be able to suggest resources or strategies to employ to bring about peak performances. Using some of these or all of these levels of processing questions can be extremely valuable at times of S-1.

As part of the awareness level, you can share with individuals the model presented here (There is an Edgework script in the section entitled Addictions: Guiding Practices that you may want to consider using). When risks are taken or we go from the known to unknown territory we come to the edge of what is no longer comfortable. Individuals can be taught to expect and become prepared for intensity in their feelings, conversations, physiology, and self-limiting beliefs. You can describe some of the primary signs and symbols they will experience at the edge and in other situations as well. The objective here is to have participants identify when they are at the edge and become aware of what specifically they are doing at these moments to decide if the experience is helpful or hindering to them.

❖ FREEZING THE S-1 MOMENT

Whenever possible, you want to stop or freeze the learning activity when you see individuals or the group at heightened emotional levels. This is when they are in S-1; usually they are frustrated, confused, tired, excited, or stuck. By stopping the process while doing, you give them an opportunity to explore what they are experiencing—what is happening at this moment before the answer, solution, or breakthrough occurs. Usually one or two words describing what is tran-

spiring is sufficient. This gives you an anchor or benchmark to come back to later, when you are in S+1, after the doing. Your group should come to expect this interruption as a means to discover what is happening at the edge, so they can take this learning back to the school, office or home.

When working with mental health or chemical dependency groups, the preferred question to ask when you stop the group is "What are your feelings right now, in a word?" It is at these moments before a success or retreat that relapse dynamics emerge for a chemical-dependent person or dysfunctional coping mechanisms may arise for the mental health client. Awareness of their feel-

ings, actions and thoughts and their inter-relationship can provide a wealth of therapeutic material.

Corporate groups will require a different set of questions at S-1. We don't want to alienate some of the participants with "touchy-feely" language, yet we need to focus on what is transpiring. Some examples of questions at S-1 for corporate groups may include:

1. "What are you experiencing right now?"
2. "What is happening for you right now?"
3. "What is going on with you now?"
4. "Go inside for a moment and discover what information or data you are generating."
5. "Can you make your thinking visible now?"

The metaphors for corporate groups at S-1 are that these moments simulate the "chaos" in the organization that Peters (1987) and Wheatley (1992) write about, the job stress, or demands of the workday, when deadlines are fast approaching, resources are cut back, and communication is strained. Peters (1987) writes, "The winners of tomorrow will deal practically with chaos, will look at the chaos per se as the source of market advantage, not as a problem to be gotten around. Chaos and uncertainty are market opportunities for the wise" (p. xiv). Wheatley (1992) writes, "There is no predictability, the system never is in the same place twice. But as chaos theory shows, if we look at such a system long enough and with the perspective of time, it always demonstrates its inherent orderliness" (p.21). "All this time, we have created trouble for ourselves in organizations by confusing control with order" (p. 22). Being unaware of these stressors or opportunities and one's reactions to them can lead to cost overruns, poor and expensive decisions, ineffectual performances where products must be redesigned, low morale and motivation, and strained interpersonal relationships.

The next line of questions for most populations, as well as the corporate groups and mental health groups, has to do with what they are doing with their feelings or experiences. In order to help individuals use the information that they currently have, you may want to ask questions similar to these: "Now that you are aware of what is going on within you, is there anything that you want or need to say to the group?" "What risk could you take to help you and the group have a success?" "What kind of out of the box thinking is necessary here?" These questions access the responsibility and experimentation levels.

In summary, even though you may stop your group for only two to three minutes while in S-1, this is the space that holds valuable ingredients for their successes or obstacles for their failures. These few moments can give you a treasure chest of gems to process which participants later can exchange for future knowledge and achievements at school, home or the office.

❖ EDGE COMPONENTS

"We what we don't know, realize or understand keeps us prisoners of the same."
—*Author Unknown*

Below are the main components at S-1 that you want to help individuals and groups become aware of and eventually alter or refine in order to become more encouraging, positive, and supportive so future breakthroughs at the edge are possible. Many of these signs and symptoms overlap and influence each other but are presented individually for the purposes of this discussion.

1. Defenses and Typical Patterns. As mentioned earlier, the defenses or patterns that emerge as protection against the anxiety or fear of hurt and rejection are generated from being in disequilibrium. At the edge, it is important to make everyone conscious of these unconscious responses, patterns, or actions. These behaviors and responses were at one time successful in combating the anxiety; however, currently they typically are outdated, limiting, and no longer useful.

For most of us, between the ages of seven and ten, we made rules or guidelines for how to control or manage our lives. These rules helped us get out of uncomfortable situations. We may have made a joke, or become angry, isolated or intellectualized. When this worked, we felt relieved and reinforced to use this strategy again in other difficult situations. As a result, we tend to rely on this pattern or defense automatically in uncomfortable situations. The problem arises when this pattern is *no longer useful* yet *we still cling to it.* Retaining these patterns is similar to having a computer that when initially introduced was state of the art technology. Now we continue to use that same computer for 15 to 20 years without updating it. While it still functions, it is no longer as efficient or effective as some recently, developed models. Another analogy would be using old eight-track tapes over and over again and refusing to accept that compact discs sound better. The same concept applies to our fixed defenses or patterns. Our experiences, knowledge and capabilities have enhanced and improved since we were younger; therefore, it is time to innovate our newer "user patterns."

Experiential learning activities, which put individuals on the edge, can challenge participants to update, refine, and alter mental programs when they emerge. An effective means to bring about these shifts is to use the awareness and responsibility level of processing questions and/or the processing activities. Participants can be encouraged to experiment with new behavior patterns when at the edge.

2. Feelings. Feelings are important for us to be aware of, understand, and befriend. Many of us have learned to "not feel" and haven't learned to feel, manage, and sometimes just tolerate feelings when they are uncomfortable, unfamiliar, and negative (See "Feelings Aren't Biodegradable" section for more information on feelings.) What we have learned is to "stuff", run from, and avoid feelings. Feelings are going to intensify when we get closer to new territory at the edge. We get anxious, uncomfortable, impatient, scared, excited, confused, and vulnerable while in S-1.

Each person has his or her unique set and sequence of feelings which will typically emerge when arriving at new territory. The awareness and responsibility for these feelings will help demystify these emotions and move them from being an enemy to becoming an ally. Because these feelings are intense while in the structured experience, we have a great opportunity to help individuals feel and learn from their emotions. What are the specific feelings each person experiences when at the edge? By the end of the learning experience, participants should know what their feelings are, how they typically respond to their feelings, and what happens when they experiment with new reactions to these core feelings.

Tracy (1987) stated that we are born with just two fears—fear of falling and fear of loud noises; the remainder we have learned. During a structured experience, we can help participants unlearn some of their fears. Some of these fears are of deeper emotions, which include: like fear of rejection, embarrassment, grief, loneliness, horror, inadequacy, and sadness. It is these fears that emerge and intensify at the edge that we must help individuals break through.

Jeffers (1987), in her book, *Feel the Fear and Do It Anyway,* gives the prescription for breaking through the "edge" in her title. She also states, " At the bottom of every one of your fears is simply the fear that you can't handle whatever life may bring you" (p.15). She suggests five statements about fear that may be helpful to share with individuals who are doing edgework:

1. The fear will never go away as long as I continue to grow.
2. The only way to get rid of the fear of doing something is to go out . . . and do it.
3. The only way to feel better about myself is to go out . . . and do it.
4. Not only am I going to experience fear whenever I'm on unfamiliar territory, but so is everyone else.
5. Pushing through the fear is less frightening than living with underlying fear that comes from a feeling of helplessness" (Jeffers, 1987, p. 30).

Epston (1989) shares another view of fear in his *Collected Papers.* He calls these the five laws of fears:

1. Fears increase in direct proportion to the time they are not confronted.
2. Fears are weak; they need good friends to feed them.
3. Fears are infectious; they need to be isolated.
4. Fears are humorless; they cannot stand a joke at their expense.
5. Fears hide in dark corners; they need to be exposed and brought out into the light.
    (p. 51)

Once individuals have identified and expressed their feelings, the next step is to go ahead and do it anyway, even though they may be scared, confused, or helpless. For example, if participants can learn to feel the feelings and move forward with them, they will experience more breakthrough's and successes. Feelings will become information for them rather than impediments to their progress or reasons to retreat. This information is like knowing how your car is running while on a trip. It's important to know how much fuel you have, if the emergency brake is on, what the tire pressure is, or if the car is running hot, so you can make any adjustments and keep moving rather than stopping or turning back. Feelings, then, are a gauge to be read and to be aware of rather than a flashing red light that means DANGER and STOP, and GO BACK. Instead, feelings can be thought of as a yellow light, which means proceed with caution. So, acknowledge your feelings, breathe, and move forward staying aware of your surroundings.

3. Physiology. People's physiology can give information on how and what they are feeling at a certain moment. Their physiology is analogous to the red light in a car that signifies something is going on under the hood and may need exploring. For our purposes, physiology will mean the internal cues of the physiological symptoms, like one's heart racing, face flushing, sweating, respiration quickening, and pupils dilating, along with external signs like one's posture, gait, voice tonality and quality, mannerisms, and eye contact. At the edge, an individual's typical physiology patterns will intensify.

When processing at S-1 you want to raise participants' awareness of what information their physiological symptoms give them. These signs are usually unconscious responses to a situation, and we want the participants to become conscious of them. There will be a specific sequence and typical pattern to these signs whether the situation is speaking in front of a group, preparing for a rock climb, or reporting to their boss. These kinds of situations may arouse the feeling of anxiety.

For example, when Betsy felt anxious, her heart would pound, her palms would sweat, she would look down, have shallow breath, and speak in a soft, tenuous voice. Being aware of and understanding this pattern allowed Betsy to have more choices in managing this feeling rather than the feeling managing her. Betsy experimented with new patterns when she was at the edge in later activities. When anxious, she stood tall, took deep and confident breaths, focused her eyes on what she was afraid of, and told herself in a powerful voice, "I can do this." We had her practice saying this out loud, along with changing her physiology. She was able to relax more, use this anxious energy constructively, and move forward through the edge—where she had previously chosen to turn back. For Betsy, these physiological signs became signals that she was anxious and triggered the association of what she needed to do to manage this emotion and stay on track. This example illustrates how we can help participants bring new resources to their edge to accomplish their goals both on the course and in other settings.

There is a reflexive quality between feelings and physiology, each influencing the other. We first want to help individuals become aware of what signs go with what feelings. These signs then become the cloud formations which indicate what kind of weather or feelings are present. Second, we encourage participants to change their postures, breathing patterns, and mannerisms to elicit new feelings and empower them to move through previous road blocks. Stopping the process in S-1 helps identify these signs or symptoms which may have gone unnoticed and therefore are unavailable as a possible new resource for the person.

4. Beliefs. Beliefs are the mental or cognitive maps that we use as our guidelines to stay on the safe and secure trail within our comfort zone. They are made up of a network of premises and presuppositions. Our defenses, patterns, or actions, described above, are the means we use to stay oriented. These beliefs, like our defenses, were formed early in our lives and may have been influenced or reinforced by our family and/or friends. Today, they may be self-limiting beliefs, when earlier in life they may have been necessary for survival and were very useful.

In this text, we have called these patterns of thoughts: beliefs, mental models, cognitive maps, and mind-sets. Kuhn (1962), in *The Structure of Scientific Revolution,* called these mental models a "paradigm." He defines a paradigm as "A constellation of concepts, values, perceptions and practices shared by a community which forms a particular vision of reality that is the basis of the way a community organizes itself" (p. 11).

What is important to recognize in this definition is the shared nature of a belief system. During the learning experience, the group can become the community which organizes itself around a new paradigm or shared vision of reality. So, aside from the new perspectives that individuals obtain from being at the edge and breaking through to new territory, the community can be a supportive audience or hungry critics. As a leader and change agent, you have the difficult task of helping individuals move into new territory, acknowledging personal achievements, along with shaping the community or group to be receptive, encouraging, and supportive, which may be a paradigm shift for the group at large.

Paradigms are very powerful in their makeup. There are many basic assumptions in life that drive us, without our conscious awareness. In essence, we may be seeing everything in our lives through smudged glasses, which we don't realize are even on our face. Kuhn (1962) observed three paradigm patterns.

- ◆ First, the dominant paradigm is seldom, if ever, stated explicitly; it exists unquestioned.
- ◆ Second, once the paradigm is accepted, it is clung to tenaciously by our mental apparatus.
- ◆ Third, the unfolding of a new paradigm is always discontinuous, meaning that it is characterized by interruptions or breaks and thus difficult to own or believe.

Intellectual and emotional resistance inevitably arise when a radical way of perceiving the world is presented (Barker, 1985). What this means to you as a group leader is that facilitating for awareness and responsibility of beliefs will be very challenging because, first, participants don't realize they are operating from these beliefs; second, there is a lot of comfort from these paradigms and, conversely, there is a great amount of resistance to looking at their world without their comfortable, smudged glasses.

Below is a list of some of the common beliefs that can be self-limiting for individuals. They are drawn from the work of Nemeth (1990), Ellis (1975), and Burns (1980). Your challenge is to facilitate students' awareness, responsibility, and experimentation of and with the beliefs that emerge at the edge. There will usually be one core belief that fits best and other beliefs that are layered around this assumption. This core, self-limiting, belief typically will not feel good to the individual, and that is why he or she will consciously or unconsciously compensate for it. Examples of core beliefs are:

1. "Something is wrong with me."
2. "I can't."
3. "I won't."
4. "I'm stupid."
5. "People are jerks."
6. "Life is hard."
7. "I don't know."

8. "I'll do it my way."
9. "I must be unfailing, competent and perfect in all I do."
10. "It's absolutely necessary that I'm loved and approved of by everyone."
11. "It's horrible when things are not the way I want them to be."
12. "External events cause all my misery."
13. "I am helpless and have no control over what I feel."
14. "I never do anything right."
15. "Everyone looks down on me."
16. "I'll make a fool of myself."
17. "I'll fail."

For the purposes of discussion, we've found the most utility with the first eight self-limiting beliefs. It's important to try to get to the lowest common denominator or what lies beneath the other beliefs. Once participants are aware of this from their involvement in the structured experience, it will be easier for them to detect such when or if it emerges in other edge situations such as at the school, office, or home.

5. Conversation. The conversations we are referring to is the self-story or self-talk expression or script we have with ourselves. It has also been called the internal dialogue or the inner committee. This conversation often becomes the structure that supports and affirms our self-limiting beliefs. The beliefs then are similar to an architect's blueprints. The conversation is the building that is erected to match the plans. Even though the blueprint or belief may be erroneous, we still blindly build a case or a structure to support it. Without realizing it, we constantly talk to ourselves, either planning, confirming or disconfirming our map of the world.

It has been noted that people generally speak at an average of 150 words a minute. Yet, the inner dialogue occurs at a rate of 400 to 650 words per minute (Tracy, 1987). When someone is speaking to us, there is a tendency to fill in the spaces between their words with many of our own thoughts, which can lead to poor listening. For the sake of illustration, let's see how much we say to ourselves in one day. At the rate of 400 words a minute, that is 24,000 words in an hour or 384,000 words in a 16-hour day. If we break this up into seven-word sentences, we come up with a total of 54,857 sentences are communicated to ourselves on a daily basis. This is a staggering amount of reinforcement, which may be directed toward erroneous, irrational or outdated beliefs, which in turn can be overwhelming and difficult to interrupt.

We want to help participants become aware of their internal dialogue or self-story and to learn how to challenge those statements that are debilitating. It is important for participants to realize that when they get to the edge of the unknown, their conversations will most likely get louder, more frequent, and that their spoken words will influence other edge components like their physiology, metaphors, and feelings. Our bodies respond to our statements, even though they may not be true. In addition, the conversation will give clues to which beliefs are being overcompensated for or supported.

As an example, one participant, Jim, frequently operated under the belief of "I can't." The conversation that supported this belief as he got close to the edge was, "I always mess up"; "I'll never be able to do this"; "People are going to laugh at me"; "This is too hard"; "No way"; "Maybe"; "I'll refuse to do it." This all transpired in a few seconds and left him scared, resistant, and pessimistic about the activity. We were able to work with him on challenging some of these thoughts and talking about his "I can't" belief. He eventually changed some of his self-talk at the edge, which lessened his feelings of fear, and he broke through to new territory, where in the past—he would have retreated.

6. Support. Support is an edge component that a person uses to get from the comfortable zone to new territory. It can be constructive or many times be something that is overused, destructive, or unhealthy. What was once effective as a strength can become overused and develop into a weakness, as it prevents the possibility for new actions. As leaders, we want to help participants be aware of what they are using for support and allow them to make healthy choices.

A person's actions and choices are usually viewed as serving a positive intention for them. Most people will choose a support because it is either self-nurturing or self-protective, or both. Some qualities or components that make up a support system include: (a) consistency, (b) security, (c) safety, (d) tension relief, (e) nourishment, (f) trustworthiness, and (g) encouragement. In this light, you can see how a person may depend on alcohol, drugs, food, work, or a relationship to provide these qualities.

Let's look at a few examples. Dan was a 17-year-old adolescent on an outdoor-experiential learning program. He had been using alcohol since he was thirteen. In going to parties with his friends, he always drank before and during the party. He reported, "I liked the way I felt; it let me talk with people better." In other words, when approaching new territory, like a party or the opposite sex, there was safety, security, dependability, and trust in the alcohol that he could feel better. Plus, there was encouragement (Alcoholics Anonymous talks about the "bottle of courage"), nurturance, and tension relief in taking new risks, which without the alcohol, would have been more frightening. Dan used alcohol, where others in similar situations may have used drugs, food, work or a dependent relationship. While on a structured experience, participants, like Dan, have the opportunity to explore what means of support they used in the past and experiment with new constructive ways of asking for and getting support.

The second example involves Mike who was participating on a corporate teambuilding program. The team had already discussed the three statements that don't get spoken in the corporate world, from McCormack (1990). *What They Still Don't Teach You at Harvard Business School.* These are: (1) "I don't know," (2) "I made a mistake," and (3) "I need help." Mike, a manager, was in the middle of a group problem-solving activity called the acid river. He was blindfolded and really struggling to move across the board by himself. The leader stopped him, while he was in this S-1 experience, and asked him what he was experiencing. He replied, "I'm frustrated." The leader asked, "What do you need from others at this moment?" Mike said he didn't know. In spite of the leader's persistence, the words "I need help" couldn't be pulled out of him, until another team member mentioned it. He then said, "Oh yeah, I need help." This request for help just wasn't a part of his repertoire or mental model. While debriefing, Mike became painfully aware of what it costs him, his staff, and his company when individuals don't know how to ask for and get help and support.

When participants can experiment with new behaviors and ask for support while at the edge during an experience, they will have a better chance of using new resources at the edge in the office, school, or at home. Some examples of positive support that participants can learn and carry home to use at the edge include:

1. A positive relationship with a friend, therapist, co-worker, boss, or sponsor, who encourages and supports without rescuing;
2. The ability to develop an inner "coach," "nurturing parent," or "wise sage";

3. Relaxation, meditation, exercise, or self-hypnosis that the individual can use at the edge to relax, recharge, and encourage;
4. Journal writing to help put the edge components into perspective;
5. 12-step programs;
6. A sense of a higher power, where they can feel support and guidance;
7. Support groups at work or in the community, where individuals can share apprehensions and fears and know that it won't be used against them. Instead, they can experience the support and encouragement to stretch into new territories.

7. Metaphors. "I feel like a million dollars." "I'm on the top of the world." "My heart is beating like a race horse." "I can see the light at the end of the tunnel." Metaphors such as these are very effective in communicating an experience. They are widely accepted, spoken daily, and usually have unconscious roots. Siegelman (1990) stated that ". . . metaphor is primary both in language and in thought. It is through metaphor that language itself develops. . . . Metaphor is not just a figure of speech but an elementary structure of thought. . . . As the quintessential 'bridging operation', metaphor links domains by connecting insight and feeling, and what is known with what is only guessed at" (p. 3).

As participants move into new territory, they have experiences that are "beyond words." The use of and facilitation for metaphors can help bring this unknown and unfamiliar experience into the known and familiar circle of comfort. Essentially, the metaphoric process entails describing one thing in terms of another and with this comparison a third thing, the new idea, is born (Siegelman, 1990).

A metaphor is something that represents something else. Creating metaphors is a natural and sometimes unconscious process humans use in thinking and communicating. It may be a symbol like a word, object, painting, statue, gesture, or mental image. A metaphor may be expressed in a story or a song, or it could be a ceremony or ritual that holds symbolic importance for the people performing it. For our purposes, a metaphor encompasses all of the linguistic and visual aspects that we create and utilize as symbols or markers for our human existence. The story and pictures that describe the metaphor have a significant influence on both what we bring to the edge, along with what we create and take back from the new experience. We saved this component for last, because a person's metaphors at the edge can include and stand for all the other edge components. One picture can stand for 1,000 words at S-1. Bateson said that a metaphor is "the pattern that connects" (Combs & Freedman, 1990, p. 16). He believed that metaphors were inescapable in living systems because every thought we have is associated with something or someone else. For example, when we think of a compass, we don't see the word, but instead we create a picture of an object that's a metaphor describing where north is located. Metaphors can be used to create patterns that connect the learning experience with the office, school, or home environment. Therefore, we need to help participants clarify and magnify the metaphors that they use to transfer and generalize their experiences.

In actuality, participants are unconsciously trying to connect or make sense of their experiences. You can help them by making the process more conscious, and thus it may become more readily transferable. This process is akin to, first, orienting the map so that it accurately represents the territory. This helps participants become aware of how they have had a breakthrough and, second, imprinting this new map or picture on the brain, so it can be quickly retrieved and utilized for breakthroughs when they are at new edges.

The American Memory Institute (1989) reports that memory is a series of pictures that we create and then recall. To improve memory, they advocate creating engaging and exciting pictures about things. We know during experiential learning the day is full of exciting and engaging activities. Our task then is to help participants connect or make conscious these pictures and have them represent the specific learning that they have experienced. In other words, to turn their learning into graphic pictures or metaphors as a means of remembering and transferring the experience. This process is elaborated further in a subsequent section entitled, "Developing and Using Metaphors."

❖ METAPHORS AT THE EDGE

When participants are at the edge of new territory, they are embarking into a land of experiences and feelings that may be without words. A great deal may be going on for them unconsciously and influencing them without their awareness. The metaphor provides a window to the experience that becomes a transitional phenomenon linking one's inner experience to the outer world. Our task is to help make implicit metaphors explicit, so they become available for association, examination, and reworking.

Stopping the activity in S-1 will help open the window to see what is inside. Without facilitating for a metaphor, the success or retreat may happen quickly and unconsciously. The information of what prevented them from taking the risk or how they motivated themselves to "go for it" is lost, as is the learning and knowledge for transfer. As stated earlier, at the edge, the first objective is to help participants become aware of what is going on. Inquiring about their physiology, feelings, patterns, conversations, beliefs, and support will help create a picture for them. Then, we ask the questions, "What is an image that you see now?" "What pictures are you creating in your mind now?" "If we videotaped you feeling and saying these things to yourself, what kind of picture would we see?" "What is it like to be where you are at this moment?"

Frequently, when participants are at the edge and scared or unsure, an old image may be reactivated. They may see themselves as the small child they once were, with foreboding or critical parents saying things to them. Now it's themselves who are repeating these statements, and feeling vulnerable as a consequence. This is the picture, or being and feeling young-childish, that we want to evoke and make conscious.

Encouraging participants to take the risk or change some of their edge components will help form the basis for alternative and more constructive metaphors. When they have had a success and are in S+1, you can ask, "What is that image like?"; "What is the picture or symbol?". This is important to identify so the participants can carry the picture to other activities and home. It is something they can flash on when at a new edge but with more helpful pictures. When participants become conscious of their process, they begin to take charge of their personal slide show. The old images appear; they are aware of it, and replace the old slides with the new S+1 slides. Changing this metaphor also can change their affect, along with their physiology, beliefs, and internal conversations.

For example, after the ropes course initiative called the "trapeze leap," we worked with participants to come up with metaphors for their experience. Some examples included; "a soaring eagle," "an angel with wings," "a person unshackled," and "someone lifted by the hand of God." These metaphors were then used in the processing of the experience and discussion for transference. Statements like, "What does your eagle need to do in order to soar at work?" "How can you get unshackled when you're at home?" "If your angel with wings was with you at home, I wonder what success you would have." When we talk metaphorically, the unconscious gets stimulated, which may help participants make connections more easily, and in the end they become creators of empowering metaphors, rather than prisoners of outdated images.

❖ MIDDLE EDGEWORK

Since first writing and presenting about Edgework, we have noticed a phenomenon among a small number of participants, who always need to be considered and encouraged. For some individuals it is more unfamiliar, risky, unpredictable, and uncomfortable to be in the middle than on the edge. These people live on the edge and thrive on the excitement, but feel very uncomfortable being quiet and alone in the middle.

It is important to visit the middle to recharge and renew so that we can push the edge at another time. In the middle is where we find the "R words", here is where we recharge, replenish ourselves, reflect on our edge actions, re-evaluate, relax, and renew ourselves. Edgework then, is like a rubber band where we constantly expand and push the edge, while at the same time, retract and come back to relax so we can be ready for the next battle at the edge. The *middle* for some individuals is *their edge,* as they avoid this necessary quiet time. It is hard for them to say NO to any new challenge or thrill on the edge. Their growth and new territory is conquering the middle realm of being by themselves with their own thoughts and feelings.

During the structured experience these individuals need to learn to take care of themselves, which in some cases is to refrain from doing an activity or being first at everything and just **be** rather than **do.** It is important for participants to be aware of their roles and know what will help them stretch and grow and as leaders we need to facilitate for this movement whether it's pushing the edge or coming back into the circle.

❖ PUTTING IT ALL TOGETHER

Edgework is enhanced by using the levels of processing. Once at the edge, you can help participants become aware of what they are saying, doing, thinking, feeling, and viewing. Then, you can focus on whether this is a typical or common pattern for the individual, so that the person can take responsibility. Participants, in other words, own their patterns. They move from "I did?" in the awareness level to "I do!" in the responsibility level. Once this is established, you can encourage participants to take some risks, experiment with new patterns, and do something different at the edge. Because the edge components influence each other and are interdependent, making a change in one component can alter the other components. Then, participants can feel more empowered; there are more choices for them and they are not "stuck."

The choice level is important for participants. Here, they realize that they can choose to stay the same or make changes; it is totally up to them. Experimenting at the edge gives them information about what is possible, so they can make an informed choice. When risks or experiments are taken, the processing focuses on "What was it like for you?", "How did it work?", "How can we support you?", "What do you need to adjust?", etc. The group focus can be on the evaluation of the experiment, the outcomes, and what, if any, adjustments that are needed to refine the experiment.

Below are some selected examples of edgework. The first column signifies the old pattern that has been owned at the edge during the learning experience, and the second column shows the new resource that the participant is experimenting with at new edges—at the office, home, or school.

George was a 30-year-old manager for a small family-run business. The new territory for him was a promotion at the office, where he will be required to manage 20 people and do more public speaking both within the company and to future customers.

Old Edge Patterns

Feelings:
Scared and feeling sorry for self

Physiology:
Heart racing and losing breath

Pattern/Defense:
Avoid, wait, hide, and people please

Belief:
"Something is wrong with me."
"I don't know."

Conversation:
"I may fail."
"I may get rejected."

Support:
Overeat

Metaphor:
Pictures self on the outside of a
circle of people as an "outcast."

Edge Resources

Feelings:
Satisfied and content

Physiology:
Take a deep breath with a long, slow exhale

Pattern/Defense:
Move forward, take the risk, and please self

Belief:
"I accept myself."

Conversation:
"I'm not a bad person."
"People like me."

Support:
Friends, self, and group support

Metaphor:
Picture self successfully speaking at a meeting.
Looks at receptive audience and sees face of
woman who complimented him on his speech.

Elizabeth was a 59-year-old woman who has been in recovery from alcoholism for the last ten years. The new territory at home for her was living alone after the death of her husband and running her own business.

Old Edge Patterns	Edge Resources
Feelings: Scared and anxious	*Feelings:* Pride and satisfaction from successes
Physiology: Shallow breathing, holding arms over stomach, and bent posture	*Physiology:* Breathe deep, move arms off stomach, and sit tall
Pattern/Defense: Avoid situations	*Pattern/Defense:* Just do it without thinking
Belief: "Something is wrong with me." "I'm stupid."	*Belief:* "I can." "I'm okay the way I am."
Conversation: "This is too much for me." "I can't handle this."	*Conversation:* "I can handle it." "One step at a time."
Support: Husband Bottle (in the past)	*Support:* Asking for help, Alcoholics Anonymous, and pleasing self
Metaphor: Pictures self as scared child in the fetal position	*Metaphor:* Pictures successes as a capable and nurturing adult helping others

Greg was a 17-year-old in a treatment center for chemical dependency. The new territory for him was doing well in school and finding new friends and activities that didn't involve drugs and alcohol.

Old Edge Patterns	Edge Resources
Feelings:	*Feelings:*
Fear, anger, pity	Excitement and the joy of discovery
Physiology:	*Physiology:*
Sighing, dropping head, and shallow breathing	Sitting tall and taking deep breaths with long exhales
Pattern/Defense:	*Pattern/Defense:*
Put things off, procrastinate	Do it right now
Belief:	*Belief:*
"I can't."	"I can."
"I don't know."	"Just do my best."
Conversation:	*Conversation:*
"It's too late."	"I'll never know unless I give it a try."
"I won't make it."	"Do it anyway."
Support:	*Support:*
Beer and cocaine	Family, sponsor, Alcoholics Anonymous, and therapist
Metaphor:	*Metaphor:*
Pictures a person in a rut or on a bicycle just "spinning my wheels and going nowhere."	Pictures success of doing a long rappel in spite of his fear

❖ SUMMARY

Experiential learning or any new learning event can put individuals at the edge of new territory. This is where it appears to be unfamiliar, unknown, and unpredictable. There are feelings of discomfort, disequilibrium, and risk. The person either retreats or withdraws from this edge or "goes for it" and may have a breakthrough or a success. Edgework puts this moment at the edge under the microscope and examines the components. Old and outdated edge patterns are recognized and altered or discarded in favor of trying some new behaviors, thoughts, and feelings. These new actions or resources can then become the gems to treasure, transfer, and generalize the experience to the new territories of the office, home, or school.

CORRECTIVE EMOTIONAL EXPERIENCE

"Initiative is to success what a lighted match is to a candle."

—*Orlando A. Battista*

In a story told by psychotherapist, Paul Watzlawick (1990), a man persisted in clapping his hands to keep the elephants away from him. A therapist tried in vain to explain to the man that there were no elephants. The man quickly responded, "You see." He assumed his solution was working. Watzlawick (1990) explains that there are four ways to try and change this man's phobia. They include:

1. In a trusting relationship with a professional or friend, convince the man there were no elephants.
2. Using insight as the agent of change. Here the unconscious motivations for this fear would be examined and brought into consciousness, which would then help him let go of this symptom.
3. Bring an elephant into the therapy session and show that clapping his hands doesn't work to keep the elephant away.
4. The man breaks his wrist and can't clap. He sees then that the elephants haven't charged him, and maybe it wasn't the clapping that kept them away.

During the structured experience, we typically use all four of these approaches to help individuals deal with their fears at the edge. The fourth approach is a life experience that happens in an unplanned random manner. This doesn't happen frequently during the experience, yet there are times that you may have observed when a random event (severe storm), a mistake (getting lost), or crisis (first aid emergency) provided an opportunity for significant learning to occur for the participant or the group. In many of those instances, the growth that occurred was an indirect result of the experience; it couldn't have turned out better if it was planned.

Given the value of significant unplanned learning, Watzlawick (1990) advocates creating what he calls "planned chance events" to bring about change. In this section, we discuss these

48

four ways of creating change and explore the "corrective emotional experience" that occurs during the learning experience directly and sometimes indirectly.

The term "corrective emotional experience", which was coined by Franz Alexander (1946), who studied how people change, aptly describes what experiential learning and therapy provides for participants. The experience is "affectively" loaded and in many cases is corrective for an individual. In other words, we help individuals "change the viewing" and "change the doing" of the problem (O'Hanlon, 1990). Participants' perceptions of the problem may change, and as a result, they act or interact differently in relation to the problem. There are two types of corrective emotional experiences: (1) the therapeutic relationship, and (2) new experiences in life.

❖ THERAPEUTIC RELATIONSHIP

For our purpose, we will call both the relationship that exists between the participant and the leader and the relationships that are developed among the group members, therapeutic. There has been much written about the curative factors of a group (Yalom, 1985). A few points that are relevant to this discussion are

1. the sense of universality—all the members of the group see how their concerns are similar to those of others,
2. group cohesiveness—the sense of connection and good feelings when the group works together well,
3. improved interpersonal communication—members feel listened to and understood, and
4. the recapitulation of the family unit—this encompasses the reparenting that transpires within a group.

Support is important for participants to experience so they can take new risks. This is similar to the recapitulation of the family unit. Our participants unconsciously wonder if the activities or experiences are safe and if it is okay to trust others. Can they gingerly move into new territory and explore such without the fear of criticism or rejection? Early experiences in the family, usually with the mother, may become reactivated. If it was hard for the person to trust his mother for safety and security, the leader may see a reticent and anxious person. In turn, if exploration as a child was prohibited, taking new risks during the experience may feel frightening. Therefore, early in the experience, you are encouraged to establish a safe and supportive environment within the group. This foundation establishes the groundwork for new risks to be taken.

Ingredients for corrective emotional experiences which develop trust and encouragement include the following:

1. *Trust Phase*
   a. Permission to feel and be
   b. Safety and security
   c. Consistency
   d. Empathy and support
2. *Encouragement Phase*
   a. Encouragement to explore and take risks

b.   Affirming individuality
c.   Failure as a necessary step for success
d.   Support for the person rather than the performance
e.   Encouragement to ask for help and support

Winnicott (1985) proposed the term "holding environment" as a metaphor for the total protective, empathic care that the "good enough" mother provides the infant during the first few years of life. You have a challenging responsibility in creating this "holding environment" for participants. Adjusting to the "ever-shifting needs" of one person is difficult, let alone adjusting to a groups' "fluctuating needs." You may be encouraging one participant to take a risk, while comforting another who requires less tension and more soothing and trust building. This is where maintaining the constructive level of anxiety, which is different for each person, demands attention to and understanding of the specific capacities and needs of each individual in your group.

❖ NEW EXPERIENCES

Providing new experiences as part of the corrective emotional experience may be the primary factor which promotes the significant learning, growth, and changes that are evident during the structured experiences. As expressed earlier, many educational theorists emphasize the value of new experiences or action. Bateson (1980) argued that new and different experiences are essential for personal growth. He suggested that all information is necessarily "news of difference," and that it is the perception of difference that triggers all new responses in living sys-

tems (White & Epston, 1990). Piaget (1954) in his book entitled *The Construction of Reality in the Child*, contends that children literally construct their reality by exploring actions, rather than first forming an image of the world through their perceptions and then beginning to act accordingly. If Piaget's perspective is accurate, then we would assume that different actions may lead to the construction of different realities.

A similar view was suggested by Erickson (1948), who believed that experience was the best teacher. As a result, he was a therapist who attempted to design experiences that allowed people to reach their goals. He wrote: "It is the experience of reassociating and reorganizing his own experiential life that eventuates in a cure . . . The patient's task is that of learning through his own efforts to understand his experiential life in a new way (1948, p. 38–39).

There are an abundance of activities and experiences that comprise an experiential learning program, most of which are new for people. Therefore, it is likely that at least one activity will be the planned chance event that provides a "change of viewing" or a "change of doing." Processing can be viewed as a coding mechanism. When the new experience is coded, it then can be more easily generalized and applied to the office, school, or home. Consequently, you want to first get participants to try something different and, second, process or codify the experience to establish exactly what was different; then this experience can be utilized in the future.

At the beginning of this section we shared a story about the man and the elephant. No amount of insight or explaining, even with a trusting relationship, could alter this man's reality or story as much as the action of breaking his wrist or being with the elephant and seeing his hand clapping didn't work. Each of these provided a new experience which had to be integrated into his conscious knowing and interpretation of reality. One is an example of a direct new experience, and the other an indirect new experience.

Direct new experiences can be facilitated by using the levels of processing format. When participants become aware and responsible for their edge components, then they can be encouraged to take new risks. This gives them an opportunity to create a new reality for themselves. They can have a breakthrough or success and expand their circle of comfort or sense of competency. This is a direct new experience in that they are fully responsible for taking the actions.

As previously mentioned, taking any new action on an edge component can alter the other components and help propel them into new territory. Support and encouragement to experiment with new behaviors and facilitation about the experimentation then becomes the main task for leaders. It is through these steps that participants are helped to evaluate their experiences and construct personal meaning from them.

❖ PLANNED CHANCE EVENTS

Planned chance events refer to indirect experiences that the person hasn't actually self-selected, yet which occur because he or she have agreed to participate in the experience or program. Usually these indirect experiences are structured by the leader. Other times, they may derive from random events. They are "planned" in that you may think this experience will benefit participants by helping them stretch to new areas where they may not go on their own. Leaders have always done this, designed an activity in a creative way. Here we are encouraging you to consider this kind of intervention more as a means of giving people breakthrough experiences. You can be very creative in generating "planned chance events." The more personal risks that you can take within the scope of good judgment (never compromising safety), the more successes you and participants can have.

An example from an experiential learning program for adjudicated youths may be appropriate at this point. The participants had been in the field for ten days of a 19-day course. There had been several incidents of stolen food, usually the cookies, without the thieves identifying themselves or being caught. The

leader decided to approach the issue in an indirect way. He sent the crew out to collect firewood. While they were away from camp, he stole the fudge cookies from one of the participant's backpack. After dinner, the group was anxiously awaiting their treats. When the individual couldn't find the cookies, a group meeting was called. All the participants were angry and upset about this. An excellent discussion ensued about trust, feeling violated, and honesty. Even the suspected thieves got involved and shared pertinent feelings. The leader then pulled out the cookies. After some initial shock and resentment, the participants all responded how it had been a great learning experience. Obviously, this planned chance event was risky and took time to plan and implement, but the outcome was very fruitful. Participants were compelled to go outside their circle of comfort and discuss personal matters of significance.

One way to set up planned chance events is to use handicaps; where one sense is taken away from an individual during an activity (see Using Handicaps section for some additional ideas). While handicapped individuals are thrust to their edge, feeling a constructive level of anxiety, something unique or significant may occur. You may not know what the person will experience, but you need to trust in the individual's ability to learn from being impelled into the new territory. In addition to using handicaps with participants, you can use any of the following suggestions to bring about planned chance events:

1. Encouraging individuals to try out opposite roles than they normally take.
2. Designing activities and discussions at unusual times, i.e., night or early morning.
3. Selecting specific participants to be leaders, followers, a person sabotaging the experience or a complainer (especially if this what the person typically does; this is called "prescribing the symptom"). Or be the worst leader you can be in the next activity. Usually, the more absurd or unique it sounds, the more potential there is for breakthroughs.
4. Making note of and emphasizing the smallest changes that are observed and which are probably seen as only random events by participants.

In summary, new experiences, whether direct and initiated by the individual's experimentation, or indirect and suggested or designed by the leader, are a major force in moving people

into new territory. Once in new territory, the processing of the experience is what gives the new learning personally significant meaning for the individual to bring back to the office, home, or school. As a result, the new territory is tamed, and the structured experience can become a corrective emotional experience. The participants may add a significant chapter of successes and increased self-efficacy to their life stories. Their unique outcomes, then, can be plotted in an alternative story, which then can alter their lives and their relationships.

FEELINGS AREN'T BIODEGRADABLE

"The first step in handling anything is gaining the ability to face it."
—L. Ron Hubbard

People frequently have a misunderstanding about the way that litter biodegrades when left in wilderness areas. This misconception also applies to how we deal with our feelings. That is, many people believe that if painful or uncomfortable feelings are left unattended, they will magically disappear. Lundin and Lundin (1993) state, "Ever since the industrial revolution employees and managers have been compelled to live a cultural myth that says emotions and feelings should not exist at work. It's a distortion of what it means to be human and it's choking us to death." (p.xii) This section explores these misconceptions and describes some interventions that can be undertaken to positively deal with feelings.

In the wilderness, many individuals have a difficult time with the concept of biodegradable. Most of us have observed individuals throwing orange peels or apples cores into the woods and when asked about their behavior, they respond, "They're biodegradable." People also bathe upstream from where others are cooking and when asked about the soap in the water they respond "It's Dr. Bronner's soap, and it's biodegradable." It seems that there's a magical quality given to the term biodegradable, which somehow indicates that instantly peels, apple cores, or soap will decompose or dissolve.

The Oxford Dictionary (1990) defines biodegradable as "capable of being decomposed by bacteria or other living organisms" (p. 109). Degrade is defined as "1) to diminish with deteriorating effect; 2) To break up into small lumps or into dust; 3) To reduce the strength of—giving a tendency to deteriorate or disintegrate . . ."(p. 367). What is often misunderstood by individuals is the time or duration that is involved in this deterioration process. During this process, the substance is a contaminate that alters the ecology. Some examples of the length of biodegradation cited in the *Instructor's Field Manual, North Carolina Outward Bound School,* (1980) are:

Glass bottle:	1 million years
Aluminum cans:	80–100 years
Tin can:	50 years

Nylon fabrics:	30–40 years
Paper containers with plastic coating:	5 years
Cigarette butts	1–5 years
Orange peels:	Up to 2 years
Paper containers:	2 weeks to 5 months
Fecal matter:	1–4 weeks

In a similar manner, unresolved feelings are a contaminate to the human system. Even though the feelings are hidden or repressed, individuals are influenced, at times burdened, or even imprisoned by them. The impact of these feelings usually occurs unconsciously since individuals are not aware that the toxin is seeping through in unrecognizable ways.

Because feelings are hidden, we often think that others won't see them. Yet, we have all met people who later we wondered: "Why is he mad at the world?" or "What's her problem?". A maxim from Alcoholics Anonymous is that "Whenever you bury a feeling, you bury it alive." It may grow in unexpected and unwanted ways.

Generally speaking, people don't know what to do with their feelings. They can be painful, uncomfortable, and embarrassing. So, why not just ignore them or run away from them? Our society promotes this. We've all received "don't feel" messages, such as:

"Be strong, will you?"
"Big boys don't cry."
"Come on now; you'll get over it."
"You are always so sensitive."
"You are just too emotional."
"It's not that big a deal."
"Why are you always crying about everything?"
"Just do this (instead of feeling)."
"Tomorrow you won't think twice about this."
"Don't let them see you sweat."
And even, "Don't worry; be happy."

While these messages are verbal, there are also many non-verbal messages to not feel, create waves, or burden others with your feelings. The ideal of the perfect family, where there aren't problems or arguments fosters this repression of feelings. Television promotes "don't feel" messages with commercials to self-medicate anytime you feel slightly uncomfortable. Contact, Anacin, Excedrin, Scope, Tums, Alka Seltzer, and Rolaids will all help you to not feel. Researchers noted that 80% of people who see medical doctors do so for lifestyle or emotional reasons. And how are most of these problems taken care of? By being given some type of medication to correct their feelings. Accordingly, it is not a surprise that most people think that feelings will somehow just biodegrade if we don't attend to them and just ignore them. We are never taught in school or from most parents how to learn from feelings or what to do with them. Instead, we learn how to avoid or "stuff" feelings.

There are some feelings that are more difficult and painful than others to experience. These feelings are the deep emotions which all of us have, but most likely we hide. We hide them with our defenses, which were mentioned earlier. Also, we hide these deeper feelings with surface feelings which are easier to experience and distract us from deeper feelings (see figure 9). The middle layer feelings also protect the deep feelings from being revealed and/or acknowledged. These deeper feelings are the ones that don't biodegrade, unless they are given attention. They can endure, like the aluminum can in the wilderness, for a lifetime. All this time, they are negatively impacting our system, although observable through attitudes, defenses, surface feelings, metaphoric language, and psychosomatic illnesses.

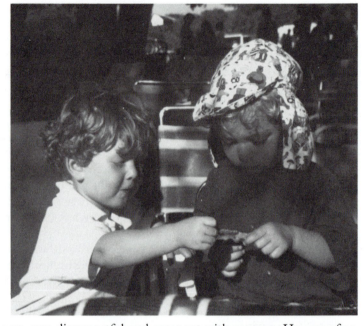

An example may help elucidate this process. Jim, a student on an 8-day adventure course, was disrespectful and arrogant with women. He was often angry or depressed. Underneath these surface-feelings he revealed an experience that housed his deeper feelings. Jim had been married for four years in what he thought was a good relationship. One day, he came home and found his wife in bed with another man. He left that night, never to see his wife again. His obvious feelings of rejection, hurt, embarrassment, grief, helplessness, and horror were all present but avoided. In the subsequent years, the contamination from the non-biodegradable emotions exhibited themselves by treating other women horribly, being obnoxious, angry, and becoming addicted to cocaine and alcohol. In talking about his ex-wife, 12 years

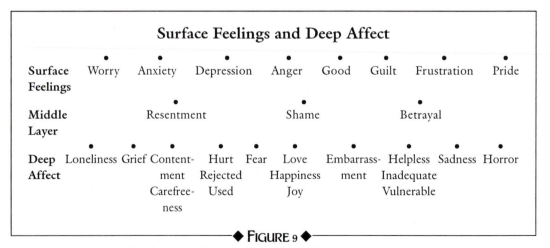

Surface Feelings and Deep Affect

Surface Feelings	Worry	Anxiety	Depression	Anger	Good	Guilt	Frustration	Pride
Middle Layer		Resentment		Shame			Betrayal	
Deep Affect	Loneliness	Grief	Content-ment Carefree-ness	Hurt Rejected Used	Fear	Love Happiness Joy	Embarrass-ment	Helpless Inadequate Vulnerable	Sadness	Horror

◆ FIGURE 9 ◆

Surface feelings and deep affect (adapted from Fabian et al. 1985)

later, the anger and deeper feelings of hurt and rejection were present, as if the incident had happened the week before, which is a strong indication that his unacknowledged and avoided deeper feelings did not biodegrade. By sharing his true feelings, he was more accepted and understood by others as a result of revealing his "secret." He began to realize that he wasn't as horrible and worthless as he had thought; rather that he was just hurt and rejected and that he could be understood and accepted by others. His deeper feelings were able to change after being released.

❖ WHAT TO DO WITH FEELINGS?

As mentioned earlier, many of us "*HIDE*" our deeper feelings. We haven't learned how to constructively deal with and manage feelings. A beneficial change would be to allow feelings that have been *HID* to surface. To do this, we can change HID to the acronym IHD. This stands for (1) *I*dentify and acknowledge feelings, (2) *H*onor and accept the feelings, and (3) *D*eliver, experience, or communicate the feelings to yourself, another, or the source. The following is a more extensive explanation of each of these steps:

1. *Identify and acknowledge feelings:* First, you need to know the aluminum can doesn't belong in the wilderness and is a pollutant to the environment. With feelings, some of this knowledge is imparted by education that feelings are a significant part of the human experience, just like the wind, rain, and animals are a part of the wilderness experience. Feelings aren't right or wrong; they are part of life and exist in their own right. Experiencing our feelings helps get through them, rather than avoid them.

    We ride out storms in the wilderness and work at getting comfortable in those uncomfortable situations. Putting extra clothes on or sitting under a tarp helps us get through storms. We usually realize it's foolish to run from every storm. We learn to navigate through and manage the elements, and usually feel more capable after weathering the storm. The next storm usually is less threatening. Feelings, like storms, come in waves of intensity followed by the quiet peacefulness that exists after the storm.

    We can usually observe signs that inclement weather is on its way, which is similar to the existence of signs to identify that deeper feelings are in the air. Some typical signs are:

    a. *Surface feelings*—usually under each of these surface feelings hides a deeper and more painful emotion. The surface feelings can begin or end abruptly or last for days. Their chief goal is to maintain the "status quo." People who are always laughing or smiling inappropriately usually will tell you that they would cry if they weren't laughing. Often, the depressed person is moving away from more painful feelings. Underneath anger towards others is usually anger at oneself or a significant other. Anxiety may be blocking a fear of rejection or of being hurt.

    b. *Psychosomatic signs*—often betray some deeper feelings. Headaches, migraines, nervous stomach, cracking voice, sweaty palms, dizziness, all may be indications that some deeper affects are being activated (see the section entitled "Enhancing Communication Skills).

    c. *Defenses*—such as intellectualizing, blaming others, charming people, being the clown, the know-it-all, the airhead, and the perfect student are all roles that protect the more sensitive and vulnerable feelings.

d. *Metaphors*—are descriptive means to describe painful experiences. Examples include: "I have a lump in my throat"; "My heart is racing"; " I feel dead inside"; "There's an emptiness or hollowness within me"; "I have a knot in my chest"; "It's like having your arms cut off"; "It was like a slap in the face to me"; "It was like I was bleeding to death and no one cared." These metaphors are very graphic. They powerfully describe the deeper feelings that may be imprisoned and inexpressible. Often these feelings occurred early in life and are communicated in the words of a child.

These types of signs can give you information about the participants who you are working with. By noting the external behaviors and communicating them to participants, you can help them identify and acknowledge their feelings. The awareness questions found in the Levels of Processing section also can be used to facilitate the identification of feelings.

2. *Honor and accept the feelings:* After we have identified the feeling, we want to honor it. Here individuals are encouraged to accept and own their feelings as being valuable components in the human system. In the ecological system, storms and rain are integral components for the continued growth of the environment. At this stage of the process the message of "It's okay to feel" seeks to take the place of the conditioned "Don't feel" messages. Honoring one's feelings is a means of owning or being responsible for this emotional domain. It is a way to be true to yourself. At times it may be appropriate to surrender to the feeling rather than to fight it. This is similar to surrendering to a storm and altering your travel plans.

People feel all the time, in differing intensity levels. Every feeling brings information about who we really are at that moment. In an effort to honor feelings, Fabian (1984) suggests that we avoid spending time doing the following:

a. Needing to explain them or find a reason for them.
b. Searching for their source or unearthing their cause.
c. Finding out what they mean.
d. "Doing something" about them or "getting something done" about them.
e. Enduring them as a kind of martyrdom.
f. Forcing deep affect into awareness. Rather, we need to take deep feelings as they come.

Other people in our life don't help in honoring our feelings when they want to become Mr. or Mrs. Fixit. Instead, we need encouragement to feel our feelings and believe that "We'll handle it" or weather this storm. So, once our feelings are identified, then we honor their existence or become honest with ourselves by admitting that we have them, in spite of the fact that they may not feel

good. In the wilderness, we first notice the aluminum can and by realizing that the can is polluting or contaminating the environment, we are honoring the ecology and thus become aware that something must be done about this toxin. To feel is natural; to avoid feelings is unnatural and presents a dam in the natural flow of emotions.

3. *Deliver, experience or communicate the feelings to yourself, another, or the source:* In this stage, we retrieve the aluminum can, put it in our backpack, and carry it out. Similarly, our feelings are retrieved, experienced, and carried out. There are times when a person is truly experiencing his or her deep affects and no words need to be expressed. A shift has occurred. The emotion is felt and thus delivered between two individuals. It can be a look, shared sentiment, hand on the shoulder, or other nonverbal communication.

Many times, though, more of an effort is needed to deliver these emotions. This may entail communication of these feelings to others or the source with whom the feelings were experienced. Expressing feelings in a responsible manner with I-statements is appropriate. Defensiveness or blaming doesn't allow the deeper affect to be delivered. Ideally, the leader will teach and role model how to express deeper feelings, while creating a safe environment within the group to make this possible. Practicing this process in the group can be very beneficial. Role playing a significant other in the group, or at home, also can help.

If a person whom you feel comfortable with or the source of these feelings is unavailable, expressing them to yourself via journal writing can be very effective. The act of experiencing and communicating deep feelings using any available mode can be very healing in itself. This provides an opportunity to let go, which in turn can create more energy for dealing with here and now relationships.

One of the fears commonly experienced by individuals in regard to dealing with their feelings is that if they really sample this forbidden feeling, it will overwhelm them and never stop. This is untrue. Feelings are like waves that have moments of intensity, then dissipate and come back in a wave. Participants need to understand this in order to give themselves permission to feel. In most cases, a participant will remain at a heightened emotional state for less than ten minutes, and there will always be intermissions. When feelings are truly felt and experienced, there is a change or shift. Fabian (1984) stated that ". . . everyone's storehouse of difficult deep emotions is FINITE. That is, people who persist in facing their difficult deep emotions will, within a period of months, finish the job!" (p. 2).

During the learning experiences, participants will engage in activities where deeper feelings are activated or elicited. This is an opportunity for each person to learn how to express and feel these feelings. This is a new skill for many people, like rock climbing, rappelling, or presenting to the steering team, and they need to become comfortable with their emotions. As expressed earlier, you are not expected to do psychotherapy. If you don't have the necessary skills or training, don't try to deal with issues that you are uncomfortable with. However, the IHD process of identifying and acknowledging feelings, honoring the feelings, and then delivering the feelings appropriately can be a resource that everyone can utilize at home.

In summary, most of us have never learned how to deal with feelings constructively. We think these unresolved feelings are biodegradable, when in reality they are contaminating us like a toxin. What we have learned to do with feelings is

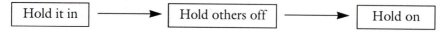

This is how the contaminate spreads. Now we can assist individuals in navigating these negative emotions, by learning how to

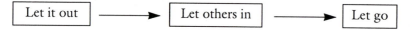

A summary of what to do with feelings is found below:

◆ TABLE 3 ◆

IHD Process

Most of us have **HID** feelings and instead we want to use the **IHD Process.**

I   1.   **Identify and acknowledge feelings:**
          "What are you feeling?"
          Stay with feelings rather than stuff or avoid.
          Look for the deeper emotions.

          Typical signs include:
          A.   Surface feelings   C.   Defenses
          B.   Psychosomatic symptoms   D.   Metaphors

H   2.   **Honor and accept feelings:**
          "It's okay to feel."
          "To heal you must feel."
          No need to explain or unearth cause.
          Ride with and through deep affect, as they come in waves.

D   3.   **Deliver, experience or communicate feelings to self or others**
          I statements, "I feel . . ."
          When expressed, feelings will shift or change.
          Moments of intensity are limited.
          "You'll handle it."

A Gestalt Approach to Experience

Craig Penner, M.A.

"If you are not aware of it, there's nothing you'll be able to do about it."
—*Gregg Butterfield*

Scott is "crossing the acid river" with his team. He is close to the other side, and gets so excited that he jumps off the last board, causing it to shift. The person behind him looses his balance and falls off. Scott wants to blame the board, or the person behind him, or perhaps even someone else for not telling him to slow down. He feels anxious and just wants to get on to the next event hoping to not have to process any of this. How would you deal about this? What do you think is going on here? Why would Scott "lose" it, when they were so close to finishing? This section will give you insight to a Gestalt approach to the stages of experience, and how we interrupt the stages.

We all seem to engage with the world through countless experiences of noticing our needs and wants, and then following a tendency to move toward "closure" or completion. We do this within a wide variety of interruptions and successes. Gestalt theory talks about our natural process of "need formation and destruction" in terms of the "Stages of Experience" (see below), which tracks our energy as we go through this process. When anything attracts our attention, we respond by investing our focus and efforts, thus our energy rises to meet the stimulus.

In the process of this movement through need development, satisfaction and closure, each of us run into our own blocks which interrupt our flow of energy in a variety of ways. These "resistances" can be either conscious or unconscious. They may stop our process at any moment, or cause us to move through so quickly that we don't really assimilate anything new from our experience. These blocks are not inherently good or bad, but rather just attempts (perhaps old and outdated) to take care of ourselves. It is valuable to note the effects of these resistances on our process in the present, so we can have the option to make more deliberate choices.

Gestalt Therapy and experiential education strongly share the value of enacting actual experiments in order to create contact and "ownership" with our own learning processes. Through an understanding of the Stages of Experience (adapted from Zinker, 1977), we can conceptualize "process" in steps. This can simplify our task of observing and helping others to process their adventure and learning experiences, in order to better embody the desired changes. The more aware we are of ourselves in the moment, and how we interrupt this natural flow of energy—the more apt we are to focus and meet our challenges.

The basis for the Stages of Experience lies in how we flow energetically. We will begin here by considering the stages and observe how we both progress and interrupt ourselves along the way. These stages may seem simple, yet there are great ramifications from what happens at each significant point. The goals for leaders using this Gestalt approach to experience include:

- ◆ Help participants understand their natural flow of energy towards closure.
- ◆ Help participants identify where and how they typically interrupt the stages.
- ◆ Give participants the awareness, tools, and experience to move through their interruptions.
- ◆ Help participants use this learning to focus their energy within other aspects of their lives.

This idea of the Stages can be observed in experiences of various lengths, from a momentary event like noticing and scratching an itch, through the process of taking a trust fall, or over the length of a long day on the ropes course. We'll begin from a hypothetical "zero point," where our energy is waiting to be invested, and our attention is open to anything.

Sensation creates the foundation of awareness and perception. The sources may be internal or external. Our abilities to use our senses

The Stages of Experience

and to clearly discriminate between sensations determines what we pay attention to, and what we ignore. Sensations are not automatic, but rather they are screened by individual differences, past experiences, culture, expectations, language and habit.

Examples of sensations include: thoughts; physical senses, like tension, pain, or warmth; sounds and words; visual images; touch; odors; and tastes. There is a wide variation of demand characteristics for any sensation. The thought of balancing on a log 30 feet high is much different than traversing a log on the ground. Height demands our attention with more urgency.

People may de-sensitize themselves, and unconsciously block themselves from the chance to effectively notice their surroundings or themselves. It's also common for individuals to interrupt awareness when fears or limiting beliefs suddenly arise that draw a person's awareness out of the present and into old reactive patterns. We don't need to know "why" this occurs in order to be able to detect it. As you observe participants in warm-up exercises and initiatives, look for signs that they may be distracted from attending to themselves or their surroundings, including the physical environment, instructions, leaders and fellow participants.

Consider how someone's lack of basic focus creates a handicap that will impact them throughout any activity. It frequently occurs that problems in the completion of an initiative or activity stem from poor attention to necessary sensations at the start. It is also common that people who de-sensitize tend to do this over and over, so you may witness this throughout a person's involvement (or lack of it). The next stage is where you can help participants identify these sensations.

Awareness is the process by which we begin to organize all the raw material from our senses. There are often many sensations competing for attention at any given moment. What stands out? What fades into the background? This is where we begin to assign meaning to the sensations. We can be aware of: emerging wants and needs; our internal environment—including memories, images, fantasies, beliefs and values; and our external environment. Here we begin to have options about where and how to direct our focus and energy, along with cognitive awareness, emotional and physical awareness starting to emerge.

If you notice a participant who appears to be withdrawn from the present experience, it is useful to draw his or her attention to some basic stimuli, either external ("What do you notice as you look off at the trees?") or internal ("Scan your body from head to toe for 10 seconds. What are you aware of?"). This is an example of a shuttling exercise, identifying internal and external cues. Other strategies and questions at this stage of developing awareness of sensations include: Stopping the activity frequently and asking;

"In one word what are you feeling?"
"What are you experiencing?"
"What's going on in your body?"
"Where in your body do you feel it, can you point to it?"
"What are you thinking?"
"What's the dialogue that you are having with yourself?"

Excitement, or Mobilization of Energy is the next stage. Our needs and wants become more defined at this point, and we should decide whether we want to move toward or away from any sensation. We may be curious, frightened, intrigued, resigned, bored or thrilled. We can begin to feel our own momentum building as we focus on the demands arising from our needs. Notice in the diagram how energy is rising in stages if we stay focused, without interruption. The energy can feel good or bad to us, and it may heighten our attraction or avoidance.

At times, as we gain more awareness of our wants and needs, we may derail ourselves due to some other sensation that enters the picture. It may be our own self-doubt or criticism, a memory of a past failure, an old rule that prohibits us from obtaining goals, objectives, or a current lack of safety or support from our immediate environment. In these cases, we may not clearly define what would help us get past this point. Often the energy goes to this unproductive thinking which interrupts the natural flow towards closure. Questions to ask at this stage include:

"What do you want right now?"
"What do you need right now?"
"Where is your thinking taking you now?"
"Is this the direction you want to put your energy in?"

Action becomes possible, in a purposeful and deliberate way, when our energy and focus rise sufficiently. We now have the potential to act strongly enough to fulfill our needs. It may entail physical exertion, speech, or simply more thought. If our focus is too scattered or insufficiently formulated, then our actions will not match our objectives.

Think of times you attempted something without sufficient attention or energy, and your efforts missed the mark. Notice the variety of ways that you can get all the way to the point of taking action, but still not be present enough to succeed (even if you feel that you ultimately possess the capability). We get distracted, our desires are low, we aren't clear enough about our focus, we hold ourselves back at the last moment (due to a competing need) or we just give up. What's different about the times you move forward with full force, maybe even in spite of significant doubt? Questions at this stage include:

"What steps do you need to take to meet the demands of the moment?"
"What do you need to do to focus your energy into constructive actions?"
"Are there any skills or resources you need to implement your actions?"

Contact occurs when we really meet the environment, another person, or an aspect of ourselves, and there is an interchange. Something new happens here, which can be assimilated as part of the self. This experience has the potential to reduce the tension created by the emerging need. The fulfillment may be from relief or satisfaction. Energy is at its highest point here. It's like a membrane opening up, where the unexpected can flow through. We may have insights or "Aha!" moments, and allow the unexpected. There is a merging of the boundaries of "sameness" and "differentness," between people, ideas, past and present experiences, expectations and current realities. We have the ability to change from experiencing something new.

When we have fully engaged in an experience, we may feel the exhilaration of realizing we can do something we thought we couldn't do. If we've held back, we may benefit from a strong experience of disappointment with "more of the same." This awareness may strengthen the desire to create a difference that will make a difference the next time. Questions to help facilitate learning at this stage include:

"How are you experiencing this moment? What is different?"
"How do you feel now?"
"What are you experiencing about yourself or others?"
"What's going on in your body?"
"What are you thinking now?"

Closure is the process by which we re-establish our boundaries; the membrane seals back up. We pull back, evaluate, and notice if we are finished. "Did I take in something new, or hang on to the familiar?" It is a period where we may let go of prior conceptions, in order to allow this new experience or idea to become integrated. This is where we assign meaning to the contact we've just had. If we are feeling finished, and the need has been fulfilled, then our energy and interest in that need will naturally decline. If some need remains, this becomes the sensation for the next cycle, and our energy can build from there.

Taking time for this experience of evaluation is essential for healthy functioning and growth. To move rapidly past this, without adequate time for reflection, is to potentially miss the chance to integrate some important changes. People pass this stage for numerous reasons, from avoidance of painful awareness of mistakes, to fear of acknowledgment and success, or simply by habit. We need to repeat, finish, close, let go, celebrate, or do whatever is ecological with the contact we've just made. This is the time processing that usually takes place and helps solidify the learning and closure. Questions at this stage are your typical processing questions which include:

"What did you want to take from this experience?"
"What do you need to remind yourself about the experience?"
"What were the success factors that let you really connect with the experience?"

Withdrawal refers to a time of quiet reflection and pulling back. We may appreciate a sense of completion and clear our senses. This enables us to be fully present and available for the next sensation. This zero point, or balance point, may be fleeting, but it is a good indication of the fulfillment of completion of the Stages of Experience.

In the United States, our culture generally doesn't respect the value of closure and withdrawal. Pressures to "go faster" and "get on to the next project" frequently exist. Such expectations and assumptions are important parts of our sensations, and they may strongly influence us. When facilitating experiential education or therapy, these factors can be brought to awareness and at times be offered up and challenged as chosen values.

Dealing with stuck points in the Stages. A stuck point is when a participant does not flow through a stage, and thus inhibits his or her ability to move on strongly, or perhaps even to proceed at all. Examples of this exist at every stage. Instead of attending to their sensations, they may numb or distract themselves, or deny present sensations so that their awareness is limited. At the excitement stage, awareness of feelings, wants and needs may be sidetracked by old beliefs like, "I'm a failure," which divert energy and focus away from creating effective action. Stuckness in the action stage may result from individuals not having the skills to express themselves or deal with the challenge, and thus they are not able to successfully engage in order to make good contact. There may be a stuck point at being frightened to truly experience a moment of beauty or success or intimacy with others. Some individuals may not be able to feel closure and withdrawal from an experience, and keep "hanging on" to it or don't effectively learn from it.

To get through these stuck points, individuals first have to identify where they are interrupting this natural process. We can strengthen our awareness by slowing down and attending to immediate sensations and awareness. These are building blocks. This is sometimes referred to as *fattening the moment*—like spreading it out so it's easier to see the details. "What are you aware of right now? What is around you? What are you thinking as you look around? What do you notice in your body? What feelings have come up? What are you expecting? Is any of this familiar?"

This is where most of the processing work occurs. When we heighten these sensations, there is a greater chance of effectively heightening our needs and wants, and defining directive action. If we pass through this process too fast, we end up with insufficient or inaccurate raw material, and later it may be harder to determine what went wrong.

Consider that the experience of focusing on a stuck point also has its own Stages, beginning with sensation and awareness. Note what occurs at each moment of the processing. Is the participant able to stay focused? Are they able to take in the information that they are at a "stuck point?" Are you as the leader able to stay present? If the leader becomes impatient, this becomes part of the sensations that the participant encounters.

Interruptions in the Stages of Experience

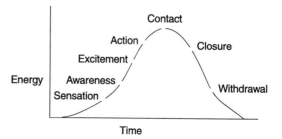

Quite often, as we heighten awareness in an impasse or "stuck point", a person has greater access to fears, limiting beliefs, judgments and assumptions that create and maintain such impasses. These blocks may be overcome by seeing new options in the present moment, and creating corrective experiences during the initiative. This experience is wonderful and exciting. These blocks also merit later attention as "targeted sensations" themselves, to help the person reprocess the issues that emerged. If we are able to make present "contact" with these blocks or "impasses", we have the chance to experience a new relationship with them, using all our present senses and resources. We can then transform them, let them go, and assimilate something new.

Back to Scott, and his leap off the board. We froze the moment of jumping off for Scott and encouraged him to imagine himself back on the board (as he had been a moment earlier), seeing the shore. He felt his excitement and anticipation of completion. As we helped him to access his whole experience, he realized that his entire focus narrowed onto himself and his personal needs. Scott then felt guilty for his "selfishness," and could have easily become lost in self-blame. We asked if this process of losing awareness of others was familiar, and Scott recalled repeated scenes in his large family where everybody had to fend for themselves in order to get their needs met. He felt how naturally his sense of urgency arose, along with the thought "I need to act fast or I'll lose." Scott held this awareness and re-connected with his current environment, thus creating a contrast that he found useful for realizing how he now wants to do things differently. He then expanded this change into situations at home and at work, and decided to shift to: "Others can win with me." We made sure to check in with Scott's self-reflections and actions at various times in subsequent initiatives.

We also noticed Scott's initial reluctance to reflect on what had just happened (avoidance of "closure"). As this is a common issue, we utilized another participant's similar experience to heighten this awareness for the whole group. We normalized the issue by asking everyone to share their thoughts or experiences about how looking at mistakes can be difficult for them. More safety emerged in the group as people acknowledged their need to know that they are respected in order to risk vulnerability. This exemplifies how a lack of emotional safety will cause "resistance" and an interruption of the Stages, and how expanding the moment of impasse can lead to a natural addressing of needs. It is helpful throughout the experience to focus on the impasses that participants are having, so they can learn how they typically interrupt their own Stages of Experience.

In order for most leaders to make use of the concept of the Stages of Experience, it takes some practice in observing behavior from this perspective. The levels of processing and processing activities within the book can give you more suggestions on how to highlight the stages of the cycle of experience. You may find it useful to watch your own process, as well as that of others. Notice the flow and interruption of energy and the various stages of the drive toward need development, contact and resolution.

P · A · R · T   III

Effective Leadership Knowledge and Skills

Leader Interventions
Building Rapport
Enhancing Communication Skills
Promoting Co-Leader Vision and Teamwork
Group Developmental Stages
General Guidelines for Working with Groups
Group Ground Rules
Levels of Processing
Additional Processing Questions
Methods of Processing
Processing Activities
Developing and Using Metaphors
Co-Constructing New Stories
Use of Reflective Teams
Increasing Effectiveness
Reluctant Individuals
Redirecting
Using Handicaps
Goal Setting and Personal Action Plans

LEADER INTERVENTIONS

Experiential educators, trainers and therapists responsible for leading and facilitating learning experiences are expected to be highly knowledgeable and skillful. They need to oversee safety parameters, assess individual and group needs, provide instruction, facilitate personal development, and evaluate the quality of the experience. Specific processing skills suggested by a sample of members of the Association of Experiential Education were reported by Brackenreg, Luckner, and Pinch (1994). Table 4 contains the list of essential processing knowledge and skills for experiential educators and therapists. For organizational purposes, these competencies have been divided into four general categories—preparation, fostering a caring environment, communication skills, and sequencing. Additional information on each of these competencies is provided throughout the text.

In the remainder of this section, we have highlighted twelve leader interventions that commonly are used to structure and process experiences. This information has been adapted from Dyer (1972) and Schwarz (1994).

1. *Content Focus.* This entails some specific introduction of information. This information may include safety issues, providing clear guidelines and parameters, addressing participant concerns and expectations, sharing a personal experience, giving an opinion, or clarifying some instructions. Content interventions are most helpful when they provide information that the group members feel they require to proceed with the activity or exercise. For example: (a) "On this activity you have a twenty minute time-limit. Then, we will take a few minutes to reflect and discuss how decisions were made." or (b) "Today's hike is going to be challenging. I would like you to monitor the statements that you say to yourself when you are feeling stretched."

2. *Process Focus.* This intervention focuses on what is happening within the group. It examines the interactions among members while they are doing certain tasks. You want to focus on the here and now process in the group. Examples may be (a) "How are you working together as a group?", (b) "I wonder why some people aren't sharing their feelings or ideas", (c) "It seems like the same people do all the work", (d) "What is preventing people from speaking their mind?", (e) "It seems like the group is more concerned with just getting done than with producing a quality product ", or (f) "Right now, I experience a lot of tension in the group."

◆ TABLE 4 ◆

Essential Processing Skills

◆ **Preparation**

Allocate time for processing.
Encourage setting of personal and group goals.
Address the most important issues and goals that have evolved during the activity.
Process immediately after major events.
Establish the ground rules in advance
Balance practical considerations.
    Example: discomfort, fatigue, hunger, time restrictions, type and ability of group.
Assess the participants.
Position the group so that everyone can be seen and heard, and no one is excluded.

◆ **Fostering a Caring Environment**

Use appropriate tone of voice.
Allow participants to take risks in speaking freely and honestly.
Show empathy by:
    responding to feeling
    responding to feeling and content
    personalizing meaning
    personalizing problems, feelings and goals
Create an atmosphere for caring, sharing and trusting by encouraging everyone to belong, listen
    and be involved.
Be genuine.
Exhibit consistent behavior to all participants.
Give praise and words of encouragement.
Respect everyone's personal limits.

◆ **Communication Skills**

Use appropriate non-verbal communication such as:
    ◆ eye contact
    ◆ facial expression
    ◆ body posture
Observe nonverbal behavior and draw information from it.
Ask for feelings about specific events.
Be an active listener.
Involve reluctant individuals but respect silence.

Questioning Skills
Provide sufficient "wait time".
Ask more open ended questions than closed.
Allow participants to reflect on experiences and draw meaning from them.
Use directed questioning to highlight issues, roles and behaviors.
Probe for self-discovery rather than tell participants how they are functioning.

(continued)

◆ TABLE 4 ◆

Essential Processing Skills *(continued)*

Feedback

Use verbal and nonverbal gestures to encourage participants to continue, and indicate you are focused and following their communication.

Check communication by:

  Asking the receiver if she/he understands what you mean.

  Giving your understanding to check if it is right.

Give feedback and encourage others to do the same.

Offer a description of what you saw and how you felt, rather than judging behavior.

Deal with the here and now.

Communication Strategies

Focus on behavior which can be changed.

Transform a groups' perceived mistakes or failures into positive learning experiences. (Reframe experiences)

Avoid giving advice, instead, communicate parallel experiences and feelings.

Allow participants to do more talking than the debriefer.

Use humor.

Vary the length and intensity of debriefing sessions.

Foster an openness and acceptance of the group and individuals to failure.

Use a variety of methods. Example, journals, dyads, drawings, role play, solo, reflection, whips, modeling.

General Skills

Redirect destructive, manipulative or dominating behaviors.

Allow only one person to speak at a time.

Give everyone the chance to speak.

Keep the group focused.

◆ **Sequencing**

Help transference to other life situations.

Provide gentle and small opportunities to disclose.

Highlight process; move from content to process.

Move from facilitator controlled processing to participant controlled processing.

Address all types of learning—psychomotor, cognitive and affective.

Provide closure.

3. *Eliciting Feelings.* This intervention helps members develop a sense of being a group. It may not only let members know that they are not alone, but also it may help them see how others feel about their behavior. Reluctance to share feelings may be based on the lack of trust, self-confidence, or the inability to identify feelings. An example of this intervention may be, "How did you feel, Mary, when the group rejected your suggestions?"

4. *Exploring.* Exploratory interventions are designed to help you understand a situation by getting the essential facts, understanding how a series of events unfolded, or finding out how an

individual or members of the group think or feel about something. Examples of questions that you may use include, "What do you think the problem is?," "Could you say more about that?," or "What do you want to accomplish?"

5. *Seeking Specifics.* People have a tendency to talk in general, abstract terms. Thus, you often need to solicit more specific information in order to clarify exactly what they mean. Examples include, "Can you give some examples of what you mean by 'a negative attitude'?" or "What exactly did she say to you that upset you?"

6. *Sequencing Activities.* Making decisions about the flow of events is an important aspect of establishing a positive, learning environment. Some of the important questions that you will want to ask yourself include: "How does the activity relate to the individual and group goals that have been set?" "Is the individual and/or group mentally and physically prepared to do the activity?" "Does the person or group have the ability to attempt the activity or to complete it?" "What is the general mood of the individual or group?" "What types of positive and negative interactions are affecting the group?" "How cooperative are the group members?" "What is the physical shape and abilities of the partici-

pants?" "How tired are they?" "What is the group's developmental stage and level of functioning?"

7. *Direct Feedback.* Individuals and groups are usually anxious to know how you view them. These concerns may be a legitimate request for feedback or may indicate that the participants have not worked through viewing you as an authority figure. Feedback is very important. It's important that members not only get feedback from you but also from their peers. You can facilitate this by asking, "Ernie, how do you interpret or view Bill's behavior now?" Once a few viewpoints are expressed, then you can respond. If the group is protective of its members, you may want to go first and then ask others for their feedback. Once the group coalesces, the group members will begin to give each other direct feedback without your example.

8. *Cognitive Orientation.* At times, you may want to offer participants a relevant theory or information in order to provide them with a conceptual framework for understanding the group process. Suggestions for topics include problem-solving techniques, conflict resolution, using the ladder of inference, stress management, 7-habits of effective people, group stages, how to express feelings, assertive behavior, defining forgiveness, and leadership styles. The extent to which you use the cognitive orientation intervention will depend on the individuals and group goals as well as your assessment of how best to help group members learn.

9. *Performing Group Functions.* You may intervene by using task maintenance functions. The purpose of these interventions is to help the group maintain itself as an effective system that

continues to promote learning. One way to do this is to have the group reflect upon and analyze what they have just accomplished. You will facilitate this by asking for opinions or reactions. For example, you might say, "O.K. what is working here? what is not working?, and what do you need to do to be more efficient?" Generally, you will reduce such interventions as participants develop a greater ability to perform these functions on their own.

10. *Diagnostic Intervention.* When an individual or a group is having difficulty getting started or functioning, you may diagnose what you see happening by thinking out loud with the person or group. The diagnostic intervention encourages participants to be introspective and speculative in order to create a better understanding. An example of a diagnostic intervention would be: "There may be a number of possible reasons to explain why we are not working together well today. One reason may be that our goals may be too vague. Another is that some people may not feel comfortable sharing their opinions because they may be criticized. Are there any other possible reasons that you think may exist?"

11. *Reframing.* Reframing helps people change the meaning they ascribe to events. As the meaning of events changes, people's responses and behaviors also change (Bateson, 1972). For example, people are often reluctant to give others feedback. They feel uncomfortable, and, if the feedback is not positive, they are worried that they might hurt the other person's feelings. You

can help group members overcome their unwillingness by working with them to reframe what it means "to care." You can explain that really caring about people means giving others feedback about their behavior. This feedback will help them improve their personal lives as well as professional effectiveness. In addition, by withholding information from people, we may be hurting them by not allowing them to make informed choices about whether or not to change their behaviors.

12. *Protective Intervention.* In some groups, members may want to share deep emotional issues (e.g., addiction, incest, physical abuse, or rape) that extend beyond the boundaries of the group. If this is not the focus of the program, these personal emotional issues may diverge significantly from the goals of the group. In addition, you may not have the appropriate training to deal with such issues. Therefore, you will want to intervene and possibly choose to speak with the member individually and encourage him or her to contact a professional counselor or psychologist. You also want to intervene when one or two members are being cruelly criticized. In general, you are responsible for protecting the emotional safety of each of the group members.

BUILDING RAPPORT

"Don't accept your dog's admiration as conclusive evidence that you are wonderful."

—Ann Landers

As educators, trainers and therapists it is important for us to develop relationships that are based on trust and comfort. Consequently, we need to be concerned about building rapport with our fellow workers as well as with the individuals that we work with in experiential education and therapeutic settings. This is true throughout the relationship, however, the initial stage is most crucial for building rapport because it is at this point that we establish either a positive or negative impression.

The key to building rapport is to make others feel accepted, supported, and comfortable. This can be a particular challenge when variables such as age, gender, race, life experiences, professional status, or reputation interfere with establishing rapport. Nonetheless, we want to reach out to others and try and develop compatibility right from the beginning of our interactions. The most effective procedure when establishing rapport is to be authentic and genuine. A good starting point is to ask yourself, "what are the things that people do that help me feel

accepted?" Some general strategies that tend to communicate acceptance are (a) use the person's name; (b) maintain eye contact; (c) appear calm, yet energized (d) use effective interpersonal communication skills—listen actively, paraphrase, summarize, clarify, and ask for more detail, (e) give credit to individuals for their ideas and accomplishments, (f) refrain from making judgments, (g) eliminate jargon terms and acronyms that others might not have knowledge of, and (h) offer information about yourself when appropriate.

Another tool to consider when developing rapport is a technique referred to as matching and mirroring. Researchers indicate that nonverbal behavior makes up 75% to 95% of communication (Egan 1986). What people are really saying or meaning can be seen in their posture, facial expressions, tone of voice, excitement level, and mannerisms. Robbins (1986) noted that, "People tend to like people who tend to be like them" (p. 9). Matching and mirroring allows individuals on an unconscious level to think "this person is just like me." Accordingly, one way of matching and mirroring is to sit or stand like the person, use the same tonality, phrasing, pitch and imitate their hand gestures, body movements, postures, facial expressions, breathing patterns, and tilt of the head. While it may seem strange to copy the person that we are having a conversation with, it is interesting to note that we all do this unconsciously. We suggest making this practice more intentional.

Another means of matching and mirroring is to use the same words, expressions, or predicate phrases that they are using. Here again, they can easily feel that you hear and understand them. Table 5 contains a list of words or predicate phrases that people may use (Robbins, 1986).

◆ TABLE 5 ◆

Commonly Used Predicate Phrases

Visual (see)	Auditory (hear)	Kinesthetic (feel)
Appears to me	Clear as a bell	Come to grips with
Looks like	Clearly expressed	Get a handle on it
Bird's-eye view	Earful	Cool/calm/collected
Clear Cut	Express yourself	Get in touch with
Eye to eye	Purrs like a kitten	Hold it!
Plainly see	Rings a bell	Get the drift of
Mental picture	Loud and clear	Keep your shirt on!
In view of	Manner of speaking	Hand in hand
Make a scene	Idle talk	Hang in there
Beyond a shadow of a doubt	To tell the truth	Lay cards on table
Tunnel Vision	State your purpose	Pain in the neck
Paint a picture	Tuned in/tuned out	Not following you
See to it	Unheard-of	Sharp as a tack
Pretty as a picture	Tongue-tied	Pull some strings
Sight for sore eyes	Voiced an opinion	Have a handle on it
Take a dim view	In perfect harmony	Solid as a rock
Staring off into space	Sounds good	Doesn't feel right
It's hazy to me	Word for word	Underhanded

They are divided into visual, auditory, and kinesthetic. Each of us use all three of these ways to communicate, but we usually have a preferred mode.

In general, people with a visual preference talk very fast, their breathing may be high in their chest, and the vocal tone is high-pitched, nasal, or strained. They talk fast because they are making pictures and want to project it out quickly. They use words like: "see," "view," and "paint me a picture." People with an auditory preference speak in more modulated tones; their voices have a clear and resonant tonality. The breathing appears to come from the diaphragm. They use words like: "sounds like," "I hear you," "that rings loud and true," and "to tell you the truth." People with a kinesthetic preference tend to speak in a slow tempo with long pauses between words. Their tonality is low and deep. These people feel as they speak. They use words like: "It doesn't feel right," "I want to get a grasp of this," and "I can't get a hold of what you are saying."

In building rapport and developing trust, if you can identify individuals' preferred way of perceiving communication and then match that, they are likely to feel as if you are speaking their language. Add to this the ability to mirror their physiology, body language, and tonality, and rapport can be greatly enhanced. As a result, it is likely that others will feel trust in the relationship and be encouraged out of the circle of comfort to the successes of the new territory.

ENHANCING COMMUNICATION SKILLS

"The most important single ingredient in the formula of success is knowing how to get along with people."

—*Theodore Roosevelt*

Communication is a dynamic and ongoing process in which people share ideas, information and feelings (Owens, 1992). Effective communication skills are the lifeblood of every relationship. When communication is open, clear and sensitive, the relationship is nurtured. When communication is guarded or hostile, the relationship falters (Bolton, 1979). Similarly, effective communication skills are considered essential for successful individuals in virtually all professions.

Due to the essential role that communication plays in establishing positive relationships and for promoting individuals' learning and development, this section includes information that we believe is extremely important for professionals. Specifically, this section includes information on the: (a) The communication process; (b) Skills that facilitate communication; (c) Barriers to effective communication; and (d) Feedback.

❖ THE COMMUNICATION PROCESS

Communication is a cyclical process comprised of five components: A sender, a message, a channel, an environment, and a receiver. The process of communication is initiated when the sender sends a message by some kind of channel through the environment to a receiver of that message. The channels for messages typically are auditory or visual. A verbal message consists of words, whereas a nonverbal message consists of actions such as gestures, body position, facial expressions, pitch and tone of voice. Senders simultaneously send both verbal and nonverbal messages to the receiver. The receiver picks up the message through a combination of visual and auditory means and gains meaning by interpreting the combined visual and auditory message. The receiver then becomes a sender and provides direct or indirect feedback to the original sender (who now becomes a receiver), which helps the original sender understand that the original message was understood. This cycle continues throughout the interaction.

79

For communication to occur, sending a message is not enough; the message must also be understood accurately by the receiver. Continuous feedback provides the means for individuals to share information and to modify messages or to provide clarification when a message is misunderstood. Without an understanding of communication as a cycle involving both a receiver and a sender, we might assume that we communicated successfully simply because we sent the message. Feedback from the receiver indicating that the message sent was understood accurately is necessary to validate this assumption. The communication cycle must be completed before we communicate.

❖ SKILLS THAT FACILITATE COMMUNICATION

LISTENING

The term hearing is used to describe the physiological sensory processes by which auditory stimuli are received by the ears and transmitted to the brain. Listening, refers to a more complex psychological procedure involving interpreting and understanding the meaning of the message. In other words, we can hear what another person is saying without really listening to him or her.

Listening skills are important particularly when engaging in educational and/or therapeutic relationships. When we listen, we are showing a concern and a desire to understand both the other person and the situation. We communicate concern for the speaker as an individual as well as the intent to understand what that person has to say. We also demonstrate that we are sensitive to the situation and to the person's perception of the situation. Another major reason for developing effective listening skills is that good listening is essential for obtaining adequate and accurate information. These are the skills that help clarify and understand the messages being sent.

The following specific suggestions to consider for improving your listening skills have been adapted from Friend and Cook (1996):

✓ *Rehearse the information being conveyed to you.* Mentally practice repeating the information being conveyed. Challenge yourself to determine whether you truly understood everything that was said.

✓ *Categorize the information being received.* Develop categories so that you can actively sort the information that you are receiving. For example, you can classify information by feelings, behaviors, current problems, family situation, goals, and support systems.

Additionally, when you begin speaking, you can use the categories as a framework to address the topics that have been raised.

✓ *Jot notes for details.* Note taking is one technique that you can use when a large amount of information is being presented to you. Although note taking may interfere with listening, it can be effective when you limit yourself to jotting down only the important concepts and details. It is beneficial to let the other person know the reason why you are taking notes.

✓ *Use a signal as a cue to remember ideas.* When you want to remember a specific thought or concern, you can use an unobtrusive signal to yourself, such as bending and holding down your little finger or turning your ring around, to enable you to temporarily store the information. When the person is finished talking, your signal will remind you of the point you wanted to make.

ATTENDING BEHAVIORS

Attending behaviors refer to the nonverbal communication that indicates that we are paying careful attention to the individual who is talking. Attending behaviors show others that we are interested in them and in what they have to say. Discussed below are eye contact, facial expressions, body posture, and physical space. General information about these behaviors is provided, however, it is important to note that these behaviors may vary among individuals as a result of cultural differences.

✓ *Eye contact.* Focus your eyes directly on speakers but be sensitive to the effect such direct eye-to-eye contact may have. Many people feel uncomfortable with direct eye contact and tend to shy away from it. Readjust your focus accordingly.

✓ *Facial expressions.* Your expressions or lack of them provide feedback to speakers, thereby prompting them to say more, to slow down, to clarify. More important, let your face tell the speaker that you empathize with him or her. Smiles, frowns, expressions of surprise or disappointment don't cost much so share them with others. Simultaneously, attend to the facial expressions of speakers. What nonverbal messages are they conveying ?

✓ *Body posture.* You can help speakers relax by relaxing your own body. Body gestures often convey meaning. When listeners lean toward a speaker a high level of interest and involvement is communicated. Attend to the body language of speakers—it also is sending messages.

✓ *Physical space.* The distance that people create between themselves has an inherent communication value. An 18-inch distance between speakers has been described as "intimate space", the 18-inch to 4-foot distance as "personal space" and the 4-foot to 12-foot distance as "social distance." Each of these distances communicates distinct nonverbal messages.

NONVERBAL BEHAVIOR

As discussed in the previous section on developing rapport, nonverbal behavior is a critical element of the communication process. Substantial valuable information is communicated without

words. Skillful use of nonverbal behaviors is considered an essential element in communicating attitudes necessary for establishing and maintaining positive relationships (e.g., interest, acceptance,
warmth) and a powerful tool in clarifying, emphasizing, or confusing the meaning of verbal messages.

Each of us communicate nonverbally in several ways. Three primary classes of nonverbal
cues are (1) body movements such as facial expression, eye contact, posture, and gestures, (2) vocal
cues such as quality of voice and the pacing or flow of speech, and (3) spatial relationships that
include the physical distance between the participants. Each of these categories of nonverbal
cues affects the nature of the communication among people. For example, without even using
words, you can communicate a wide range of attitudes and feelings through gestures and facial
expression. Similarly, paralanguage, the vocal—rather than verbal—component of language, also
communicates a great deal of information separate from the verbal content of the message.
Paralanguage includes voice tone, pitch and volume, speech rhythm and pacing or tempo, as
well as the use and timing of silence.

Many or all of the elements of paralanguage may reach extremes when we experience intense
emotions. For example, pitch results from the tightness of one's vocal cords. When you are calm,
depressed, or tired your vocal cords are relaxed and your pitch is lower, whereas excitement or
anxiety tends to cause your pitch to be higher. The pace of speech also may indicate emotion;
rapid speech can signal excitement and enthusiasm or nervousness and insecurity. Thus, you may
observe that someone anxious or uncertain about a situation may speak very rapidly at a high
pitch while someone more confident and relaxed is likely to speak slowly at a lower pitch.

When a person is dealing with or talking about something important to them, tactile sensations, body movements, and paralanguage are important signals to unconscious feelings or motivations. These signals are not within their awareness and can provide us with insight into the
person who we are communicating with and possibly help guide us in our processing. Table 6 contains some examples of nonverbal information and learning that have been adapted from Norton
(1978). It is important to note that these behaviors may vary according to cultural differences.

Brief Verbal Acknowledgment

It is valuable to occasionally interject brief verbal acknowledgments, such as: "I see", "Uh-
huh", "Oh", and "That's too bad." The goal is to express interest and concern without interrupting or interjecting personal comments. Keep the reaction brief and quickly refocus on the
speaker. These statements provide others with an invitation to continue talking. Statements of
encouragement such as the following are short indicators to others that you interested:

- Tell me more.
- For instance . . .
- Really?
- I see.
- Right.
- And?
- Then?
- Sure.
- I hear you.
- I'll bet that's frustrating.

◆ TABLE 6 ◆

Examples of Nonverbal Behavior

Head

Hair hiding face reflects low self-concept or insecurity at that point in the person's life.
Hand on head means the person is holding something back, so ask is there more he or she wants to
   say about it.

Eyes

Dry tears (wiping invisible tears) signifies sadness and/or insecurity.
A dominant person maintains eye contact more than a submissive person.
Looking to the side is avoidance.
Looking up is intellectualization or they are creating or remembering pictures.
Looking down means the person is dealing with feelings.
Looking up and to the side is looking for approval.
Large irises mean the individual is emotionally expressive and sensitive.
Small irises mean that individuals conceal their emotions or think with their head rather than their
   heart.

Mouth

Fingers held to the mouth, stroking the lips, shows a need for nurturance or for support.
Hand in front of the mouth while talking reflects the attitude "I'm not important."
Continual smiling means the person is anxious or nervous and not showing real feelings.

Chin

Person with a strong, extended chin will most often be a stubborn person.
Person with the chin in or recessive tends to be more passive and submissive.

Jaws

A person with a strong chin will also tend to have rigid jaws which show assertion.
Chewing can be an act of hostility, anger, and/or aggression.

Throat

Pulling down is choking off.
Hand on throat is choking off.
"Lump" represents a need to cry or shout. It may also mean that something is stuck there. There is
   an unwillingness to "swallow" some feeling or expression imposed on one by others, or an
   unexpressed wish to tell someone off.

Arms

Crossed arms are holding feelings in.
Holding oneself is a need to be comforted.
No gesturing (arms rigid) shows inhibition of feelings or depression.
Excessive use of arm and hand movements indicates a need for attention.

(continued)

◆ **TABLE 6** ◆

Examples of Nonverbal Behavior (continued)

Hands

Represent emotions.
Sitting on hands turned up means the person is tucking in his/her feelings.
Sitting on hands turned down means feelings are being hidden (more severe).
Hands on chest are holding in feelings.
Running fingers or tapping or drumming fingers shows impatience.
Fist and hand show that the person is putting the lid on his/her aggression.
Picking lint is an attempt to be rid of something.

Legs

One leg bounce sometimes means the person would like to kick someone.
Two leg bounce shows impatience or ambivalence.
Rubbing thighs may also precede any conscious feeling or thought about sexuality.

Voice

Soft voice shows lack of self-confidence.
Fluctuating volume—what is said softly is an area where person doesn't feel secure.
Whiny voice shows a need for nurturance, a need to know that people care.
A person with a monotone voice is most likely the type of person who has difficulty making
    commitments.
Laughing is many times covering up a need to cry.
Talking fast is running from something.

Body orientation

Body positioned toward the other person, facing the person with forward trunk lean shows
    involvement.
Lack of involvement is shown by moving away, turning away, backward lean of trunk or by putting
    any object between the two people.

PARAPHRASING

In paraphrasing, we restate in our own words what we think another person has just said. This provides the sender with an opportunity to agree or further refine the message. Paraphrasing focuses on relatively small units of information that were discussed by the other individual, and it involves little or no inference. By accurately restating the main points of a person's statement, we demonstrate that we have been attending to and accurately understanding what the person has been relating thereby conveying an interest in the message as well as in the person. When paraphrasing, we want to try to (a) be concise—including only the essential ideas, concepts, themes of the speaker's message, and (b) focus on the content of the speaker's message—deal with the facts or ideas rather than the emotions the sender is expressing.

REFLECTION

Reflection makes use of clarifying statements that are more complex than paraphrasing. In reflection, we describe what another person has said and try to capture the affective meaning of the message. We focus on the emotions because feelings are the energizing force that help us sort out data, organize it, and use it effectively. Reflection demonstrates that we understand another's feelings.

Because we cannot observe another's feelings, we examine the verbal and nonverbal information provided and infer what this information communicates. When reflecting a speaker's apparent message, Bolton, (1979) suggests that you try to concentrate on four things:

1. Focus on the feeling words.
2. Note the general content of the message.
3. Observe the body language—facial expression, tone of voice, gesture, and posture.
4. Ask yourself, "If I were having that experience, what would I be feeling?"

Reflection is usually best when it is kept to a single short sentence. A rambling response hinders communication. When first learning to reflect meanings, people often find it beneficial to use the formula "you feel [insert the feeling word] because [insert the event or other content that is associated with the feeling]." For example, "You feel disappointed because the group did not listen to your idea." As you become more comfortable with the technique of reflection, you may decide to stop using the "You feel . . . because . . . formula and integrate less awkward variations such as the following:

"You are confused by . . ."
"Sounds like you are thrilled that . . ."
"You're angry about . . ."
"You're discouraged by . . ."
"You're really clear about that. You're friend . . ."
"You sound like you feel anxious about . . ."
"I'm not sure I understand. Do you mean you're disappointed that . . ."
"I see, you mean that you hoped she would . . ."
"Are you saying you're so frustrated that you . . ."
"I get the idea; you want to . . ."
"It's frightening to . . ."
"It seems unfair to you that . . ."
"It hurts when you . . ."
"When it happens, your resentful."
"I hear you saying you're unhappy with . . ."
"Sounds like you're excited about . . ."
"That's embarrassing for you to . . ."

CLARIFICATION

When engaged in dialogue, there are times that we need to seek clarification in order to gain greater understanding of the information being provided. Confusion can occur for two reasons. First, the manner in which our partner is sending the message can lead to confusion. When people are upset, concerned, or excited they often jump around—having several different thoughts. Consequently, they send messages that contain parts of each of these thoughts simultaneously. When this happens, we have to slow down the person, ask some key questions, and, in the process, help the person begin to sort out what's really important. Second, we may need to seek clarification because of our own lack of attention. After listening to a person for a while, we may find that we have begun to think about other things not related to what the individual is saying. Trying to pretend that we were listening is a mistake.

SILENCE

"A closed mouth gathers no feet."

—*Anonymous*

When used appropriately, silence is a valuable asset to communication. It can give both parties a chance to stop and reflect on what has been said. It may encourage speakers to say more. Too often listeners feel compelled to make an immediate response, and; consequently, they begin searching for a reply before speakers have concluded. Wait a few seconds to be sure that speakers have completed their thoughts.

SUMMARIZING

Summarizing consists of one or more statements that restate, in succinct form, several preceding statements made by the individuals involved in the interaction. By feeding back to speakers the gist of their message, we validate the communication, which often inspires further communication. It also is a means of ensuring that all individuals involved understand what has been said. Specifically, it gives all individuals a chance to hear the key points and to agree on what was said or to disagree and revise the content of the interaction and make some clarifications regarding key ideas or events.

USE OF I-MESSAGES

"Relly, I can't believe that you don't have the section on Levels of Processing finished yet. Here it is one week from our deadline and you still haven't completed the work that you are responsible for."

This is an example of a "you-message." When we send "you-messages" to people, they feel embarrassed, angry, hurt, put-down, or worthless, and most likely, they don't feel like cooperating. "You-messages" often don't work because: (a) individuals who continually receive negative messages may begin to believe them, (b) when we put the blame for our feelings on others, we risk their refusal to accept the blame, and, (c) when we criticize others, we may be reinforcing the behavior that they are demonstrating.

"I-messages" meet three important criteria for effective confrontation: (1) they have a high probability of promoting a willingness to change; (2) they contain minimal negative evaluation of the person; and (3) they do not injure the relationship. When we express our feelings and concerns in "I-messages," we appeal to the individual's good nature and desire to cooperate. We are asking for their help. We say, "I'm worried", "I'm concerned", I'm afraid", "I'm disappointed"—and we tell why rather than making an evaluative statement such as "You're a rotten, self-centered egotist who won't listen to anyone else's ideas." We take responsibility for our own feelings and leave the person's behavior up to them. At the same time, "I-messages" avoid negative impact that accompanies "you-messages," freeing the person to be considerate and helpful, not resentful, angry, and devious. For those reason, in the example above, it would have been more appropriate to say "Relly, I am feeling stressed. Our deadline is a week away and all of our sections aren't finished. What do you think we should do?"

Constructing I-messages. "I-messages" are composed of three parts:

1. First describe the behavior—Don't blame, just describe. "When people are not paying attention while belaying. . . ."
2. Then state your feelings about the possible consequences of the behavior. ". . . I get worried"
3. Then state what those consequences are or might be. ". . . that someone might fall and get hurt."

We can vary the format. The three parts don't have to be delivered in order, and you may sometimes eliminate the statement of feelings. For example: "When we don't take time to plan, our work sessions don't seem to be effective." Similarly, sometimes when you speak to an individual, your statement will contain the word you. It is still an "I-message" if the "you" is descriptive and not critical or blaming. An example is: "Todd, when you take off down the trail ahead of everyone else I get worried that you might take a different route than the group and that we'll have to spend lots of time trying to find each other".

❖ BARRIERS TO EFFECTIVE COMMUNICATION

To communicate effectively, we must also recognize barriers to communication and try to eliminate them from our interaction style. The following are examples of behaviors that often interfere with effective communication. This information has been adapted from Friend and Cook (1996).

REHEARSING A RESPONSE

At times, we think that we have a sense of what the person that we are talking with is discussing, and we proceed to work on framing what we will say when we have the opportunity to speak. Consequently, we may miss the true essence of what is being said.

FALSE REASSURANCES

Perhaps one of the most well-intentioned errors that may result in serious consequences is giving false reassurances. This occurs when we indicate to an individual that everything is going to work out and there is nothing to worry about or that we are sure the problem is going to be solved.

CLICHÉS

"Don't worry, just go for it." is an example of a frequently overused cliché. Responding to an individual's problem with a cliché is certain to inhibit communication. Clichés diminish the feelings of the person with whom we are interacting. When we hear ourselves using a cliché, we should try and backtrack and clarify the response.

MISDIRECTED QUESTIONS

In order to help individuals reflect upon what's happening in their situation, so greater understanding can be gained, we often rely on the use of questions. Questions are a primary means of directing conversations and of developing mutual understanding. However, if too many questions are asked or the questions lack a consistent direction, they will inhibit the quality of the conversation.

DAYDREAMING

We are capable of receiving information more rapidly through listening than the average speaker can convey. The result is that we have extra time to think, even while we listen. Unfortunately, we may use this time to think about things other than the conversation—what the other members of the group are doing, what you will do when the structured experience is finished. Obviously, this shared mode of thinking does not benefit our conversational partner.

❖ FEEDBACK

"Honest criticism is hard to take, particularly from a relative, a friend, an acquaintance, or a stranger."

—*Franklin P. Jones*

Feedback is a way of providing people with information about their behavior and how those behaviors affect others. As in a guided missile system, feedback helps individuals keep their behavior "on target", and thus they are better able to achieve their goals. To be effective in working with others, we need to become skilled at giving, soliciting, and accepting feedback. When giving feedback to others, specific criteria should guide us. The following are criteria for effective feedback:

✓ *It is descriptive rather than evaluative.* People are more likely to listen when someone describes what has been observed. Avoiding evaluative language reduces the need for individuals to react defensively. For example, "I noticed that you lost interest in participating." is more appropriate than "Why did you quit taking part in the activity?"

✓ *It is specific rather than general.* It is easier for us to understand specific statements as compared to general comments. For example, to be told that one is "dominating" will probably not be as useful as to be told that "When we were making a decision about what to do first, you did not listen to what other people said. I felt pressure to accept your opinion or be ready for an argument."

✓ *It takes into account the needs of both the receiver and giver of feedback.* Feedback can be destructive when it serves only our own needs and fails to consider the needs of the person on the receiving end.

✓ *It is directed toward behavior which the receiver can do something about.* Frustration is only increased when people are reminded of some shortcomings over which they have no control such as physical traits or situational aspects. Information such as "I notice that you usually wait to see what Cameron thinks about an issue before you share your opinion." is information that may be acted upon if a person chooses.

✓ *It is solicited, rather than imposed.* Feedback is most likely to be used when someone has formulated specific questions and requested information. Nonetheless, there may be situations when it is appropriate to ask, "Are you asking for some feedback?" or "Would you like to hear some feedback?"

✓ *It is well-timed.* In general, feedback is most useful at the earliest opportunity after the relevant event or given behavior, depending, of course, on such variables as the person's readiness to hear it and the type of support available from others.

✓ *It is checked to ensure clear communication.* An effective method of checking others' understanding of the feedback is to have receivers try to rephrase the feedback they have received to see if it matches what the sender has tried to express. A statement such as "I want to make sure that I'm communicating clearly; would you sum up what you understood me to say?" can be used to initiate the clarity check.

✓ *It is cross checked for accuracy.* When feedback is given in a group, both the giver and the receiver should have an opportunity to check with others in the group for the accuracy of the feedback. Is this one person's impression or an impression shared by others?

❖ SUMMARY

> *"Good communication is as stimulating as black coffee, and just as hard to sleep after."*
>
> —*Anne Morrow Lindberg*

Effective communication is crucial for success in all aspects of life. The more we understand the communication process and the more skills that we have within our arsenal of communication strategies, the greater our options will be for effectively communicating in any situation. In this section, we discussed the communication process, delineated skills that foster communication, identified barriers to effective communication, and provided information about giving and obtaining feedback.

PROMOTING CO-LEADER VISION AND TEAMWORK

Co-instructing can be very exciting and highly rewarding. It also can be extremely stressful and incredibly draining. Each pair of co-instructors have a unique relationship. Factors such as personality, philosophy, experience, expectations, and chemistry of the group impact the relationship. Yet, it is generally believed that the characteristics of flexibility, communication, problem-solving, and commitment to the relationship are essential for promoting co-leader vision and teamwork.

The vitality of instructional teams can be enhanced by having each individual take the time to understand the expectations, strengths, likes and dislikes of your partner. By initially discuss-ing as well as periodically reflecting on topics that effect co-instructing success, you can im-prove your skills, strengthen your professional relationships, resolve disagreements, and pro-vide quality learning experiences for participants. Responding to statements such as those pro-vided below, which have been adapted from the Voyageur Outward Bound School (1994) and Schwarz (1994), can promote self-assessment and serve as a guide for dialogue and reflection with your co-instructor. Your responses will point out potential strengths in your relation-ship as well as alert you to potential barriers.

PERSONAL INVENTORY

1. My personal strengths are . . .
2. My personal weaknesses are . . .
3. My personal values and goals which may affect the experience are . . .

90

4. My positive expectations about working with you are . . .
5. My hesitations about working with you . . .
6. When I am stressed, angry, or threatened I . . .
7. My approach to planning and organizing is . . .
8. My goals for students involved in this experience are . . .

EXPERIENCES AND BACKGROUND

1. The types of groups that I have worked with are ...
2. The best experience I had as an instructor was ...
3. The worst experience I had as an instructor was ...
4. The problems that I have had before working with a co-instructor were ...
5. We resolved those problems by ...
6. The specific areas in which I am trying to improve as an instructor are ...
7. You can help me improve in those areas by ...

ORIENTATION/STYLE

1. The major beliefs and principles that guide me are . . .
2. In working with this type of group, the things I find most satisfying are . . .
3. The things I find most frustrating in working with this type of group are . . .
4. When someone talks too much, I usually . . .
5. When the group is silent, I usually . . .
6. When an individual is silent for a long time, I usually . . .
7. When someone gets upset, I usually . . .
8. Where there is conflict in the group, I usually . . .
9. When the group attacks one member, I usually . . .
10. When members seem to be off track, I usually . . .

CO-INSTRUCTOR COORDINATION

1. When we need to make decisions, I would like to see us . . .
2. If we have a conflict, I would like to see us . . .
3. The kinds of disagreements between you are I that I am willing to show in front of the group are . . .
4. If changes need to be made to our plan, we should . . .
5. With regard to giving and receiving feedback, I would like to see us . . .
6. When you have something to add to my presentation, I would like . . .
7. When you disagree with something that I presented or said, I would like . . .
8. With regard to pacing, I prefer . . .
9. If you want me to teach something, my preference for preparation lead time is . . .
10. The things that I think are nonnegotiable for each of us as co-instructors are . . .
11. With regard to the division of labor (e.g., teaching, facilitating, taking personal breaks), my preference is to ...

GROUP DEVELOPMENTAL STAGES

"It's not knowing what to do but it's knowing what to do with your group and when to do it. This is the difference that truly makes the difference."

—*Gregg Butterfield*

Groups are composed of many individuals with different personalities and needs. Generally speaking, though, groups develop an identity of their own. In so doing, they tend to go through a series of stages. While it is possible that all groups will not go through the same stages, the following are the group stages elaborated by Cohen and Smith (1976). Knowing where your group and the individuals in the group are in the process can help in structuring your facilitation. Once you have an in depth understanding of how your group develops, you can use the popular brief model of Forming, Storming, Norming, and Performing stages. These are explained by Scholtes (1988) and inspired by Tuckman (1955), and presented at the end of this section. This model we find, is easier to explain to your group and for them to identify with and remember.

❖ GROUP STAGES: IN-DEPTH PERSPECTIVE

Stage 1: Acquaintance Individuals are looking for something in common, a way to categorize one another. Outside roles and status often determine inside roles. Group members share names, background, residence, occupations, likes, and dislikes. This is a time of sizing up each other and thinking "Am I going to fit in here?"

Stage 2: Goal ambiguity and diffuse anxiety Group members may feel confusion, uncertainty, anxiety, and difficulty in understanding directions or the purpose of group activities. Members may feel very unsure of themselves. Some may feel helpless and become self-deprecating and express inadequacy. Some members will attempt to establish bonds with others who seem to have similar problems, interests, attitudes, and backgrounds. Self-centered communication, hesitant and resistant behaviors may also be noted. The situation is new and ambiguous, so values and attitudes may go into a state of flux.

Stage 3: Members' search for position Power may shift rapidly during this stage as various assertive members try to influence and/or control the group or engage in leadership struggles. The initiators become leaders, while fearful members may intellectualize and generalize. Indirect discussions and outside concerns are the topics of discussion rather than immediate necessary tasks or feelings. The first here and now feelings expressed tend to be negative, frequently toward the leader or the experience. This may be in the form of a challenge. There's fear in this stage of discussing the real self. Anger may be at the perceived dependence on the leader.

Stage 4: Sharpened affect and anxiety—confrontation In this stage, some individuals may clash with one another for leadership, while others may play more passive roles. Anxiety and fear are expressed by anger and defensiveness. This may feel like a mutiny to you, or it can be as simple as one negative statement by one individual. Interactions may only focus on tasks, with isolation or cliques forming after the endeavors. If you successfully handle the negative feelings, the group then has permission to get more positive and intimate. You need to be able to say, "I hear that you are angry at me"; or "I see that you are overwhelmed by the demands of the experience; can you tell me more about it?" This is the most important and critical stage for leaders to successfully get through.

Stage 5: Sharpened interactions—growth Original group leaders re-emerge. Some members behave in ways that encourage total group involvement. Group members become more involved. Misunderstandings are sharpened as frequent communication occurs. Group members share significant personal experiences. Here and now concerns about power and leadership develop. Trust grows between you and the group and among group members. Members begin to talk more openly and test their perceptions and assumptions with you and the others.

Stage 6: Norm crystallization Norms develop as the group works on and evolves rules and standards for behavior in the group. Group attention stays on interaction and processes within the group, not on outside matters. One person may assume the role of disciplinarian who punishes group members deviating from the group norms. Daily routines are established and members become self-disciplined and self-regulated. A unique culture develops that includes jargon, rituals, and group-consciousness and cohesion. In general, there is a willingness to work together on tasks and goals. Individual identity is submerged in the group. Members subjugate their own identity in pursuit of group unity.

Stage 7: Distributive leadership Members accept each other as equals. Members accept the authority of your role and there is less acceptance or nonacceptance thinking in regards to you. Group members will use you more freely as a "skilled resource" who can observe the group process and help them deal with personal issues. You will be seen both as a person and as a member of the group. Members become observers of the group process and thus become more self-regulating and self-determining. Decisions become more based on consensus. When conflict occurs, it is over substantive rather than hidden issues. Formalized structure tends to dissipate and informality prevails.

Stage 8: Decreased defensiveness and increased experimentation There tends to be a dropping of masks and protective facades at this stage. Insight into others develops and becomes common. There is a freer flow of feelings and thought. Tension and expressions of negative and positive feelings are expressed and worked through in a more open manner. Members tell each other their reactions and perceptions. There is an increase in empathy and a nonjudgmental atmosphere prevails. Less regard for power and status exists in the group. Group members discuss and work on personal problems. They try out new ways of behaving. Risk taking increases and members have better self-esteem. Members are more willing to compromise for greater solidarity.

Stage 9: Group potency The group in this stage accepts individual members and rewards their positive changes. Members know when it's appropriate to use the group. Cooperation and shared responsibility is common. Interdependence increases interpersonal solidarity. The loyalty and affection to each other is increased. The group may deal with highly intense interpersonal interactions without becoming defensive or changing the subject. Intense joy and pleasure may also be experienced. Members become confident that the group will accept them as they are. The members also accept the group as a potent change agent.

Stage 10: Termination There are expressions of over-optimism about the power of the group. Individually and collectively the members are optimistic. Denial of the impending termination is expressed by disbelief and regret. As a defense against the pain of separation, some members withdraw before the group actually ends. Other members experience happiness over leaving and returning to the outside world. Still others attempt to plan ways for the group to get together in the future. Testimonials to the power of the group and the experience are expressed. Some members feel that they have completed the task of the group and they are now ready for the outside world, while others continue to explore the mechanics of the transfer of learning.

As the experience ends and the group terminates, it may be useful to talk about the death of the group and how individuals deal with grief in their lives. The group will never be the same, and developing some rituals and giving participants the opportunity to share their feelings and learning with each other will help to bring some closure to the group. You can discuss how individuals make contact in their lives and what "letting go" of the connection feels like for them.

❖ GROUP STAGES: BRIEF PERSPECTIVE

It is useful for your group to be able to identify where they are in their team development. We like to use the forming, storming, norming, and performing stages when we present to groups, because it is easy to follow and remember. Groups can usually reach consensus around which stage they are at. The four stages adapted from Scholtes (1988) are:

FORMING

Forming is characterized by team members cautiously exploring boundaries of what is acceptable in and by this group. They are moving from individuals to member status. This stage is where trust is being built, and it is full of excitement, anticipation, and anxiety of what is ahead and "will I fit in." Attempts are made to define the task at hand and discussions are abstract, lofty, and problem-oriented. Little is accomplished in regards to project goals, which is normal. This is a group of individuals versus a team.

STORMING

Storming is the most difficult stage, and it is characterized by arguing, defensiveness, and questioning the wisdom of others because the task is different and more difficult than imagined. Impatience with the lack of progress leads to tension and indecision about what needs to be done. A pecking order may be established and disunity is common. It feels like members are choosing sides for what needs to be accomplished. It's almost like people are saying "I will show you my worst side and see if you leave me."

NORMING

In this stage members reconcile their differences and competing loyalties. Criticism is expressed more constructively The group has become a team by agreeing and accepting each other by developing their ground rules or norms. Competitive relationships become cooperative. Friendliness and sharing personal issues are more prevalent. There is a sense of team cohesion, common spirit and movement towards shared goals. The tension from above has turned into trust and collaboration.

PERFORMING

By this stage the team has settled its relationships. They begin to perform well solving problems and implementing actions by using each other's strengths. People know their roles and responsibilities and begin to synergize. They get more things done by working in a coordinated fashion. There is a strong sense of loyalty and satisfaction in the team. They know each other well and can comment on their team development, and as a result, they can constructively bring about team change.

Having your group identify and normalize what stage they are in can help move them to the next stage and prevent overreactions and unrealistic goal setting. Some groups will move quickly through these stages, while others will move painfully slow. It is important for the group to know this is a dynamic process of change, full of interruptions and lapses to previous stages.

GENERAL GUIDELINES FOR WORKING WITH GROUPS

There is so much information to remember, so many logistical details to attend to, and so much coordination that needs to take place." Statements such as this are often heard within circles of experiential educators, trainers and therapists. And, it is true. To be really experiential requires significantly more work than traditional approaches to education or therapy.

The purpose of this section is to provide direction—to help prioritize what is important when working with diverse groups. The following suggestions for working with groups have been adapted from Schwarz (1994), the Voyageur Outward Bound School (1994) and Rohnke and Butler (1995). These are general suggestions to consider and to revisit on occasion. We believe that by keeping these guidelines in mind, they will help you structure positive meaningful experiences for each group that you work with.

1. When planning and implementing experiential learning opportunities, take in consideration four key factors (1) The age and maturity of the group—the more responsible people can be for themselves, the more space you can provide for them to develop on their own. For example, a group of elementary students generally needs more coaching than a group of adults, (2) The length of the program—usually, a group develops better skills over time. You need to be more directive and visible in a shorter program, (3) The goals of the program—a day of fun and activities for a college orientation program requires one level of involvement; a day of team building with a corporate group who are at odds with each other dictates a different approach. It's essential to understand the goals of the group so that your actions can be focused on the outcome desired, and (4) The readiness of the group—some individuals and groups are able to manage safety issues, resolve conflicts, and process their own experiences. When this happens, you can step back and provide guidance and support. When groups are not at this readiness level, you will need to be more hands-on and directive.

2. Time is extremely valuable (a) plan your work and work your plan—use a checklist to keep yourself organized, (b) examine all equipment prior to using it, (c) have all necessary props available, (d) attend to logistical details, (e) develop suitable contingency plans, (f) become familiar with the area in which you are working, and (g) know your material and refine the progression of your presentations.

3. Plan more activities than you need, but always be ready to change the plan. Having more ideas than you could ever use may make you feel more secure and confident, but you need to remember that you can't always predict how groups and individuals will react.

4. In your introduction, let individuals know what to expect. Participants' pre-conceived expectations often create barrier to learning.

5. Be clear about what your role as a leader is. That being, to ensure safety, instruct, facilitate, observe, raise issues, and clarify. Simultaneously you need to be clear about what it is not. That being, to judge people and to preach and require others to accept your values.

6. Be clear about where a group can have input and make choices, and what you will not change about the experience. When giving the group a choice, spell out any parameters which they need to consider in their decision making, and be prepared to live with the choice they make.

7. Finding the right balance is an on-going challenge. You want to establish parameters that are safe, yet flexible; challenging, but not overwhelming; thought provoking while still being fun; focused yet allowing for diversity; and planned but not rigid.

8. You provide the spark to the potential of the group. You will want to maintain momentum, striking a balance between action and discussion, between experience and learning. Gear your attention towards maximum involvement and participation to keep everyone engaged at a high-level of interest.

9. Right from the beginning of the experience help participants relate what they are thinking, feeling, and learning back to their lives at home. Some of the questions that you may consider asking are: "Do you feel this way in other environments?" "Is this pattern one you see at work/home?" and "What are the consequences of your behavior?"

10. Timing and pacing are essential. Reassess goals, individual's needs, and the group's needs regularly.

11. Help individuals turn negative feelings into positive learning experiences. Remember disequilibrium is the catalyst for growth.

12. Try to suspend judgment and refrain from assuming someone's motives, Being nonjudgmental and sensitive to someone else's point of view entails believing that all people are of equal worth, and all values and lifestyles are equally valid.

13. Use descriptive words rather than evaluative words whenever possible. Evaluative words contain some built-in judgment, implying that you either approve or disapprove of a behavior or idea. For example, "you made an excellent presentation" is an evaluative statement, while "you appeared poised and confident of the material throughout your presentation" is descriptive.

14. Avoid the use of imperatives, such as "you must", "you should", or "you have to", except in issues related to safety. Imperatives discourage groups from making free and informed choices, and they put you in an "expert" role.

15. Avoid experiential education jargon. Terms such as OB, NOLS, AEE, PA, the crux, initiatives, debrief, belay and beaners are shorthand that participants may not understand and of which they have little need to learn. Whenever possible, it is best to use everyday language instead of using jargon.

16. Avoid humor that puts down or discounts members or that can be misinterpreted. Humor can be a valuable tool for relieving tension, emphasizing a point, and helping individuals to examine their behavior. However, certain types of humor can reduce your effectiveness. Sarcastic humor about individuals' inappropriate behavior can decrease their trust in you because they are likely to interpret the humor as unsupportive.

17. You can only take others as far as you have gone. The more in touch you are with your own feelings, patterns of communication, methods of resolving conflict , and personal strengths and weakness; the easier it will be to facilitate learning in a group setting.

18. You can't expect to relate to the life experiences and problems of all individuals that you work with. Be honest. Don't pretend to have answers you don't. Ask good questions. Often group members can use each other as resources, and usually people can find their own answers, espe-

cially when encouraged to listen to their own inner-wisdom. We can point out behavior and offer options for handling a situation, but individuals need to make their own decisions.

19. When honesty and respect are demonstrated and trust ensues, honest confrontations and open questioning are usually met with appreciation. Realize that for many people it takes a lot of courage to let down defenses and engage in open and honest communication. We need to respect people for who they are. Some will disclose and share deeply their feelings with others; what appears to be superficial and non-risky may be a large emotional risk to them.

Group Ground Rules

One of the primary roles of educators, trainers and therapists who use experiential approaches to education and therapy is to provide a safe environment for learning to occur. Both physical and emotional safety are critical for inviting participants to take risks and to use the experiences for learning and developing.

As group members interact and become comfortable, they usually develop a set of norms that establish the kinds of behaviors that are acceptable, expected, and not expected of them. Unfortunately, when these norms are unspoken, some group members may misinterpret the rules and negatively impact the safety of the learning environment. To decrease problems and to foster a safe space, group members can develop a set of ground rules.

The ground rules, or ways of relating to each other, provide a consistent set of standards for interaction. The agreed upon ground rules help participants feel safe and knowledgeable about what to expect and provide you with a guide for observing behavior and for intervening. Some ground rules that you may want to consider are as follows:

1. When using a large group session, group members should sit in a circle where everyone can see each other.
2. Ask participants not to lie down. Try to keep the energy of the group within the circle.
3. This is a safe environment to explore feelings and learning from the experience.
4. Both feelings and logical ideas are important.
5. Each person has the freedom to say no or to pass.
6. It's okay to listen and not have to talk.
7. What is spoken in the group will remain confidential among the group members, unless the individuals give their permission to share their situation and feelings with others outside the group.
8. One person speaks at a time without interruptions from others.
9. Allow people to express complete sentences without interruption.
10. Pause after someone speaks to allow less vocal people a chance to enter the conversation.

11. "Put downs" are prohibited.
12. Speak only for yourself—use "I" statements.
13. There is to be no physical violence in the group.
14. Everyone in the group belongs in the group. Only the leader can change this rule. If the group is unhappy with one person, this does not change the individual's membership in the group. The unhappiness is what needs to be worked through.
15. Everyone is ultimately responsible for his or her own behavior. No one should be forced into anything. Sometimes members need encouragement and support to try new things.
16. What is true for individuals must be determined for themselves. People may have different perceptions about an event that they have shared with others. As a result, peoples' emotions belong to them and should be considered true for that person.
17. Respect people's different backgrounds and styles of learning.

◆ Levels of Processing

W hen working with groups and individuals, it is often difficult to know how to foster intro-spection and help them become conscious of their behavior, thoughts, and feelings. A flow chart that you can use to help guide you and those that you work with is found below. It graphically displays a sequential progression that we refer to as the Levels of Processing. In order to progress through the levels, we need to reflect, analyze, and communicate our perceptions by actively focusing on Level 1 issues prior to moving to Level 2, and Level 2 prior to Level 3 and so forth.

The first level focuses on developing an awareness of the unconscious feelings, thoughts, and behavior patterns that get projected onto the experience. You want to help individuals identify and become aware of typical feelings, thoughts, and behavior patterns. Second is the responsibility level. Here participants consciously own their patterns, thoughts, feelings, and actions. In this stage, they become aware of the old patterns. Fritz Perls (1969) called responsibility "ability to respond." This ability to re-spond leads to a choice at the third level. Individuals can continue with the old patterns

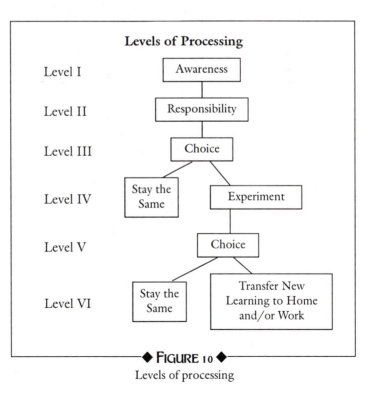

Levels of Processing

Level I — Awareness

Level II — Responsibility

Level III — Choice

Level IV — Stay the Same / Experiment

Level V — Choice

Level VI — Stay the Same / Transfer New Learning to Home and/or Work

◆ **Figure 10** ◆

Levels of processing

or experiment with new emotional, cognitive, and behavioral risks. Experimentation is the fourth level, followed by the fifth level of choice again. Participants choose between maintaining the existent patterns or transferring the new learning back to their daily lives at home. Again, processing the experience can help individuals move through each level. Specific exercises and activities that may help you work with individuals progressing through different levels are presented in the section entitled "Processing Activities."

❖ LEVELS OF PROCESSING QUESTIONS

The following are some examples of questions that will help you facilitate participants' movement through the different levels. The overall intent of these questions is to: a) provide opportunities for new perceptions, new directions, and new options for individuals; b) have individuals' become interested in their own interaction patterns; c) connect and link the structured experience with transferable knowledge for home application; and, d) have individuals' experiment with new behaviors. Some of the questions use Tomm's (1988) "circular assumptions," Bateson's (1979) "double descriptions," and White and Epston's (1990) approach. Circular assumptions look at the interactional principles and systemic approaches, while double descriptions attempt to get more than one view of the same event and thus open up space for more differences and options. This is not a finite set of questions. Rather, they should be viewed as examples that will help you develop an understanding of the concepts and start your own creative processes flowing.

AWARENESS

The objective is to focus on here and now behavior, patterns, and others' perceptions and roles in a non-threatening manner and simultaneously build trust.

Did you notice your role in this activity?

Are you aware that you were (leader, in the background, interrupting others, etc.)

What were you feeling during the experience ? What were you stopping from feeling during the activity? How do you feel now?

How did others see (name)'s role in this activity?

When you felt _____, how did you behave?

What was your intention in this activity? Did anyone else notice that?

Did you respond automatically to anything in this activity?

Are you aware of your (point out posture, voice quality, expression, etc.)?

How do others feel when you see (name)'s behavior?

Are you aware that you did _____ again?

Right now I am experiencing you as _____ (angry, defensive, passive, etc.).

Does anyone else experience ___(name)___ as _____?

How can we help you raise your awareness about this pattern?

Who do you think most noticed your role in this activity?

How do you imagine that others react to you when you do _____?

Who in the group do you think was most rooting for your success?

When you did _____ what do you think (name) was experiencing?

What was different about your role or experience?

If you were miraculously able to _____, how would your life be different?

What effect does _____ have on your life?

RESPONSIBILITY

The object is to have individuals make the bridge of how their roles and behaviors are similar to what they do at home, school, or work. We seek to have them become responsible for what they were previously doing automatically or unconsciously.

Did you notice that you were controlling, withdrawing, interrupting, etc., again? Do you do this at home, school or work?

Is this a typical role for you?

Have others at work or home ever given you feedback about your _____?

I wonder if at home or work when you feel _____, do you _____?

What do you think you get out of doing _____ or how does that serve you?

What strengths do you bring to this group?

Do you ever use your strengths to excess?

Can you accept that _____ (controlling, withdrawing, etc.) may be a pattern of yours?

What would it be like if you were always _____ and never changed? How would others respond to you?

Does your style fit in well with others? How do others feel when ___(name)___ acts this way ?

How is your behavior self-protective or self-nurturing?

When you typically do _____ at home, who notices first?

How does your (wife, husband, parents, friends) react when you do _____ at home?

I wonder who else in the group realized that _____ may be a pattern for (name)?

Can you recall a time when you didn't react in this manner? What was different about that situation?

What aspects of this pattern have you felt most pushed around by, and how is this pattern influencing your life?

How long do you want to be pushed around by _____ before you stand up and protest against it?

Who will be the first to notice when you stand up against it?

How much influence does this _____ pattern have over your life? (1–100%)

How much influence do you have over the _____ pattern? (1–100%).

EXPERIMENTATION

The objective is to give individuals the opportunity to create new options and choices for themselves.

Are you willing to try something different today?

What would be a risk for you today?

What's preventing you from being more _____ (assertive, expressive, etc.)?

How will you sabotage your attempt to take a new risk today?

Can you tell others in the group what you are going to do today?

How can we support you in your risk today?

How would you evaluate your risk today?

Would you like feedback from others when they see you _____ ?

With your experimentation what went well? What would you adjust for next time?

How did it feel doing _(new behavior)_ ?

What did you learn by taking the risk?

What was the hardest part about doing _____?

(To others) How do you imagine (name) felt today in trying something different?

What do you think this might tell you about your ability that you wouldn't have otherwise known?

What else do you think you could now do after you successfully completed this risk?

What do you think others will say is the hardest part for you to continue with?

What do you think your risk tells the group that they can appreciate?

Holding the two pictures of yourself, the old you with the _____ pattern and the new you, and by comparing them what do you discover about yourself?

Now that you didn't let _____ push you around what difference will this make in your future?

Who do you think first noticed you were successful in your experiment?

Who do you imagine is most surprised by your successful experiment?

How much influence do you now feel you have over the_____ pattern (1–100)?

GENERALIZATION AND TRANSFER

The objective is to maximize what has recently been learned so that it can be used back at home, school or work.

What are you blind to, handicapped by, speechless about, etc., at home, school or work ?

How can you use this learning at home?

What will prevent you from using what you have learned at home?

What will you need from others to implement your plan at home? What helped on the experience?

What are the positive forces that you have at home? How can you enhance them?

What visualization symbol, anchor, or ritual can you use at home to remind you of what you have recently learned on the experience?

What statement or affirmation can you use to remind you of what you learned on the experience?

Write down goals that you have for yourself at home.

Are you willing to hear feedback from others as to trouble spots that they anticipate for you back at home ?

Are you willing to role play some of those trouble spots?

Develop a tool box and describe what's in it to help you attain your goals at home.

When you act differently at home, who will be the first to notice?

What will they see in you that is different?

What will be the first signs for you at home that will tell you you're on the right track?

What do you think it says about you that at home you don't let the _____ pattern push you around anymore?

How will this experience keep you on track at home?

Now that you've tackled the challenges on the experience, what issues will you tackle at home?

What do you think your changes at home will tell your (wife, husband, parents, peers) about you?

How much influence will you have over the _____ pattern at home? (1–100%)

What will you need to do to reinforce your influence over _____ ?

What aspects of yourself makes you think that you will make significant changes at home?

◆ ADDITIONAL PROCESSING QUESTIONS

In addition to using the levels of processing questions, there are times that you will want to ask questions that focus on specific thoughts, feelings, and behaviors. The following questions, some of which have been adapted from Knapp (1984) and Rosenthal (1995), are useful to refer to when preparing for discussions.

TRUST AND SUPPORT

1. What did it feel like to have your physical safety entrusted to the group?
2. What are the similarities and differences in the way you supported each other here and the way you support others back at home, school or the office?
3. What impact does trust have in your relationships with others at home, school or at work?
4. What is the relationship between managing risk and establishing a support system?
5. What needs to happen for you to trust people?

COMMUNICATION

1. What were some of the effective forms of communication that you used in completing this task? Ineffective forms of communication?

2. How were differences in opinion handled?
3. In what ways could the group's process of communication be improved to enhance its problem-solving skills?
4. How could you improve your communication and networking?

MAKING DECISIONS

1. How did the group make decisions for completing the tasks?
2. Were you satisfied with the manner in which you made decisions?
3. Were decisions made by one or several individuals?
4. Did everyone express his or her opinion when a choice was available?
5. What did you like about the manner in which the group made decisions? What didn't you like?
6. What is the best way for this group to make decisions?

COOPERATING

1. What are some specific examples of when you cooperated?
2. How did it feel to cooperate?
3. How did cooperative behavior lead to the successful completion of the tasks?
4. What are the rewards of cooperating?
5. What can you personally do to produce a cooperative environment at home or work?
6. When cooperating with others, what guidelines would you want to establish for yourself?

TEAMWORK

1. How well do you think you did?
2. How effective were you in completing the task?
3. How efficient were you?
4. How did you develop your plan of action?
5. What is the relationship between input into the plan and commitment to action?
6. What were the differences between having a common vision versus not having a common vision?
7. Did the team IQ go up or down? What was it? 100 is average, 115 above average, 85 below average.

PROBLEM-SOLVING

1. Have you noticed any patterns in the way you solve problems? Are they productive? Unproductive?
2. What effect did planning time have on the process?
3. How well did you execute your plan?
4. On a scale of 1–10, how committed were you to executing the plan?

5. What are the similarities and differences between the ways in which you have approached solving problems here and the way that you approach them at home, school, or work?
6. What would need to change in order to enhance your problem-solving ability?

LEADERSHIP ROLES

1. Who assumed leadership roles?
2. What were the behaviors that you would describe as demonstrating leadership?
3. How did the group respond to these leadership behaviors?
4. When and how did the leadership role change?
5. Was it difficult to assume a leadership role in this group? Why?
6. What are the characteristics and qualities of a good leader?
7. What specific skills do you need to develop to become a more effective leader?

FOLLOWING OTHERS

1. Do you consider yourself a good follower? Was this an important role during the activity/day?
2. What type of leader was it easiest to follow?
3. Did the manner in which the feedback was given make a difference to you? Explain.
4. What was difficult about being a follower?
5. What are the characteristics of a good follower?

SELF-STATEMENTS

1. Did you criticize yourself or put yourself down during the activity/day?
2. What did you say to yourself?
3. Do you usually get upset with yourself when you make a mistake or do not achieve perfection?
4. What could you say to yourself to counteract the put-down message?
5. What are some ways in which you were successful during the activity/day?
6. What self-messages did you give yourself when you were successful?
7. How can you increase your positive self-messages in the future?
8. What percentage of time are you "on your case" vs. "on your side"? Do you prefer this style?

GIVING AND RECEIVING FEEDBACK

1. What are some examples of when you received feedback during the activity/day? How did it feel?
2. Did the manner in which the feedback was given make a difference to you?
3. What are some examples of when you gave feedback during the day?
4. How did you express appreciation for another during the day?

5. What are some appreciations that you did not express?
6. Do you typically express appreciations?
7. How can you improve your skills in giving and receiving feedback?
8. What is the best way for someone to coach you or give you feedback?

RESPECTING PERSONAL DIFFERENCES

1. What are some of the significant differences among group members?
2. How did these differences strengthen the group-as-a-whole?
3. What would this group be like if they were very few differences among the group members?
4. What specific instances did being different help or hinder the group from reaching its objectives?
5. How can you increase your ability to respect and use personal differences?

PERSONAL RENEWAL

1. How could you lessen the burden that you carry around?
2. How could you challenge yourself to improve and grow?
3. Are there things that you do to anesthetize yourself and your emotions? If so, what are they?
4. What are some things that you could do to improve your diet and quality of nutrition?
5. What are some things that you could do to feel more sexually alive and vital?
6. What adventures would you like to undertake in the future?
7. How could you enjoy your work more?
8. How could you enjoy your daily tasks, chores and responsibilities more?
9. What could you do to feel better about your home environment?
10. What could you do to optimize your level of health, fitness and well-being?
11. What could you do to improve your relationship with your partner?
12. How could you have more energy, vitality and moment-to-moment aliveness?
13. What are the career goals that you are shooting for?
14. How could you improve your relationship with your children? How might you be a more involved and loving parent?
15. Are you satisfied with your level of spirituality? Could you do anything to improve your spirituality??
16. How could you have fun and enjoy your life more often?
17. How could you improve your relationship with your parents and/or your extended family?
18. Do you permit yourself time to occasionally relax, slow down and smell the flowers? Do you take good vacations? Is there anything you could do to improve on this?
19. How could you improve your relationship with your colleagues, co-workers, boss and/or employees?
20. How could you invite deeper and more meaningful friendships with people in your life?

21. In which areas of your life are you out of balance? What would assist you in being more in balance?
22. What could you do to add greater meaning and purpose to your life?
23. If you could do one thing that would significantly change your life, what would that be?

CLOSURE QUESTIONS

1. What did you learn about yourself?
2. What did you learn about other group members?
3. What did you do today that you are particularly proud of?
4. How can you use what you learned today in other situations?
5. What beliefs about yourself and the other group members were reinforced during the day?
6. What specific skill are you going to improve as a result of this experience?
7. What obstacle(s) will you need to deal with to effectively use this learning? How will you remove this obstacle?

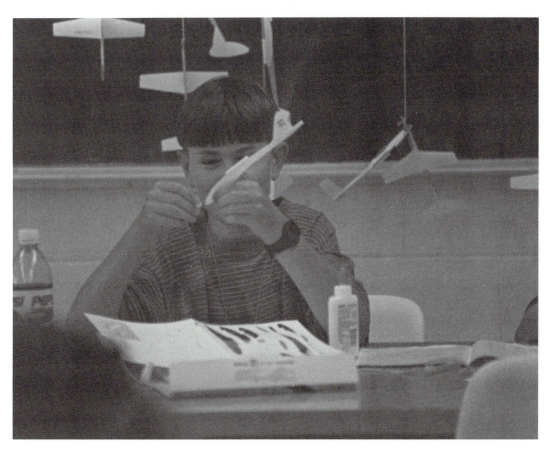

Methods of Processing

"Success won't just come to you. It has to be met at least halfway."

—*Frank Tyger*

There are many ways to process experiences. Most of us are familiar with the approach that involves having a large group sit around in a circle and talk about what they are going to do or what they recently went through. This is one effective technique. Yet, it should not be the only approach that you use. Think about what a house would look like if the only tool that a carpenter had to build with was a hammer. So while the hammer and the large group discussion are important tools for the jobs that you want them to do, they aren't the only ones to use. The following is a short explanation of some different ways that you can use to structure your processing sessions.

❖ Framing

Framing or briefing the experience sets the stage for what is about to take place. Framing provides individuals with lead time before an activity or experience so that they have an opportunity to think about it and prepare for it. Depending on your assessment and the goals of the group, a briefing may cover some or all of the following information (a) safety issues, (b) needed equipment, (c) skills instruction, (d) a short explanation of the activity, (e) identification of activity goals, (f) a tone setting message, and/or (g) a metaphoric introduction.

Group Contracts

Often, the focus of a briefing is on nuts and bolts issues such as what type of clothes to wear, what time to meet, who is bringing what, what is going to happen, how it is going to happen, and what will be expected of people. Yet, only to focus on logistics may mean missing a golden opportunity to facilitate significant group and/or personal learning to occur. This learning may transpire among group members by establishing a common social contract. For example, Project Adventure uses the "Full Value Contract" (Schoel, Prouty, & Radcliffe, 1988) to help establish a supportive environment and to promote goal setting. According to Schoel, Prouty, and Radcliffe (1988, p. 95) an effective "Full Value Contract" contains a commitment from each group member to: (1) work together as a group and to work toward individual and group goals, (2) adhere to certain safety and group behavior guidelines, (3) give and receive feedback, both positive and negative, and (4) work towards changing behavior when it is appropriate. Other conditions that can be included in group contracts can be found in the section on Group Ground Rules.

INDIVIDUAL GOAL SETTING

In addition to establishing a group contract prior to the activity or experience, individuals can be helped to identify what they want to achieve, how they are going to accomplish this, and how they will demonstrate that they have achieved a specific goal as part of the briefing. This can be done by asking questions such as some of the following or by using some of the procedures and activities provided in the section entitled Goal Setting and Personal Action Plans:

a. What are your expectations for this activity/experience?
b. How will you define success for yourself on this activity/experience?
c. What will be the hardest thing for you to do on this activity/experience?
d. What will be the easiest thing for you to do on this activity/experience?
e. How can others support you on this activity/experience?
f. How are the challenges of this activity/experience similar to other challenges in your life?

READINGS

Another technique that can be used to help frame an activity or experience is to share readings. Readings are quotes collected from well-known individuals or from people who have been in similar situations. They can be used for motivational purposes, to set a tone, or to plant a seed for future thought and reflective consideration.

We have included a variety of quotes throughout this text. A few more of our favorites include:

"Never doubt that a small group of committed humans can change the world. It's the only thing that ever has."
—*Margaret Mead*

"Few people learn from success, but there is often much to learn from failure."
—*Steven Muller*

"The truth shall set me free, but first it will make me miserable."
—*Author Unknown*

"A diamond is a piece of coal that did well under pressure."
—*Author Unknown*

"A wishbone ain't no substitute for a backbone."

—*Ken Alstad*

"Argue for your limitations and sure enough they're yours."

—*Richard Bach*

"If you run, you might lose. If you don't run, you're guaranteed to lose."

—*Jesse Jackson*

"Take care of the means and the end will take care of itself."

—*M. Gandhi*

"Life is like an onion, you peel off one layer at a time, and sometimes you weep."

—*Carl Sandburg*

"The most human thing that we can do is comfort the afflicted and afflict the comfortable."

—*Clarence Darrow*

"The aim of education is to impel young people into value forming experiences."

—*Kurt Hahn*

"Go out on a limb, that's where the fruit is."

—*Will Rodgers*

❖ LARGE GROUP DISCUSSION

Large group discussion is the approach that most people think of when the word processing comes to mind. There are several different ways for you to structure the discussion. They are:

1. *Open Forum*—within this approach you pull the group together and provide an opening statement in anticipation that the group will volunteer their perceptions and insights. An example of an opening statement that you might want to use is "I'm interested in hearing peoples' reactions to today's activity.

2. *Questioning*—this entails the development of a set of questions that you would like participants to respond to after they have completed the activity. The value of pre-planning is to establish specific objectives that you would like to achieve for the session. Through the identification of objectives, you can develop questions that focus on the specific issues that you would like to see addressed. The sequence of questions that you use will vary according to your personal style. However, we suggest that you begin with the concrete and slowly move on to more insightful types of questions. A general sequence that you may want to consider involves the use of three simple questions: "What happened?", "What did you learn?", "How can you use this knowledge in the future?" Supplemental questions that you may want to consider appear in the section on questions for the Levels of Processing and also in the section entitled Additional Processing Questions.

3. *Rounds*—a round is an activity in which every member of the group is asked to respond to a stimulus that you present to the group. According to Jacobs, Harvil & Masson, (1988) there are three types of rounds. There is the (a) designated word or number round, (b) word or phrase round, and (c) the comment round. The following is a brief explanation of each:

    a. *Designated Word or Number Round*—this can be done very quickly since each member is asked to respond with either a single designated word or a number on a scale, which is usually from 1 to 10. A few examples that we have used include: "I would like each of you to think of your role during the last event and choose one of the following labels to describe it: "Leader," or "Follower." "On a scale from 1–10, how would you rate your commitment to the experience right now," or "On a scale from 1–10, how comfortable are you being a member of this group right now? A 1 means that you are not comfortable at all and a 10 indicates that you are very comfortable."

    b. *Word or Phrase Rounds*—group members are asked to respond with only a word or a short phrase. A few examples that we have used include: "I would like each of you to think of an adjective that describes how you feel right now," or "I would like you to think of a word or a phrase that describes how you think we handled the last initiative."

    c. *Comment Rounds*—group members are asked to share more than a few words, either because the question calls for more than a word or phrase or because there is a desire to have individuals express more than just a few words. Examples that you may want to consider using are: "I would like to hear a brief reaction from each of you about how you feel about your experience on the ropes experience? Let's do a round and hear from everyone."

Rounds are a very valuable tool. When time is an issue the use of a designated word or number round or a word or phrase round is really useful for getting people to reflect and communicate in an expedient manner. It also gives you some important information about individuals and/or the group that you can use as you decide which activity to do next. Other advantages of using rounds are that they can be used at the beginning of group discussion to get members focused. Rounds give each person time to think about what they are going to say, and they also present a chance to hear what other people think about the topic of discussion. They allow you to get everyone involved and they also encourage individuals to think in greater depth about a specific issue. Finally, the use of rounds permits you as the group leader to survey the group for a general reading of how people are thinking and feeling. This gives you a quick survey of how things are going and provides stimulus for deciding which issues to focus on with individuals and/or with the group either at this time or in the near future.

When using rounds, it is a positive practice to vary the starting point so that different members get to speak both first and last. At times, you will want to begin with the person who you know is comfortable sharing his or her ideas. This will get the conversation flowing with energy and enthusiasm. This train of thought may also be extended to negative and positive-energy people who are members of the group. By beginning with a positive-energy person and trying to end with a positive-energy individual, you can avoid the pitfall of allowing a negative-energy member to shift the focus of the group if this is not appropriate at this given time. Finally, you may want to think about where you want to end the round, especially if you have an individual that you know is reluctant to talk, or who you know is in need of some additional time and attention. By ending with that person, you can focus on that member's comments without spot-lighting him or her.

❖ JOURNAL WRITING

Journal writing is a strong tool that can be used for processing the experience. Journal writing promotes exploration of personal knowledge. Without threat of criticism by an external audience, individuals are free to concentrate on and explore their thoughts and feelings. Writing captures and preserves thoughts and feelings, creating a record of individuals' progression through an experience. The act of writing compels the individual to express in symbols specific knowledge originally represented and stored in memory in a different form.

Because of its active and personal nature, cognitive demands, and feedback characteristics, writing makes possible unequaled forms of extended and involved thought. Journal writing creates situations that encourage reflection and explicitness, which often leads to a renewed awareness of a person's knowledge. Journal writing also promotes an awareness and possible clarification of feelings and emotions.

If you choose to use journal writing as a way to process during experiences, you will have to provide time for individuals to do this. If you do not set aside time for people to write, then you can not expect them to find the time on their own. Also, if you want individuals to use journals, then you must begin very early in the experience. Otherwise, it becomes difficult to get people involved at a later time and as a result you may have missed a golden opportunity for them to experience a different way to reflect and communicate their thoughts and feelings. When structuring journal writing time, you can choose between using free writing or assign processing questions. The following is a short explanation of each.

1. Free Writing—prior to or following an activity or at designated times throughout the experience you can ask individuals to take out their journals. They can write about (a) their goals, thoughts, and feelings about an upcoming experience, (b) their thoughts and feeling about what they recently experienced, or (c) their thoughts and feelings about their performance over a period of time. Ask them to find a comfortable spot and to write down what comes to mind. If you want them to share this information with other members of the group, it is important to let them know that before they come back. This way they can decide what they would like to share rather than being put on the spot when they return to the group.

2. Assigning Processing Questions—an alternative to fee writing is to give individuals some specific questions that you would like them to respond to in their journal. Again, these can either be kept private or they can be shared with the group after everyone has taken the time to respond individually in writing. Two advantages of assigning questions are that they provide a degree of focus on the issues that you may want to raise and that they also get everyone involved. This is especially valuable when you have an individual or two who tend to sit back and not get actively involved. Giving them the questions that you want to discuss prior to the discussion potentially allows them the opportunity to feel more comfortable and confident when the group reconvenes. Some examples of questions that you may want to assign include:

a.   What do you think it will feel like to have your physical safety entrusted to the group or a group member?
b.   What did it actually feel like to have your physical safety entrusted to the group or a group member?
c.   How are decisions being made by the group?
d.   What could be done to improve the way that the group goes about solving problems?
e.   What are some of the effective ways of communicating that you used in completing the tasks?
f   What would you like more of or less of from the group?
g.   What could you do to improve the quality of this experience for yourself?
h.   Describe the kind of person you'd like to be. Name some characteristics you'd like to have.
i.   What are the three biggest challenges in your life right now?
j.   Describe the good relationships you have with others, how they came about and what you did to bring about that relationship.
l.   Think of one person in your group you are having a difficult time with. In what ways are you different from that person? In what ways are you similar to that person?

❖ DYADS

Dyads occur when you pair up group members to share their perceptions with each other. The value in using dyads is that they allow for more personal interaction. Dyads provide more time for each member to talk and also provide the setting for individuals to discuss things that they may not be comfortable in sharing in a large group setting. Dyads are particularly effective at the beginning of the experience to help people become better acquainted and more comfortable with each other. You can structure dyads in several different ways. You can allow group members to choose a person they want to talk with, or you can choose the person for them to work with. This can be done by having them pair up with the person sitting next to them or by assigning them to be in a dyad with another person. For example, you might say "We are going to take the next ten minutes to talk about our run through the rapids this morning. I would

like Mike and Alice to pair up, Ernie and Jerrod, Bill and Beth, and Sue and Lorraine. Take about five minutes each to talk about what you were feeling and thinking about this morning."

When using dyads, you will want to make sure that you give clear directions regarding the topic that they are to discuss. Also, let groups know how much time they have for this discussion. Whenever possible, let them know when they have reached the halfway point so that one individual does not monopolize the conversation. In addition, it is a good practice to try and circulate while the dyads are in progress to make sure that they are staying on task. At times, you may want to make yourself a member of a dyad so that you can get to know someone better or if you see that someone would benefit from your undivided attention. This arrangement provides you with a good opportunity to isolate with him or her so that you can get a sense of what he or she may be thinking or feeling.

❖ SMALL GROUP DISCUSSION

As an alternative to a large group session or to using dyads, you may choose to use small groups of 3 or 4. An advantage of using groups of 3 or 4 is the fact that they are small enough for people to feel comfortable, yet, they are large enough to share multiple perspectives on a problem or situation. In addition, if you are using role playing or problem solving activities, two people can participate and one or two people can function as an observer and provide feedback to the participants. A final advantage of using small groups has to do with conflict. If conflict arises between two members, the other person or two people can function as the mediator(s) between the quarreling pair. Most of the considerations for structuring dyads should be kept in mind when using small groups as well.

❖ WRITTEN ACTIVITY SHEETS

Written activity sheets are papers in which group members are asked to answer questions, fill-in sentence completion items, or make lists in relation to an issue or topic. The advantages of using written activity sheets are that it provides an alternative approach to processing, it focuses attention on the task, provides immediate responses when individuals are done, and, finally it gives people an opportunity to think about what they may want to say before sharing it with the group. As suggested earlier, it is important to let people know that you want them to share their responses with other members of the group when you give out the activity sheet. An example of a written activity sheet adapted from Hagberg & Leider, (1982) is found in table 7. An example of a sentence-completion exercise is found in table 8.

❖ ISOLATION

Providing time for individuals to reflect and communicate with themselves is another form of processing. On Outward Bound courses this time alone, solo, is a standard part of every experience. However, you don't have to be on an Outward Bound course or wait until this designated component of the course to provide individuals with some time to themselves. It is

◆ TABLE 7 ◆

Sample Written Activity Sheet

What are the three most important things you've learned about yourself during this experience?

People that have truly helped me in my life are: (include how they have helped you)

Three words that describe my personality are (not roles):

What would your best friend say is your most positive attribute?

What do you want to achieve in relation to career/work before you die?

What do you want to achieve in relation to education, travel, adventures before you die?

What do you want to achieve in relation to relationships before you die?

What do you want to achieve in relation to lifestyle before you die?

What would you most like to be remembered for in your life?

How do you allow others to support you? How do you let others know that you need support?

What was the last significant risk that you took?

◆ TABLE 8 ◆

Sample of Sentence-Completion Exercises

Today I am

A wish of mine is to

My friends are

Something I worry about

Three turning points in my life have been

Love is

In five years I

The biggest thing that gets in the way of doing the things that I want to do/be is

I get upset when

When I don't like people I

The hardest thing for me to do is

I am happy when

The main, overriding concern at this stage of my life is

My hero/heroine is

I feel important when

Life is

During my life, the goals I am going to accomplish are

During this experience I want to

By the end of this experience, I hope to

Something I wish I could do better is

I find these things easy to do

I find these things difficult to do

Some qualities that I like about myself are

Some qualities that I want to improve about myself are

A decision I'll have to face is

Something I wish people would understand about me is

Other people see me as

The ways I'll sabotage this learning are

Some ways that I can prevent myself from discounting this experience are possible to structure short blocks of time to give individuals time to think about what they are going to accomplish, what has been accomplished, or to get themselves to refocus if that is what they need to do. Short blocks of time can be established at several points during the activities or on short courses—at a vista if you are hiking, spread everyone out and tell them that they have 15 minutes to focus on the hike, the functioning of the group, and/or their performance. The same can be applied for rafting or canoeing. On even shorter experiences, you can find a place for peo-

ple to take a 15-minute respite, by having everyone go off on a solitary walk, or designate quiet time when walking from element to element, or from the lunch spot back to the ropes course. The shorter the experience, the more important it is to make use of each of these precious minutes.

❖ DRAWING

Drawing is another alternative technique that can be used to help individuals get in touch with what they are experiencing. People don't have to develop beautiful pieces of art in order to get in touch with themselves, the group, or the environment. In fact, some of the silliest stick drawing that people create have great meaning for them and others. A fun activity is to give individuals time to draw and then to share their drawings with other members of the group. The explanation of words and the visual depiction of those words or concepts are usually a very creative and enjoyable way for group members to share their perceptions. Examples of stimuli that can be used for drawing are:

a. Draw a picture that shows how you want to feel at the end of this experience
b. Draw a picture that shows the personal strengths that you bring to this group.
c. Draw a picture that shows how the group is working together and what your role in the group is.
d. Draw a picture that indicates what you consider your greatest accomplishment so far on this experience.
e. Draw a picture that shows what you would like to gain from this experience.

❖ VIDEOTAPING

In this era of technological advancement, frequently, there are opportunities to use video-taping as a method of providing stimuli for discussion of thoughts, feelings, and behavior. For example, you could record while the group is planning to solve an initiative activity, while they are implementing the plan, and when they complete the activity. You could begin the discussion of how they attacked the problem and what each person's role was in the process. At the end of the discussion, you could play back the videotape and compare their perceptions with the information on the screen. In addition, participants could set goals for how they want to approach an upcoming activity. The videotape could be used to document their success or lack of success. Finally, you could use the videotape to identify patterns of behavior that you have noticed. This may allow them to move from the level of awareness to that of responsibility as discussed in the section on Levels of Processing.

❖ USING OBSERVERS

Using observers is a powerful way to bring new information and knowledge to the group as they process the experience. In most organizations and agencies people react to others in an automatic way, and they don't have the opportunity to observe the process of their interactions to develop proactive strategies for the future. Benefits of having an observer of the structured experience include:

a. The observer has to step out of the experience and take a systemic or "big picture view" of what is going on.
b. The observer's comments are heard differently from those of the leaders', because they are "one of them."
c. Often the observer is more direct and effective in giving feedback than the leaders, as the leaders may "couch" their observations where the observer may "hit the group between the eyes" with his or her comments.
d. Rotating observers for different activities not only allows the "fresh eyes" to bring new thinking to the group, but it also focuses and builds skills of looking at the process versus content that generalize to the home, school, or office.
e. The observer's comments can be structured by you to relate to the learning and themes you have designed for the experience (See the examples below).
f. Rotating observers allows participants who don't usually speak up to have their voices and critical observation skills recognized and heard.
g. Functioning as an observer allows participants who have chosen not to partake in the physical experience to be actively involved in the learning process.

It is important to structure the observation process, we like to take observers to the side and explain what their purpose is and what is expected of them. They are encouraged not to interact with the group, they are observers and should remain in their role. At the end of the activity, the observers' comments are heard first. If there are more than two observers, it's helpful to have one of them just respond to one point. Then, move to the next observer who discusses the same point in order to keep the flow of the debrief moving. Below are some examples of questions that we have given to observers to respond to in writing. You will want to use your own set of questions that engender your learning points.

a. Was there an overall vision or shared purpose stated by the group?
b. What were examples of members listening to each other?
c. What were examples of members not listening to each other?
d. How was the leadership of this group structured?
e. Who were the leaders that emerged from this group?
f. What were examples of the things that worked well with this group in completing their task?
g. What were some examples of actions that they could improve upon?
h. Were basic assumptions challenged by anyone in the group?
i. What were examples of people being proactive or taking risks in this activity?
j. What are some examples of care and concern for others being demonstrated?
k. Were there any examples of creativity or "out of the box" thinking?
l. In regard to the synergy of the group, how would you rate it?
m. Are there any other observations you want to comment on?

After hearing from the observers, you want to elicit responses from the members of the group. Keep the conversation going. To this end, at times, it may mean asking the observers only to comment on a few points.

❖ FISH BOWL

The fish bowl processing method is useful for bringing out different points of view in a constructive manner. You identify the topic you want to focus on and determine which participants should be in each group. Usually, you will divide the group in half-forming two groups. There are four main sequences to this method of processing.

1. One group is in the fish bowl, which is an inside circle, doing an activity or talking about a topic, and the other group is outside the fish bowl in an outside circle observing.

2. When the activity or conversation is completed, the outside group moves into the fish bowl, while the inside group goes outside the fish bowl and listens. The group in the fish bowl discusses out loud among themselves what they observed in the other group, without interacting with the outside group. You previously structured what they will be commenting on to make sure people aren't being labeled or judged.

3. Now the outside group comes back into the fish bowl, and the inside group goes outside again. The inside group talks among themselves about their reactions, feelings, and thoughts to what they heard. Again, they are not to address the other group, who are just listening to the discussion.

4. When the inside group finishes, open up the conversation to see if any outside group members want to comment and allow the whole group to partake. At this point, you facilitate like you would any group discussion allowing the differing perspectives to be heard, understood and accepted.

This method is good for "us and them issues" such as gender, college-educated or not, or size and body. You can also combine groups that aren't getting along to demonstrate how easy it is for us to get into "either or" thinking. The fish bowl can be very effective for people to hear perceptions of others in a constructive way. Leaders must structure it well and use their skills to keep the conversations focused on learning and understanding.

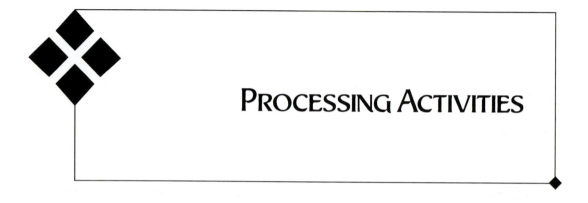

PROCESSING ACTIVITIES

"Never let the fear of striking out get in your way."

—*Babe Ruth*

Similar to each of us, we're sure that you are always searching for activities to use with the diverse groups you work with for the varied settings that you find yourself working in. This section contains a variety of activities and exercises for you to experiment with. They are presented in a sequential manner that compliments the information discussed in the levels of processing section. Specifically, this section is broken-up into exercises and activities for trust, awareness, responsibility, experimentation and transfer. It ends with a few comments that we've labeled "Keynotes and Cautions" which can serve as reminders of how these activities are best used.

DILBERT ® by Scott Adams

DILBERT reprinted by permission of United Feature Syndicate, Inc.

❖ Trust Building

The following processing activities can be used to build trust and bring individuals from awareness through responsibility to experimentation and the transfer of learning. The exercises can be used as stimuli for your processing groups and as the thread that binds and weaves together diverse activities with participants' emotional experiences.

Trust is an essential and vital component of experiential learning or therapy because of the essential role that it plays in group development. The development of a group follows a sequence that consists of trust, data flow, goals, and social control. Each stage is dependent on the stage prior to it. Without trust, people won't speak freely of their concerns or personal life (data flow). If data flow hasn't developed adequately, it will be very difficult to set group goals and make group decisions. Social control or procedures of a group is the final stage. It is contingent on the ability of the group to establish goals. Therefore, trust is the foundation of a successful group. The purpose and objectives of trust building are to allow individuals to (a) speak freely and honestly about their feelings, (b) take new risks, such as rock climbing, changing behavior, leading a training session, etc., and (c) feel comfortable enough with the group to feel the sharing, warmth, and power of being a cohesive entity.

Trust building is most effective when accomplished early in the experience, and then gradually continues throughout the experience. Some trust building exercises that you may want to experiment with are the following:

1. *Adjective game*—To learn everyone's name, one person starts by saying an adjective for how he or she feels now and his or her name. The next person repeats the first person's name and adjective and then his/her own. The third person repeats the first and second persons' name and adjective and then his/her own name. This process continues around the entire circle. Other ways in which this activity can be used are to pick a fruit, vegetable, or animal that you most identify with and your name; or, pick something you're good at and then your name. "I am a singer, Tom."

2. *Introduce each other*—This is an excellent early in the experience activity. In dyads, one person talks about himself/herself, i.e., interests, his/her family, why he/she is on the experience, and dreams. The other person just listens for four or five minutes. Switch the roles, then back in the group, have individuals introduce their partner to the crew. In addition, when individuals introduce each other, they can state what aspect of their partner they were most impressed with. Finally, everyone can discuss how it felt having someone talking about them. This is also a good way to focus on using appropriate listening skills.

3. *Talk about trust*—First in animals. How do you know an animal trusts you? What behaviors do they exhibit? How does an animal know you trust it? How do you know when people trust you? What are the behavioral cues? How do you know when you trust someone? What behavioral cues exist?

4. *Trust statements*—In dyads have individuals complete this sentence, while the other person just listens. "In order for me to trust you, you should _____, i.e., look at me when I speak, help me on the trail." Have each person do this for four or five minutes. Encourage individuals not to engage in conversation. Let them struggle with continually completing

the sentence. "What things came out?" "What commonalties do you share?" "How did it feel struggling for answers?"

5. *Appreciations*—There are several different types of appreciations. Here are a few that we have used with great success. (a) Individuals can share something positive about the person to their right or left, and then continue to go around this way. This is a good way to end a group session around the fire; (b) Select a person who has had a hard day, either from the activities or from the other group members. Each person shares an appreciation with this one person. He/she should be encouraged not to sabotage compliments, but just listen and accept them. On a longer experience, try to bombard each person at least once.

6. *Trust fall*—Have the whole group do a trust fall from a stump or rock. One person falls backward into the arms of the others.

7. *Trust walk*—(a) In dyads, one person is blindfolded and the other leads him/her through a variety of experiences; (b) Form a line and have everyone blindfolded. You are not blindfolded, and you are the only one who can speak. Everyone holds on to whatever they can.

8. *Feeling word*—To help individuals become more aware of their feelings and also to get a feel for your group, have each person say the first feeling that is with them right at the moment. This is effective if it's done quickly. You can utilize this activity to start group sessions and also end them.

9. *Blind line*—Have each person put a bandanna over their eyes. Give each person a number (1–10 or 1–12) secretly and have them line up in order non-verbally. Whatever way they can do it without talking. Questions to ask include: "How did you feel?" "Were you frustrated?"

10. *Nourishing game*—Have each person share with the group someone that has made them feel good today and how it was accomplished.

11. *Good trait*—Have everyone in the group share a good trait they have. Another alternative is to share their greatest success of the day, week, month, or year.

12. *Interviews*—Break up into groups of three or four. Each group selects one person to be interviewed. Other members of the group can ask him or her any question that they may want. The person being interviewed has the option to pass on any question. Change roles until every member of the group has been interviewed. Ask "What kind of questions are easiest for you to answer?" "Hardest?"

13. *Concentric circle unfolding*—Count off by 2's. Form two circles facing each other, one inside the other. Discuss topics with one person listening, the other talking, then switch. Practice non-judgmental listening. Groups move opposite ways, so each topic gets different people together. Topics can be anything that you want. Here are some suggestions:
    a. Most memorable experience in the last two weeks.
    b. Someplace in the world I'd like to go.
    c. Hero or heroine of childhood.
    d. Person I most want to impress.
    e. What skill would I like to master.
    Follow this up with a discussion. Some questions that you may want to include are: "Who was easiest to talk to?" "Hardest?" "What made them so?" "Any difference talking first or second?" "What topic was hardest?" "Which gender was easier to talk to?"

14. *Sentence completions*—To help process any experience, have group members complete some of the following sentences.

    a.   I learned today
    b.   I was afraid when
    c.   I liked
    d.   I disliked
    e.   I'm unhappy when
    f.   I'm cool when I
    g.   I feel good when
    h.   When I'm mad I
    i.   My favorite place is
    j.   Something I never told anyone is
    k.   What people like best in me
    l.   I'd like my parents to
    m.   I'm concerned about
    n.   Other people in this group
    o.   I usually avoid
    p.   What I hate most
    q.   My friends are
    r.   When I'm frustrated I usually
    s.   What I fear the most
    t.   I am really
    u.   Most people don't know that I

❖ AWARENESS

The following segment includes activities that have been designed to help individuals learn more about their thoughts, feelings, and actions. Each person is provided with information regarding the interdependence and integration of thoughts, feelings, and actions in the learning process. The intention is to achieve personal relevancy that can emerge from the activities and the experience. This can happen when participants learn from activities about themselves and others, as opposed to retaining fond memories about activities.

Repeated actions to the same thoughts and feelings are called patterns. Patterns are unconscious or conditioned roles or ways of being that we fall into during our interactions with superiors, the opposite sex, fear, alienation, groups, or whatever the situation may be.

Some traditional patterns are: the know it all, the loser, the competitor, the dumb role, the passive one, the macho, the arguer, the intellectual, and the compromiser. Whatever patterns that individuals possess usually surface more in an experiential setting than at home because of the intensity of the experience. This makes patterns a vital educational or therapeutic tool. As discussed previously, the more a person learns about his or her patterns when in disequilibrium, the more conscious control and responsibility they'll have in making the transfer of learning personally relevant at home, work, or school. The purposes and objectives of awareness exercises are to: (a) allow individuals to become aware of and integrate their thoughts, feelings, and actions, (b) allow individuals to see patterns that arise; (c) explore the relevancy of patterns on an experience and at home; (d) make unconscious roles and patterns conscious; and, (e) allow individuals to see how patterns are serving them and what alternative actions are available.

These exercises should be started when you feel that there is a sufficient trust-level in the group. Continue to work with the awareness exercises throughout the experience.

1. *Patterns discussion*—Have a brief discussion as to what roles or patterns are. We all have them, and this experience is an opportunity to look at some of them. Plant a gentle seed.

2. *Briefing prompts*—During group activities and opportunities for group decision-making, you can try some of the following interventions:
   a. Keep journals—ask each person directly after an activity to jot down a few notes. "What were your feelings during the activity?" "What did you like and dislike?" "What were some of the statements that you were telling yourself during the activity?" "What were you doing?" "Were you uncomfortable doing anything? If so, what?" "Were any of your reactions typical of you? If so, what?" The first time just let them write, ask if there are any reactions. The next time talk about how a person's thoughts, feelings, actions work together and stimulate each other. Let them write down the thoughts, feelings and actions that they assimilated. "How typical is this?" is an appropriate question to ask.
   b. Sometimes preface an activity with "Be aware of the role that you're taking here." "What part are you playing?"
   c. Other times at the end of an activity, ask each person to share what role they thought they took. Ask them to think if this role is similar to what they do at home, school, or work.
   d. Something to try once is to have each person play the opposite role and do the same activity.
   e. Discuss with individuals early in the experience how rare an opportunity they have to experiment with different behaviors. Statements such as, "No one knows you," "Be whoever you want," "Try things differently on the experience," help to set an open and free atmosphere. Do exercises when you feel it's a good time. Be in touch with yourself and the participants' levels of disequilibrium.

3. *Forced choice*—Make two parallel lines in the dirt, or on a trail about eighteen feet apart. Ask people to decide on one choice or the other and move to the respective line. Ask them would you rather be:

ice cream or cake	chair or table
hammer or nail	spender or saver
pitcher or batter	forest or ocean

lover or loved one	helper or helpee
doer or thinker	talker or listener
fast or slow	calm or excitable
flexible or rigid	sun or moon
trusting or cautious	videotape or still photograph
loner or people person	night or day
planner or a "wing it person"	logical or sentimental
mountains or beach	outdoors or indoors

"What were your feelings?" "Which were hardest and easiest?" "What were the statements that you were telling yourself?" "Did you move quickly or hesitate?" "Did any patterns emerge in your choices?"

4. *Line continuum*—Make two lines on the ground parallel to each other. One line is the highest point on a straight line and the other the lowest point. Participants should line up in a straight line, one person per slot by rating themselves on this continuous line for the characteristics of:

leader-follower	optimist-pessimist
aggressive-passive	listener-talker
giver-taker	sensitive-cold
energetic-lethargic	flexible-rigid
serious-playful	introvert-extrovert
confident-insecure	independent-dependent
brains-brawn	conventional-unconventional

Select any combinations that are apropos, or create your own. Once people are in a straight line in rank order, ask if anyone disagrees with the order. If so, have them put people in the spot they feel they belong. Let any person who wants to change the order do so. This allows individuals to rate themselves and see how others perceive them.

Discussion questions can include: "How did you feel about the spot you put yourself at?" "What were your feelings in lining up?" "Were you uncomfortable or did you feel fine?" "How did you feel when someone moved you?" "Are there other times that you feel this way?" "What were some of your reasons for putting yourself where you did?" Keep things focused in a positive manner. Ask individuals if they see any specific patterns. You can use this exercise a number of times on the experience as a benchmark to show growth or change.

5. *Ten Commandments—Discussion*
   a. "What were the rules of your house as you were growing up?" "What did you have to abide by?"
   b. "What were the 'shoulds' and 'shouldn'ts' of your peer group as you grew up?"

6. *Opposite roles*—Ask each person to pick a partner. Ask them to be aware of their pattern of choosing or waiting to be chosen. Each pair is to have a thumb wrestle, slap fight, and push fight. When they have finished, have each person identify his/her pattern in those activities; the competitor, playful, apathetic, serious, etc. Follow-up this activity by having each person choose a new partner and play the opposite role in the activities. Discuss how the new role felt, hard or uncomfortable, and what they liked about their original role. This exercise can be fun.

7. *Postures*—Ask individuals to pick partners and non-verbally have one acquire an inferior posture and the other a superior posture. Actually have them stand over or on top of each other. Have them switch, nonverbally being aware of how they feel making the transition. Discuss how they felt about being superior and inferior. "Which role was most comfortable?" "Which role do you usually take?" If you select a leader of the day, this can lead to a discussion of how you feel about being the leader and follower, and how would you like the leader to lead.

8. *Benefit of patterns discussion*—In a group discussion have individuals share a personal pattern that they have become aware of on the experience. Then, have people share how this pattern serves them. What is the benefit or "goodies" they get by holding that pattern? Examples are, "I compromise myself all the time with people; what I get from it is that people like me, I'm easy to get along with, and I don't create waves." "I'm always a leader and tell people what to do. I get attention, and it feels good." This exercise helps individuals become aware and take responsibility for their patterns. Do this activity towards the latter half of the experience when the trust is built and individuals have a good feel for patterns. It is best if you go first and model the type of statement that you want people to make.

9. *Sculpturing*—In this exercise, participants will position themselves as a multiperson sculpture or statue. They will have to decide who stands next to whom and in what posture or stance. For example, one person may be standing, pointing a finger, while another is kneeling below, with his or her hands out, palms up. You can do the whole group or subgroups. When they are positioned, they are nonverbal and should be asked to be aware of their thoughts and feelings in this position.

    You may want to have a director who positions people and shapes them to have the appropriate expression and stance. You may want to pick a scene to depict, like working on a project, cooking dinner, or using a map and compass. Processing questions can include: How do you feel in this position? What would you like to say to anyone in the sculpture? What stops you from saying it? What postures and positions would you rather be in? How can you bring this about when you find yourself in the original position?

❖ RESPONSIBILITY

To some degree, many of us live in a cloud. This cloud limits our present awareness and personal responsibility. The disequilibrium that is created by participating in an experience provides an opportunity to wake up, reown, and make changes in our lives. The theory and techniques from Gestalt therapy can help us facilitate participants' ability to take more responsibility on the experience and in their life. Gestalt means wholeness. A Gestalt premise is that our cloud is made up of unfinished situations, resentments, dreams, and projections, which rise to emergence, at times seeking a form of expression. When we focus on these elements, we're ignoring or blind to what we're currently experiencing, i.e., our environment while hiking, blisters on our feet, the beauty of nature, or how we are affecting others.

A goal of Gestalt is to return to wholeness by helping individuals to become aware of, responsible for, reclaim, and integrate their fragmented parts. Integration releases a surge of energy that was used to suppress these emotions. People become more aware of themselves and the environment. This permits more responsibility for their feelings, thoughts, and actions. The following activities are valuable to use after the awareness phase of the experience or when issues emerge. The objectives and purpose of the responsibility exercises are to allow the person to: (a) take responsibility for their thoughts, feelings, and actions; (b) be aware of their "here and now" experience physically, mentally, and emotionally, (c) discharge and deal constructively with their resentments; and, (d) take more control and responsibility for their lives. Ways in which you can facilitate for awareness and responsibility are:

1. *Use I-statements*—Ask individuals to speak in "I statements" as opposed to "you statements." This encourages each person to own what they're saying. "When I get tired of hiking, all I want to do is sit down," as opposed to: "When you get tired of hiking, all you want to do is sit down."

2. *Responsibility discussion*—Talk about responsibility and "Who controls you?" and "Who makes you do things?" One of the values of experiential education is the immediacy of consequences. If a person doesn't pack a raincoat and it rains he or she will get wet. Individuals need to become responsible for all their actions.

3. *I am aware . . .*—When you're taking a break during activities, have each person complete this sentence. "I am aware of _____." Allow them to say it about five times, filling the blank with whatever they are aware of right then. Statements that they might make include: "I am aware of the wind"; "I am aware that John's boot is untied"; and "I am aware of a fly on my leg." This helps people cut through their own clouds. When possible, this activity should be coupled with a solo walk afterwards, this promotes an increased awareness of the environment.

4. *Projection exercise*—(a) Ask each person to bring back an item from the woods. In the circle, have them become that object and make "I statements" about it. Examples include: "I am a leaf"; "I am yellow"; and "I am old and used." This allows each person to become more in touch with the item and some of their projections that come up. What they choose to say at times can be profound self-description; (b) Do the same exercise but have them choose an animal they would like to be, and make "I statements" for that. Statements like "I am a squirrel," and "I'm quick" are likely to occur. Ask individuals, "what part of the projection was the object and what part did they feel was them?"

5. *Can't do discussion*—An exercise before an emotionally or physically strenuous activity is to have each person think of three things they can't do. Have them report one to the group. Have each person change the word "can't" to "won't" and repeat it to the group. Discuss how they felt saying "won't", and owning their shortcomings.

6. *Bitch Session*—This activity can be used at the first sign of tension within the group. It promotes constructive discharge and dealing with potential problems. The session needs to be well structured. A person with a bitch expresses it as a resentment to the specific person or the whole group. The person then states his/her demand of that person. This is where the person with the resentment can tell the other person exactly what he/she wants from them to help extinguish the problem. When the demand is through, the person shares an appreciation with the person, similar to the resentment. Example—"Randy, I resent you cooking every meal. I demand that you give someone else a chance and demand that you try some different jobs. I appreciate that you take the initiative every night to start cooking, and I appreciate that you are a good cook."

7. *Fantasy of getting in touch with fear*—This activity is good to use before a physically or emotionally challenging activity. Have each person relax with his or her eyes closed. "Take a deep breath and let it all out. Now do this again. Take a trip in your body and find where your fear is located. How big is it? What shape does it have? OK, now breathe through that spot. Get

some deep breaths right through that spot. When you're ready open up your eyes." Have them share on a 1–10 point basis what their fear was before and after they focused on it.

8. *Wall fantasy*—This is best to use directly before rock climbing, solo, or the wall initiative. Tell people that you're going to take them on a guided fantasy, and at a certain point they are to complete it themselves. Have everybody get in a comfortable spot and close their eyes and relax. Use as many details as possible to provide them with a good representation. Here is an example of a scenario that you might use: "Imagine yourself in a big field. It is very open and it's warm outside. How does the sun feel on your shoulders?" "You can feel the grass on your legs. There are some flowers; what colors do you see? On your right is a footpath. You walk over to it and follow it. You walk up a rise, and in front of you, you see a wall. Walk up to this wall and complete the fantasy on your own from here. Don't censor, but let whatever comes into your mind come."

When they have finished the fantasy, have them share their visualization in small groups. In the large group explain that the wall can signify a block, challenge, risk, or problem, like they're going to have on the challenge course, while rock climbing or on solo. Each person creates his or her own wall, the size and what it was made of. Some will have huge walls and some small. Some people will make it over easily, while others won't even try. It is important to share with them how this is their own creation, how they put up their own blocks and created their own difficulties. It's also interesting to see what people have created on the other side of the wall, or their reward. Let people get whatever they can from this, without your interpreting it for them.

9. *Bragging*—Arrange participants in groups of three. Have them pick one quality they do well. Then have them brag about how great they are at it. Sabotage—Now with the same quality, have them tell how and in what way they use it to not believe in themselves.

10. *Alter ego*—While in group discussions, a person may have difficulty expressing his or her feelings. You or another person can go behind him or her and put your hands on his/her shoulders. Then, say what you think or feel he or she might be experiencing as succinctly as possible using "I statements." If it fits for the person, have him or her say it. This exercise helps people identify their feelings more and speak from the heart.

❖ EXPERIMENTATION AND TRANSFER

The following activities are presented to encourage individuals to experiment with new behaviors. One of the keys to success is to have the support and encouragement of the group to try out these new behaviors, without the fear of ridicule or criticism. The atmosphere you want is that of a safe laboratory where failure is impossible and constructive learning is guaranteed.

Role-playing is a good technique for promoting generalization and transfer. Role-playing is used to portray another person or for exploring a different side of one's self. It is best, when used in the middle or end of the experience, when the trust level is high. Role-playing can be a high-risk activity and some people are more comfortable with it than others. The purpose and objective of the experimentation and transfer exercises are to: (a) allow individuals to experiment with new behaviors and receive support and constructive feedback; (b) identify the ingredients necessary to encourage risk taking; (c) allow individuals to see how others perceive them; (d) allow individuals to become more aware of different sides of themselves; (e) allow participants to have a clearer perception and practice of their re-entry back home; and, (f) help transfer what has been learned on the experience to the home, school, and work-setting.

Ways in which you can facilitate for experimentation and transfer are:

1. *Safe environment discussion*—Hold a discussion about the ingredients the group would need from each other to guarantee that it would be a safe laboratory for all to take the risks necessary to be "peak performers."

2. *Acceptable vs. unacceptable comments*—Discuss the type of comments from others that would sabotage or inhibit taking emotional risks.

3. *Verbal commitments*—Have each person make a verbal commitment that they will provide a safe environment for others to experiment with new behaviors.

4. *Pattern identification*—Ask people to pick a pattern that they are willing to experiment with as a behavior change and share what their plan is with the group, i.e., "I will speak up more and offer my ideas", or "I will give others a chance to lead and work on being able to follow today." Ask each person how the group can "help or support you in taking this risk?"

5. *New behavior reflection*—At the end of the day, ask each member of the group how experimenting with this new behavior went. Get feedback from others and refine what worked and didn't work. Recommit to do it again, or try a new behavior.

6. *Support partners*—Develop support partners who can coach and support each other on behavioral changes. This will help to diversify the type of processing groups you hold. You may want to consider creative matching of your pairs. For example, a leader who wants to be less assertive could be paired with a passive person who wants to be more assertive. You can have them teach the other person how to accomplish such. A passive person teaching another how to be passive can no longer be unconscious using this process.

7. *Coaching discussion*—In the bigger group discuss how individuals can give and receive good coaching on the experience and back at school, work, or home. How can you guarantee your coach will be successful?

8. *Sub-personalities discussion*—Hold a discussion on sub-personalities, subselves, different sides of a person, or the different voices or conversations that we hear inside our heads. Have individuals be aware of the fact that we all have different sides and this is normal. The conversations may not go away, but we can get better at managing them.

9. *Fantasy of sub-personalities*—Have people relax with their eyes closed. The setting is in a field. Give many details including that they see some woods in front of them. They walk up to the trees and find a footpath. It leads to a cabin in the woods. Have them fantasize how big is the cabin? "What is it made of?" "What kind of windows does it have?" They walk up to the door. "What does the door look like?" Inside the cabin are all their sub-personalities or different sides of themselves. When they open the door, all their sub-personalities are going to come out. Ask them to identify these sub-personalities, and have each sub-personality say something to them.

When people finished their fantasies, ask each person to share them in small groups. When back together as a large group, anyone can share their fantasy with the entire group. This exercise is very effective because it allows them to become aware of themselves and their internal voices that they will invariably hear when they are by themselves.

10. *Role-play each member of the group*—split up into two groups, and pick half the people to role-play. Set up a scene such as at a meeting, working on a project, dinner time, breaking camp, or group discussion, and have each group role play the same scene portraying the characters that they have selected. In order to role-play the whole group, this process has to be completed twice. In the role-play, try to capture the characters' body posture, mannerisms, voice, and what the person may say. One group enacts their role play, and then the other group per-

forms theirs. When this has terminated the people playing the same parts, as there should be two of every character, share how they felt playing their role. Ask "What was hard or easy for you?" In the large group, have the two people share what they found about the role, and person, and then have the person they portrayed give their impression of how it was to watch himself or herself, as others may have perceived him or her.

11. *Re-entry Role-play*—Have people describe a situation that they are going back to, such as, school, their parents, work, or special relationships, that is causing them some anxiety. The person whose role-play it is can describe each of the people, their role, and the scene. This person also can play many of the characters, by switching roles and thus allowing the other players to get more of the flavor of the character.

12. *Coaching*—In small groups of two or three, have people pick a behavior or situation they want to change at school, work, or home. Each person can receive coaching from group members about the situation and strategize ways to deal with the problem at home or work. Have them develop a list of strengths and/or supports that they have or will need along with a plan to counteract the negative forces. This small group can support each other on the new behaviors when the experience is over, by deciding to write letters, make phone calls, or arrange meetings. Each member can share their plan back in the big group and receive more feedback. Here they can role-play situations that will need more practice.

13. *Visualization*—Using their visualization skills have individuals go back and experience the successes of the experience. What did they see? The activities, environment, people's faces, etc. What did they hear from others or nature? How did it feel and where did they feel it? Is there a metaphor that goes with it, an object or a special word? How can they carry this feeling, visualization, and metaphor with them when they get to a new edge?

14. *Anchoring*—When individuals feel the feelings, hear the positive words and sounds, and see the successful sights and they are all at their peaks, have them touch their hands in a unique way to "anchor" or associate these sensations to this touch. For example, hold their little finger with the fingers of their other hand or make the "OK" sign, but use a different finger. Each time they visualize their success, have them hold their anchor until holding their anchor will be conditioned to bring up their successful experiences. People can then use their anchor when they are in a new or uncomfortable situations as a positive resource. In addition, they can anchor many positive emotional states for future use.

15. *Positive visualizations*—Have people use their positive visualizations of past successes and their anchor as a preconditioning to visualizing the situations at home, school, or work which they are committed to changing. Then have them visualize the new situation and doing it perfectly, and handling any of the issues that may come up. Have them continue to replay the future scene over and over until the results are exactly what they want.

KEYNOTES AND CAUTIONS

You cannot teach humans anything. You can only help them discover it within themselves.

—Galileo

1. Each person is the best authority on him or herself. All we can do is bring things to his or her awareness.

2. Let people know that they can pass on participation in an exercise. It's their responsibility to make their own decisions.
3. Stay with "what", "how", and "where" type of questions. Why's tend to receive rationalizations and lose focus on the experience.
4. There is no need to force these activities. Stay with the concerns of group members'. Use these activities only where they fit.
5. Use exercises that you feel comfortable with and do them in your own style.
6. It is a good idea to let participants lead some of the activities.
7. Use levity and humor when and where you can.

DEVELOPING AND USING METAPHORS

"The metaphors through which we organize our work have a powerful influence on both what we perceive and what we do."

—*Jill Freedman and Gene Combs*

Using metaphors and stories have become very popular in the psychotherapy and mental health field. It appears that the use of metaphors is becoming a bridge between various psychological disciplines. There have been many publications written on using metaphorical communication (i.e., Combs & Freedman, 1990; Freedman & Combs, 1996; Grove, 1989; Siegelman, 1990; White & Epston, 1990,), along with framing learning experiences metaphorically (Gass, 1995). This section will look closely at some of this work, plus give some practical suggestions on how you can use metaphorical communication and develop new stories with your participants. The section is divided into three segments: (1) Using Participants' Metaphors and Stories; (2) Leaders Using Metaphorical Communication; and (3) Creating Metaphors for Experiences and Feelings.

How reality is viewed is important to the learning we take from an experience. Freedman and Combs (1996) identified three different stances regarding human knowledge of reality. They are:

1. "Reality is knowable—if elements and workings can be accurately and replicably discovered, described, and used by human beings;
2. We are prisoners of our perceptions—attempts to describe reality tells us a lot about the person doing the describing, but not much about external reality; and
3. Knowledge arises within communities of knowers—the realities we inhabit are those we negotiate with one another" (p. 20).

A gradual evolution of these views of reality has occurred over time. Currently, an increased number of theorists support the third perspective—that of co-creation of reality. It is this third world view we are embracing in our approach to working with participants' metaphors and stories. Leaders and participants co-influence and co-construct the learning from any experience.

❖ USING PARTICIPANTS' METAPHORS AND STORIES

"A single word can possess multiple meanings, yet as the common saying goes, one picture can be worth a thousand words. And if one picture can be worth a thousand words, then one experience can be worth a thousand pictures, then one metaphor can be worth a thousand experiences. But in the end, a metaphor only possesses value when:

> *It is able to interpret the experiences*
> *in a manner that provides the picture*
> *that produces words*
> *that have meaning*
> *for that particular person."*

—Michael A. Gass 1995, p.XV

We are defining a metaphor as a mental bridging operation that links the unknown with the known, describing one thing in terms of another or the pattern that connects two different things (Combs & Freedman, 1990; Siegelman, 1990). A metaphor usually follows, when someone says "It's like. . . ." A story is the development and elaboration of a metaphor into more of a discourse or dialogue. It is important to train your ears to recognize peoples' metaphors and then try to incorporate these metaphors in your responses. Using participants' metaphors will help them know they have been heard and honored. People have a special relationship with their metaphors, like they do with their names. We know communication can be enhanced when we use the person's name. The same is true for metaphors and stories as they are your window into how people perceive their world. The success of storing experiences provides persons with a sense of continuity and meaning in their lives, and they rely upon this for the ordering of daily lives and for the interpretation of future experiences (Combs & Freedman, 1990).

All stories have a beginning, middle, and ending or a history, present, and future. So, peoples' interpretations of current experiences are as much future-shaped as they are past-determined. It is in knowing and understanding the participants' stories that help us process their new experiences. Ask yourself how this new success can fit into the existing theme. You can help individuals rewrite their scripts as a director or producer would. However, maintain caution and understanding that reordering and changing the script may result in some disequilibrium, and like some writers, individuals may find it difficult and disturbing. The dominant story of a person is contained within the comfort and known circle. Being at the edge and into new territory creates new stories and metaphors that will take time to be accepted, so the dominant story can expand. Then, new chapters or choices in life are the result. The art of processing the experience brings about a richer story for the participant, which can have broad appeal and application at home.

Having participants tell their stories helps create the new story. If it's untold or not put together well, only bits and fragments will exist. This point reinforces the suggestion of stopping participants while they are in S-1. The edge components can then be exposed and included in the story to shed light on the retreat or the success. In S+1, the telling of the story, helps construct the full meaning of the experience. Bruner (1988) believes that in telling the story there is an opportunity to be in the experience again and create new meanings. He states that "It is in the performance of an expression that we re-experience, re-live, re-create, re-tell, re-construct, and re-fashion our culture. The performance does not release a pre-existing meaning that lies dormant in the text . . . Rather, the performance itself is constitutive" (p. 11).

Some examples of using participants' stories and metaphors will help illustrate this process. Nancy was a woman in her mid-thirties, and she spoke about feeling like she "was in a barrel and barely peeking over the edge" when she was in new situations. The barrel was her metaphor, and the story was the dialogue built around the metaphor. We took notice of her description and used her metaphor of the barrel and gave her the following feedback: "It seems like you came out of the barrel during the last activity. What was that like for you?" Jane was a woman in her sixties and spoke about a "knot" in her stomach when she felt her pain and loneliness. We continued to explore her "knot" with her during the experience, i.e., "Is your knot there now? How big is it? What do you imagine your knot would like to do?" Jim was a 34-year-old man, who said, "Each time I achieve a new success at work, it's like grabbing an ice cube above me, and by the time I bring it down, it's melted, and I have to look for another." We talked with him about how he could savor this "ice cube" or the success longer, before it melts. He decided to "treat it more like a treasure and keep it in an ice box with a window where I could view it and use it as a trophy to propel me further." Dan was a 48-year-old man who worked in a flower orchard for the past ten years. We talked to him about "pinching back the old growth when it gets in the way," listening to others as "fertilizing his soil", when he'd withdraw as "a freeze outside and all the flowers are closing up", and when he risked into new territory "as the emergence of a new petal unfolding."

After completing the ropes course, Susan, a 28-year-old in recovery, talked about feeling like an "agile cat." We continued to speak to her about using "her balance of a cat" in other aspects of her life. "What would your cat do when things get shaky?" She responded "hold on tighter, like I have to do with my program and keep showing up; then, I know I'll always land on my feet."

In all these cases, we either used their metaphor or an aspect of their life story and utilized it as a symbol and means to enhance the communication and processing. The metaphor or story tells you the type of boat that they are navigating down the stream of their lives. We then jump in with them and use their specific language to help improve their steering and propulsion so that they can arrive at new territories, landings, or choices in their lives.

❖ LEADERS USING METAPHORICAL COMMUNICATION

". . . Retellings are what culture is all about. The next telling reactivates prior experience, which is then rediscovered and relived as the story is re-related in a new situation. Stories may have endings, but stories are never over."

(Bruner 1986, p.17)

When you use metaphorical language and narrative, there is always an element of ambiguity that accompanies the language. This is because there are a number of ways it may be interpreted. People tend to want to resolve ambiguity or tension because it creates disequilibrium; thus more balance and stability are desired. People will listen closer, think harder, and become more experientially involved when you use a certain amount of ambiguity when expressing information that is not safety related. Finding oneself in the unknown new territory can lead to a very active kind of participation where individuals are reassociating and reorganizing their internal experiential lives to find some order in the message that has been conveyed.

A metaphor or story is a nonlinear, indirect way of expression. It encourages the participant to be actively involved in personally interpreting what has been said. Generally, becoming much more involved than when direct statements are used. The individual must search through a number of stored or imagined experiences in order to find some personal meaning in the symbols or stories that have been told. The searching stimulates mental associations which make the messages more memorable. The creative process involved in searching through and reorganizing new experiences helps individuals become active collaborators in processing and generalizing their learning (Combs & Freedman, 1990).

In school, when a teacher stated, "If you don't all be quiet, some of you will stay after," it was easy to take this indirection as pointing a direct finger. Milton Erickson, the famous hypnotherapist, was renowned for using metaphors and indirection with his clients. He frequently told them to climb a nearby peak where they would learn something significant. Typically, they would come down with a profound experience, discovering why he sent them there. He used these experiences metaphorically, allowing them to come back with whatever learning they needed.

As a means of briefing an activity, you can use metaphors and indirection. Below are some examples:

1. "An individual on the last experience discovered an important personal strength on this next activity."
2. "Some of you may learn some significant things about yourselves today."
3. "Leadership can emerge from unexpected places."
4. "Don't be surprised when something extraordinary happens to you."
5. "I think many of you will really get what you came for from this activity (or course)."

When people are on the edge, the natural inclination is to move back into the circle of comfort. It's as if there were a magnet pulling them back to the safe territory. To combat this natural tendency, you may need to encourage people unconsciously and indirectly, in addition to doing it directly. Metaphors can help with this process. Since ideas are not presented directly, it is more difficult for individuals to object to them (Combs & Freedman, 1990). The use of unconscious and indirect encouragement can help individuals to take those big steps and have the break-throughs and successes they want.

❖ REVERSE SYMBOLISM

People who have been involved in experiential learning personally know the impact, po-tency, and learning that occurs from a course or program. It is possible that one of the major fac-tors for this growth and relevancy comes from a process referred to as "reverse symbolism." That is, in almost all other educational situations, a learning, insight, or meaning is connected with a lived or real experience that acts as a symbol. For example, an educator may say to a student or friend "learning to use a computer is like riding a bicycle; you have to take many falls before you really get your balance and can go some distance" or "getting an advanced degree is like climb-ing a mountain; you just keep walking one step at a time." We take a concept or meaning and try to match it with a lived, active, or real symbol.

In outdoor experiential programs, we have the unique opportunity of engaging people in diverse real, active, and lived experiences. Reverse symbolism is one of the skills of processing where these lived or real experiences are taken as symbols and matched or connected with per-sonal meanings for the individual. So, the symbolic or metaphoric experience goes from real life experience to meaning, where typically the analogy goes from meaning to a similar experience. If reverse symbolism doesn't take place, the activity stands as an unconnected, irrelevant, and unor-ganized experience for the person. When the experience is bridged with personal meaning for the individual, then the third thing created is the experience as a metaphor which can then stand for the learning and be used in an abundance of ways and situations. The reverse symbolism helps organize this new chapter within the dominant story for the person and becomes a valu-able and useful resource. The experience becomes a symbol which is the golden nugget that now has value and can be exchanged, bought, and sold.

We have already established that our minds think in metaphorical or associative ways. In processing activities, leaders need only ask the right questions to facilitate what is a natural human process, making connections. When you use metaphorical communication, participants are compelled to think and listen in symbols and soon learn to make bridges from the experience to their life.

The direct and traditional way of processing may be to ask the question, "What did you learn about this experience that you can apply at home?" This approach beckons linear and ra-tional modes of thought with limited symbol and picture making. Some examples of using metaphorical communication for processing the experience include:

1. "What are the walls that you face back at work or home, and how can you get over them?"
2. "What mountains in your life are you still climbing?"
3. "When do you need to re-orient your map at home?"
4. "When in your life do you need to get out of your boat and scout the rapids?"
5. "Who are your spotters or belayers back home?"

Each of these examples creates a picture for individuals from the real, felt, and lived experiences of the learning program and asks them to make connections and meanings with other aspects of their life. The experience then becomes a metaphor for them. Siegelman (1990) writes, "What gives metaphor its usefulness is the possibility of bridging or generalizing so that thought can cover a larger domain than originally. But what gives metaphor its vividness and resonance is its connection with the world of sensed and felt experience" (p. 7).

Below are some words that can be used to facilitate the use of metaphorical language. Carefully select your words to enable participants to make pictures when they hear your words. This can help arouse their affect and connect unconscious processes.

1. poison	10. burned	19. explode
2. imprisoned	11. wounded	20. whipped
3. strangled	12. betrayed	21. struggle
4. burst	13. starving	22. speeding
5. liberated	14. thirsty	23. violated
6. isolated	15. overflowing	24. abused
7. stranded	16. submerged	25. reborn
8. suffocated	17. trapped	26. smothered
9. drowning	18. set free	27. slapped

An example that contrasts the use of metaphorical language versus not using it would be the following. "It seems like the trapeze leap was a good experience for you" versus "Climbing up the ladder you seemed terrified and trapped, but once you jumped you seemed unshackled and set free." You could then follow up these statements with "What were the chains that were keeping you stuck?" This type of question can provide stimuli for a rich discussion.

❖ METAPHOR THEMES

There are some basic themes that metaphors and stories communicate, which are common to all humans. These themes can be used as a resource because people have already experienced them and need only apply this universal knowledge to their particular situation. We are then using each person's common knowledge of these themes and bridging them with their current experience. This process is an example of the utilization approach. We are taking something that is already there and finding a way to use it as a metaphor. Below are some basic themes which are in no way exclusive. They are presented as stimuli to further promote your creativity and personal style in using metaphors and telling stories.

A. *Journey Theme:* This can be used when individuals or a group are beginning a new project, endeavor, task, career, or life course.
   1. *Types of Journeys:*
      a. Train
      b. Automobile
      c. Ship or Boat
      d. Plane

      e. Bicycle

      f. On foot

  2. *Trip Planning and Beginning:*

      a. Planning and gathering information—research

      b. Gathering supplies

      c. Conditioning for the journey

      d. Setting a goal

      e. Orienting the map

      f. Breaking inertia to get started

      g. Taking the first step

      h. Setting the sails

  3. *Navigation:*

      a. Taking charge or responsibility—"who is the skipper, who is behind the wheel, helmsman, driver, pilot or conductor?"

      b. Skills and attitude—concentration, patience, paying attention, effort, focus, and ability to self-correct or re-orient.

      c. Direction—staying on track, one foot after another, getting lost, wrong path, off the track, going in circles, put it in reverse, turning around, asking for and receiving directions or feedback, self-correction, and staying on course.

      d. Refueling—resting, recharging, eddying out, making stops, missing the stop because too focused on time and destination, care of or lack of care for vehicle, maintenance issues versus task issues, and making the most of layovers.

      e. Dealing with obstacles—how do you or your group deal with obstacles or crises? What kind of ride is it? Bumpy road, storms at sea, rapids, getting derailed, air pockets, debris on the track, blizzards, white out, fogged in, blacked out, out of gas, broken down, dead battery, and grounded.

  4. *Destination*—pulling into port or station. Who is there to meet you? What is there? What are the rewards? What are the feelings—relief, exhilaration, accomplishment, or anxiety to head out again?

      Example: "The group appeared to get derailed when Steve and Barry started arguing; no one emerged to be the conductor and get you back on track. What do you think is needed here to get this train going and arrive safely at our destination?"

B. *Healing Theme*—This can be used when there has been a setback, hurt, or when an emotional wound exists. It is a valuable metaphor to use for interpersonal relations with couples, groups, and families.

  1. Healing is a process that takes time and effort. Paying attention to the wound and particular stages of healing will expedite the process.

  2. Grief model for any kind of loss. From Elizabeth Kubler-Ross, we know the stages of grief: (a) Denial, (b) Anger, (c) Bargaining, (d) Depression, and (e) Acceptance.

  3. Medical Model—this is taken from the medical pathology of tissues, or standard first aid. When there has been a deep cut or wound, the following stages of healing occur:

      a. The pain, hurt, and bleeding of the injury.

      b. There is the bridge of new skin to cover the wound, the scab. It is extremely sensitive and can easily fall off, and open the wound, and start the bleeding again. In human relations, one party may cause the other's scab to come off and open the wound again. People need to be sensitive with each other when there has been a wound. The scab is the bridging of one party to patch it up, but this bridge needs to be attended to by both parties. Understanding and commitment by both parties to heal the wound is necessary.

   c. The initial scab is knocked off and cleaned out, so the new skin can heal better. This is the airing of resentments and hurts to be able to start fresh without any dirt in the wound. It may be painful for the parties involved, but it will heal better than in the initial clotting stage. It is the resolution versus the covering over of the wound.

   d. The new skin emerges fresh, revitalized, and clean.

   e. There always will be a trace of a scar; you won't forget it, but you can forgive the people involved.

    Example: "There appears to be a deep hurt or wound between the two of you. You have continued to knock each other's delicate scab opening the hurt and causing bleeding again. Would you like some support in cleaning out this wound, so you can both heal better, get some new skin, and get beyond this hurt?" Later you can just use the work "scab" to evoke this healing process.

C. *Systems Theme*—This can be used with groups or families. The central point is that everyone is a member of a team or family and needs to work together.

   1. If one player, family member, or part of a machine is down, it affects all other parts and the total efficiency of the system.

   2. As in a factory, there are inputs, outputs, human resources, materials, and procedures, all of which are necessary and dependent on the other parts for success.

   3. The care of the machine is vital. Changing the oil, lubing and greasing, making sure the engine runs properly, keeping the tires inflated, gas in the tank, not racing the engine, and making sure all parts of the machine are being attended to. This will make a smooth and efficient team, or group. Sports analogies can be used. Casey Stengel said, "It's easy getting the players. Getting them to play together is the hard part."

    Example: Bob worked as an auto mechanic manager and felt very stressed out at work. The leader used the systems theme with him. "Bob what happens when you run your autos without oil or without changing the spark plugs? How efficient can you be when you are constantly racing and never take time to grease your parts?"

D. *Cyclic and Natural Phenomena Themes*—This metaphor can be used with groups to point out the processes of nature and to expect the unexpected.

   1. Time and change are dynamic processes. What is new today is old tomorrow. Time never stops, and the world is in constant motion.

   2. Seasons, flowers, and crops follow and endless consistent cycle. Birth, life, production, fruitfulness, old age, death, and rebirth again. Death of one animal is life to another.

   3. Natural calamities—survival of the fittest. Storms, fires, avalanches, lightening storms, tornadoes, and death. We all experience crises and losses. It's the process of getting through these struggles safely that forces us to grow. New growth is the result of a fire. Starting over again is the continual rebirth.

    Example: "The best way to get through the storms of your life is to be ready and prepared for them. What do you need in your personal first aid kit to get through the storms and reach the calm that follows them?"

The process of becoming aware of the value of communicating metaphorically and developing your metaphor style and skills starts by asking yourself questions similar to the following:

1. "What does this situation remind me of?"
2. "How is this like something else?"
3. "How did I learn this?"
4. "What most clearly and completely symbolizes this experience?"
5. "How have other people or groups resolved this problem?"
6. "What could this situation or problem mean in terms of the development of the group?"
7. "How can the problem be a symbol for the entire group?"
8. "If the feelings among the group were a picture or image, what would it be?"
9. "Is there anything from the metaphor themes I can apply here?"
10. "How do I know this idea or suggestion is valid? What is the evidence that makes it convincing?"
11. "How can I reframe the problem into a resource or strength?"
12. "Is there an experience I can design for participants that would symbolize and be instrumental in developing a needed resource?"

After thinking about your answers to these questions, it's important to listen to yourself and to trust what comes up. There may be a story, experience, symbol, or ceremony. Many times it's just asking some new and different questions that engenders some new thoughts. Some of the ideas may seem crazy and illogical, but remember working with metaphors is not a linear and rational process. Much of their power comes from being indirect and stimulating the unconscious. Many of a leader's most creative and effective ideas have remained only a thought and have been prematurely censored from actually trying it. So, it is important for you to take some risks and manage your own discomfort at the edge to create breakthroughs for participants and yourself.

❖ CREATING METAPHORS FOR EXPERIENCES AND FEELINGS ────────────────

This section explores how metaphors can be created from participants' experiences and feelings. The purpose is to: (a) Give individuals a symbol, image, or story that can easily encapsulate their present experience and be easily retrieved at a later time; (b) Help individuals be aware of the metaphors they are making unconsciously which may prevent them from breaking through new edges; and (c) Improve participants' capability to change their metaphors to foster more breakthroughs.

METAPHOR TRAINING

In developing metaphors for and from the structured experience, participants need to learn what a metaphor is and the reasons for creating them. We encourage you to have a discussion early in the experience which focuses on the value of making metaphors. Below are some of the points that you many want to cover. These have been mentioned earlier in the text.

1. A metaphor is an image, symbol, story, or ceremony that stands for something else. It is the bridge or connection between two or more things. So, metaphors can help connect the experience back to the home, school or office.

2. Metaphors can enhance the transfer of the experience. One reason for this is the fact that our memories are enhanced when they are linked with images and pictures. If one's pictures are clear, graphic, and engaging, they will be easier to remember and use at a later time.

3. People think in images and metaphors unconsciously, and sometimes these images may prevent them from achieving personal growth. Being aware of one's metaphors can help in replacing old or outdated images with more useful ones.

4. At various times during the experience, discussions will be held to explore and create metaphors for what is transpiring.

Once participants understand the importance of creating metaphors, you can begin metaphor training. Below are some exercises that you may want to do with groups in the beginning of the experience. The exercises will help create an understanding of the value of making metaphors and train the associative mind to make connections in this way. Only a few are presented here; for more suggestions, see Combs and Freedman (1990).

1. Pick two things or objects and have the group brainstorm how they are alike or similar. Start with some easy ones, then have participants pick two things, and let the creative mind stretch in finding similarities.

Examples: Tree and a blade of grass: Each are alive, growing, longer than wide, stand erect, point to the sun, move with the wind, can be a source of nutrients to animals, can serve as protection for animals, and at times are cut down.

Stove and Car: Each are a type of machine, use fuel to operate, have moving parts, take something from one point to another (stove: liquid to steam) and get hot while in use.

2. Have participants pick an object from the outdoors and bring it to the group. Then have them create a simile about it. "This _____ is like a _____." Then take it the next step by saying "This _____ is like a _____ in that _____." You can have each person do it for their object, and when the group gets efficient, have the whole group do it for one person's object.

Examples: "This stick is like a building." ". . . in that it is straight and erect." "This pebble is like a marble in that it rolls away easily." "This feather is like a backscratcher in that I can reach hard to get areas."

3. Participants can build on the above exercise by using emotions as the simile stem.

Examples: "Sadness is like a stormy day in that it's gray and full of moisture." "Happiness is like a bird in that it can take you many places." "Anger is like a volcano in that when you explode, people get hurt."

4. Pick certain outcomes from an activity, like cooperation, trust, compassion, understanding, and exhilaration. Pick one word first and ask participants, "If this was a picture or image, what would it be a picture or image of?"

Examples: Cooperation could be a picture of one hand helping another." "Exhilaration could be an image of an air balloon floating upwards." Hopefully, from this start, you can create your own metaphor-training exercises that are specific to the people you work with and the setting you are working in.

METAPHOR AND AFFECT

During an experiential-learning program, we know that emotions are intensified; sometimes to the point that words can't describe what is going on. If an individual is in this new territory, a metaphor can be discovered or created to bring the experience back into the circle of comfort, where the experience can be familiar and known. Here, the metaphor becomes a bridge from the unknown new territory back to the known and predictable.

Siegelman (1990) found that figurative language springs from strong feelings or affect that is unable to be conveyed in any other way. By staying with the metaphor and nurturing it along, the participants' responses to it deepen. When we hear an individual use a metaphor, especially in a time of strong affect, it becomes a way of making sense or connecting this experience with the rest of his or her life story. Be gentle and easy with the metaphor, allowing the person to ease it out and take its own form. Your role is that of a midwife helping the birthing process. Using the metaphor later with the individual will help retrieve these deep feelings.

Metaphors and feelings are initially experienced in our bodies. This is because our first affective experiences as a child were housed in the body. Our "lump in throat", "the pounding heart", and "knot in the stomach" all describe feelings. We can facilitate the expression of feelings and metaphors if we can get individuals to focus on their bodies and describe that phenomena. In a way, learning to identify feelings from the bodily experience is an affective education, especially for some people who are unaware of their emotional domain. Sensitizing the person to their differing body experiences can help illuminate what they are feeling. One participant, Mary reported, "When I was younger and experiencing many physical symptoms, I went to a doctor. He told me they were all in my head and to forget about it. I thought then I was just a head case and crazy." When Mary felt things in her body, she then felt crazy. This kind of miseducation about the body and feelings is common. The doctor would have been more helpful if he said, "Your symptoms are all in your body and that tells me that you're feeling a lot, and it's very natural. It may help to talk to someone about your feelings." As mentioned earlier, the learning experience can become an excellent vehicle to learn about one's feelings. Creating metaphors from feelings will not only help during the experience, but they will be a valuable tool to bring home.

MAKING EXPERIENCES AND FEELINGS INTO METAPHORS

Experiences and feelings can be made into metaphors when we can create an image, picture, or symbol. Grove (1989) wrote, "You know when you have a metaphor when you can draw it" (p.7). The objective then is to ask the right question and take the time to allow participants' experiences and feelings to emerge into images. The flow chart for this process is below:

Experiences   Feelings
↓   ↓
Images   Body
                   ↓
                   Images

Some questions to help guide you when making metaphors for participants are found below. Try to catch people when their experiences and feelings are heightened. This will usually be in the S-1 experience, the moment before the success or retreat, or as they move into the success and S+1 experience, the moments after the success.

METAPHOR-MAKING QUESTIONS

Some of the following questions draw from the work of Grove (1989).

1. "What are you feeling now?"

2. "When you're feeling _____ , where do you feel it in your body?"

3. "Where about in your _____ do you feel _____?" (Get specific location.)
4. "Is it on the inside or the outside?"

5. "When you're feeling _____ and it's in your _____, does it have a size or shape?"

6. "When you're feeling _____ and it's in your _____, what is it like?"

7. "What kind of _____ could it be?"

8. "If you had to draw a picture of your _____(feeling) when it's in your _____ (body part), what would it be?"

9. "Is there anything else about _____ (images created)?"

10. Talking to the metaphor: "What would _____ like to have happen?"

11. To the metaphor: "What would _____ like to do?"

12. To the metaphor: "And as _____ (metaphor) moves, what happens next?"

13. To the person as a way of redirecting to the metaphor: "What would you like to

    have happen with _____ (metaphor)"; "When you want to _____

    (get rid of metaphor), what does _____ (the metaphor) want to do?"
14. "If this experience was an image or picture, what would it be?"
15. "If you had to draw a picture of this experience, what would you draw?"

16. "When you are experiencing _____ , what are you feeling?"

17. "When you are experiencing _____ , and feeling _____ , where are you

    experiencing _____?" (Follow feelings into metaphor questions.)

18. "Is there anything else about _____ (experience into an image)?"

In establishing a metaphor and then talking to the metaphor, you can create and define the metaphor. It then has its own identity with certain intentions and qualities that can give participants more information about themselves. Many times a metaphor in the body has been an ineffective way to solve a problem. Talking to the metaphor and allowing it to change, facilitates a change in feelings and promotes more constructive use of the metaphor.

Some examples will help clarify the process. Brian, who was 28 years old, felt very nervous and anxious at the start of a corporate teambuilding day. When he located this feeling in his body, it was in his heart, which was "moving fast." When we asked, "Moving fast like what?", he responded like a "sleek locomotive." The sleek locomotive wanted to move and get going; it had a schedule. We asked the sleek locomotive if it could "stand waiting at a station to get fuel and directions about the destination"? He laughed and realized how his locomotive wanted to move but wasn't sure where it was headed. Throughout the day, we returned to his locomotive meta-phor and asked questions, like, "How could it slow down when it's necessary?"; "Are there stops that would be important to make in life versus racing to the destination"; "Who is the conductor of this locomotive?"; "Can you slow down for this next activity and possibly let others get on with you?"; and "When you are at the office, when does your locomotive get away from you?"

Obviously, Brian's locomotive didn't just emerge for the corporate teambuliding day. He was able to see that it was with him at many moments in his work day. Also, he was able to ex-ternalize it and look at it, rather than having the locomotive drive him, unconsciously. He had fun playing with the metaphor and experimented with slowing down during the day. This helped change some of his feelings associated with it and let him feel empowered by being in charge of the locomotive's schedule.

Maxine was a 32-year-old woman on a course for individuals in recovery from drugs and al-cohol. Whenever a new activity commenced, she felt anxious about her performance. When she located this feeling in her body, it was in her chest and It felt heavy. In response to "heavy like what?" she said like a "rock." When asked, "What kind of rock could this heavy rock be?", she said like a "heavy brick." We then asked the metaphor, "What would it like to do?" She said, "Go out and let her breathe." We asked, "Can the heavy brick move out?", and she responded, "No." "What could help the heavy brick move off your chest?", we then asked. She responded, "If I take a deep breath and exhale hard, I can move it off." Once outside of her, the brick be-came a "shiny shield" to help fend off others' demands of her. We eventually helped her trans-form "shiny shield" into a "talking shield" that could assertively tell others to give her space and let her feel more protected. Later, during a private discussion, she discovered that the "heavy brick" had been there since a time of sexual abuse with her uncle at an early age. It had served as a protection for her for all those years. Now she knew that it was possible to expel the "brick" and use a "talking shield" to take care of herself. As we mentioned, many of these metaphors were created as a means to solve some kind of problem, and then the metaphor itself became a symptom of the problem. During the experience, Maxine was encouraged to breathe deeply and expel her brick and tell the group from the "talking shield" what she needed. When she did this, she breathed better, felt empowered, and went ahead and took risks.

Using metaphors can help make important affective shifts for participants, even without knowing the content or the purpose of the metaphor. In working with Maxine, we didn't need to know about the abuse, since she was making initial gains without divulging this trauma. Similarly, it is best to try to help participants find additional resources rather than exhume prob-lems, unless that is the focus of the experience and within the scope of your skills and training.

In summary, you can help create metaphors from the experiences and feelings of participants which will assist them in remembering the experience and also help promote transfer and gener-alization. We suggest that you use the information presented in this section as a jumping-off point for creating and using metaphors, and that you go ahead, get wet, and have fun in the water.

Co-Constructing New Stories

*The stories that we enter into with our experience have real effects on our lives.
The expression of our experience through these stories shapes or makes-up our
lives and our relationships*

(White, 1992, p. 81).

As discussed in the section on Why Process, people think and store information in the form of a story. Our stories include information about events, characters, and settings as well as purpose and importance. Each story that we create is the product of an interpretive process that allows us to make sense of each experience. In essence, stories provide each of us with a format that enables us to capture the intricacy of an experience and connect it in a personally, meaningful manner.

We can help individuals co-create new stories that are developed as a result of their experiences as well as help them re-create more positive perspectives of old stories. By helping them become aware of and articulate the narratives they have developed to give meaning to their lives, individuals are then able to examine and reflect on the themes that they are using to organize their lives and to interpret their own actions and the actions of others. The reflective awareness of one's personal narrative helps individuals realize that past events are not meaningful in themselves but are given significance by the configuration of one's story. This realization can release people from the control of past interpretations that they have attached to events and open up the possibility of renewal and freedom of change.

LISTENING

If we are going to help participants create new stories for themselves, we need to listen in a new manner. When we listen, it is impossible to do so without interpreting what they are saying through the filter of our own story. We take their representation of their experience and fit it into our preconceived notions of what is therapeutically or educationally appropriate. Freedman and Combs (1996) noted that,

> *"Given our stories about therapy, which are formed within these prevalent discourses, it is hard for most therapists to learn to listen to people's stories as stories. Our stories about therapy conspire to make us listen with our ears cocked and our mouths set to say "Aha" when we recognize a "clinically significant item"—something that we know what to do with"(p.43).*

Because of our "expert" training, some of the foundational filters that we listen from become a natural part of our assumptive process. Some of those foundational filters include:

- ◆ "What is the underlying problem this person is expressing?"
- ◆ "What is the chief complaint here?"
- ◆ "What is the root of this issue?"
- ◆ "This seems like an alcoholic family problem."
- ◆ "I wonder if they were abused?"
- ◆ "This person has low self esteem."
- ◆ "This doesn't sound normal."
- ◆ "I am hearing DSM IV criteria, I wonder if they have other symptoms?"
- ◆ "They are really in a lot of pain, I'll get them to express it more."
- ◆ "Their inner child has really been ignored."
- ◆ "This sounds like a trauma case."

Each of the internal questions or statements you make to yourself opens up a different track of questions and new myriad of assumptions. This happens automatically as we listen from our own autobiography, which reinforces our certainty, sense of the known, and what to do next. We may feel better, but it may take the participant on a journey that reinforces our map of the territory and ultimately can be unproductive, limiting, or a dead end for them.

So what do we do instead of listening to our education and knowledge? We try to put ourselves in their shoes and understand their lives from their perspective. We listen from a "not-knowing position" (Andersen & Goolishian, 1988, 1992a). This means not asking questions from a position of pre-understanding or looking for answers to our questions. An attitude of curiosity and humility is necessary as we listen for what is unique, different, or not fully expressed or understood. This then leads us to many new questions. Andersen and Goolishian (1988) suggested:

> *"The goal of therapy is to participate in a conversation that continually loosens and opens up, rather than constricts and closes. Through therapeutic conversation, fixed meanings and behaviors . . . are given room, broadened, shifted, and changed." (p. 381)*

DECONSTRUCTION

This is a process in our questioning, where we try to find the holes or cracks in a story with the purpose of opening space for aspects of the narrative that haven't yet been storied (Freedman & Combs, 1996). The idea is to help participants realize that they play an active role in creating their stories rather than being shaped by the story. Deconstructionists talk of the slipperiness of meaning (Derrida, 1988) and focus on the gaps and ambiguities of meanings. We try to have the participants fill in the gaps and question or reconsider their interpretations or meanings. Deconstruction questions examine a belief, feeling, or action of a person, and the influence or results on the person. Some examples of the questions that can be used for the purposes of deconstruction include:

a.   What experiences did you have in the past that encouraged these (feelings, beliefs, or actions)?
b.   In what situations does this feeling, belief, or action take over?
c.   If you were to step further into this feeling, belief, or action, how would this affect your future?
d.   What does this idea, feeling, or action have you doing?
e.   In what ways does this feeling, belief, or action take you for a ride?

EXTERNALIZING THE PROBLEM

White and Epston (1990) popularized this concept of externalizing the problem. Some of the questions above move the participant in this direction. Externalization is the practice supported by the belief that the person is *not* the problem, but the problem *is* the problem. The problem operates on the person's life. They contend that externalization is more of an attitude than just a technique. It is a belief system of the leader in how you look at the person and the problem. Externalizing takes the verb, quality, or emotion and turns it into a noun. Below are some examples:

◆   Angry becomes "anger".
◆   Guilty becomes "guilt".
◆   Irritable becomes "irritability".
◆   Co-dependent becomes "for other's lifestyle" or "people pleasing."

◆ Having an addiction becomes "the addiction", "the beast", or "the bottle."
◆ Having bulimia or anorexia becomes the "stuffing lifestyle", "starving pattern", or "anorexia" or "bulimia."
◆ Being pushy or aggressive becomes "the bully lifestyle", "the tornado", or "the volcano."

Externalizing helps participants treat the problem as an object or an "it"—outside of themselves that they now need to stand up against or exert influence over. Externalizing creates a different "receiving context" for the story (Freedman & Combs, 1996). When you speak in this manner participants will eventually mirror you and will began to label "it" the same way. Then, you know you have succeeded in the externalization process, and the participant can now begin to focus on the strengths, training, and strategies to withstand the force of the "it." Some examples of using externalizing questions are the following:

Was there a time when "perfection" wanted to take over and you denied it? How did you do it?
What does "irritability" keep you away from _____ ?
Do you prefer how "the addiction" controls your focus?
How much influence did the "stuffing lifestyle" have over you today?
How is "anger" keeping you a prisoner?
What steps will ready you for taking back your life from "pleasing others"?
What training and skills do you need to withstand the "volcano's explosion" again?
What helped this week in standing up to "the stuffing lifestyle"?
On a 1–100% scale how much influence did you have over "anger" this week?
What allowed you to be successful with "people pleasing" yesterday?
What do you imagine "the addiction's" strategy will be to challenge this success you have had over it?
How will the "discounting lifestyle" try to take away or minimize your success here?
Who else noticed that you are taking back your life from "bulimia."

When externalizing the problem try to use the language of participants as frequently as they may use their own names for which they call the "problem." Often you can use "lifestyle," "pattern", "habit" or a graphic metaphor or word picture to mean that it has been around for a long time. Now the focus of the conversation is on: (1) how it (externalized problem) is loosing it's grip on the person, and (2) building a new story of opposition and expansion of the successes.

EXPANDING THE STORY

The goal of the narrative approach is to expand the "alternative story" which is in contrast to one's dominant story. The focal point of attention should be on the information that is useful, constructive, helpful, and empowering. We can assist in the reconstruction of individual's narratives that have been too restrictive in several ways. First, we can ask questions about the quality of existence and the freedom of choice that an individual's narrative allows. Second, we can draw attention to events and attributes, from the experience, not accounted for by the individual's narrative, which can challenge and test the story as told. And, third we can offer alternative narratives that more fully incorporate an individual's strengths, capabilities, and life events in a more coherent and powerful narrative.

Sample questions to ask participants to help them construct new self stories, that have been adapted from White (1989), are provided below. These questions can be asked in a group, individually, or through journal writing assignments.

Responsibility and owning the success—The goal is to internalize, document, and codify the unique outcome.

How do you account for this success?
How did you get this to happen?
What steps did you take to ready yourself for this success?
What does it say about you that you did *(the success)*?
How did you stand up to the influence of the old story?
What support or resources did you use to have this success?
Was there a moment that you could have given in to the old story and refused to be taken? How did you free yourself?
When were you first aware of your decision to take this risk?
Do you think this new story about you suits you better than the old story?

Expand the temporal plane—The goal is to situate the unique outcome or success in time by giving it a past and a future.

What sort of training did you do to prepare yourself for this kind of endeavor?
How do you see this success fitting in with your hopes and aspirations?
What in your past would let us predict that you are the sort of person who could do such a (success)?
When in your past do you think you started moving in this new direction?
What steps will you have to take to employ this learning at home?
What will be the first road sign that you see that will tell you that you are still on track at home?
What other accomplishments await you down the road?
What other possibilities are closer to you now with this success?

Increasing descriptions from the audience—The goal is to open up space for as many alternative stories as possible by including other's viewpoints.

How did others see (name) prepare for this success?
Who in your past would be least surprised that you accomplished such a feat?
What did they see in you then to predict this success?
Who will be first to notice your changes at home?
What will they see?
Who else in this group might have known that you were ready for such a big step?
What do you think this tells me about you?
What do you think (other's name) saw as the highlight of your accomplishment?

Meaning and Difference—The goal is to help participants make distinctions in how they will make sense of the learning and apply it.

> What difference will this make for you now that you know you can accomplish this
> success?
> What does it say about you now that you have accomplished this?
> How will others see you differently?
> What difference will it make in your relationships when you stay on the new path?
> Did you surprise yourself with anything today and what does that mean about you?
> How do you see yourself now after completing this task?
> What difference will it make to you knowing that you have written a new chapter
> about yourself?

USE OF REFLECTIVE TEAMS

An innovative technique that you can use to help individuals create new stories or re-create old stories is the use of reflective teams. Reflective teams were first used by a group of Norwegian family therapists (Andersen, 1991). While working with a family, several members of the team were observing from behind a one way mirror. When the team began to consult with the therapist, who was working directly with the family, they were unable to reach consensus about what they observed. Consequently, they had the family and the therapist listen to their conversations, or differing stories, about what they had witnessed during the recent session with the family. The result became a quick way to obtain multiple descriptions of an event with the goal of expanding the alternative story for the family. Andersen (1991) wrote that the reflective team should search for the "appropriately unusual questions." He stated, "If people are exposed to the usual, they tend to stay the same. If they meet something un-usual, this un-usual might induce a change" (p. 19).

❖ CREATING REFLECTIVE TEAMS

This method can easily be adapted to any learning experience. Often, when a group is involved in an experience, not everyone is engaged at the same time. Anyone who is observing can become the reflective team, rather than just waiting for their opportunity to participate in the activity. This way, the observers are more involved and can provide unique descriptions or new stories for the other participants to consider and possibly incorporate into their own story of the experience. Groups then can alternate between being the participants and serving as the reflective team. A sequence of events that you may want to consider using is the following:

1. The group, or reflective team, witnesses or observes others in an activity or learning experience.
2. When the activity is finished, the involved participants create their own story about the experience that they recently had, possibly responding to some of the questions presented throughout this book.
3. The group or designated reflective team has a conversation among themselves, while the participants listen to their stories without commenting on what they hear. The

reflective team starts by asking unusual questions to generate some alternative stories, for example:

◆ What surprised you most in observing this activity?
◆ What strengths or resources did you notice being used during the activity?
◆ Who surprised you in this activity and why?
◆ In the activity, what roles or interactions were you the most curious about?
◆ What are some of your wonderings about future successes for this group or specific individuals?
◆ What surprised you the least about this activity?
◆ What comments from other reflective team members were most interesting to you and why? Ask them for clarification, if necessary.

4. The participants in the learning experience have a conversation with each other about what they just heard from the reflective team.

◆ What comment from the reflective team most caught your attention and why?
◆ What did the reflective team notice that you didn't?
◆ Which comment holds the most promise for your future?
◆ Hearing these comments about yourself or group, says what about you?

5. The participants ask the reflective team for clarification about their perceptions or about the statements that they made. The reflective team has the same option.

The facilitator will need to structure this well and keep it moving, as the questions may be difficult for some people to answer. This process can be very successful in getting the whole group to become co-authors with the individuals in their new story as each person may notice a different or unusual strength or resource. Guidelines to consider when using reflective teams are presented below.

❖ GUIDELINES FOR USING REFLECTIVE TEAMS

1. The goal is to maximize the numbers of alternative stories and unusual unique outcomes witnessed and give a voice to them. Comments should be generative.
2. Be curious about how people were able to achieve what they did. Describe what you were surprised by in individuals or the group; wonder what future changes may be.
3. Focus on experiences that are judged by the participants to be preferred developments or developments that the reflective team believes might expand the individual's personal story.
4. Reflective team members should actively interview each other. They should not merely point out the positives (White, 1992b).
5. Remain aware of the various histories, narratives, and metaphors that were expressed by the person or group and use the language that they used.
6. Try to suspend judgment or the urge to "analyze", assess or diagnose others. The goal is to open up space for new discoveries and stories by asking for "hard thinking" rather "easy thinking" (Andersen, 1991).
7. Keep the process short and void of jargon.

INCREASING EFFECTIVENESS

"What we think or what we believe is, in the end, of little consequence. The only thing of consequence is what we do."

—*John Ruskin*

How can the individuals we work with get the most benefit from the processing sessions we structure? This is the question we continuously need to ask ourselves and our colleagues. The following are some sample suggestions. By no means is it an exhaustive list. Hopefully, each of us can use this list as a starting point and continue to add to it as we work with different groups and accrue more experiences.

1. *Structure regular periods of time throughout the experience.* Prior to beginning any activity or experience, it is important to establish an expectation that we will take time to be introspective and reflective and share our thoughts and feelings. We want participants to consider processing as an integral component of every activity or experience.

2. *Let group members do most of the talking.* Processing sessions are most effective when the participants are doing most of the talking. Occasionally, the discussion will need some prompting from you by using some of the techniques presented in this section and in the section on Methods of Processing. At other times you want to monitor the frequency of your contributions to the discussion. If you find yourself doing most of the talking or hear yourself specifying the learning that has occurred, it may be a good time to re-examine your approach to facilitation. Effective processing does not mean telling people what they will or have learned. Rather, it is the establishment of an environment that encourages people to create new learning for themselves.

3. *Vary style and method used.* As a member of the human race, we tend to get comfortable with certain ways of doing things. As a result, we develop our own patterns and habits. This frequently causes us to do activities, such as processing, in a similar manner all too often. Therefore, we need to become aware of our own behaviors and monitor how we choose to structure our sessions. Make a personal goal to try some of the different approaches delineated in the section on the Methods of Processing. Using different styles and methods provides for a good change of pace and increases your chances of reaching all members of the group.

4. *Alternate the times of day.* For experiences that are longer than a day or two, you have the luxury of bringing the group together at various times for the purpose of processing. However, we often wait to process until the end of the day. This decision has a few shortcomings. First, if your day is full and you are running late, processing is the activity that gets eliminated. Second, at the end of a good day of experiential learning, people are tired. Often, when we bring the group together, they begin to "zone out" and think about other things (which is frequently a nice warm sleeping bag).

The suggestion that we are making is not to eliminate using the evening but to make use of other times during the day as well. Spend time before breakfast. Plan a break in the morning or the afternoon. Give participants a journal, a short solo or a dyad break after a high impact activity. Have a group discussion before beginning dinner. It increases on-task behavior and succinct discussion. Or, have one of the leaders get the food cooking while the other facilitates the group discussion.

5. *During discussions provide sufficient wait-time for people to think.* There is a tendency for instructors to ask a question and then expect individuals to immediately respond. Research indicates that the mean amount of time that educators wait after asking a question is one second. If individuals are not quick enough to come up with a response, the educator repeats the question, rephrases it, asks a different question or calls on someone to respond.

When we break out of the pattern of bombing individuals with questions and increase wait-time to five seconds after asking a question, people give longer, more thoughtful responses. More people take the time to think, and individuals feel more confident in sharing their thoughts. As a result the quantity and the quality of the discussion improves.

6. *Ask open-ended questions.* If you decide to use a processing format in which you want to have a discussion and you choose to ask the group, dyads, or individuals a few questions, it is best to try and ask questions that invite discussion rather than one or two word responses. The first step is to recognize that questions have distinct characteristics, serve various functions, and create different levels of thinking. Questions such as, "Who felt that they were challenged today?" or "Did you enjoy the hike today?" call for one word responses. Questions such as "What personal challenges did you encounter today?" or "How would you compare today's hike to yesterday's?" set the stage for individuals to think in greater depth and provide opportunities for sharing more personal information. An additional consideration when forming questions is to try to be explicit enough to ensure an understanding of your question, but at the same time, try to avoid using so many words that people forget what the actual question was.

7. *Ask one question at a time.* In trying to get to the core of an issue, sometimes, we blurt out a series of questions rather than raising a single question, discussing it, and then moving on. For example, "How do you think that you worked as a team and what can you do to improve this in the future?" is a bit too much stimuli. Discussing part one of the question and then, if appropriate, moving to part two is a more effective practice.

8. *Own the questions that you ask.* Most of us have gone to school for long periods of our lives. Through the process of educational enculturation, many individuals come to think of answers to questions as being either right or wrong. Even though the setting is different, you are still the teacher in the eyes of most of the individuals who you work with. Therefore, many times when you ask a question, course participants believe that there is a right or wrong answer to the question. So whenever possible, it is a good practice to try to de-emphasize the right or wrongness and set a tone for open discussion. One way to do this is for you to own the questions that you ask. For example, you could begin the discussion by saying, "We seemed to be having some problems getting the interviews of senior citizens transcribed yesterday. I was wondering if anyone had some ideas about how to remedy the problem today?" or "I'm curious, how did you feel about the trust fall activity?" By simply letting them know that this is a personal question, it lessens the potential that individuals will only tell you what they think you want to hear.

9. *Give individuals specific feedback.* As expressed in the section on Enhancing Communication Skills, whenever possible, try to be specific with your praise and/or criticism. To tell individuals that they did "a great job today," you have given them a positive message but little more. The day was composed of many hours and many interactions. What aspect of the day made it great? Getting out of their sleeping bags? Putting their packs on? Getting into the rafts? Using the latrine? A more specific statement, such as, "It was super to see the way that you supported each other on the high ropes course. You talked about what order to go in. You let the people who expressed concern go first, and you made sure that everyone was ready before having the person go. It was enjoyable to see you work together like that."

10. *Guard against small talk.* If you are using the large group format and people begin to have their own private conversations, there are a few things that you can choose to do. First, you will want to make a quick survey of what may be causing these conversations. Is one person dominating the discussion? Has the discussion been dragged on too long? Are you doing all the talking? Are people comfortable sharing their thoughts and feelings with the group? Some interventions that you can consider include (a) making a short comment about the difficulty of lis-

tening to someone when other conversations are occurring, (b) asking if people want to divide up into dyads to discuss this point first and then come back to the group (c) establishing a "power object" which is held while talking and placed in the middle of the circle for the next individual to pick up and hold while he or she is talking, reminding group members that only one person should be talking, or (d) terminate the discussion since people are beginning to get scattered and unable to attend.

11. *Maintain an awareness of group and personal goals.* Awareness of group and personal goals allows you to stay focused. When individuals have goals in mind, the discussion can center on those goals and thus permit people to plan and/or examine the experience as it relates to their goals.

12. *If people are not in the mood, cut the session short.* Making every session into an "encounter group" makes many individuals resistant to getting together for a debrief. Don't try to make every session intense and profound. Don't expect people to talk or push them when they are not ready. It's not uncommon after an intense group meeting for the next group session to be more superficial. If you bring the group together and try to structure a session and you realize that they are not into it, ask if they want to cut this session short or think about using an alternative method of processing, such as rounds or giving people a short, isolation opportunity.

◆ Reluctant Individuals

Most individuals are cooperative and motivated. However, on occasion you will work with individuals who are reluctant to share themselves—their thoughts and feelings with other group members. In which case, you will want to search for ways to actively involve them and have them contribute to the group experience. The reasons for wanting to get hesitant individuals involved are:

a. if we believe that the structured experience is a vehicle for learning and growing, and that reflection is part of the learning cycle, then, we must find ways to help individuals analyze, present, and support their own ideas;

b. it helps people explore issues in greater depth—through discussion and questioning we can assist individuals in being more introspective and possibly help them gain more from the experience;

c. it is likely that members who have a difficult time sharing in this group also have trouble talking in front of others in other environments. By getting these individuals to participate, they may develop a sense of confidence about speaking up;

d. other group members will benefit from hearing the thoughts and feelings of the reserved member; and

e. the verbal exchange and sharing of ideas is an essential part of the group experience.

Often, group members want to speak but do not because they are afraid of what other members might think of them. They envision people laughing at them or thinking that they are stupid. It is important to find ways to involve these individuals so that they may be able to recognize that they are focusing on the worst possible scenario which is not likely to occur at all. Other reasons why people might be reluctant to get involved are that they are not committed to the group; they do not trust the leaders or some of the other group members. The leaders or another member of the group may dominate discussions, which causes others to sit back and listen rather than contribute.

On occasion, it has been extremely beneficial to socialize with reserved individuals during breaks. It gives these individuals the message that you are interested in them and on occasion that brief one-on-one interaction has been sufficient encouragement for them to feel comfortable enough to participate more. At other times, you will have a sense that members either want to or need to be invited to speak. When this happens, you can elicit their comments by simply nodding your head or gesturing in their direction. Whenever possible, follow-up their comments with some form of positive reinforcement to encourage additional future responses.

If neither of these suggestions work, you can try using some of the following statements, which have been adapted from Eitington (1989) and Jacobs, Harvill and Masson (1988):

a.   "I don't think that we have heard from Bonnie yet on this issue."
b.   "Go ahead," "It looks as though you are thinking. Would you like to share your thoughts?"
c.   "You seem to be reacting to something. Is there anything that you would like to share?"
d.   "It seems that you were relating to his statement. What are your thoughts?" and
e.   "Julie, you have been rather quiet today. Is there something on your mind?"

The challenge to drawing out members of the group is to get them to speak and share their thoughts and feelings. At the same time, they will need to have the option to decline and not be "put on the spot." One technique is to look at a member who is being quiet for a brief moment, and with your eyes invite the person to speak. If the person does not choose to talk, then you can shift your eyes away which will then give the person the right to pass.

You can invite the person to speak by using a tentative voice and trying not to focus the attention of the group on that person. For example, you may say "Bert, I notice that you have been quiet throughout our discussion. We would like to hear from you if you want to comment." At this point you should scan the group with your eyes rather than staring at Bert. If he doesn't comment in a reasonable amount of time, you can open things back up and say something such as, "Who would like to share what they are thinking about?"

According to Jacobs, Harvill, and Masson (1988) there are two primary ways to draw out reluctant individuals. They are called the direct method and the indirect method. A brief explanation of both methods and some specific examples follow:

❖ Direct Method _____

The direct method refers to the procedure of simply asking individuals if they want to comment or react to what is going on. Some specific examples of direct questions that you could use are: (A) "Kent, you seemed to be having lots of fun working on your project this morning. Would you like to tell us about it?", (b) "Barbara, we have heard a lot of different perspectives on how the wall went. Is there anything that you would like to add?", (c) "Richard, you have been very quiet since we got back from the peak ascent. Is there something on your mind?"

As suggested above, using eye contact is a valuable technique for eliciting comments from group members. This is especially true when people are waiting to talk. By acknowledging people with your eyes and a light head-nod, you can often let them know that you are looking forward to their comment. This technique can be used in a more direct fashion when necessary. When speaking to the entire group, you can maintain eye contact with a specific member; this acknowledges that you would like that person to speak. It also gives him or her an "out" should he or she not want to comment. For example, while looking mainly at Molly, you say, "Does anyone else want to say something about the service project?" You can then scan the group and return your eyes to Molly. If she is not ready to respond, then you can shift your eyes to other members of the group.

❖ INDIRECT METHOD

There are three indirect methods that you can use to involve reluctant members. They are the use of dyads and triads, rounds, and written exercises. The value of using these techniques have been explained earlier. When the dyads or triads come back together, you may want to use some of the following types of questions to invite individuals to talk: (a) "Who would like to share what you were talking about?", (b) "What were some of your thoughts about solo?", (c) "What kinds of things came to mind when you talked about how you resolve conflicts with your partner?", (d) "Does anyone want to comment on what you have discussed in your pairs?", and (e) "Mike, would you mind sharing with us some of the things that you talked about in your triad?"

This procedure is usually effective because individuals have something to say as a result of the discussion that they have just completed. Another way to structure this activity is for you to be a member of a dyad with the reluctant individual. During your discussion, you can either seek to find out why the person chooses to be silent and/or give the person encouragement for his/her ideas and suggestions that you would like him/her to share his/her information with the larger group.

Rounds are another valuable technique for getting hesitant members to contribute. If while doing a round the reluctant individual appears to be uncertain or anxious, you can skip that person by saying something like "we'll give you a little more time to think" and then come back to him or her after everyone else has contributed. Also, you can make it easier on this person by starting the round with the person sitting next to him or her and ending up on the reluctant individual. This also makes it possible for you to ask for more information from this person since he or she will be the last to comment when the round is ended. An example of a round that you could use is: "In a word or a phrase, what was the most difficult part of the acid river for you? Think about that for a moment, then I'm going to ask everyone to share their thoughts."

Written exercises also can be used to help reluctant individuals contribute. This activity tends to be indirect and nonthreatening because your are only asking members to read what they wrote. You can structure the activity around a journal entry, compiling a list, or giving the group a series of sentences to complete. After individuals have completed their writing, you can ask them to share their responses. With their ideas written down in front of them, individuals are less likely to mind—since they are now simply being asked to share their written responses. An example of a written exercise that you might want to consider is to say something like: "In your journals, I would like for you to respond to the following incomplete sentences:

a. My high point of the day was _____,

b. Something that I did today that I feel proud of is _____,

c.   Something that I would like to work on tomorrow is _____, and

d.   One way that the group can help me is _____.

Additional examples of stimuli that can be used for written exercises are provided in the section on Methods of Processing.

❖ SUMMARY

Trying to get everyone actively involved in processing sessions can be challenging at times. A variety of ways for inviting hesitant individuals to participate have been discussed in this section. We encourage you to try some of these suggestions so that you might develop more confidence in working with reluctant individuals, and at the same time you may increase your ability to establish learning environments where all group members are involved.

REDIRECTING

On occasion, you may interact with an individual who you wish would talk less or not be so negative. In this section, we will use the term of "redirecting" to indicate that you are trying to intercept the flow of communication in a nonpunitive manner to help individuals and/or the group move in a specific direction. Some possible reasons that you would want to intervene are when an individual is (a) rambling, (b) arguing, (c) consistently negative, (d) overly sarcastic, or (e) dominating the conversation. Other reasons that you may consider redirecting the flow of conversation are if you want to shift the focus of the discussion, or if you are running out of time.

Timing is one of the most important and difficult factors to consider when trying to redirect an individual's or group's energy. Whenever possible, you want to intervene quickly before someone rambles too long or argues for an extended block of time. At the same time, you want to be careful not to cut off worthwhile statements. Your personal experience and awareness of the patterns of speakers and the responses of the group will help guide you in making the right decision.

Equal in importance to timing is control of your tone of voice. If it is viewed as critical or angry, it is likely to have a negative impact even if the words that you use are carefully chosen. Calming yourself, and trying to understand the motives of the speaker are helpful steps prior to intervening.

A positive practice to use when redirecting is to explain to the individual and group why you are trying to stop what is occuring. By taking the time to discuss your motives, you are preventing members from having to try to create their own reasons for your actions. Without providing a rationale, they are likely to wonder such things as, "Why doesn't the leader like me"? or "How come my opinion doesn't matter"? For example, if the discussion has begun to get a little heated and you are concerned about the direction it is going, you may want to say something like, "Dave, let me break in here if you don't mind. I want to remind you of some of the ground rules that we have set. That is, we listen to each other, and we try to accept that everyone has a right to their own ideas and ways of doing things." Or, if you are concerned about time you could interject something along the lines of "Marion, I wonder if it would be possible for you to sum up your discussion in the next minute or two. We're running short of time and energy, and we need to move on."

Two nonverbal techniques that you can use are (1) to avoid eye contact while the person is talking, or (2) to give a slight hand signal, similar to a traffic cop which you hope will let the speaker know that you would like him or her to "wrap it up." If these types of subtle hints do not work, then you will need to use a more direct verbal approach. The following are a list of potential statements that you might use to get the flow of conversation away from one specific person and back to the other group members:

a. Kent, let me cut in and stop you in order to give others an opportunity to speak. What reaction did some other people have to the . . . ?

b. Marilyn, let me stop you here to say a couple of things. First . . .

c. How about others? What were some of your perceptions of how the day went?

d. Mike, I would like to hold off on your comments until we have heard from a few other folks first.

e. Darren, I notice that you are always ready to speak first. I'm wondering if there is any specific reason behind that?

f. Let me stop you, because I don't think that we are listening to each other.

g. Kristi, you have some valid points and I want to give others an opportunity to speak also.

h. Hunter, I'm aware that you're first to speak often. I wonder if you'd be willing to experiment with going last and see how that feels.

i. Leah, I notice that you are always ready to speak first. I'm wondering if you would like some feedback from the group about how they feel about this pattern?

j. Alright, you've told us how poorly things are going. Can you think of anything that you feel positive about? Just one thing?

k. Would you mind if we got another opinion on this?

l. Could you hold on a second, several others haven't had a chance to respond yet?

m. Anyone want to reply to that?

n. I understand your position. You believe that . . . Can we agree to disagree on this one?

o. How do the rest of you see this? Is there another side to it?

p. I see that you have some strong feelings on this issue. Are you interested in hearing other people's opinion?

q. I didn't understand your joke. Could you tell me what you meant?

r. I would like to stop, since it doesn't seem like we are getting anywhere.

❖ SUMMARY

Redirecting often feels uncomfortable. Therefore, it is easy to want to ignore or avoid these situations. However, we need to keep in mind our overall intention is to have the group continually moving forward, together, in a positive direction. We may be hindering group progress and possibly compromising the quality of the experience for everyone by not intervening with some individuals.

USING HANDICAPS

"I have learned that success is to be measured not so much by the position that one has reached in life, but by the obstacles which they have overcome while trying to succeed."

—*Booker T. Washington*

Handicaps are challenges or tasks given to participants that take away one or more of their senses or abilities. Handicaps are usually unfamiliar and unexpected and, as a result, raise the level of disequilibrium in participants and the group. This disorientation can facilitate the restructuring of individuals' cognitive maps.

You can use handicaps at any time or with any event. The educational and therapeutic uses are unlimited. Deciding who, what handicap, which event and at what point in the event to use handicaps creates endless possibilities. It's important to know the individuals well, so the handicap creates a constructive level of anxiety, and it is not a destructive one. The stretching of the limits is vital, as is trying to ensure success for the individual and the group. Handicaps can be used to make events more challenging for the individual, such as being blindfolded while climbing, or for the group, like doing an initiative with everyone non-verbally. However, if the level of anxiety becomes too high, you should consider removing the handicap.

Another reason to use handicaps is to help individuals expand their potential. Now, they are unable to rely solely on their strengths, like being verbal, being a leader, or using their physical power. The disequilibrium caused by handicaps compels participants to develop other abilities. When using handicaps, processing the experience is extremely important in order to raise individuals' levels of awareness, responsibility, and increase the possibility of transferring the learning home, to school or to the office.

Below is a list of some of the common handicaps that can be used, and issues or themes to be gleaned when processing:

1. *Blind*—Participants are given a blindfold to put over their eyes. *Issues:* Powerlessness, being out of control, trust in others or a higher power, sense of the unknown or unexpected, and use of new senses or ways of knowing. Processing questions for the activity include:

"What are you blind to in your future or recovery?"
"In the absence of vision what was necessary for you to use in order to keep going?"
"In what ways did your partner empower you?"

This handicap is particularly well suited for individuals in recovery from chemical dependency, or for corporate groups focusing on their vision and empowerment.

2. *Nonverbal*—Participants are unable to speak to others. This is good to use with a leader or take-charge type of person. *Issues:* Powerlessness, communicating in new ways, reliance on others, awareness of new senses, and being in new roles. Processing questions include:

"What things in your life are you speechless about?"
"How did you react to losing a main resource?"

3. *Paralyzed*—Participants are unable to use one of their arms or legs. This is good to use with someone who relies on their physical strength. *Issues:* Disabilities, powerlessness, reliance on mind versus body, feeling like a victim, dependency, teamwork, sense of the unexpected, and vulnerabilities. Processing questions include:

"What paralyzes you in work, relationships, or life?"
"Where do you feel most immobilized?"

4. *Siamesed*—Participants are hooked together at the side like Siamese twins and must move together without any individual getting between them. This is a good handicap to use in couple or family work. *Issues:* Compatibility, dependency on others, cooperation, enmeshment, consequence of how one affects the other and commitment. This handicap can be used to get a passive and unengaged person involved when siamesed to an active leader type. Processing questions include:

"What issues are you and another stuck on?"
"What part of others at work, home, or school have you incorporated?"

5. *Singled Voice*—Participants can only talk through another person. Somebody else is their voice, and they can only share ideas with this person who will then vocalize the idea to the whole

group. This handicap, like the one above, is a good way to get a quiet person involved by sharing ideas with a leader who can use his or her voice. Couples and families are well suited for this handicap as well. Also, it can be used with bosses and employees, where the boss has to share the employee's ideas. *Issues:* Communication, listening, cooperation, not being heard, and being a leader. Processing questions include:

"What do you really want to say to others in your life?"
"How does it feel to only share other's ideas and not your own?"

6. *Questions*—Participants are asked only to ask questions rather than make statements. This is good when some individuals are dominating the process, but you don't want to take their voice away. It lets them stay involved but in a challenging manner. *Issues:* Communication, dominance, the importance of clear communication, and cooperation. Processing questions include:

"What was this like for you?"
"Who in your life do you need to ask more questions of, rather than making statements?"

7. *Killer and Suicide Statements*—Killer statements are ones like: "This won't work."; "That's a dumb idea."; while suicide statements are ones like: "I can't do this," "I'll never get over the wall." One or two participants are asked to make either of these statements to observe the effect on the group process. It's good to let it go for only five to ten minutes and then stop the group and ask them what they noticed. *Issues:* Negative forces within the group. People avoiding offering their ideas because they are afraid they'll get rejected. Processing questions include:

"What happened to the team spirit when these statements were introduced?"
"Who makes killer and suicide statements in your life?"

8. *Confusion technique*—Participants are asked to say the opposite of what someone else says. Usually one or two people are asked to assume this handicap. One member says "stop and go right.", the handicapped member says "let's go and go left." *Issues:* Opposition in the group, people talking at same time, poor communication, and inability to resolve conflict. Processing questions include:

"How did the group experience this confusion?"
"Where in your life do you get mixed messages and become confused?"

9. *Prescribing the Symptom*—A participant or two is asked to do the role he or she normally plays, especially when it's an unproductive role. Prescribing the symptom makes them conscious of what they are doing and what effect it may have on the other group members. *Issues:* Unproductive group role and raising awareness of the group process. Processing questions include:

"What effect does this role have on the group process?"
"How does it feel to take this role?"
"What do you think a person with this role gets out of it?"

GOAL SETTING AND PERSONAL ACTION PLANS

"Your past cannot be changed, but you can change tomorrow by your actions today."

—*David McNally*

This section of the text has two purposes. It can be used to help participants develop personal goals for themselves during or after they complete the structured experience; it also can be used to help you establish personal goals that you would like to accomplish in order to become a bet-

ter experiential educator, trainer or therapist. Using some of the information that you have gained from this text and feedback that you receive from people you work with, you can develop a plan for increasing your knowledge and skills.

When working with individuals or groups you can begin by having a discussion on the importance of goals. A statement that you may want to use to begin the discussion is "How does having meaningful goals reduce tension and foster personal satisfaction?" Additional questions that you may want to ask participants as well as consider for yourself include:

1. What are your dreams and aspirations? What do you want to do, have or be?
2. What are you excited about?
3. What gives you the most satisfaction?
4. What values guide you?
5. What do you need to "unlearn?"
6. What new information do you need?
7. What new technical skills do you need?
8. What new "people skills" do you need?
9. Where is your best learning environment?
10. Who are your real teachers and mentors?

In addition to using the suggested questions, you can ask participants to identify behaviors, thoughts, or emotional patterns that they have become aware of during the structured experience. Discuss alternatives to those patterns, identify sources of support and ways to reward themselves for meeting their goals. Each person can do this activity on their own, in discussion with you, or this can be undertaken as a group activity; using the brainstorming abilities of all the members to help generate potential action plans for each individual.

The activity sheet found in table 9 has been adapted from Gerstein (1988). It can be used to assist individuals in identifying aspects of the patterns that they would like to change or modify

---

◆ TABLE 9 ◆

Personal Action Plan Worksheet

A. *What Are You Doing Now?*—Describe what you are doing that you would like to change?
B. *What Do You Want To Do?*—Describe what you want. Explain how you would like to change the situation.
C. *Goal Development*—Develop one or two goals based on the changes that you would like to make.
  1.
  2.
D. *Make A Plan*
  1. What is the first step to take in order to reach your goal(s)?
  2. What additional steps do you need to take to reach your goal(s)?
  3. What obstacles could prevent you from reaching your goal(s)?
  4. How will you overcome these obstacles or roadblocks?
  5. What types of support (friends, colleagues, training opportunities, materials, organizations) will help you reach your goal(s)?
  6. How can each person, organization, or training opportunity support you? Be specific.
  7. When and how will you implement your plan?
E. *Make A Commitment*
  1. What positive outcomes may occur if you attain your goal(s)?
  2. What negative outcomes may occur if you attain your goal(s)?
F. *Succeeding*
  1. How will you know when you have attained your goal(s)?
  2. What reward will you provide for yourself when your goal(s) has been attained?

to help them develop a strategy for making these changes. When developing goals and action plans, the following points should be kept in mind. Goals should be:

1. Desirable—based on something that individuals truly want.
2. Achievable—able to stretch a person, but not beyond the bounds of what is reasonable given an individual's strengths and limitations.
3. Concrete and Specific—includes what, when, how, where, and who.
4. Measurable—able to be evaluated in some quantitative and/or qualitative way.
5. Broken Down Into Smaller Steps—stated in a manner that allows individuals to take one small step at a time.
6. Immediate—can be initiated in the very near future.
7. Written—an unrecorded goal is only a wish.

— P ⋆ A ⋆ R ⋆ T ⋆ IV —

APPLICATION
AND PRACTICE

❖ INTRODUCTION _____

Experience is not what happens to you; it is what you do with what happens to you.

—Aldous Huxley

In this section we present "hands on activities" that are practical and attempt to answer the age old question, "How do we make this learning stick after the experience?" The models introduced are easy to follow and full of ideas, activities, and strategies for experiential educators, trainers, and therapists who are looking for diverse ways to improve on what they are doing in the training room, classroom, or the outdoor setting. Learning crosses all disciplines. We are all looking to increase our knowledge, utilization, and retention. Peter Senge quoted Arie De Gues, the former head of planning for Royal Dutch/Shell, who stated that "The ability to learn faster than your competitors may be the only sustainable competitive advantage." (Senge, 1990, pg. 4) This is true for organizations as well as for the individual, especially now in our information age. Your success comes from not only what you know, but how well you continually learn and apply your new knowledge. What follows are the main components of this applied section.

The **Learning Activities and Retention Strategies** section has been inspired by the work of Garvin (1996), from Harvard University who is helping corporations around the world develop curriculums for learning **before** doing, learning **while** doing, and learning **after** doing and by the work of Broad and Newstrom (1992) who have been studying the transfer of training for more than a decade. They too have broken training down into the same time periods **before, while,** and **after** the training or learning experience. We have adapted this model as a map to organize activities around the before, while, and after time periods and have identified activities and strategies for the main roles in the learning system. This section presents these activities in the **Learning before Doing, Learning while Doing,** and **Learning after Doing** sections.

The **Leadership Topics to Enhance Processing** section is a collection of teaching units, that leaders can utilize to integrate cognitive content into experiential learning. The content can anchor the structured experience, while the experience can bring to life the cognitive content. The purpose of these units is to provide you with various topics to present in a traditional training-setting that will broaden your services and overall impact. They are easy to read and written in a "how to" format. These units can be implemented either before, while, or after doing.

The last section is **Expertise from the Field,** where you will find guiding practices and special topics from experts who are applying their unique learning, knowledge and skills to various populations, on a daily basis. These contributions are divided into two areas: (1) Best practices about specific groups that you can use in your programs, and (2) Typical scenarios that occur frequently with responses from one or two experts. The purpose is to allow you to "get inside their head" to witness their thinking as preparation for what to do in similar situations. We feel very honored that these individuals were willing to share their knowledge and expertise.

LEARNING ACTIVITIES AND RETENTION STRATEGIES (LARS)

❖

True wisdom is to know what is best worth knowing, and to do what is best worth doing

—*Edward Porter Humphrey*

Learning Activities and Retention Strategies (LARS) facilitate the expansion of the learning experience from an isolated event to a string of coordinated learning activities which improve retention and application by enlarging the time frame and increasing support and reinforcement. At each time period, there are specific activities and topics to be covered that will provide a holistic and continuous learning experience. Broad and Newstrom (1992) make a distinction of the main roles or stakeholders in the learning process. Specifically, they identify transfer activities for the manager, trainer, and trainee to enhance learning.

Although, this model was developed for the corporate and organizational arena and will have the most applicability to practitioners in this area, we feel the model and activities can be adapted to all settings, and populations. Specific examples of applications to a variety of groups and/or settings are included. The development of the model and the research supporting it are presented next.

❖ RESEARCH AND RATIONALE: TIME PERIODS AND ROLES

Research indicates that corporations, nonprofit agencies and governments spend about $50 billion each year for human resource development and yet only 10% of classroom learning is applied in the work place (Broad & Newstrom, 1992). Cynicism always exists among employees when they must leave their real work to go to training that they know their management team either hasn't been to or won't support in a few months. The experience easily falls into the "flavor of the month training". If this happens more than a few times, workers come to the learning experience with a mental model of "this is a waste of my time" and feeling jaded and ripped off by management. The best training or learning experience in the world will fail with these preconceived attitudes and lack of applied knowledge and learning. Consequently, the challenge to all educators, trainers, and facilitators, is finding out how we can retain learning and increase the return on investment for all the hours and money spent on learning and development.

Broad and Newstrom (1992) have researched the "technology of transfers". Their work helps us develop new strategies for implementation, evaluation, adjustment. The matrix presented in Figures 11 and 12 delineate strategies for each time period and each individual's role.

A panel of five experts in transfer of training were asked to place 79 transfer strategies into the before, while, and after categories. They were then asked to report which time role combinations were used most frequently in their organizations. These results were corroborated and endorsed by a wide range of organizational groups both nationally and internationally (Broad & Newstrom, 1992). Figure 11, adapted from Broad and Newstrom, (1992) shows these results.

| | Time Periods | | |
Role	Before	During	After
Manager	5	6	9
Trainer	2	1	7
Trainee	8	3	4

Key: 1 = high; 9 = low frequency

◆ FIGURE 11 ◆

Perceptions of most frequently used role/time combinations for using transfer strategies

The most significant effort to stimulate transfer came from the trainers during the training and before the training. That was followed by the trainee during the training and after the training. The lowest ranking (9) was that of the manager after the training, which perpetuates the participant's feeling ". . . if they are not into it why should I be?" For the managers, support for the training prior to the training was also low with a ranking of a (5).

The panel of experts were then asked which role/time combinations would be the most powerful for transfer if used properly. These results are presented in Figure 12.

As you can you see, the most significant role change is that of the manager, before being ranked number (1) and after as number (3). The least powerful role was that of the trainer after the experience (9). It also shows that the trainer's preparation along with strategizing with the manager is more powerful than what they do during the training. Broad and Newstrom (1992) summarize the principal learning as, "Clearly, in the eyes of these trainers and many others with whom we have consulted, managers do not consistently and powerfully support the transfer of

| | Time Periods | | |
Role	Before	During	After
Manager	1	8	3
Trainer	2	4	9
Trainee	7	5	6

Key: 1 = high; 9 = low frequency

◆ FIGURE 12 ◆

Perceptions of most powerful role/time combinations for using transfer strategies

training in the work environment. We believe that this represents a fundamental problem, and also a substantial opportunity for improvement." (pg. 53)

ASSUMPTIONS AND APPLICATIONS

As we look at this research, there are immediate applications that we can use to improve the learning and retention from experiential learning, training classes, and educational classes. To make this learning applicable to multiple settings, we will use the title of "sponsor" instead of manager, although at times it may be a manager, "leader" instead of trainer to include experiential educators, teachers, and trainers, and "participants" to include students, family members, and trainees.

The main assumptions that can be drawn from Broad and Newstrom's (1992) work are listed below:

1. We are under utilizing the network or system of learning supports. We need to develop more learning support-teams for participants to help cement the learning. They can be co-participants, sponsors, or past participants.
2. The stages of doing need to be delineated with tasks or actions to expand the learning event into learning retention and applications. See the learning activities and actions for each time period.
3. If managers play a critical role in transferring the learning in organizations, wouldn't that be true for a designated sponsor for participants in other settings also, like the classroom, the ropes course or adventure program, hospital or group home, youth group, or family program. We need to identify a sponsor for each participant. It may be a manager for a corporate or organizational employee; at times, this could also be a co-worker. It may be parent or sibling for a younger participant or a spouse for a husband or wife in a program. Educators may have their principal or direct supervisor be their sponsor.
4. Sponsors need to be educated about the value of their role, and what is expected of them.

5. Leaders have to change their mental models and see that the program delivery is only one phase. The true learning and changing depends also on the leader's ability to develop and work with these learning support-teams.

❖ LEARNING BEFORE DOING

In this section we look at actions that the sponsor, leader, and participant can do to help ensure the use and retention of the learning that occurs from the experience. You are encouraged to take these ideas and modify them for your particular setting and clientele.

ACTIVITIES PERFORMED BY THE SPONSOR

As the sponsor, your role is to help the participant become a better learner and utilize this learning when back at the office or home. You are vital for the participant's success because for learning to be retained it needs to reinforced. The participant has selected you to be his or her sponsor and you are the champion of the learning experience. Your job is to provide:

◆ Support for the learning experience.
◆ A sounding board to help establish a strong purpose for the learning experience.
◆ A plan for integrating and utilizing the new knowledge.
◆ Encouragement to take risks, assimilate the learning, and put the learning to use.
◆ Coaching the participant when a relapse or obstacle presents itself.
◆ Logistical help in getting the learning and freeing-up the time from other responsibilities.

The goal is for the participant to sit down with their selected sponsor and have a conversation responding to the questions 1–5. This structure will provide a positive framework for the partnership that is needed to help sustain, use and retain the learning. It is a good idea to write down the answers for these five questions and use this as an agreement between the sponsor and participant.

1. **Establishing the "Why."** It's important to have a strong reason for sending or encouraging a participant to go to a learning experience. The "why" can be initiated either by the sponsor or the participant. The sponsor needs to take a strong interest in understanding how this experience will fit into the future development of the participant. Explore your reasons thoroughly with the participants or their reasons if they initiate the request. Questions to answer to help establish the "Why", include:

    Why do you and the participant think this kind of learning experience is beneficial?
    What is the desired end-result for you and the participant?
    What do you expect will be different after the learning experience?
    What does the participant think will be different after the experience?
    What do expect them to learn?
    What do they think they will learn from this learning experience?

2. **Establishing support guidelines.** As the sponsor, what are the guidelines of interaction for you and the participant?

> Answer these questions to help generate the guidelines:
> What are your expectations of the participant, for example to be on time, try his or her hardest to be attentive during the experience?
> What does the participant need from you to be successful?
> Hold a conversation about what you shouldn't do? What shouldn't the participant do?

3. **Establishing what resources are available to each of you.** This includes other participants, present and past, financial support, educational, other individuals who can be supportive.

4. **Establishing the measurement of success.**

> How often will you meet with the participant?
> How will you know if there is change and learning?
> What metrics will you use to measure progress?
> What is the current baseline of performance or behavior?

5. **Establishing positive and negative consequences.** If you and the participant are successful in the experience and in implementing the learning, what will happen: career wise, project or promotion, future training, financial, pride, self esteem, respect of others, for the customer or colleagues, or family members and friends? If you are both unsuccessful or fail at implementing the new learning what will be the negative consequences: career wise, project or promotion, future training, financial, pride, self esteem, respect of others, for the customer or colleagues, or family members and friends?

   This initial conversation is very important to demonstrate commitment to the learning experience and to clarify expectations in an attempt to prevent problems and promote learning. Below are additional actions for the sponsor to take once this conversation is finished.

6. **Involve the participants** in the program planning, wherever possible and appropriate.

7. **Provide orientation** about the learning experience to others who can act as members of the learning support team, such as supervisors, co-workers, family members.

8. **Build transfer of learning** into supervisory performance requirements, that is the sponsor will be evaluated on how well they support the learning of the participant.

9. **Brief the participants** on the importance of the learning and on course objectives, content, process and applications back to the job or home.

10. **Review learning experience content** and materials.

11. **Provide coaching** and encouragement where and when necessary.

12. **Provide time to complete pre-learning assignments** and paper work where and when appropriate.

13. **Arrange meetings** with prior participants to clarify expectations.

14. Where possible send co-workers to the experience together to act as a support-team.

15. **Provide a positive learning environment** (timing, location, facilities).

16. **Plan to participate** in or visit the learning experience if possible.

ACTIVITIES PERFORMED BY THE LEADER

1. **Spend time with the sponsor** to explain the learning experience and align the goals of the learning experiences with the organization's strategic plan.
2. **Involve sponsors and participants** in the design of the experience.
3. Try to **provide learning experiences that closely mirror** the real world issues or problems of the participants.
4. **Develop the readiness** of the participants with orientations, conversations, reviewing materials, or talking with past participants.
5. **Plan learning activities** using the language and specific slang of the group you are working with.
6. **Design a peer coaching** component for the learning program, where the participants teach others what they learned in "best practices" follow-up activities.
7. **Utilize the Leadership Topics** (see following section) to enhance the preparation and learning. Bringing in new thinking can help them take more risks and frame what they will learn.

ACTIVITIES PERFORMED BY THE PARTICIPANT

1. **Provide input** into the learning program that is consistent with your specific needs and with the organization's strategic plan.
2. **Actively explore** and familiarize yourself with the learning curriculum and material.
3. **Participate** in all advance activities and orientations.
4. **Meet with your sponsor** to discuss the overall goals and expectations you have. Under the sponsor section is a list of questions for the two of you to answer and establish a LARS agreement.
5. **Visualize yourself** at the learning experience having all your goals met, enjoying it, supporting others, and being very open to the new information that you are receiving. Doing visualizations prior to your arrival is a great way to prepare yourself for the experience. The mind can't distinguish between what is real and imagined, so you can program yourself to be just like you want

during the structured experience. This skill has been used frequently and effectively by Olympic and professional athletes to enhance their performances.

❖ LEARNING WHILE DOING

This section identifies actions for the sponsor, leader, and participant to undertake during the structured experience. This time period is the one most of us are familiar with, but looking at all three roles and the activities will give you new ideas for promoting transfer and generalization.

ACTIVITIES PERFORMED BY THE SPONSOR

1. **Prevent interruptions** for the participants, so they can focus on the learning.
2. **Transfer work** assignments of the participants to others.
3. **Communicate supervisory/managerial support** to the participants for the program.
4. **Monitor attendance** and attention given to the learning, if this is possible.
5. **Recognize the participants** attendance and work with certificates or some other kind of visual reinforcement.
6. **Participate in a learning retention and action planning session** with the participant before the learning experience is over. This is a review of the initial agreement that the sponsor and participant had in the "learning before doing" actions. Responding to the following questions will help:

   What does the participant want to implement as changes once back at home, school, or work?
   What obstacles exist in implementing the learning?
   What steps or actions are necessary to eliminate the obstacles?
   What resources are needed to put the actions in place?
   Review your guidelines again: What do you (the partnership) want to continue doing?
   What do you (the partnership) want to stop doing? What do you (the partnership) want to start doing?
   Review again, will you measure progress?
   Review the consequences, anything you need to add or delete?

7. **Plan assessment** of the new skills to the job or home and come up with a time line for measurement and the next meeting.
8. **Maintain support** by contacting, writing, visiting, or phoning to demonstrate your commitment to the learning.

ACTIVITIES PERFORMED BY THE LEADER

1. **Develop application-oriented objectives,** which are the skills that the participants will take back and use rather than the knowledge or resources. Focusing on skills forces the leader to think of real applications and examples during the learning and not just present concepts.

2. **Manage the "unlearning process."** This means to acknowledge that participants already have preset knowledge or mental models that need to be "unlearned" before the new learning takes place.

3. **Answer the "WIIFM" question,** which means "what's in it for me?" Having an answer for the WIIFM, means that the leader has put himself or herself in the shoes of the learner. As the learner sits, stands, or hangs there, they are asking themselves: Why am I here? What difference is this going to make in my life? Can I use this learning or experience? Leaders need to ponder these questions and be able to give responses that will invite participants into further involvement.

4. **Provide realistic work-related tasks.** Broad and Newstrom (1992) discuss two ways to help participants apply their learning, (1) Through basic principles that can be repeated and used as foundations for related problems and learning situations, and (2) "Identical elements", which is the key to experiential learning, providing similar experiences that mirror the real, life/work task or situation, or create a tight metaphor for the learners. Leaders can develop basic principles that can be the summary card for the participants to take home with them to reinforce and remember the learning. The "Identical elements" can be accomplished by knowing the participants work site or home situations well and spending time to create simulations that embrace their main elements.

5. **Provide integration processing.** During the learning experience, let the participants know that you will be stopping the experience to help them make connections between what they currently are experiencing and how they can apply this knowledge. This is a scheduled time to focus on the following questions:

    ◆ "How is this learning similar to what happens at work or home for you?"
    ◆ "What is the main insight or learning from this experience that is different for you?"
    ◆ "What strength or resource was present here that you want to take back with you?"
    ◆ "What can you apply from this learning back at home or work?"
    ◆ "What will you or anyone else see that will signify that you have made changes?"

    These questions force participants to create space for these answers because they are not typical questions people ask themselves. The questions provoke and initiate participants to think about their learning in new abstract ways. Usually there isn't an immediate answer and the leader has to encourage people "to think out of their box." Aside from emphasizing your focus on transfer and generalization, these questions start the process of the brain to search for these connections throughout the learning experience. Other resources are the Processing Activities which are in a later section and Levels of Processing questions and Additional Processing Questions in an earlier section.

6. **Utilize the Leadership Topics** (in a following section) to enhance the processing and learning. Bringing in new thinking can help them take more risks and frame what they have learned.

7. **Provide visualization experiences.** Participants are encouraged to visualize themselves applying the knowledge and skills at home or work. Help them see themselves coping with all the obstacles that may be present in the learning transfer.

8. **Give individuals feedback,** ideally a few times throughout the learning. Focus on the strengths and areas of development. Help them structure a plan to attend to the development areas.

9. **Provide reminders** of key learning points that participants can use or put up back at the office or home.

10. **Provide "Insights and Applications" notebooks** or **journals.** Document any thoughts or actions that relate to their transfer of the leaning. Give them time daily to reflect and write in their journals or notebooks.

11. **Create opportunities for support groups and peer coaches** to get together to discuss their learning as a "learning community", and how they will apply the knowledge at home or work.

12. **Help the participants prepare group action plan** where they exchange ideas of what they realize as being most relevant for work or home.

13. **Have trainees create individual action plans** that detail their specific plan to apply the learning. Get a copy of this and mail it back to them within a month.

14. Give time, **design,** and **implement Relapse Prevention** sessions. (See the Leadership Topics for the teaching unit on Relapse Prevention).

15. **Help participants** write an ongoing "group lessons learned" in a communal journal that later can be circulated to all the participants as a reinforcement.

ACTIVITIES PERFORMED BY THE PARTICIPANT

1. **Connect with a learning buddy,** who will help discuss lessons learned and contribute to the "new story" for you. Make commitments to each other about the new behaviors and new mental models that you are experimenting with in order to increase your motivation and risk taking.

2. **Utilize an "Insights and Applications" notebook** or journal to jot down your thoughts, insights, and applications. Usually trainings are packed with information and it's beneficial to take reflection time to allow all the new data to settle in. If each day you took this integration time, your retention and application would be richer. Pay attention to your patterns of behavior during the learning experience. How are they holding you back? How typical are your responses and what would you like to change?

3. **Form learning support teams** to discuss learnings and applications. These participants can become co-authors with you of the new story you create from the learning experience. Ideally, you should meet daily and have no more than two or three participants on your team. Share your insights and actions from your individual action plans and strategize how to deal with potential obstacles.

4. **Meet with your sponsor** to go over your LARS agreement, talk about your learning and planning for the changes and implementation of the learning, and how he or she can help you. If this is your spouse, co-worker, supervisor, or parent, this update of your experience, and what you need from them can help the transition back home or at work. If you can't meet in person, a phone call can give them the information.

5. **Participate actively and take risks** to try out new behaviors and let go of old mental models. The more involved you are the more you will learn and retain.

6. **Plan for your goals and applications** after the learning experience. You can answer these questions: What will be first steps you need to take to stay on track? Who will be the first to notice you have made changes and what will they notice? Prepare your plan and give it to the leaders to send back to you in a month.

7. **Anticipate a lapse** to the old behaviors and develop your relapse prevention program toward the end of the learning experience. (See Leadership Topics for more information on developing a relapse prevention program).

8. **Create behavioral contracts,** with your learning team, sponsor, and learning buddy. The more commitments you make; the harder it will be to return to the old behavior.

9. **Visualize yourself implementing your new skills** back at home or the office. See yourself responding to challenges that will be present in a constructive manner, like dealing with others who are cynical about your new learning. The more time you can do this; the better prepared you will be for your re-entry and dealing with obstacles.

❖ LEARNING AFTER DOING

In this section, the main strategies for the sponsor, leader, and participant are listed. This time period is where the skills and knowledge can be applied and reinforced. It is easy to get caught up in day to day activities and not take this time, but this time is crucial for the investment made into the learning. Tracy (1993) after reviewing the time-management literature has stated that, one minute of planning and preparation saves five minutes of execution. The planning and the activities presented here can have a significant payoff, not only for the participant but for the entire organization, family, or classroom.

ACTIVITIES PERFORMED BY THE SPONSOR

As discussed in the research and rationale section, the sponsor is critical to furthering the learning and facilitating the application of new skills. All too often, participants don't have a sponsor; or, if they do, the sponsor doesn't assume responsibility for the investment just made in the participant. There is tremendous potential for increased learning if participants have a sponsor, and if they use the strategies presented below.

1. **Hold a reentry debrief,** where you hear about the participant's experience and learning. Go over your LARS agreement and see if the experience met his or her expectations. Coach them how the road ahead may be difficult as the people around them have not changed and won't necessarily be excited to hear about their experience. Schedule some ongoing "one on ones" after this debrief.

2. **Psychologically support the learning,** by communicating support and endorsing their learning. Monitor their agreement and progress.

3. **Provide an opportunity to teach** parts of the learning as soon as possible to others to help cement the learning. This can be a group or just one other person.

4. **Provide opportunities to practice** new skills. This isn't always easy, but they need to quickly assess that you and the organization are serious about incorporating this new knowledge. Have them take responsibility for some projects where they can use their new skills

5. **Reduce pressures initially** by not having a pile of actions for them to do. They will need to settle in and have some reflection time for integrating and implementing the learning.

6. **Hold a debrief with the leader,** where you can get feedback on the participant's performance and inquire into the leader's perceptions about the next steps.

7. **Give positive reinforcement,** when you see actions that are new and are in line with the initial agreement that you talked with the participant about. Your reinforcement especially when it is tied to specific behaviors or performance will be very important. Do this early on and intermittently to maintain the behaviors and performance.

8. **Provide role models** of past participants who have successfully integrated the learning and have dealt with transfer strategies. They can provide another source of what "reality" will be like for them, when they return to home, school, or the office.

9. **Schedule "lessons learned" sessions.** If you had a team of people go, this is especially helpful in distilling the learning and coming with applicable actions to implement. If only one person went, schedule a learning session to teach the main concepts to co-workers or family members or other interested parties.

10. **Reclarify expectations for improvement** by updating the LARS agreement. Evaluate how reentry is going, and establish what else is needed for both the sponsor and participant to be successful.

11. **Schedule practice sessions** if the skill learned is a perishable skill. Time may have to be allotted to practice the learning to keep it present.

12. **Provide and support the use of a learning aids.** This is a checklist, flow chart, notebook or key concepts that may have been given out in the learning experience. If not, encourage the participant to make his or her own.

13. **Support participant reunions.**

14. **Publicize small successes** as a way to keep the learning momentum going and continually showing your support.

15. **Give preferences to the participant,** be it promotional, financial, special projects, or additional training.

ACTIVITIES PERFORMED BY THE LEADER

This is the time period where leaders haven't traditionally been involved. A change in your mental model from deliverer of a training to a facilitator of behavioral change is necessary. Any attention given to the participants after the experience will pay high dividends. After looking at these strategies, pick the ones you can effectively do within the constraints of your situation and develop a plan to implement them. A series of these strategies over a period of time can be very effective without spending a lot of your time.

1. **Maintain high expectations** by reminding participants that they have the skills and capabilities to implement the changes they wish. Your faith and hope in them can help when they are challenged and feeling self-doubt.
2. **Provide continual support.** This can be accomplished through the use of phone calls, cards, visits to their home or office, sending them their action plan or copy of the group journal with your personal note.
3. **Use evaluations surveys and interviews to provide feedback.** After a learning experience acquiring data for the participants and sponsors on their progress can provide helpful information and serve as a reinforcer. It also provides information for the next steps that they may want to accomplish with you in order to move the event into a learning curriculum arena.
4. **Suggest, develop and administer recognition strategies.** Your relationship with the sponsor can help establish some recognition activities for participants. Certificates, awards, lunches, picnics, parties, slide shows are examples of activities that you can use.
5. **Provide refresher follow-up sessions.** This is where you can cover key concepts, give some new experiences, or expand on items that you did not have enough time to develop fully.

ACTIVITIES PERFORMED BY THE PARTICIPANT

These are strategies participants can do on their own to help reinforce their learning.

1. **Practice self-discipline** to follow-up on the actions from the individual action plan, attend all the support meetings, and spend time with your sponsor. To utilize the learning information in many instances is to break old habits and substitute new, more constructive habits. This is not easy work. It starts with making and keeping small promises to yourself and to initiate some of the actions presented in these activities.
2. **Review the learning content,** skills, individual action plan, and your journal by going over the synthesized and high impact insights and strategies you have developed. If this is done weekly, initially, and then monthly (after the first month) you will be able to move the learnings from short term memory to long term memory. You will create new habits for yourself along the lines of living the "new story" you wrote for yourself.
3. **Develop a mentoring relationship.** In these strategies, you have had a sponsor, a role model with the organization or system, and learning buddies. These experiences

should let you see the value of having multiple perspectives and developing role models. The goal of this strategy is to select one of these people or someone new who is in a place where you want to be in future. Continue to use this person as a sounding board to bounce your ideas off and get a clear direction of what lies in front of you for the future.

4. **Maintain connection with your learning buddies.** The goal is to use your learning buddies as accountability supports. If you can make a verbal commitment to them about your behavior changes, they can help support, challenge, and reinforce you. This can be done weekly by phone calls or meetings.

5. **Develop the next learning interest.** This is a way to continue the cycle presented here by exploring more training or classes that are relevant to your overall goals. This could be a new interest or more advanced learning.

We presented an array of activities and strategies for you to choose from and implement. You probably will not be able to do all of them depending on your specific circumstances. We hope that you see the value of the time periods and the different roles that you are able to apply, and also a few of the strategies in each category. Then, as a field of educators, trainers and therapists we will increase our impact and significance in the lives of the learners we teach.

Think of yourself as on the threshold
of unparalleled success.
A whole clear, glorious life lies before you.
Achieve! Achieve!

—*Andrew Carnegie*

SECTION 2

LEADERSHIP TOPICS TO ENHANCE PROCESSING

❖

The topics presented in this section are teaching units to help integrate cognitive content into experiential learning. The content can enhance the learning and retention from the experience, while the experience integrates and strengthens the content. These units can help you broaden your services, magnify your impact, and generate better processing by expanding the one day event mind-set and adding value to your clientele. You can select to integrate these units before your experiential program, during it, or use them as follow-up activities. They are easy to read and written in a

"how to" format to be used in a traditional training-room setting. Each topic will take approximately two hours to conduct and integrate your current organizational and leadership expertise along with indoor experiential activities to maximize learning.

CREATING A SHARED VISION

Terry Horsmon, M.B.A.

"In the long run men hit only what they aim at. Therefore, though they should fail immediately, they had better aim at something high."

—*Henry David Thoreau*

GOALS

- ◆ To choose an image for the team that it will want to strive to achieve.
- ◆ To create a vision for the team that is inspiring, sincere and beyond their present grasp.
- ◆ To allow the team to establish a collective set of values that support the image.
- ◆ To provide an action strategy for the group to use in bringing the vision to life.
- ◆ To provide team guidelines for the drafting of an inspiring shared vision statement.

TIME FRAME

Two, two hour sessions

MATERIALS NEEDED

White board, flip chart or blackboard and individual notebooks. A prepared list of values.

PROCESS

1. Ask the team members to individually take five minutes and think of what the team might represent if it were being described as a metaphor or an image. Typically, the word "like" can best link the image to the group. For example, "we're like the pit crew of a finely-tuned race car."

2. Ask each team member to take the image that they devised and compare each of its components to a part of their organization. For example, if they have chosen a tree as an image, the

roots might represent "our customer", the trunk "our management team" and the leaves "our individual team members."

3. Ask the group to take five more minutes and try to visualize what this image will look like one year from now. Each member should now be prepared to share what image they chose, why they chose it, and to describe it to the group.

(Note: As the facilitator of this process, your job is to help the group to give meaning and clarity to the image that each person is describing. In doing this, ask "why questions for you to help them develop this image. For example "why would you say that? or "why does that fit what you represent?". Your questions will help each person understand his or her own images.)

4. After team members have described their image, ask everyone to select their top two choices from those images described. Create a ranking system for selection. Give a person's first choice two points and second choice one point. Total up the results and present them to the group for a final consensus.

(Note: Be careful to make room for consensus. If one image was everyone's second selection but did not receive the highest total score, you may want to re-poll the group by asking for only one choice from each person.)

5. Now you have the team prepared to attach values to the vision. Based on the image the team has chosen, ask the group to take five minutes and individually select five personal values that most strongly represent this image. You can use the values list from the "Personal Mission Statement" section. However, let the group know it can add any value that is not on the list.

6. Compile the list by having each member of the team come up to the board and write their five choices. Where a choice has already been identified, have the individual put a mark next to that choice.

7. If more than five or six values stand out, your job as facilitator is to get the team to come to a consensus on which values are most important to them. Use this time to ask the team questions about what meaning they gave to each of the values they chose.

8. Expect some interesting dialogue from the group. You will be responsible for helping them differentiate one meaning from another as they select five values. After approximately ten minutes of team dialogue have the group vote on their top values. Have them pick their top three if the group is large or top five if the group is small.

9. For each value the team has selected, have team members use their individual notebooks to write a statement that describes how this value shows up in the team's work. As the facilitator, your job is to get each person to describe how he or she acts toward others when using that value, and how the team interacts as a whole when the value is in place.

(Note: You may want to use the following model to accomplish this exercise: "We demonstrate integrity by treating each other and the customer with respect and by always considering everyone's point of view before we act as a team." Another example is, "we demonstrate teamwork by cooperating, communicating, asking for and giving help consistently").

10. Ask members of the team to read their value statement. As the facilitator, you must pick up key words and modifiers and put them up on the white board for the group to see. Cluster the words as they begin to shape a theme. For example, if you hear the words "honesty", "integrity" and "fairness", you would cluster them separately from "communication", "teamwork" and "consensus."

11. After you have received feedback from team members, ask them which clusters they think most accurately reflect the image they chose for the team. Ask the group to explain how these words fit the image they selected.

12. Get feedback from every team member, even if you have to go one by one and even if you can only get one comment from each person. The value of this exercise is to get "buy-in". from everyone.

(Note: If the group remains enthusiastic during this process, you will know that "buy-in" is being achieved. If the team begins to lose energy, stop and remind the group that a vision is supposed to be inspiring. Ask them "why they don't seem excited about the words and images they are choosing." Be sure to determine if they are only confused about the process or uninspired. If they are confused, step back and try to determine where you lost them.)

13. Using the clusters of words you have created for the group, break them down into small teams. If you have four clusters, for example, break them into four teams. Take ten minutes and have each team develop a definitive value statement for each cluster.

14. If the team has done a good job, many of the words contained in the cluster will appear in the statement of value. Have one member from each group read their statement to the entire team.

15. As a facilitator, be aware that you have actually deconstructed their original value statements, redefined and reassigned some additional meaning and reconstructed the value statement. It may not look any different than when you began this part of the exercise. However, through this process, you have achieved "buy-in—**shared vision**—from the entire group.

16. As a final exercise, use the image the team first selected as the foundation for helping them create a vision statement. For example, if the team chose a tree as its image, write on the white board "As the _____ team, we see ourselves as a tree with strong roots and branches reaching new technologies, ... At this point, the team will insert the value statements to complete it's vision statement.

17. Have the team break down into groups of three people to craft examples of what they want. Give them ten to fifteen minutes and bring them back together. Have each group read their example and have the team chose what best represents their view.

18. Read back to the team what they have selected. As the facilitator, try to determine whether the excitement is still present. Look at the expressions on their faces.

19. Finally, ask the group to answer "yes" or "no" to the following questions: Does this statement:

- ◆ have depth and meaning to you?
- ◆ inspire you and pull you towards it?
- ◆ give you a clear sense of how great you could be if you achieved this vision?
- ◆ make you feel like it is your own vision?
- ◆ give you a sense of responsibility toward yourself and your teammates?
- ◆ communicate a strong sense of why you are doing what you are doing in this organization?

If you get a rousing round of "yes" votes, the team has created a strong, compelling, shared vision for the future.

CREATING A PERSONAL MISSION STATEMENT

Being, Doing, and Having
We can think of life as having three dimensions: being, doing and having.
Often we attempt to live out lives backwards. We try to have more money in
order to feel we can do more of what we want, so we can be happier. The way it
*actually works is the reverse. We must first **be** who we really are, then **do** what we*
feel guided to do, in order to have what we want.

—*Shakti Gawain*

GOALS

- ◆ To have the opportunity to answer questions about what is most important to them.
- ◆ To establish participant's top values.
- ◆ To provide reflective time to create or review their life plan.

TIME FRAME

It is best if you divide this session into two 2 hour sessions. In the first, you want to give an introduction to writing a mission statement, establishing values, and then have time to start responding to the mission statement questions. A week between sessions is needed for participants to complete their mission statement and then come back with a draft.

MATERIALS NEEDED

White board, flip chart, or black board and overheads of this material.

PROCESS

First Session

1. Introduction: You want to spend some time introducing what a mission statement is and does for someone. Creating a personal mission statement is a task that a small percentage of the

population ever does. This exercise is enhanced if you have done an orienteering course or have been sailing with a group, as the metaphors of "taking a bearing," "following a bearing" and "staying on course" are useful as a kinesthetic imprint. You can have the reading above on an overhead or handout or just read it as part or your introduction.

What *is* a mission statement?

> *The greatest thing in this world is not where we are, but in what direction we are moving.*
>
> —*Oliver Wendell Holmes*

- ◆ It is a direction, path, or desirable state you want to create with your life.
- ◆ It includes your top values and your main roles.
- ◆ It helps you establish who you want to *be*, so you can *do* what you want, to *have* what you want.
- ◆ It is a personal vision of your head and heart working together.

What does a mission statement *do* for someone?

> *He who has a why can endure any how.*
>
> —*Nietzche*

- ◆ It provides an ideal or best plan for yourself to follow.
- ◆ It is something to aspire to and bring out your best.
- ◆ It is inspirational and should have a magnetic pull towards the future.
- ◆ At times of confusion and chaos, it helps you reorient, redirect, and adjust your course.
- ◆ It provides the "why" for your life to do the "whats."

2. Values provide a foundation for the mission statement as they help identify what is most important to people. Below is an opportunity to establish individual's top values.
Have the group pick their top *ten* values from the list below and make sure they know they can add any values they feel are not included in their list.

Achievement	Freedom	Money
Accountability	Excitement	Productivity
Adventure	Empowerment	Purpose or mission
Balance	Expediency	Pride
Challenge	Excellence	Quality
Change	Friendship	Recognition
Continuos learning	Fun	Reward
Commitment	Goalsetting	Respect
Communication	Honesty	Risk
Cooperation	Integrity	Sense of community
Contribution	Isolation	Teamwork
Creativity	Loyalty	Trust
Ethics	Love	Understanding differences
Family		

3. When they have selected ten, ask them to choose five and put those five in rank-order with number one being the most important.

4. Have the participants pick a partner and share their list of values, and answer why they picked what they did. When they have finished answering the question, have them answer how effective have they been in living by these values?

5. Creative tension is what Peter Senge (1990) describes as occurring when there is a gap between the vision and the current reality. The vision is where you want to be, and the current reality is where you are now. Creative tension is experienced by emotional tension, such as frustration, confusion, apathy, pain, and anxiety. It is important to have a vision, but it is also important to be honest about current reality. This creative tension can be the fuel to motivate you towards your vision, if it is recognized and accepted. If not, the creative tension can facilitate lowering your vision as that is easier than moving towards what you really want. Explain this concept to participants and ask them:

- How do you experience your creative tension?
- What is helpful for you in working through your creative tension?

6. Mission statement exercise

Below are a series of questions needing responses to that will help the participants establish what is most important for them. The answers to the questions will be data for the mission statement. It is best, if they take some reflective time to respond to these questions. Ideally, in a quiet, natural setting away from phones and interruptions. These questions have been adapted from Covey, Merrill, and Merrill's (1994) *First Things First*.

It is very helpful if you have some examples of a finished mission statement to read to the group, so they can get a picture and impression of what they will end up with. If you don't have your own, do this process first for yourself and write one. Covey, Merrill, and Merrill (1994) have some examples in their book.

Some of these questions may take a few minutes, some considerably more time. Have them answer all the questions or just the ones that seem to be the most intriguing. The most important thing is to get in touch with what really matters to each individual. This will take some time anywhere from one to two hours, you can start it in your session, or just explain it and have them complete it outside the session. Here is the task for them:

1. Read the questions and write down your answers.
2. Reflect on your answers and write a *rough* draft of your mission statement.
3. Look back at your mission statement and decide:
    - Are all your most important roles covered with this statement?
    - Do you feel direction, inspiration, and challenge when reviewing it?
    - Does the statement represent the best that is within you?
    - Are all your main values covered by this statement?

Take time now to go on a personal retreat and deeply consider these questions:
(Answer any and all that you can.)

What are your greatest strengths?

_____

_____

What have other people noticed as your strengths?

_____

_____

When you are over 80 and on your death-bed, what do you think will have been most important to you as you look back on your life? Why?

_____

_____

What qualities do you admire in others?

_____

_____

Who is the one person that has had the greatest influence on your life?

_____

_____

Why was that person able to have such an influence?

_____

_____

What have been your happiest moments?

_____

_____

What was it that made them so happy?

_____

_____

If you had all the money and time you needed, what would you want to do?

_____

_____

What are you usually doing when you start daydreaming?

_____

_____

What would you say are the three most important things to you?

_____

_____

When you look at your work life, what activities give you the greatest pleasure?

_____

_____

When you look at your personal life, what activities give you the greatest pleasure?

_____

_____

What gifts or talents do you have that have been invisible to others?

_____

_____

Are there desires, things, or activities that in your deepest heart you feel that you really should do? What are they?

_____

_____

Physically what desires or goals do have for yourself?

_____

_____

Socially what desires or goals do you have for yourself?

_____

_____

Mentally what are your desires or goals?

_____

_____

Spiritually what are your desires or goals?

_____

_____

What important roles are you currently fulfilling? (mother, father, friend, daughter, son, co-worker, supervisor, etc.)

_____

_____

What lifetime goals do you want to make sure you accomplish in each role?

_____

_____

What results or successes are you currently receiving in your life that you want to continue?

_____

_____

What are you doing to achieve these results?

_____

_____

What would you really like to be and to do in your life if you were guaranteed success?

_____

_____

Any other dreams, desires, or goals that you want to document?

_____

_____

How are you feeling now after answering all these questions?

_____

_____

Your answers to these questions should give you some excellent input for your mission statement. Start to write your rough draft now. Good Luck!!!

Second Session:

1. Have the group get in groups of three. They will discuss the following questions, you can have them on the board or an overhead.

◆   What was the most significant insight you had about yourself?
◆   What was the hardest question(s) for you and why?
◆   Any metaphors or word pictures surface that represent the "best you."

2. Hold a group discussion to hear the highlights of the subgroups. Put the commonalties on the board.

3. Back in their groups of three, each person will have the opportunity to read their mission statement to the others. Ask the listeners to respond after hearing the following questions:

◆   What was inspiring about the mission statement for them?
◆   Was there a part that you didn't understand?

4. Give the following guidelines for the mission statement to the large group.

◆ It should be stated in present terms, i.e., "I am, I do, I value", versus "I'd like to or I will."
◆ It should be positively stated, i.e., "I live very healthy" versus "I don't smoke or I won't be angry."
◆ All the stakeholders should be covered, meaning if your spouse, boss, or co-worker read it they would see something about your relationship with them mentioned in some way.
◆ Your top values should be represented in your statement.

5. Have them go back to their small groups and read them again. This time, the listeners will act as consultants and give the reader more feedback regarding the guidelines from number 4. Give them time to rework their statements from the feedback they receive.

6. Back in the big group, see if there are any volunteers to read their mission statements in front of the whole group. Hear from 3–4 people and tell them what you like about each one. Encourage them to read their mission statement every day in the morning as a way of starting the day off on the right course. It should be a "living and breathing document"—meaning for some it is never finished, but reworked as you grow and change.

7. Have them go back in their group for the last time. As a support for each other discuss the following topics:

◆ What could each person do that would sabotage their good work and dilute the potency of their mission statement? When they have all finished with this, then ask:
◆ What plans or actions can your group brainstorm to prevent this sabotaging from happening?

One day Alice came to a fork in the road and saw a Cheshire cat in the tree. "Which road do I take? she asked. His response was a question: "Where do you want to go?" "I don't know," Alice answered. "Then," said the cat, "it doesn't matter."

—*Lewis Carroll*

Genius is the ability to put into effect what is in your mind.

—*F. Scott Fitzgerald*

RESOLVING CONFLICT

"Nothing in life is to be feared. It is only to be understood."

—*Marie Curie*

GOALS

To discuss the role of conflict in human interaction.
To discuss the impact of conflict on our lives.
To have participants identify personal and professional situations in which conflict exists.
To examine two processes for resolving conflict.

TIME FRAME

Two, two hour sessions

MATERIALS NEEDED

Flip chart, blackboard or white board, copies of the problem-solving and negotiation process for each participant.

❖ CENTRAL POINTS OF KNOWLEDGE RELATED TO RESOLVING CONFLICT____

Conflict is part of human existence. It generally occurs when people perceive that others are interfering with their ability to meet their goals (Friend & Cook, 1992). Conflict often arises when two individuals want different outcomes but must settle for the same one, or when they want the same outcome, but it cannot be available to both.

Though most of us would like to find a way to avoid conflict, no such path seems to exist. At best, conflict is disruptive; at worst, it can be destructive. However, at times conflict can be constructive and helpful. What should you do when you are experiencing conflict? Unfortunately, there is no simple formula that will lead to satisfactory solutions for all conflicts. In fact, some conflicts cannot be resolved.

Many approaches to conflict resolution stress the importance of rationally examining the important issues. However, this may be very difficult to do when emotions are so strong and evident. Therefore, when an issue involving conflict raises strong emotional responses, you may find that it is not possible to proceed, and temporary avoidance is needed. After calm has been restored and the emotions recede, then you can move on to the substantive issues of concern (Bolton, 1979).

Try to focus on issues, not people, whenever you experience conflict. You can sometimes diffuse emotions by responding positively to others' negative comments, by not responding to comments that might cause you to become angry, and by acknowledging the feeling that others are expressing.

For particularly serious conflicts in which there are far-reaching implications, you may find that it is helpful to ask a third party to assist in resolving the conflict.

You have the option to adapt to the issue or exit the situation. At some point it becomes self-defeating to continue to try to address a conflict if the other person does not view the matter as an issue, or if you cannot influence the conflict situation. Resolving the matter within yourself, so that you no longer worry about it may be the most viable option. If that is not possible and the issue is critical, you may choose to remove yourself from the situation.

❖ PROCESS–PROBLEM SOLVING

A. Working in groups of two, ask participants to generate a list of personal and/or professional situations in which conflict existed or currently exists for them, i.e., problems getting along with his or her boss, neighbors with a loud barking dog, a co-worker who is always sarcastic.

B. Ask them to volunteer to share a few of the situations. You can write them on the board as they explain the situation.

C. Ask the large group to try to identify common themes that exist across the examples provided. i.e., differing opinions, poor communication, lack of understanding.

D. Introduce the following problem-solving process as a constructive way to think about conflict resolution. Walk them through each step providing them with specific examples appropriate to the group and the situations that they shared with each other.
1. Identify and define the problem
   a. Use I-message to express your opinion nonjudgmentally.
   b. Use active listening to help understand the other person's perspective and to reduce anger or defensiveness in the other person
   c. Verbalize the other person's side of the conflict.
   d. Be sure both parties accept problem definition, which should be stated in terms of conflicting needs, not competing solutions.

2. Generate alternate solutions.
    a. Initial solutions may adequate, but they may also stimulate better ones.
    b. Get a number of possible solutions before evaluating.
    c. Keep at it, even restating the problem, until you have a number of feasible solutions or one that appears far superior.
3. Evaluate the alternate solutions.
    a. Use critical thinking, with both parties being hones.
    b. Examine flaws, barriers, difficulties in implementing the plan.
4. Make decisions.
    a. Mutual commitment to one solution is essential.
    b. Don't persuade or push a solution because if it isn't freely chosen; it's unlikely to be carried out.
    c. Restate the solution to make certain that both parties understand.
5. Implement the solution.
    a. Talk about who does
    b. Trust that the other will carry out the responsibilities rather than stating consequences for not carrying them out.
6. Follow up with an evaluation of the solution.
    a. If either of you discover weaknesses in the solution, more problem solving is in order.
    b. Ask how each is not feeling about the solution.
    c. Understand that decisions are always open for revision that are mutually determined.

E. Choose one specific situation from those that were volunteered earlier in the discussion. In the large group, go through each step of the problem-solving process demonstrating the application of that specific step.

F. Divide the large group into dyads. Have each dyad choose a situation in which conflict has existed for them. Role-play the situation using the problem-solving process.

G. Have the group get back together and share their current thoughts about dealing with conflict and their perceptions of the problem solving process.

❖ PROCESS–NEGOTIATION

This begins the second two hour session.

A. Use some of the situation which involve conflict that were identified at the previous session as stimuli for this discussion.

B. Introduce the conflict resolution technique of negotiation of the group. Share with them the following definition of negotiation:

Negotiation is a process that begins with each person involved in the conflict asking fore more than is reasonable to expect and then, using a series of offers and counteroffers to reach an agreeable resolution (Rubin, 1989).

C. Introduce the following process of negotiation as a way to handle conflict. Walk them through each step providing them with specific examples appropriate to the group and the situations that they have shared.
    1. Examine the situation using the following questions as a guideline:
        a. What is your own motivation as well as that of others involved in the conflict.
        b. Is the basis of the conflict a value difference?
        c. Is it an issue of limited resources and the stress caused by the situation?
        d. Is it a matter of differing opinions?
    2. Try to clarify the issues. Chances of resolving conflict increase when everyone involved understands what the real issues are. Without a mutual understanding of the issues, it is unlikely that you will resolve the conflict.
    3. Set expectations. Determine your ideal solution to the conflict and then temper it with your understanding of motivations as well as other factors influencing the situation.
    4. Make and respond to offers. This involves "give and take" among participants.
    5. Monitor for ethics and integrity. Withholding information or manipulating others' words, will worsen the situation instead of improving it. The final goal for negotiation should be to enable everyone to "save face," while simultaneously resolving the predicament.
D. Divide the large group into dyads. Have each dyad choose a situation in which conflict has existed for them. Role-play the situation using the process of negotiation.
E. Have the group get back together and share their current thoughts about dealing with conflict and their perceptions of the process of negotiation. Develop a list of "lessons learned" from the sessions that participants can use again at home, school, or work.

STRESS MANAGEMENT

GOAL

◆ To explain the difference between stress and stressors.
◆ To have participants identify stressors at work and in their personal lives.
◆ To identify coping strategies and develop a resource list that the group can draw from.
◆ To identify a stress strategy map for coping with stress.

TIME FRAME

One and a half to two hours

MATERIALS NEEDED

White board, flip chart, or black board

PROCESS

1. Explain that stressors are present in the environment and affect people, while stress is how we manifest that stressor within our body. You may want to write these down on your flip chart or white or black board. Add examples specific to your situation. Some examples are:

Stressors:	Stress:
Traffic	Frustration
Work deadlines	Anxiety, tension headache, little appetite
Downsizing	Problems sleeping at night, knot in your stomach
Big presentation	Sweating, dry mouth, butterflies
Sick child	Problems concentrating at work, anxious to get home
Responsibility without authority	Heart pounding, headache, and neck ache

2. Ask the group to write down individually what are their main stressors in their life, both at work and at home. Give more examples if they need to (2–3 minutes).

3. Pick a partner and have them share their lists. Then, after two minutes, have them choose one stressor that they have in common and one that is unique.

4. Suggest to the group that it may be helpful to know what stressors their team or co-workers go through typically. Then, have each pair share their list of common and unique stressors out loud to rest of the group. Write these down on the board and make comments about how similar many of the stressor are and other appropriate observations.

5. **Copers**—Now ask them to change their focus and write down their own favorite coping techniques. What are their typical ways of coping with the stressors mentioned? You may have to give some examples such as exercise, talking to a friend, smoking cigarettes, getting organized.

6. Have the participants pair up with a new person to compare their coping resources. After two minutes, have them choose one skill that they have in common and one that is unique to each partner.

7. Talk about the wealth of coping resources in the room, and now is the time to hear about some of the strategies. Have volunteers share the skills that they have in common, and list them on the board.

8. Then, have each pair in turn share their unique coping strategies. Each person must name a skill that has not been mentioned. Write these on the board. If negative copers are mentioned, like drinking or kicking the dog, distinguish them on your list by a circle or some other manner. Then, talk about the benefits and costs of some of the copers mentioned. This is a good time to talk more about stress management concepts.

9. **Stress management talk**—tie in comments that people have already made as you illustrate some of these points. You could put these points on an overhead projector to punctuate and organize your discussion.

   ◆ **We all have stress.** Each day we experience stressors and internalize it as stress. External forces have to be adapted to produces stress, as does exercise, danger, and interpersonal relationships.

   ◆ **Perception shapes and is a source of stress.** If a situation appears threatening, our body initiates the fight or flight response, just the same way it did in prehistoric times, when situations were really more issues of survival. Our reaction is to prepare for the battle with our predator or to flee as fast as possible. We will react in this life-threatening manner even with embarrassing and emotionally painful situations. When we see a flashing red light and hear a siren behind us, or our boss disapproves of something we did at work, or we make a major mistake on a project, we get stressed, panicked or pumped-up with adrenaline. Our perception influences the intensity and duration of the stress response. We all know people who have the exact same stressors as we do, but don't appear to be bothered by them in the least.

   ◆ **Our negative feelings or bad habits** can cause stress. Our body reacts to our perceptions or feelings about the situation and not the real event. Bad habits such as smoking, drinking, not getting enough sleep, and being angry and reactive to people are examples that increase our stress level.

   ◆ **Stress helps us stretch.** We all need it. The stress response protects us in times of real danger and motivates us to take risks, try new things, and reach our goals.

◆ **Too much stress can be devastating.** Stress can take a serious toll on our health, emotional stability, relationships with others, productivity, and sense of personal mission.

◆ **The goal is not to eliminate stress, but modulate it.** Eustress is what positive stress is called, and we have it at happy and stimulating times, such as recognition at work, getting married, and excitement about going on vacation. The goal is to: (a) be aware of the stress in your life, (b) know what your optimal level of stress is, and (c) manage your stress level to this point.

◆ **Know your stress signals.** There are many ways to detect how much stress you are experiencing.

   a. **Listen to your body.** Insomnia, chronic anxiety, poor appetite, always getting sick are ways your body is telling you that you have had enough stress.

   b. **Listen to your feelings.** Are you frustrated and irritable much of the time? Are peaceful and enjoyable moments few and far between?

   c. **Listen to your spirit.** Are you apathetic, cynical about everything, or find a loss of meaning in what you are doing? You may be on stress overload.

   d. **Listen to your relationships.** If your relationships are strained and full of short and irritable interactions, it may be time to focus on managing your stress levels while you still have some relationships.

10. Have each person gauge what kind of stress detector they have and rank their ability to know when they have had too much stress on a 1–10; 10 being that they are experts at knowing how much stress they experience. Have the participants now pair up with a new person and discuss: (a) how effective are they at detecting stress, sharing their rankings, and (b) what are their key stress clues that let them know they are on overload. For example, losing their keys or walking in a room and forgetting what they came in it for may be clues that they are on stress overload.

11. Hear from the different groups and write down the specific stress clues that they come up with on the board. Point out commonalties and uniqueness' to the stress clues that people come up with.

12. **Stress strategy map—AAAbc's of stress.** Now talk about how you will go into more detail about a model that will help distinguish which strategy to use in regards to the stressors in your life. These points can also be put on an overhead or as handouts for the group.

   ◆ **How we deal with stress is a decision-making process.** When we are under stress, there are three major ways to deal with that stress, all beginning with letter A:

      *A*lter it
      *A*void it
      *A*ccept it by
      *B*uilding resources
      *C*hanging our perceptions

      All three of these methods can be helpful as coping strategies. The decision is which to use in which situation. The facilitator will need to come up with specific examples that illustrates these coping techniques.

◆ **Alter implies removing the source of stress,** by changing something. This is done by problem-solving, organizing, planning, time management, and direct communication. All of these could be listed as prevention activities that either remove the stressors or lessens its intensity or duration. For example, planning and organizing your taxes in January will cause less stress than waiting until April 14th to start, or communicating with your team about some of the possible "what if scenarios" that could occur with a project and plans to attenuate these problems before they become surprise stressors.

◆ **Avoid implies removing oneself from the stressful situation,** or figuring out how to not get into the situation to begin with. Strategies here include:

1. Walking away from the situation to clear your head and bring back a fresh perspective.
2. Saying "no" to more work or responsibility.
3. Delegating to someone else who could do it at least 70% as well as you could.
4. Knowing your limits and abilities so you don't get yourself in over your head.

◆ **Accepting the stressors is what is necessary when you can't alter or avoid them.** To facilitate this process, you need to equip yourself both physically and mentally. Building resources and changing your view-point will help and represent the b and c of the model.

Building resources—you can do this in many different ways.

✓ **Physical** resources can be improved by a number of methods, such as exercise, to give you more energy, practicing relaxation exercises, such as progressive relaxation, meditation, or yoga, and getting massages or some other kind of body work.

✓ **Mental** resources are built by meditation/relaxation, positive self-affirmations or self-stories, taking time-out to just reflect and digest your days or just let your mind wander, and clarify your values and priorities so you know what to "stand up for" or say "no" to.

✓ **Social** resources are strengthened by building and maintaining your support systems, putting time in others, and letting them know how they can support you, and when they are not being helpful. A good listener rather than an advise giver is usually what people are looking for.

✓ **Spiritual** resources can be enhanced through prayer, worship, faith, and fellowship.

Changing your viewpoint—is something you can control when you have to accept the stressor. Changing unrealistic expectations, irrational beliefs, or overgeneralizing from specific situations are all ways to reduce your stress. Reframing the situation by putting a different meaning to the event or stressor can be less intense and possibly more constructive. For example; by getting stuck in traffic, you can reframe as a time to relax or mentally prepare for an upcoming meeting or, the customer adds new requests without changing the delivery deadline, can be seen as a challenge or an opportunity to demonstrate added value and build a better relationship with the customer. Optimistic people are known to view situations as temporary versus permanent, and specific versus all encompassing or pervasive, these changes in pereption give more hope to people and reduce their stress level.

13. Have participants apply this stress strategy map to their real life stressors. Break the group up into smaller groups of three people each. They should discuss real stress scenarios and talk about the different strategies which they suggest could be used to deal with the stressors. You can either elaborate on the stressors from number 2 or create your own scenarios specific to the group that you are working with. A few are listed below as examples for the group to use. When the groups are finished, have one person from each group share the best option strategy that he or she used for the scenario and explain why?

14. **Sample scenarios**

   Scenario 1: You live fifteen minutes from work. Every morning you get up at 7:10, get ready for work, and you are out of the house and in the car by 8:10. Since you are due at work by 8:30, you find yourself speeding to work. When traffic is normal you have enough time to get to work on time. But when traffic is heavy, you almost get yourself killed by passing slow moving cars on a narrow winding highway. When you stop for a red light or train, you "feel like exploding." By the time you get to work, you feel like a "complete basket case."

   Scenario 2: You have a new boss at work after a reorganization. She doesn't seem to like you and anything you do is not good enough. This is disturbing for you as you never have had performance or boss problems before. You have had an initial talk with her that went nowhere. You are beginning to wonder if you will ever please her. What can you do?

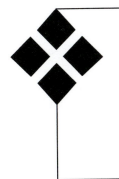

THINKING ABOUT THINKING— MENTAL MODELS

"No problem can be solved from the same consciousness that created it."
—*Albert Einstein*

In this section, we look at the process of how we think, as it is arguably the greatest influence over our actions and our lives. Yet, we take very little time to explore our thinking style. Is it effective? Are we achieving the results we want from our thinking? Are there ways that we can improve our thinking and the inferences that we make? There are four units presented to take a deeper look at our thinking process; they include: Becoming Aware of Mental Models, Understanding the Ladder of Inference, Using the Ladder of Inference, and Breakthrough Thinking.

❖ BECOMING AWARE OF OUR MENTAL MODELS

"We don't see things as they are, we see them as we are."

—*Anais Nin*

GOAL

- ◆ To understand what a mental model is.
- ◆ To see how limiting our thinking can be.
- ◆ To understand why we have thinking strategies.

TIME FRAME

Two hours

MATERIALS NEEDED

White board, flip chart, or blackboard and individual notebook, tooth picks

PROCESS

1. Start with the above quote by Anais Nin. Place it on the board or overhead and ask the group, "What does that mean to you?" Field their answers and tell them that this session is about how we think. Ask them to step back and observe their thinking process; something many of us never do.

2. *Exercise:* Tell the group there are two parts to this exercise. Put the Roman numeral VII on the board and ask the group by adding only 1 line to make an VIII. They will add a line to the end to make the VII and think this is some kind of trick. Now for the second and harder part ask them to only add 1 line again and make the Roman numeral nine (IX) into a six. Put "IX" on the board.
    Solution: The main answers are to put an "S" for SIX and a "6" for 1X6. The answer we want is to make an "S" in front of the "I". To understand this, people have to think outside the dominant model and go from Roman numerals to Arabic numbers, which takes a mindshift. The first part of the exercise sets them up to think in Roman numerals which doesn't lend itself for the critical thinking necessary for the answer.
    Process Questions:

    > What was necessary to come up with that answer?
    > How did the presentation of this exercise influence what you saw as a solution?
    > How does presentation of data influence what you see at work?
    > How often do we fall into these thinking ruts, especially when new thinking is needed?

    Create a short dialogue around these questions getting people involved. Getting stuck in this thinking rut is what we will call a "mental model."

3. *Lecturette:* Use this information for your presentation.
    A. *What is a mental model?*
        Deepak Chopra stated that we have as many as 60,000 thoughts a day. Ninety-five percent of those thoughts are the same ones we had yesterday (Robbins, 1996). Why is that ? The same thoughts keep recycling which is one reason why we use only five to ten percent of our brain power. These same or similar thoughts form patterns or clusters of our beliefs, yet leave out a plethora of other possible views. Senge (1990) defines "mental models" as . . . "deeply ingrained assumptions, generalizations, or even pictures or images that influence how we understand the world and how we take action" (pg. 8).
        The term mental model has been used by psychologists since the 1940's. Cognitive psychologists, cognitive scientists, and more recently corporate managers use the term. Senge (1990) popularized the term as one of five disciplines in his book *The Fifth Discipline*. In the *Fifth Discipline Fieldbook*, a mental model is defined as ". . . both the semipermanent tacit "maps" of the world which people hold in their long-term memory, and the short-term perceptions which people build up as part of their everyday reasoning process" (Senge, Roberts, Ross, Smith, & Kleiner, 1994, p. 237).
    B. *Why is understanding our mental models important?*
        The mental models we carry within us are usually *invisible* to us and others yet they are very powerful in their influence over our actions and responses to anything

that occurs in our world. Often these mental models may hold us prisoners to the "same old story", when "openness" to new learning is necessary to grow and advance in our careers. To continually learn and grow, we must *think* and *act* differently, and our invisible mental models hold us back, sometimes like a prisoner's ball and chain.

In many organizations, learning and training are vital for survival. If individuals only interpret new information through the same lenses and don't challenge their invisible mental models, what "gets through or in", is just what supports their worldview or autobiography. Culbert (1996) comments on all the current new management models to help organizations survive and prosper, such as "reengineering", "leadership that empowers", "transformational change", "reinventing the organization", and "becoming a learning organization" are all limited unless a mindset change goes along with them. These new models he states:

> "... are so intellectually attractive that they can lead you to believe that you have taken a critical step forward without having left the spot you are on. The reason can be stated quite simply. You'll think that you are enacting them because you are behaving differently, but that's not all they require. They require that you actually think about people differently— about their nature and motivations at work, and about how to go about influencing them. When you employ new models using the former mentality, you may, in fact, be in the boat, but your oars won't be in the water. The new models require you to do some things with people that reasoning in the former mentality won't permit" (Culbert, 1996, p. 5).

As the above Anais Nin quote infers, how can we possibly see, report, conclude, decide, act on anything that is not strongly influenced by our history, psychology, preferences, and life situation? Our world is subjective, and we interact with others like there is an objective reality. To be accurate, we would need to keep words like "objective", "real", "correct", and "truth" in quotation marks. Instead, we present our interpretations as facts and our preferences as impartial decisions. "In an organization, personal politics and subjective interest determine how each event, problem, and opportunity gets portrayed; they influence and determine every action that someone advocates as essential" (Culbert, 1996, p.xiii).

What is needed then, is for the organization and individuals to unearth these mental models, bring them to the surface and scrutinize them with others (Senge, 1990). Then, it is possible to move toward a collective knowledge, shared perspective, that opens up possibilities for fresh wisdom. Voicing these mental models lets one's thinking become more visible. Commitment is enhanced as the team or organization moves toward more of a "shared vision."

The goal then is for individuals to:

- ◆ Become aware of their own mental models.
- ◆ Understand how much influence unexamined mental models exert on one's immediate world.
- ◆ Become responsible for communicating these mindsets into the thinking and communication process.

Ask for questions or comments regarding the material you just presented. You can then ask: "What is one example from work that demonstrates a common mental model?" Examples could be "management doesn't know where we are going," "nothing changes here," "all they want is more work from me," "what are we doing about new business," people don't care about one another, every person is trying to get ahead at the expense of others."

Get as many examples as you can and write them on the board.

Ask: Are these mental models helping you or hindering you and how so?

4. *Exercise:* Divide the group into pairs for this exercise. Put six toothpicks lying flat down in front of each pair. Ask them to create *four* equal sided triangles. Give them a time limit of five to eight minutes (Sweeney & Meadows, 1995).

Solution: Put three toothpicks flat on the table in a triangle and take the other three and make a teepee structure with all of them leaning on each other. This exercise like the "IX Exercise" takes looking at the problem from a different perspective, three dimensional, versus two dimensional.

Process questions:

What mental models were evident from this exercise?
How did the presentation of the problem influence your thinking?
As a partnership did you challenge assumptions or collude in your mental models?
What strategies are necessary to free yourself from the constraints of your mental models?
Develop a resource list and put it on the board.

5. *Lecturette:* Use this information for a continuation of your presentation.
   Styles and strategies of thinking
   A. *Our need to know and be certain*

   As we talked about in the Edgework section, people don't like the feeling of being out of control, uncomfortable, or not knowing. The sense of not knowing something or being uncertain creates tension, and this is very difficult for us to endure for any length of time. It may put us at the "edge" of the known and the unknown, and there, we feel the magnetic pull-back into the middle where our comfortable and predictable mental models warm us like a cozy fire on a cold, winter day.

   Isn't learning though, going from the known to the unknown? If we continue to be seduced by our certainty of knowing, where is the space created for new learning? We have a hard time staying in "I don't know." Why is this? Robert Fritz (1991) helps explain, as humans we have an instinctive "tension resolution" system. If there is any tension, be it hunger, thirst, or exhaustion, we instinctively need to resolve it. As we grow from infants to adulthood, the instinctive quality changes to the self-conceived, or we *invent* ways to reduce our tension. So, if we don't know, rather than experiencing that tension and holding that space, we interpret, infer, abstract, concoct, speculate, and manufacture theories that we state as facts or explanations. What happens to our thinking then, is that we would rather have a reason even if it is *distorted* or *inaccurate* than *feel* the *discomfort* and *uncertainty* of not knowing. This process usually happens rapidly and without our realization. We then become victims to our thinking process without understanding how and what *we did* to ourselves. David Bohm (1965), a physicist and leading, quantum theorist, described this phenomenon as happening because of the very nature of thought. "Thought continually deludes us into a view that this is the way it is." He asserts, "Our thought is incoherent and the resulting counterproductiveness lies at the root of the world's problems" (Senge, 1990, p.245 & 240). We are unable to stand apart from our thoughts and assess what they are doing to us.

B. *Thoughts traveling the well-worn path*

Our thinking creates neural pathways within our brain. When we think in a particular way, these pathways get deeper and more worn. Therefore, it's easier for other thoughts to travel the same pathway rather than create new ones. Many of us have had the experience of hiking and coming to a fork in the trail. One is well-traveled but going in the wrong direction. While the other is faint and overgrown although going in the right direction. Which path do you take? The well-worn trail will be easier to hike on and you can go faster, and *MAYBE* it'll turn and go the right way. The faint trail will be slower and could end. So, the choice often is to go down the well-worn trail even though it's not in the right direction. The thinking process is like this, although less conscious. It's very hard to trail blaze even though frequently that is what is necessary. Before we realize it, we are down the same trail because it may have worked in the past, and it's easier than bushwhacking.

The uncertainty and the unknown as mentioned above become the traffic police pointing us down that old familiar path to quickly attenuate our tension or disequilibrium. Our past learning plays a major role in this as "thinking" tells us this is an efficient and "tried and true" strategy. Problems arise when new directions and new mental models are needed, yet, we still go down the same path.

This wrong path is what Bohm calls "incoherence." He delineates three kinds of incoherence:

◆ Thought denies it is participative in the process.
◆ Thought stops tracking reality and just keeps going.
◆ Thought establishes it's own standard of reference for fixing problems, the same problems it contributed to creating initially (Senge, 1990).

Using our trail analogy, "thought" points us down the wrong trail, but it denies responsibility for it. "Thought" then does not take notice of any of the landmarks that may indicate that we are on the wrong trail. And finally, if there is a question, "thought" picks out mountain tops and then finds them on the map to squelch doubt and reestablish that this is the right direction. "Thought" has to distort facts, the mountain tops, to fit the existing map of reality.

C. *"Hiccup" thinking*

"Hiccup" thinking exists when we go with the first thing that pops up in our mind. Usually people don't take much time to really think. We respond to others' questions in fractions of a second. A thought emerges almost spontaneously like a hiccup, and we treat it as an "AHA", and attribute value and credibility to it. Often it is an irrelevant, capricious, or arbitrary thought, but because we thought it, we manufacture a story to justify it. When we hiccup, we don't interpret it as having any special meaning; it just popped up and we let it go, almost unnoticed. But a thought, even an arbitrary one, serves the purpose of not experiencing uncertainty and not knowing, so we'll take it without scrutinizing it. The examining of this capricious thought is important to make the distinction if it is worthwhile or irrelevant. At work, we are often asked to set a deadline of when to get a task finished. Often we blurt out, "Oh I'll have that for you by Wednesday." Then, you leave the situation and realize "what a constraint I put on myself by saying Wednesday" versus the following Monday. The person receiving the material probably would have been fine with Monday especially if you made your thinking visible. This quick "hiccup" of a thought dictated your reality for the near future, and your own thinking put you in this jam. Was that response based on data analyzing what the task involved, examining your other commitments and resources available, or clarifying any expectations with the person who asked you? No! This happens all the time to us. Time management experts say that most tasks take thirty percent longer than we plan. Many of these plans may actually have been just a "hiccup", rather than good critical thinking.

D. *Summary of thinking styles and strategies*

Both thinking strategies of traveling the well-worn path and "hiccup" thinking bring some resolution to the perceived tension we experience. They also bring unintended consequences that could be eliminated by examining our thinking process closer than taking the easiest and quickest thoughts that present themselves.

6. Ask if there are any questions, then have the group divide into pairs. Have them come up with examples from their own lives of:

◆ Thoughts traveling down the well-worn path and the consequences.
◆ "Hiccup" thinking and the consequences.

7. Bring the group back together and hear some of the examples they have come up with. Ask why they used those thinking strategies. Try to bring out any feelings of uncertainty or the unknown that may have existed.

8. Go back to your list of strategies that are necessary to free yourself from the constraint of your mental models. Any other tips they can add to this list?

9. Summarize what you have discussed and put up the following strategies to review on the board or on an overhead transparency.

◆ Mental models need to be unearthed and made visible.
◆ Communicate your assumptions and inference to others.
◆ Take time to really think, reflect, and kick ideas around.
◆ Share your thinking with others.
◆ Be open with other viewpoints.
◆ Challenge and scrutinize your own and other's assumptions.

UNDERSTANDING THE LADDER OF INFERENCE

"People only see what they are prepared to see."

—*Ralph Waldo Emerson*

GOALS

- ◆ To slow down and become more aware of your thinking and reasoning process.
- ◆ To make your thinking and reasoning more visible to others when you are communicating.
- ◆ To learn the ladder of inference as a thinking and communication tool.
- ◆ To better inquire into othersí thinking and reasoning.

TIME FRAME

Two hours

MATERIALS NEEDED

White board, flip chart, or blackboard, individual notebook, copies and overhead transparency of the ladder of inference.

PROCESS

1. Introduction: "As a follow-up to the session on mental models, today we will be learning about a thinking and communication tool called the Ladder of Inference, created by Chris Argyris (1993) and popularized in the *Fifth Discipline Fieldbook* (Senge, et. al., 1994). This tool is very helpful in unearthing mental models and making your inferences and thinking processes visible." The model we are presenting has been adapted from the Argyris model of seven ladder rungs to one that only includes five rungs. See Figure 13.

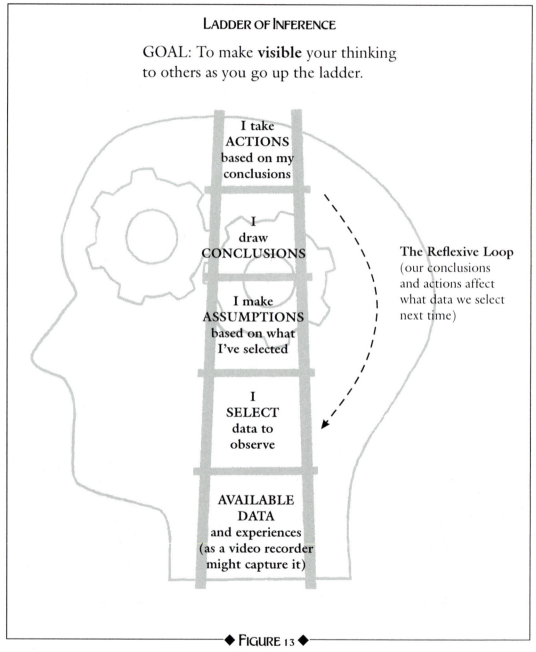

LADDER OF INFERENCE

GOAL: To make **visible** your thinking
to others as you go up the ladder.

I take
ACTIONS
based on my
conclusions

I
draw
CONCLUSIONS

I make
ASSUMPTIONS
based on what
I've selected

I
SELECT
data to
observe

AVAILABLE
DATA
and experiences
(as a video recorder
might capture it)

The Reflexive Loop
(our conclusions
and actions affect
what data we select
next time)

◆ **FIGURE 13** ◆

Ladder of Inference

2. *Exercise:* This exercise is called two "Truths and a Lie." Have your sponsor within the corporation or organization and either yourself or another person in the organization, select two truths and a lie about yourself. This is a good way for people to learn interesting tid bits about their leaders. The truths should be true things that people don't know, while the lie is something that also is plausible, but not true. Examples may be events, hobbies, or experiences such as, you played the lead in a college play, have run a marathon, rode a bicycle through Greece and Italy, collect stamps, or appeared on the Love Boat TV show. Tell the group the three things and ask them to select the one that is the lie. They should write down their answer and any of the reasons why they selected the one as a lie. You will come back to this exercise later in the session.

3. *Lecturette:* Use this information for your presentation to explain the ladder. The Ladder of Inference is a tool for clarifying our mental models. Each of us quickly add meaning to conversations and jumps to conclusions as a way of life. In fact, in our society and culture, we are rewarded for surmising a situation quickly and developing an action strategy.

   This pursuit of the quick assessment and action plan leads to taking short cuts in thinking. The mind takes the path of least resistance, and it wants to be able to say, **"Been there, done that, know that."** When we take short cuts, it becomes easy to abstract, generalize, and distort the data. Without really knowing it, we may alter or omit the data to fit our preconceived thoughts. We become invested in our opinions and these opinions then become filters for how we view other new data in our life. The ladder is a powerful communication tool, which can help change the way we think and interact with others.

4. **A case example:** We will use this example to highlight the rungs of the ladder. First, tell this story and then show one rung of the ladder at a time on the transparency, starting at the bottom—as you walk the group through the explanation. Have the story on a transparency or handout so participants can continually refer to it.

   Steve, Mary, and Robert all work for Arrow Systems Engineering, a technology engineering firm of 400 people. They receive the following notice on their CCMail that went to all employees.

   To: All Employees
   From: Management
   Re: All Hands Meeting
   At 3:00 PM tomorrow there will be an important meeting at Carver Auditorium, we want to make sure that everyone is there to hear the announcements.

   Mary has been with the corporation for five years, and she is looking for an advancement. She has heard that the company is going to move from a functional organization to cross-functional process teams and would like to be a team leader. She reads the notice and thinks that I have to be there to show my enthusiasm for the change and demonstrate that I can be an individual team leader.

   Robert has been with the corporation for fourteen years and is wondering if he should take an early retirement package, as he thinks the company is going to be sold and moved. He doesn't want to move his family, and he is angry about the situation. He reads the notice and thinks this is it; the announcement of the sale. I better be there and make sure they are gong to take care of me and my family.

Steve has been with the corporation for eight months and has been working in an office by himself and wants more contact and involvement with others. He would like to be on a team and exercise his organizational and people skills more. He reads the notice and thinks that I have to be there to hear what's going on and try to get on a team.

The five rungs are presented below with an explanation for each rung.

Available Data: These are the "facts" or information presented as you would see from a video without any interpretation. We know from the previous session on mental models that even with the same data people will see it differently depending on their own autobiography. If someone runs into the training room screaming about his or her boss, each person would recount it slightly different, depending on their viewpoint. We would get different descriptions of the person, what they were wearing, and why they were upset.

What are the mental models that Mary, Robert and Steve brought into the reading of the notice and with them into the meeting? Ask the group to think of the most overt mental models or mind set that color the available data for each of the three workers. Have people play the roles of Mary, Robert and Steve and listen to their responses about what they are thinking.

Mary—Company is changing and here's an opportunity to show them I am a good individual performer.

Robert—We are going to get sold and moved and they owe me.

Steve—I am bored with what I am doing, and I need to show that I can be a good team player.

At the Meeting

At 3:00 P.M. all of the leadership council were on the stage, except for Joe Stevenson, the CEO. In the back of the stage, there was a table with a large cake on it. Bill Moore, the second in command took the mike and said that Joe Stevenson was out of town on business and that he would preside over the meeting. Bill introduced the members of the steering team again to the employees, and he had each of them stand up and say what they have been working on currently. When this was finished, Bill shared some new business prospects and read the mission statement for Arrow Systems and encouraged all to live by it. He then called up Jennifer Eslinger, who was the team leader for a group of engineers who had just developed some new hardware for combined FAX, printer, scanning, and copy machines, called the "MDA" project for multi-dimensional applications. She explained how the team completed the project in less time than planned, and how both Domingus Enterprises and Brother were very interested in the technology. Mary called up the team and introduced them and then had the audience come up and get some cake to celebrate Arrow's success. Bill quickly grabbed the mike before people left their seats and reiterated how proud he and the leadership team were of everyone. He said, "After eating your cake go home early and celebrate our success with your family."

I Select Data to Observe: At this rung each one of us select something from all the available data. Problems occur when we select something, but do not let others know what it is that we have selected before we start reading things into it. In the example above, Mary, Robert, and Steve each anticipated the same event happening, yet selected different aspects of the presentation to focus on and subsequently make different assumptions. Listen to what the role players selected before moving on.

Mary: She selected that the team leader was a woman while the team was mostly males. She also noticed that no mention was made to the move to cross-functional process teams.

Robert: He noticed that the CEO was missing and that Bill Moore was very active in his absence.

Steve: He was aware that the team was made up of employees with more than five years in the company and Jennifer and the team seemed to be having fun.

I Make Assumptions Based on What I've Selected: This is the rung where people begin to manufacture, concoct, or construct their view of what is going on. This is the *theory making* stage, yet we don't admit that or communicate it in that fashion. Our theories sound more like facts. If we are confident in our theory, it takes a brave person to challenge us. Mary, Robert, and Steve are now on separate ladders as they diverged when each selected some different data from the meeting. Reality is completely different for them now. Most of us quickly make assumptions or interpretations, but usually don't share what facts or specific data that we are focusing on when we make our assumptions. What assumptions did the role players make?

Mary: She assumed that they liked women team-leaders, because Jennifer was also a woman and seemed to do a good job with the mix of male and female members. She assumed that they did not mention the cross-functional process teams because they wanted to let the success of the teams to sink in with the "MDA" project, and later roll-out the new initiative.

Robert: He assumed Joe Stevenson, the CEO, was out negotiating the sale of the company and that was why he was gone. He also figured that the success of the "MDA" project made them more attractive. Bill Moore was so excited, Robert figured, because either he or Joe Stevenson had to leave, and that Bill was probably the one who will go with the new company.

Steve: He assumed these fun team positions were for the people who had more seniority than he had, and his chances of getting on a team were very slim.

I Draw Conclusion: At this rung, people draw what seems to be logical conclusions based on the assumptions and the limited data they examined. These conclusions are made hastily, but they resolve the tension-resolution cycle. As mentioned earlier, the decision may be erroneous or the assumptions distorted, but the person feels better. There is a sense of certainty, security, and possibly efficiency to this conclusion process. Hiccup thinking and traveling the well-worn path thinking are very likely here. When doubt creeps up, "thinking" uses the same data, which could be skewed or limited to assure us it's *right*.

Another problem may occur at this rung, even when all the data and assumptions lead to a useful and constructive conclusion (Notice we didn't say right or wrong decision.). The problem is that no one knows how you have arrived at your decision. You are *alone* on your rung, without anyone supporting you, therefore to stay with the metaphor, you are likely to fall flat on your face. A great decision without any support, buy in, or shared conviction is a very shaky decision. When you don't get other viewpoints on your conclusions, there is a good chance that this is an old "been there, done that, know that decision", lacking in freshness and new, creative thinking.

Mary, Robert, and Steve all went to the same meeting and heard the same words, yet all heard different words and took away different meanings. Each is at the top of a different ladder. What conclusions have each role player made?

Mary: The conclusion that she drew for herself is that she has a good chance to be a team-leader and that *when*, not if, the cross-functional process teams initiative is announced, she will do all she can to get one of these positions.

Robert: He is convinced, now more than ever, that Arrow Systems is on the way to being sold and moved. His conclusion is that the writing is on the wall, even though it looks like his writing. Taking his early retirement now is the conclusion he drew from the all-hands meeting.

Steve: The conclusion he drew is that he is stuck in his boring position, and he doesn't know how much longer he will be able to stand it. They want more senior people than him for these team positions. He decides that his search for a new job is on.

I Take Action Based On My Conclusions: At this rung, people take or plan actions based on their conclusions. What we spoke about at the conclusion rung applies here. The action can resolve the tension that has been building up, even if it's just a decision to do something at a later date. The action *feels* like it's the next likely step in the logical-thinking process. We have already demonstrated how the foundation for the conclusion and action may be rushed, not validated with others, and based on sketchy and distorted data. This can lead to a conclusion and action founded on top of "quicksand." What actions would each role player take?

Mary: As result of her conclusions, she decided to go up to Jennifer after the meeting to set up an appointment with her to talk about getting a role as a team leader. She also decided to talk with Bill Moore to let him know her interests and to talk with her supervisor about her career planning. Mary left the meeting feeling very invigorated and hopeful.

Robert: As a result of his conclusions about this meeting, Robert scheduled an appointment with the HR department to talk about his early-retirement package. That night he talked over his future plans with his wife and started to look at a file he had on fishing vacations. Robert left the meeting feeling discouraged about Arrow's future and relieved that he was getting out before it was too late.

Steve: As a result of his conclusion, he decides to update his resume and pass the word that he is looking for new work. He plans to get together with friends for some drinks. He is excited that one friend is a lawyer and reminds himself to talk to this friend about a possible age-discrimination case. Steve leaves the meeting angry and let down by Arrow.

The Reflexive Loop: Once at the top of the ladder new data is looked at with old eyes and people quickly ladder jump. In conversation, many times it's a race to see who gets up to the top as quickly as possible. The old conclusions and actions influence what new data gets selected each time. These are the mental models that Mary, Robert, and Steve erroneously inferred when reading the notice.

Summary: Three different mental models view the same event and come away with three unique inferences and interpretations of what it all means. The ladder helps slow down this process and helps people get confirmation and more stability as they climb higher, when their thinking is made visible to others.

Elliot Cohen (1991) in *Caution: Faulty Thinking can be Harmful to Your Happiness*, states "Whether we realize it or not, you make hundreds of inferences every day. When too much of this logic is bad, your life can suffer. . . . Moreover bad logic has a cumulative effect. Faulty thinking today leads to decisions, actions, beliefs, emotions, and attitudes that can send you into a tailspin tomorrow, which can then affect you the next day, and so in. After many years of thinking illogically you can well imagine the damage that is done to your happiness" (p.1).

    Our insurance plan for this faulty thinking then is to share your thinking with others and get some fresh eyes and ears on your thinking, before you race up the ladder.

5. Ask the group how accurate of a portrayal is this case study? Can they think of a time that they jumped quickly to the top rung? What was the reaction of others when they did this? Create a group discussion getting numerous people to comment on the questions.

6. In groups of three, talk about the two truths and a lie exercise from above. Use the ladder to walk each other up to the conclusion rung. One person says which statement was the lie and describes what data he/she used and selected. Then discuss the assumptions that were made and how each came to this conclusion. In the small group have them point out the differing data each person based their decisions on.

7. In the big group, hear what they came up with for the lies. Use the ladder to highlight their thinking for the answers. Have the people, who first stated the truths and lie to state which one is the lie. Ask the group to consider how often we make quick assumptions that are inaccurate and that we are unaware of?

8. Summarize the session by going over the "do's" and "don'ts" using an overhead transparency.

Do's

- Get as many others as possible to "hold your ladder" to develop shared meaning of the information you are exploring.
- Try to open space for multiple points of view.
- Invite others to challenge and clarify your thinking.
- Listen and inquire more than you talk or advocate.
- Practice walking up the ladder as much as you can.
- Ask for feedback about how well you're doing by utilizing this tool.

Don'ts

- Don't use the ladder as a weapon. For example, "see how much data I have for this, therefore, my conclusions are correct."
- Don't throw "hand grenades" (your opinions or beliefs) from the top of your ladder to another at the top of their ladder with the intention of knocking them off their ladder.
- Don't expect this to be easy, or to be a quick fix.
- Don't get defensive when someone inquires into what data, etc., you are examining.
- Don't advocate your view without inquiring into the meaning and assumptions of others' views.

9. In preparation for the next session, have the participants bring in situations where there was a communication breakdown or conflict to use as a role-play by using the ladder of inference.

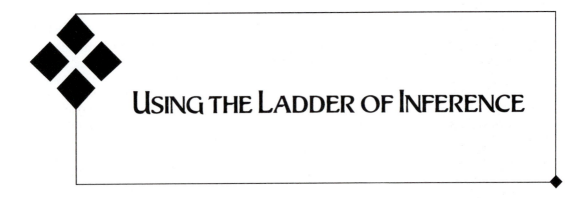

USING THE LADDER OF INFERENCE

"Unless you see something differently, you'll always see it the same."
—*Gregg Butterfield*

GOALS

- ◆ To become aware of your particular inference—style and preferences.
- ◆ To practice using the ladder of inference as a thinking and communication tool with others.
- ◆ To better understand others' thinking and reasoning by using the ladder of inference.

TIME FRAME

Two hours

MATERIALS NEEDED

White board, flip chart, or blackboard, individual notebook, copies, and overhead transparencies of the ladder of inference, ladder of inference applications (see figure 14), and inference styles.

PROCESS

1. As a follow-up to the last session on Understanding the Ladder of Inference, in groups of three, have participants talk about times that they found themselves and others jumping up the ladder quickly and how they dealt with it? Did they do anything about it and if so what effect did it have? If they didn't do anything about it, how did rung jumping affect the conversation?

2. *Lecturette:* Use this material as an introduction to learning about inference styles.

   As you become more familiar with walking yourself and others up and down the Ladder of Inference, you will notice patterns in your thinking. People tend to draw similar inferences or interpretations from the data they select.

The journey up the ladder occurs automatically, a few rungs at a time with specific and discrete messages. These messages possess the power to entangle us in emotional fears, distort things, and create blinders to other possible interpretations of certain data. Our mental models and daily conversations are filled with these bomb shells which amazingly are invisible to us; they are beyond our awareness. To gain more influence over our thinking, moods and interactions with others, we must identify our main inference style. Equally important, is discovering how the meanings and assumptions we add sometimes distort observable data. Only then, can we replace the re-created meanings and assumptions with clear, constructive, positive alternatives. This will help build shared meaning with others, as not only will our thinking become more visible, but it will include fewer distortions. As a result, group problem-solving will be faster, effectively enhanced, and more accurate. Consequently, we will be able to quickly convey our point and better understand others.

Cognitive psychology has established a solid research foundation about how our cognitive process affects our emotions, and therefore, our interactions. No matter how irrational our thoughts may be, these distorted and automatic thoughts are almost always accepted. They may manifest in incomplete sentences, several key words, a visual image, or a flash. As mentioned before, we complicate matters, when we use this initial thought as a reference point to direct subsequent thoughts. Future thoughts and actions are influenced by this automatic distorted thinking.

When you are under stress at work or at home, feeling time pressure and anxieties, it is easier to rely on your inference-style which then allows distortions to flourish. These feelings are automatic responses to stimuli. With practice, you can create a gap between the stimulus and response and catch yourself from rung-skipping. This will help you straighten out your distorted thinking patterns and when you go up the ladder others will support your inferences.

3. Listed below are typical faulty thinking patterns designed to help sharpen your awareness of the kind of inferences you draw upon. They have been adapted from Robert K. Copper's (1988) *Health and Fitness Excellence* and Elliot D. Cohen's (1991) *Caution: Faulty Thinking Can be Harmful to Your Health*. Hand out the copy of inference-styles, table 10, and have participants read through them and select the *top five* that they most often use.

4. In a group of three, share your top five inference patterns with some specific examples. Which one do you utilize the most?

5. Still in small groups, have participants figure out which rung you skip the most and describe how you do that.

6. *Lecturette:* Continue to use this information for educating about inference-styles.

Your inference-style is closely related to your explanatory-style, the way we describe experiences to ourselves and others. According to psychologist Martin E.P. Seligman (1993), if you explain bad things that happen to you in terms that are: internal ("It's all my fault"), stable ("it's going to last forever"), and global ("It's going to spoil everything I do"), you increase your risk for depression, poor performance, and illness. People who explain things as *temporary* set-backs versus permanent, *specific* problems versus global, and *correctly assess responsibility* to themselves or the situation are more optimistic, healthy, and productive.

Your inference-style is contagious, the habit spreads. When you consistently respond to events in a pessimistic manner, Seligman (1993) states that negative style can actually **increase** your feelings of helplessness and spread to other areas of your life. The best advice? It comes down to building new habits of mind.

◆ TABLE 10 ◆

Inference Styles

Each of the following inferences quickly move you up the ladder by distorting, omitting, and altering the data and by falling in assumption ruts when you make conclusions. They happen automatically, and, therefore they are invisible to you or to anyone else.

1. **Half truths:** You state some parts of the situation and leave out other parts, so there is a false understanding of the actual case. Your assumptions and conclusions are stacked in your favor.

2. **Magnification (catastrophizing) and minimization.** You exaggerate risks or percentages, anticipate disaster; you overplay your mistakes or the importance of someone else's achievements; or you erroneously shrink your positive attributes or another person's imperfections until they appear insignificant.

3. **Overgeneralization.** You make a sweeping assumption based on only a shred of evidence, a single negative event becomes a never-ending pattern of defeat. Use of strong emotional words like "always, never, every time, everyone, totally" are used to distort the frequency of events and data.

4. **Oversimplifying:** You make complex situations out to be simpler than they really are. Ignoring the complexity, other's involvement, and how the decision will be made over time can lead to a weak conclusion. Words like, "all that is necessary," " in a nut shell," or "the only thing" are signals you are oversimplifying.

5. **Mind reading:** Without checking to find out the truth, you assume that you know precisely what and why other people are thinking, feeling, and acting the way they do. You quickly leap to negative interpretations of statements and situations even though you usually lack the facts to support your conclusion.

6. **Fortune telling:** Here you jump to conclusions by anticipating a future event will turn out badly, and you act as if this is a predetermined fact, without ever questioning or analyzing the validity.

7. **Ignoring the past:** When you predict something you are going to do without ever considering if this has ever been accomplished or happened in the past. The past yields valuable information for future capabilities and decision making.

8. **Insisting on the past:** While ignoring the past can result in poor conclusions about the future, you can also misuse information about the past and not give the new endeavor any hope for occurring. Just because something has happened in the past does not mean that it *MUST* continue in the future. By insisting that the future must be like the past new opportunities can be lost.

9. **Being right:** You *need* to always prove that your statements and actions are correct. You are quick to launch into defensive rationalizations whenever your "rightness" appears questionable, and you distort data and make assumptions just to defend your ego.

10. **Change illusion:** Your happiness and success depend on other people changing their bad habits and "bad" comes from your perspective of reality. You mistakenly believe that they will make these changes if you keep pressuring them enough and then you finally will have more happiness. Their changing is *your* responsibility.

(continued)

◆ TABLE 10 ◆

Inference Styles *continued*
---

11. **Control illusion:** You either feel externally controlled; therefore, you are always victimized by other people and circumstances. You blame them for your conclusions and actions. Or, you may feel internally controlled, which leaves you always believing that you are the cause or blame for everyone else's unhappiness.

12. **Disqualifying the positive.** You reject positive experiences on the grounds that they somehow "don't count" when compared with the endless list of problems or negatives experiences in your life.

13. **Either or thinking.** There is no middle ground, things are either good or they are bad. Either you perform perfectly or you are a total failure. Many possible choices are eliminated with this kind of thinking.

14. **Emotional reasoning:** You automatically assume that your self-evaluations are accurate and therefore, reflect reality. If you feel incompetent and unattractive, then you must *be* incompetent and unattractive.

15. **Fallacy of the Whole:** This occurs when you assume that because a part of something is a certain way, then, the whole thing must be that same way. There may be some similarity, but to think that it *must* be totally so is a mistake.

16. **Fallacy of the Part:** This is the opposite of the above fallacy. It is to suppose that what's true for the whole *must* be true for ech and every part.

17. **Fairness illusion:** You think you know exactly what is fair in all situations, but you feel victimized when other people often don't agree with you. You make assumptions based on your own set of fairness or principles.

18. **Labeling and mislabeling:** This is an extreme version of over generalization. When things don't go right or you become irritated with others, you emotionally assign a label to: yourself ("I'm a loser"; "I'm an idiot"), another person ("He's a quitter."; "She's a cheater."), or situations. These are based on select events, yet inferred on your or others' whole personhood.

19. **Ultimate reward illusion:** You talk and act as if monumental, daily sacrifices and self-denial are what will ultimately bring you great rewards. You feel resentful when others don't notice what you are doing or the rewards don't seem to come to you.

20. **Vague terms:** This is when you use terms that don't have clear meanings. Terms have many different meanings, so it's difficult to follow you up the ladder. For example, "my boss is not normal." Or "she's in her own little world."

21. **Misuse of authority:** This occurs when you think that a person is an authority in one area and infer that they are an authority in a different area.

22. **Jumping on the Bandwagon:** When you decide because others are doing something, that it's permissible for you to do the same. As mentioned in the mental model section, many people do things without much thinking, so it is a mistake to do something just because others are doing it.

Begin to catch yourself jumping up the ladder, be aware of the meaning and assumptions you add to a situation. Look at the way you distort or infer meaning to yourself and others, and begin to change your assumptions to ones which are more positive, helpful, and constructive. It comes down to being aware of your thinking and creating new habits for your mind.

7. **Clarifying intent:** In getting started, to use the ladder, it is very important to clarify what your *intent* or purpose is in the communication. Think with the end in mind. What is it that you are trying to accomplish?

    For example, you may begin the conversation by saying: "I'd like to be able to understand your point-of-view more, can you help me?" "I am hoping that we can work out this situation between us." "My intent here is that we can work out this situation between us." "My intent here is that we all work as one team." "What I'd like to accomplish here is that we all cooperate."

    Use the learning values of curiosity, humility, empathy, self-esteem, and trust. This will help you stay on the lower rungs of the ladder. It is nearly impossible to be certain of your opinion and assumptions while you are, at the same time, being humble and curious with others.

8. **Ladder Sentence stubs:** Put figure 14 on the overhead or pass it out. Go through the rungs and the sentence stubs for each one. These are examples of what the speaker can say to help make their thinking visible, and how the listener can help illuminate the thinking of the speaker.

9. **Practice Session:** Ask the group for examples of communication problems they have had recently. Get enough information so that you can develop a scenario for them to role play. Another suggestion is to have a scenario already developed, like the one in the previous session, to hand out to the group to role-play. Divide the group into smaller teams of three people, for the roles of speaker, listener, and observer. The speaker will start with the scenario, while the listener will try to get them down on the ladder to reveal what data and assumptions they are generating. Do this for ten minutes and have the observer comment on: what helped in getting the speaker down the ladder? What could they do to improve getting the data and assumptions and clarified? Then switch roles until all roles have been experienced.

10. In the bigger group, inquire what was helpful in using the ladder of inference. Encourage the group to use this learning when speaking and listening. The following expressions can be a short cut in unearthing mental models and assumptions back at work, when people are familiar with the ladder:

    "You seem to be up at the top of the ladder."
    "Can you walk me down the ladder and tell me the assumptions you are making?"
    "Let me make my thinking visible to you."
    "Here's the assumptions or interpretations I am making."

We have found it useful to have a poster made of the ladder, so it can be visible in the meeting rooms when the teams get back together at their work site. Seeing it over and over when they are in discussion helps assimilate and utilize the learning. The team facilitator can be encouraged to use and point to the rungs during their meetings when certain ideas need to be clarified.

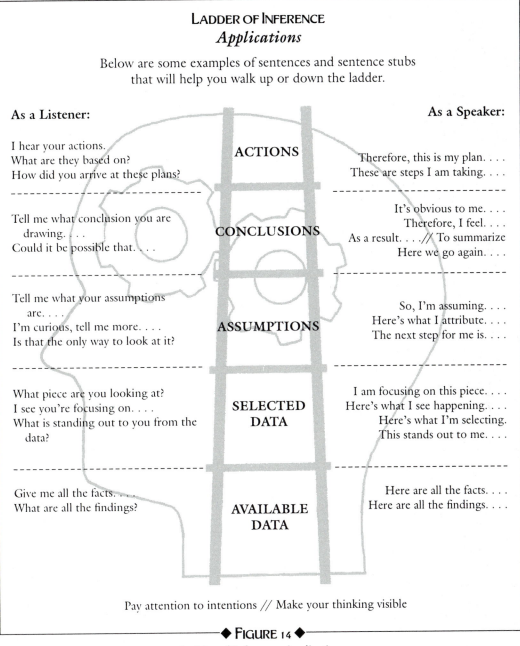

LADDER OF INFERENCE
Applications

Below are some examples of sentences and sentence stubs
that will help you walk up or down the ladder.

As a Listener:

I hear your actions.
What are they based on?
How did you arrive at these plans?

Tell me what conclusion you are
    drawing. . . .
Could it be possible that. . . .

Tell me what your assumptions
    are. . . .
I'm curious, tell me more. . . .
Is that the only way to look at it?

What piece are you looking at?
I see you're focusing on. . . .
What is standing out to you from the
    data?

Give me all the facts. . . .
What are all the findings?

ACTIONS

CONCLUSIONS

ASSUMPTIONS

**SELECTED
DATA**

**AVAILABLE
DATA**

As a Speaker:

Therefore, this is my plan. . . .
These are steps I am taking. . . .

It's obvious to me. . . .
Therefore, I feel. . . .
As a result. . . .// To summarize
Here we go again. . . .

So, I'm assuming. . . .
Here's what I attribute. . . .
The next step for me is. . . .

I am focusing on this piece. . . .
Here's what I see happening. . . .
Here's what I'm selecting.
This stands out to me. . . .

Here are all the facts. . . .
Here are all the findings. . . .

Pay attention to intentions // Make your thinking visible

◆ **FIGURE 14** ◆

Ladder of Inference: Applications

BREAKTHROUGH THINKING

"No amount of sophistication is going to allay the fact that all your knowledge is about the past and all your decisions are about the future."

—*Ian E. Wilson*

GOALS

- ◆ To gain a perspective for the history of problem solving.
- ◆ To understand the seven principles of Breakthrough Thinking.
- ◆ To identify and apply Breakthrough Thinking in problem solving endeavors.

TIME FRAME

Two hours

MATERIALS NEEDED

White board, flip chart, or blackboard, individual notebook, copies and overhead transparencies of "Obstacles to Solution Finding", and the "Seven Principles of Breakthrough Thinking."

PROCESS

1. This unit presents thinking principles for problem solving that can be used by teams or groups when approaching unique situations, dilemmas, or problems. In helping teams to think better, this unit is most beneficial when used in conjunction with the other "Thinking about Thinking" units. These principles help participants break-out of old mental models and inference styles described earlier. Breakthrough Thinking provides seven principles to facilitate better problem solving, and thus better solutions than traditional problem solving methods. It provides the "how" for getting out of thinking ruts, like "Well-worn path thinking" and "Hiccup thinking."

230

2. A lecturrette follows that explains the principles along with questions to help facilitate applying these principles to problem-solving activities. The material is drawn from the work of Drs. Gerald Nadler and Shozo Hibino, presented in their texts (1990) *Breakthrough thinking: Why we must change the way we solve problems, and the seven principles to achieve this,* and *Creative solution finding: The triumph of full-spectrum creativity over conventional thinking* (Nadler, Hibino, & Farrell, 1995). You may want to examine each of these texts for further information on this topic.

3. **Lecturrette:** Use this information as an introduction to Breakthrough Thinking. The process of Breakthrough Thinking attempts to change our automatic responses for finding solutions, from identifying what is wrong, to starting with finding the biggest purpose to achieve and describing the solutions after-next for accomplishing it. This involves rethinking our world in an entirely new way. As stated by Nadler and Hibino (1990):

    > *"A breakthrough idea seldom just occurs as a 'bolt out of the blue.' Instead, it occurs most often through* preparation of the mind. *Breakthrough think-ing can be characterized as a way of preparing the mind to increase signifi-cantly the likelihood of obtaining a quality concept or 'light bulb' idea, of being be able to get that idea implemented, and of doing so in less time, at less cost. It is a way of removing barriers to real progress"* (p.59).

4. **Types of Problem Solving**
    There have been many types of problem solving approaches throughout the years. Four main approaches have been identified (Nadler, Hibino, & Farrell, 1995):

    ◆   Do nothing approach—This is characterized by the belief that human beings can not or should not control events, because fate is capricious or God will solve it.

    ◆   Chance approach—This is characterized by two methods, passively relying on insight and stumbling on the right answer, or constantly expecting the unexpected that leads to an open-ended and flexible approach to problem solving.

    ◆   Affective approach—This is characterized by using emotions, feelings, intuitions, and hunches to solve problems. People use whatever comes spontaneously to mind, rather than follow a pre-established, structured approach.

    ◆   Research approach—This is characterized by single-factor reasoning, objectively, structured decision making, following systematic logical processes.

5. **History of Problem Solving**
    The research approach has been around for over 400 years as the predominant problem solving approach. It arose as a response to the other methods described above in an attempt to be more scientific, and to have solutions that can be generalizable, predictable, and repeatable. The research approach replaced theological dogma that ignored natural phenomena and which focused on a faith-based view of the spiritual and supernatural. Thinkers such as Rene Descartes, Francis Bacon, and Isaac Newton building on the ideas of Copernicus, Galileo, and other Renaissance thinkers, developed generalizations and theories about their world. These ideas led to the Scientific Revolution and eventually to the Industrial Revolution. The success of the research approach over the years has led to it's acceptance and application to most problems (Nadler & Hibino, 1990).

The focus of the research approach is to plan, design, improve and solve problems. Today, it is often presented as a seven-step problem-solving approach: 1) Identify the problem, 2) Define the problem clearly, 3) Analyze the problem, 4) Brainstorm possible solutions, 5) Select a solution, 6) Develop an action plan, and 7) Reevaluate, refine, and improve on the solution and plan. This approach has been successful in the physical sciences and research settings because of certain basic themes that have been accepted as conventional thinking to problem solving. These themes are elaborated on by Nadler and Hibino (1990), they include:

◆ **Positivism**—the conviction that only a scientific and rational approach can solve all problems. Only things that can proved in a cause and effect manner, rather than a faith-based approach are actually veritable.

◆ **Reductionism**—if you can break the problem down to its smallest component and solve that, the larger problem will dissipate. Quantitative, hard-data are sought and gathered, while subjective data is relegated to be interesting but not relevant. People become experts about the problem rather than an expert about the solution.

◆ **Expertise**—as an outgrowth of the specialization focus in the United States, we attribute unquestioned support of expert's solutions—because of their wealth of data, information, knowledge, and years of learning. The social sciences have demonstrated that the observer influences the observed and the observer's subjective state influences what is seen. Experts contend that they are not "guessing", but that they are only responding to the facts, just like a machine would. This reliance on expertise leads to fixed solutions, limited perspectives, and minimal alternatives.

◆ **Determinism**—the research approach promotes the perspective that once a single solution is found, through scientific research it will solve the problem and continue to solve the problem into eternity. Just keep doing the same thing that once worked. This determinism blinds people to subtle changes in the problem and to unintended consequences of the solution.

Limited and ineffective thinking process, such as those just described, has also created many of our insoluble problems. This method is an example of a mental model passed down for over 400 years as the only way to solve problems today. Once very successful, it is now outdated to deal with the complexity of our problems. Albert Einstein once said "No problem can be solved within the same consciousness that created it."

6. Introduce Table 11 entitled "Obstacles to Solution Finding with Traditional or Conventional Thinking."

7. Ask the group to think of and write down a problem that was unsolvable and persistent for them. Now, have them go through the obstacles, and identify as many that apply to their problem. In groups of three have them share what approaches they used that were limiting or ineffective for them using conventional thinking. Have representatives from each group share what was *similar* in their responses, and then what was different or *unique* in their responses.

8. Table 12 includes the seven principles of Breakthrough Thinking, also called "Full-Spectrum Thinking." These are the new mental models, assumptions, or mind-sets to hold and consider when solving problems in an effort to get better solutions. Share this information with participants.

◆ TABLE 11 ◆

Obstacles to Solution Finding with Traditional or Conventional Thinking

- ◆ Not realizing the assumptions and approach to the problem are ineffective, outdated, and preventing a "fresh approach."
- ◆ Looking for similarity in how a past problem was solved.
- ◆ The subdivision of the problem into smaller parts minimizes the possibility of finding broader and more invisible yet inclusive solutions.
- ◆ Excessive analysis prevents solution finding.
- ◆ There is a loss of synergy by dividing the problem into distinct elements.
- ◆ There are blinders to the interdependence and interrelatednes of problems by looking at discrete elements.
- ◆ Confrontation is enhanced when the mutual understanding between problem elements are lost.
- ◆ Incomplete or limited solutions are accepted too quickly because the solution is familiar and comfortable, while the problem is painful and unfamiliar.
- ◆ Fear and risk are enhanced by only seeing parts of the problem.

◆ TABLE 12 ◆

Seven Principles of Breakthrough Training

1. *Uniqueness:*
    - ◆ Assume that the problem you are confronting is different and unique from any other past problem.
    - ◆ First approach the problem by looking at differences rather than copy old solutions.
    - ◆ No two situations are alike, a solution in one area doesn't automatically work in another.
    - ◆ Each problem is embedded in a unique context. The mind wants to quickly link the problem to past problems, and this "association bias" limits looking at the uniqueness of the situation.
    - ◆ Only if the purpose within the unique context shows it is useful, should you use an old solution. You can "reinvent the wheel" *only* after finding out that a wheel is what you really need.

2. *Purpose:*
    - ◆ Always and continually ask, "What is the purpose of solving this problem?" Then ask, "What is purpose of that purpose?"
    - ◆ Expand as far as possible the purpose of the purposes and then select which purpose is the one of your focus.
    - ◆ Explore and expand the purpose of working on the right problem. Don't fix what shouldn't even exist. You don't want to efficiently do what you shouldn't do at all.
    - ◆ Edward Deming (1986) said "It is not enough to just do your best or work hard, you must know what to work on."
    - ◆ Focusing on the purpose lets the uniqueness stand out and strips away nonessential aspects of the problem.

(continued)

──────────────◆ TABLE 12 ◆──────────────

Seven Principles of Breakthrough Training *continued*

3. *Solution after Next (SAN):*
   ◆ Make changes today based on what might be the solution of the future.
   ◆ Design an "ideal system" that incorporates changes that will be necessary in the future, possibly two-to-three years from now, and work backwards from that solution.
   ◆ Stimulate questions to lead to alternative ideal solutions. What ought to exist instead of what exists? And what would be perfect or ideal?
   ◆ A target solution in the future gives direction to short-term solutions, and injects them with larger purposes.

4. *Systems:*
   ◆ Systems Principle states that nothing exists by itself. Successful problem solving hinges on consideration of interrelated elements and dimensions.
   ◆ Every solution or system is part of a larger system, and solving one problem inevitably leads to unintended consequences in another area.
   ◆ Understanding the complexity and interdependencies in advance lets you develop a complete action plan to account for all these elements.
   ◆ Purposes, inputs, outputs, sequence, human resources, environmental setting, equipment and facilities, and instructional aids are the elements in the system which are planned for over six dimensions.

5. *Limited Information Collection:*
   ◆ Determine what purpose will be achieved by gathering data before collecting and analyzing it.
   ◆ Study the solution and not the problem. Excessive data-gathering may create an expert in the problem area, while limiting creative solutions. As an example in Chicago, the Postal Service spent $23 million to study how late the mail was. They became experts about the problem, but could that money have been better spent on finding solutions?
   ◆ Collect only what is necessary, avoid information collection as an end in itself, and lessen unneeded documentation.

6. *People Design:*
   ◆ Give everyone who will be affected by the solution an opportunity to take part in its development.
   ◆ People are willing to explore purposes and solutions-after-next, rather than just gather data about what's wrong with the current system.
   ◆ Those who carry out the solution should be involved at all levels.
   ◆ The proposed solution should include only the critical details to not limit creativity.

7. *Betterment Timeline:*
   ◆ As you design today's solution, schedule future changes and improvements necessary to its continuing success.
   ◆ To preserve the integrity and vitality of the solution, build in time to monitor, evaluate and adjust the solution.
   ◆ The sequence of purpose-directed solutions and knowledge of the solution-after-next are the bridges for the betterment timeline.
   ◆ Encourage constant looking for new beginnings.

Below are some examples of the "Purpose Principle", and the "Solution After Next" Principle.

Case Example for Purpose Principle: Partial membership of two separate boards, which both oversee a non-profit health and home care organization, came together for a joint meeting. The organization recently called-off talks with the board of a local hospital about a potential future affiliation. The facilitator started the meeting by asking, "What do you think the purpose of this meeting should be? Let's all agree on this before we start" The participants stated:

a.   To develop an agenda for the next meeting of the joint boards.

b.   To understand the reasons why the meeting with the hospital was called off.

c.   To understand the differences between the two boards.

d.   To get some clarification about who, and how many representatives should go to the next meeting with the board of the hospital.

Although each of these agenda items are related, each item would lead the group down a different path; which would affect the solutions and the quality of the meeting. With each of the purposes of the meeting listed on the board, the facilitator asked, "Which of these purposes is best to start with?" The group agreed on number 2. The facilitator then asked, "What is the purpose of understanding the reason why the meeting with hospital was called off?" The answers to this question focused on having a shared understanding and "all being on the same page." This underlying purpose of the stated purpose then became a unifying focus of both groups to have as an overriding goal or vision and started the meeting off in a positive manner.

Case examples for Solution after Next principle: This principle is best explained with various examples of solutions after next.

a.   An information-technology provider needs to downsize its work force to match the decreasing number of customers. The steering team discussed their options of how to do this. They decided that in the future they would move to being a "process centered organization", and that cutting staff now would just be a "quick fix." Instead, they decided to use the resources to not only solve the current problem, but move to their solution after next . They documented their processes and reengineered them so that they were more efficient in their business and needed less people to do the same work.

b.   The government of a nearby town, ten-years ago, was able to project into the future when they redid their sidewalks. Every new sidewalk had a handicap ramp on it for people in wheel chairs to navigate easily. They saved thousands of dollars by doing the ramps when they did versus waiting until federal law mandated it.

c.   The same town government used the solution after next principle when the first highways were built in their town. They knew that there would be more people driving on the highways in the future. Consequently, they left extra land available so that they could easily go from two lane highways to three lane highways.

9.   Nadler, Hibino, and Farrell (1995) state the benefits of using Breakthrough or Full-Spectrum thinking as:

◆   "It emphasizes synthesis, not analysis;

◆   It focuses on solutions in the future, not on problems in the past;

◆ It takes the attitude of belief, not doubt;

◆ It asks initially: Are we doing the needed thing? rather than asking: Are we doing things efficiently?

◆ It generates a larger solution-space;

◆ It provides full-spectrum creativity;

◆ It emphasizes implementation;

◆ It offers all the participants a rich, multi-faceted role in developing and implementing solutions;

◆ It provides for continual change and improvement;

◆ It deals with positive methods of getting people involved" (p.12).

10. **Applied questions using Breakthrough Thinking**

The following questions can be asked after your structured experience as a means to focus the processing around the Breakthrough Thinking principles. The questions highlight the seven principles. Pick a few questions for each principle or use these questions as the theme for a series of learning activities, and apply one or two principles for each activity.

Uniqueness Principle:

◆ Was the problem approached in an unique fashion with fresh eyes?

◆ Were the unique aspects of how this problem is different from other problems discussed?

◆ What people, timing, and context make this unique from other problems?

◆ Were the assumptions about the problem made visible to others (i.e., using the ladder of inference)?

◆ Did participants try to clarify someone's assumptions about the problem before deciding on the actions?

◆ Was the association bias of linking previous information to this problem present?

Purposes Principle:

◆ Were the questions asked, "What is the purpose of solving this problem?" or "What are we trying to accomplish here?"

◆ Were all the possible purposes listed or clarified before selecting which one to work on?

◆ Were the purposes expanded on to the next level?

◆ Were the larger context of purposes discussed and understood by all?

Solution after Next Principle:

◆ Was the solution after next discussed as a way to design the ideal solution?

◆ Were questions asked about future considerations while solving this problem?

◆ Were only short-term solutions discussed without concern for changing environments and situations in the future?

◆ Did the team look for a second and third right answer before moving into implementation?

◆ After the problem was solved did the team talk about what would be a better solution for the future?

Systems Principle:

◆ Was the solution viewed in the context of the "big picture?"

♦ Were the reactions of other stakeholders considered in the problem solving (i.e., team members, other departments or teams, management, suppliers, customers, family members)?
♦ Were unintended consequences talked about before moving forward?
♦ Are there related problems that are attached to this problem?
♦ If this problem was "fixed" what could be other possible problems emerging?
♦ Was time, costs, resources, inputs, and controls considered in the problem solving?

Limited Information Collection Principle:
♦ Was time wasted trying to learn all there was to know about the problem?
♦ Was information gathered that wasn't useful or relevant to the situation? If so, give an example of such.
♦ Was time wasted looking to find a person to blame for the problem?
♦ Was the question asked, "What would be the purpose of gaining this information?"
♦ Were questions asked like "How can we make this work?" "What do we need to know to solve this?" "How will that information help us?"

People Design Principle:
♦ Were all the participants involved in defining the purposes, uniqueness, and solution after next of the problem?
♦ Were all ideas heard when the team was trying to solve the problem?
♦ Was there consensus from all on how to proceed, before doing so?
♦ Was there a good mix of cross-functional skills and learning styles in the group?
♦ Was there open communication and a method to inform all the pertinent stakeholders (i.e., other teams involved in the same activity)?
♦ What was the overall team IQ? Good teamwork leads to synergy where the team IQ is higher than any one individual IQ. An average IQ is 100 + or − 15, high average is 115 to 130, over 130 is genius, low average is 70–85, and retarded is below 70.
♦ Was a reward structure in place, and did individuals get recognized for their contributions?

Betterment Timeline Principle:
♦ Did the group question how and when this solution can be changed to incorporate the solution after next?
♦ Was it discussed to have plans and a schedule to fix it before it breaks?
♦ What were the lessons learned from this problem that can be applied to other solutions?
♦ Have the needed betterment plans been built into the strategic plan?

DEVELOPING A RELAPSE PREVENTION PROGRAM

"One pound of learning requires ten pounds of common sense to apply it."
—*Anonymous*

GOALS

- ◆ To explain the learning process and normalize lapses.
- ◆ To identify the areas where a relapse to an old learning may take place.
- ◆ To develop a plan to protect the new learning.
- ◆ To increase the support system to reinforce and implement the new learning.
- ◆ To practice the new skills in a safe environment in order to promote retention and transfer.

TIME FRAME

One two–three hour session, executed at the end of the training session.

MATERIALS NEEDED

White board, flip chart, or blackboard, individual notebooks, and overheads of the pertinent material below.

PROCESS

This session is appropriate to use in a traditional indoor training session or in a more experiential format where behavioral change is the focus.

1. Introduce the session as a way to develop a plan to prevent relapses to the previous learning. Go through the goals of the session as presented above. Explain the learning

process, how long it takes to learn new skills, and how reinforcement is necessary to assimilate and synthesize any new learning.

2. Explain to the group the change model, developed by Kurt Lewin (1951) that, since it was first introduced, has been widely used in organizational development programs to demonstrate the learning process. It has three stages:

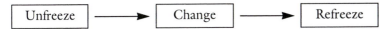

| Unfreeze | ⟶ | Change | ⟶ | Refreeze |

Unfreezing: This is the "unlearning process" that needs to take place before new learning can take hold. You have already been facilitating for this stage if you have been using the levels of processing to raise the awareness of participants' patterns, mental models, and behaviors. Also, you have been helping them identify whether or not these are typical ways of behaving. The old learning has to "melt down" or become less rigid to allow room for the new learning.

Changing: Disequilibrium occurs in experiential learning when experimenting with new actions, behaviors and thoughts. It can also be new information that is being presented in traditional training sessions. Lewin (1951) talks about the "restraining forces" that pull the individual to stay the same while simultaneously trying to increase the "driving forces" which are encouraging change and learning.

Refreezing: Newly acquired skills become habits, ingrained, and part of the individual's set of skills. The relapse-prevention program is primarily focusing on ways to reinforce the refreezing stage. This is the difference of knowing what to do and actually doing it.

3. Establish the conditions that are conducive to learning in your setting, and contrast these with the conditions people will encounter at home or the office. These are the driving and restraining forces. Ask the question, "What do we have here that is conducive to your learning that you don't have at the home or office?" Write these on the board. Some examples are:

  ◆ All sharing the same experience.
  ◆ Common language
  ◆ Risk taking is promoted
  ◆ Individuals are supportive of each other
  ◆ Novel and challenging experiences
  ◆ Open to new learning

  Help participants see the differences between the learning environment that they are in and the one that they are going back to. Some of the success factors present in the structured experience don't exist back at the office or home, and they are necessary to structure in order to prevent relapse.

4. Broad and Newstrom (1992) delineated a five-step relapse-prevention program, which we adapted and present below. They adapted their model from relapse-prevention programs that started with inpatient, chemical-dependency programs as a means to prepare patients for the rigors of applying their treatment skills once back home in their "using" environment. The five steps are:

- Accepting that lapses are normal and inevitable
- Identifying relapse signs
- Assessing coping skills
- Scenario-playing challenging situations
- Follow-up strategies

Each of these steps are discussed below for you to present to your group.

5. **Accepting that lapses are normal and inevitable.**

    a. Participants need to understand that within the process of learning that it is normal to fall back to old learning. This new learning is on the "edge" of the circle of comfort for them. Reviewing the concept of "edgework" can be helpful in accepting the "why" lapses happen. Ask the group, "Why is it so easy to fall back to the old ways?" If it is a big group, divide them into smaller groups of three, and then have them come up with as many reasons as they can in five minutes. Write "new learning" and "old learning" on the board, and then write the reasons they identify. You can draw from the following list of factors if they don't mention any:

    New learning:
    - Is unfamiliar and uncomfortable
    - There is uncertainty and unpredictability putting it to use
    - They may embarrass themselves trying it out
    - The skill level is undeveloped
    - They are unpracticed at it
    - It takes a lot of effort and feels painful
    - Have little support for it
    - They fear being wrong

    Old learning:
    - Is comfortable and known
    - Is predictable
    - They have been doing it the same way for many years
    - They are good at it
    - Is automatic and easy
    - Have support for it
    - Fear of changing

    Hearing how others also are apprehensive about making changes can help normalize the belief that making mistakes and lapses to the old way is not wrong but just part of the learning curve.

    b. **Learning from the lapse.** Once a lapse is normalized and accepted it becomes easier to use as information for future improvement. This is data versus a depiction or evaluation of the person's personality, i.e., "I am a loser" or "I'll never learn this." Have the participants develop a list of questions that they carry with them, to ask themselves after a relapse. They can include questions such as:

    "What happened here?"
    "What or who do I need to stay away from the next time?"
    "What can I learn from this lapse?"

"How will I prevent this in the future?"
"What did I do that was on track?"
"Who do can I share this information with that can be a support for me in the future?"

6. **Identifying relapse signs.** In groups of three, have each person talk about his or her situation at home or the office. Ask them to identify the main areas of stress where they may revert back to the old learning and behaviors, rather than using their new skills. In the work environment, there are five factors that make someone vulnerable to a relapse (Broad & Newstrom, 1992). These are similar if the person is returning home to their family.

   ◆ A backlog of work—where the desk is piled with work collected while the individual was in training.
   ◆ Non-support from co-workers or family—who stayed the same while the participant changed in some way. This lack of support for the new behaviors pulls the person back into the old practices. It's not uncommon for a recovering alcoholic to return home sober and committed only to find his or her family uncomfortable and disliking this "new person" and consciously or unconsciously wishing for the "drunk" to return, who often does.
   ◆ Situational pressures—like change of job assignment, a reorganization, merger, personal problems at home, or interpersonal conflicts—that distract the participant from practicing the new skills.
   ◆ Lack of confidence and competence in implementing the new learning.
   ◆ Little or no management support or encouragement for implementing the new knowledge.

7. **Assessing coping skills.** In their small learning support groups, the participants will develop an action plan that addresses each of the relapse signs mentioned above. If the person's sponsor is available, the participant will share his/her plan for feedback, modifications, and support. The plan should include the following strategies:

   ◆ Identifying resources—such as their notebooks, pocket cards listing questions to ask self, support team and sponsor's phone numbers, audiotapes, journals, pictures, software programs, books, etc.
   ◆ Identifying and reviewing a strength list of new insights and capabilities that the person learned from the structured experience.
   ◆ Indicate how they will manage their time more effectively—which will include setting up realistic expectations and prioritizing the things which are most important rather than only doing the urgent. Covey (1994) stated, "The main thing is to keep the main thing the main thing."
   ◆ Communicating to others effectively what their priorities are and how these people can support their learning activities and retention strategies. Establishing with others upfront what they are going to say "no" to, so they will have the time to say "yes" to their new practices.
   ◆ Identifying their learning-support team and sharing this relapse plan with them to help the participant stay on track.
   ◆ Building in rewards for "small wins" along the way. This should be done individually and with their sponsor and learning-support team.

◆   Avoiding self-blame and activation of old stories when a lapse occurs. Expect it will happen and have them learn from it by using their relapse questions card.

8. **Scenario play challenging situations.** In their learning-support group, the participants are each asked to pick one real scenario to role play. They should look at their relapse signs and coping skills information, and then they should pick the most likely situation where they need to practice their coping skills. Once the scenario is selected, they will share the scene with others in their group and describe what is difficult about this situation for them. One individual will observe and give feedback after the role-play while the other will play a character in this same situation. The participant plays his or her self in the role play, and practices the new behavior. After the role-play, the group will process it to illuminate the learning. The two other participants will share their scene and go through the same role-play procedure.

An **alternative** to this procedure is to have other group members play the individual in the scenario to provide that person with some visual learning of how to apply his/her new skills. There are many options for role-playing, like doing one in front of the whole group or using a fish bowl method.

9. **Follow-up strategies.** While the participants are still in the training session, they should plan out their follow-up strategy. How will they keep on track, utilize and retain the new learning? In their learning-support group, they can work on this last aspect of their plan and get feedback from the others. This plan should include answers to the following questions:

"How often will they meet with their sponsor and learning-support team?"
"When will be the first meeting for both of these supports?"
"What kind of support (i.e., phone calls, letters, meetings,) can they work out with the trainer and when?"
"How will they know they are on track? What will be some of the road signs along the way?"
"Who will be the first to notice the changes and what will they see?"
"What will be the first indication that they are starting to slip or lapse?"
"What will they do when they notice this?"
"How will they sabotage their relapse-prevention program from working?"
"What do they want their sponsor and learning-support team to do if they notice the participant slipping?"
"What are some of the rewards the participant will implement for him or herself to celebrate small wins?"

10. Select a few volunteers to hear their follow-up plans in front of the large group and give some feedback.

11. End the session by having everyone state one thing that they have learned from the session that they will implement to maintain their learning.

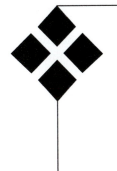

TEAM LEADER FACILITATED FOLLOW-UP

"We do not meet with success except by reiterated efforts."

—*Francoise de Maintenon*

GOALS

- ◆ To have the team leader from the organization facilitate the "lessons learned session" without the trainer, or leader from the learning experience present.
- ◆ To renew, revisit, and reinforce the learning from the structured experience.
- ◆ To allow the sponsor of the training to communicate his or her support for the training.
- ◆ To help transfer the learning into the work site.

TIME FRAME

One and a half to two hours

MATERIALS NEEDED

Pictures and, or video of the structured experience, white board, flip chart, or black board, handout of the team ingredients, and individual notebooks. The trainer or leader needs to provide the team leader with this outline and with pictures or a video of the experience, if available.

PROCESS

A. **Sponsor of the training:** The sponsor is the person who actually arranged and provided the financial support for the training. This individual should "kick-off" the start of the meeting and then turn it over to the team leader. The talk could include:

- ◆ Why he or she support the training that was just completed.
- ◆ What the expectations are of the group and how he/she will support the training.

◆ How he/she wants to see the learning applied at the work site. And, in this session he/she will help identify the "how's" or the action steps to do that.

◆ As the sponsor of program he/she is the key person to drive the learning and ensure that the investment pays off as applied learning, rather than just being a one time event.

B. The team leader or supervisor will need to lead the session. The idea is to foster communication, collaboration, and problem-solving similar to what occurred during the structured experience and determine how best to apply the learning at the work site. In some cases, the sponsor and team leader may be the same person. The team leader may want to go through the following outline to facilitate the session.

C. Pictures from the structured experience or "the day on the ropes course" will be very helpful. A video of the experience is also a great follow-up tool. You can help reinforce the learning by showing the pictures and/or video at a strategic part of the "lessons learned session." Below are suggestions on how to lead the session once the sponsor finishes his/her talk.

1. **Start by giving the "end in mind."** "We want to show you the pictures and/or video from the teambuilding experience. Then, we'd like to talk about some of the learning from the day and how it applies here."

2. **Pass the pictures out** or begin the video and let people see them to help remember the experience. Let them talk informally for awhile. Pass out the pictures so that everyone has a few to view at the same time.

3. **Start with the question,** "What did you learn at the ropes course or structured experience, that you want to continue to do here?" Write the answers on the board.

4. **"How well are we doing on each of these now?"** Ask the group to go through each item from #3, on the board, and rank it on a scale of 1–10, 10 being a high score. Get an overall average for each item, even if it is a rough average. You could also get a show of hands to make it more expedient—"Who thinks we are at a ten, nine, eight, etc.?"

5. **Pick the lowest scores,** or the area that the group feels is most important to **improve. Focus on no more than three or four areas.** Then, you want to ask; "What actions do you think we need to put in place to get at each of these?" Start with one area at time and go through the following questions.

6. "Anything we need to **stop doing** that will get in the way of our improvements?" Write the answers on the board.

7. "What do we need to **start doing** that hasn't been mentioned yet?" Write the answers on the board.

8. "What do we need to **continue doing?**" Write the answers on the board.

9. To make sure that you have covered all the important areas of successful team-work, have the team fill out the "Successful Team-Work Ingredients", (see Table 13). Look at the items with the lowest scores on the items that the team gave themselves and add those items to the stop, start, and continue lists.

10. Look at your stop, start, and continue answers and ask: "What plan or actions do we need to put in place to get at these, especially what we need to start and stop?"

11. "What are the next steps and timelines to ensure that these actions are getting done?"

◆ TABLE 13 ◆

Successful Team-Work Ingredients

Read and respond to each item using the following 5-point scale:

1 = *never* happens
2 = happens *infrequently,*
3 = happens *occasionally*
4 = happens *frequently*
5 = *always* happens.

	Never 1	Infrequently 2	Occasionally 3	Frequently 4	Always 5
1. Our team has a shared vision, we all understand and accept.					
2. There is high trust among team members.					
3. Communication is open, thinking is made visible, people listen well, and differing ideas are encouraged and accepted.					
4. Conflict is dealt with openly and resolved.					
5. Our team is able to establish, prioritize, and work on what is most important.					
6. Risk taking and being proactive are encouraged and supported among team members.					
7. Collaboration is high and team members seek win-win solutions.					
8. Our team maintains a one team perspective, or awareness of the bigger system that all teams and departments are on the same team.					
9. Our team is constantly learning and trying to improve.					
10. Leadership is participative, shared by all where no one person dominates.					
11. Our team has established values and guidelines for how we operate together.					
12. We are able to hold each other accountable for the performances agreed upon.					

Total Score _____

12. Close by complimenting the group for their participation, here and on the structured experience. Ask each individual for one commitment that he/she is willing to focus on that will continue the progress in building the team.
13. Have all the notes from this session typed and distributed to the participants. At the next meeting start by checking in on how each person has done on the team commitment that he/she stated to the group.

LEADERSHIP CHECK-IN TOPICS

"Keep away from people who try to belittle your ambitions. Small people always do that, but the really great make you feel that you too can become great."

—*Mark Twain*

GOALS

- ◆ To give team leaders and trainers a tool to start meetings, set the tone, and reinforce the learning gained from the structured experience back at the work site.
- ◆ To give the leaders across the organization a similar way to lead their meetings.
- ◆ To warm-up the group and get everyone to say something. This helps the team get to know each other better and develop camaraderie.
- ◆ To specifically focus on topics that you want to **breathe life into** and continue the on-going leadership focus and learning.
- ◆ To have a process check during the meeting, or at the end, to gauge the effectiveness, and identify what needs to be improved.

TIME FRAME

At the start of meetings—should take only fifteen minutes.

MATERIALS

A copy of the Leadership Check-in Topics.

PROCESS

The following can be used as a warm-up topic to start your meetings around a leadership topic. It is best to do a "round", which is to go around in a circle and hear everyone's response to the question, passing is always an option. The responses should be brief, allowing the discussion to move briskly.

Team Work

- How did a member of your team help you this past week?
- What have you done to foster collaboration with others?
- Give an example of some systems thinking that you have done?
- What is an example of some small wins that you created for your team?
- How have you walked your talk in regards to your team?
- Give an appreciation to the person on your left or right for something that you have thought of or felt, but never mentioned to him or her before?
- How effective is your team on a 1–10 ranking? How could the team improve?
- Where is your team in the forming, storming, norming, and performing stages of team development? Why?
- Our team's main strength is . . . ?
- One area of weakness for our team is . . . ?

Risk Taking

- How do you challenge the process, to confront or improve the status quo?
- What experiments or risks have you taken in the past week? What have you learned from the experiments or risks?
- What have you done to empower your co-workers or people you supervise to take risks?
- What have been some ways that you have rewarded others for their accomplishments?

Relationship Building

- What have you done recently that contributed to your relationship with the customer?
- What have you done that contributed to the relationship with a team member?
- What has someone else done with or for you that contributed to building your relationship with them? Be specific, especially if the person is present.
- What is the value of building better relationships with others for you?
- From your perspective, what is the best thing someone else can do to build a better relationship with you?

Passion/Vision

- What is the most meaningful part of your work-day? Give an example.
- What have you or others done that has envisioned an uplifting future for your team or the organization?
- Where do you see the team or organization in 3–5 years from now?
- What do you see as your contributions to the team and the organization?
- What do you truly get excited about at work and outside of work?
- What was one of your earliest dreams of what you wanted to do in your life that you remember?

Trust

- In the group have each person fill in the blank for, "For me to trust you, you should _____." Give at least four answers. For example, "For me to trust you should not talk behind my back, etc."
- Who on this team do you have a lot of trust for and why?
- On a one-to-ten scale, how do you rate your team with regard to trust?
- What actions could increase your rating one point?
- What actions does someone need to do for you to feel that they are trustworthy?
- Share an example of a trust story about someone or some incident at work.

Leadership

- Who is a role model for you as a leader? What is it about him/her that you admire?
- Can you give an example of something you did recently that exemplified your leadership abilities?
- What has someone else done that demonstrates leadership to you and why?
- Which leadership attribute or practice, i.e., building a shared vision, being a role model, taking risks and challenging the process, encouraging and empowering others to act, acknowledging the accomplishments of others (Kouzes & Posner, 1987) do you feel you use the most?
- Which leadership attribute or practice do you feel that you need to improve?

Values/Mission

- Pick one of your team's or organization's shared values that you used at work in the last week (Use the values the organization has developed, if there are none you may want to do an exercise first, see the "Shared Vision" leadership topic.). Select a different value at each future meeting.
- What is your top personal value and why?
- What is a value that you avoid or move away from; i.e., rejection, humiliation, or embarrassment?
- Which value is the easiest for you to demonstrate?
- Which value is the hardest for you to show?
- What is one example of how you actualized the organization's mission with the customer?
- What is one example of living the organization's vision with your people?
- What is one example of demonstrating the organization's vision for the business?

Self-awareness sentence completion

- You know I am under stress when . . . ?
- I am most motivated when . . . ?
- The biggest challenge of the day is . . . ?
- I feel at my best when . . . ?
- Something I learned this week was . . . ?
- One mistake I made this past week was . . . ?

◆ I am most happy when . . . ?
◆ What I fear the most at work is . . . ?
◆ I am most frustrated when . . . ?
◆ What I like most in other's is . . . ?
◆ Most people don't know that I . . . ?
◆ I try to avoid . . . ?
◆ My biggest highlight this week was . . . ?
◆ When I am angry, I . . . ?
◆ What irritates me the most during the work day is . . . ?
◆ I feel one of my strengths is . . . ?
◆ One development area for me is?

Self-renewal habits

◆ The way I recharge myself is . . . ?
◆ What brings me balance in my life is . . . ?
◆ What I do to get in the gap between stimulus and old reactions is . . . ?
◆ Once in the gap, I . . . ?
◆ My way of saying no to doing more is . . . ?
◆ The hardest thing about saving time for myself is . . . ?
◆ I know if I don't sharpen the saw, I feel . . . ?
◆ The value of self-renewal for me is . . . ?

Process checks Here are various ways to make sure your meetings are effective. It is good to vary the way you do the process check.

◆ On a scale of one-to-ten how effective or satisfied were you with today's meeting? (Ask people, who give low scores, to state what they think needs to be improved.)
◆ What was good, bad and needs to be better with regard to the meeting?
◆ At the half-way point of the meeting, have each person rate the quality of the meeting using a scale of 1–10 regarding how on-track is the meeting? What needs to be improved?

P • A • R • T V

NOTES FROM EXPERTS IN THE FIELD

SECTION 1: ADVENTURE BASED LEARNING: GUIDING PRACTICES

- Case Study
- Case Study Invited Response—*Jeff Nelson*
- Case Study Invited Response—*Christian Bisson, M.Ed.*

SECTION 2: ADOLESCENTS: GUIDING PRACTICES

SECTION 3: FAMILIES: GUIDING PRACTICES

Families on the Ropes: Programming with Families—*Suzanne Rudolph, Ed.D.*
- Case Study
- Case Study Invited Response—*Michael Gass, Ph.D.*
- Case Study Invited Response—*Jackie Gerstein, Ed.D.*

SECTION 4: COUPLES: GUIDING PRACTICES

- Case Study
- Case Study Invited Response—*Dene Berman, Ph.D.* and *Jennifer Davis-Berman, Ph.D.*

SECTION 5: ADDICTIONS: GUIDING PRACTICES

- Case Study
Integrating the Twelve Steps of Alcoholics Anonymous with Ropes Courses—*Paul Suding*
Disordered Eating, Body Image and Adventure Therapy: Guiding Practices—*Juli A. Hayes, R.D.*

SECTION 6: CORPORATE PROGRAMS: GUIDING PRACTICES

Sales and Marketing of Your Program—*Tom Vache't*

The topics in this section are from experts in the field who are applying their unique knowledge and skills to various populations on a daily basis. We are pleased and honored that they have agreed to share their insights and thinking. Their experience "from the trenches" will provide guidance and multiple-view points to help enhance your learning and the quality of the programs you deliver. Our goal is to afford you the opportunity to witness their thinking about various topics. There are two types of contributions:

1. Best practices about specific groups and topics, and
2. Real life scenarios that one to two experts comment on.

A full list of the contributors and information about their background is listed in the front of this book.

ADVENTURE BASED LEARNING
GUIDING PRACTICES

❖

"Security is mostly a superstition. It does not exist in nature . . . Life is either a daring adventure or nothing . . ."

—*Helen Keller*

In this section, we define adventure based learning and discuss the benefits of participating in these types of experiences. We attempt to answer the question "Why is adventure based learning effective?" and provide a model that we think summarizes what commonly occurs on adventure based learning experiences. A case study is presented and responses to the case study are contributed by Jeff Nelson and Christian Bisson.

❖ WHAT IS ADVENTURE BASED LEARNING?

In general, adventure based learning is a type of educational and/or therapeutic program in which adventure pursuits that are physically and/or psychologically demanding are used within a framework of safety and skills development to promote interpersonal and intrapersonal growth (Bagby & Chavarria, 1980). Examples of adventure based activities, suggested by Ewert (1989), are found in Table 14.

◆ **TABLE 14** ◆

Examples of Adventure Activities

Backpacking	White-water canoeing	Hot-air ballooning
Mountaineering	Kayaking	Rock climbing
Rafting	Ropes course	Backcountry snowshoeing
Rappelling	Orienteering	SCUBA
Sailing	Wilderness camping	Sea kayaking
Spelunking	Sky diving	Hang-gliding
Wilderness trekking	Bicycle touring	Cross-country skiing

❖ BENEFITS OF ADVENTURE BASED LEARNING

Adventure based learning provides opportunities for learning and experiencing in a unique social and physical setting. The activities are holistic, involving all the senses and accommodate a variety of learning styles, with clear goals that provide immediate feedback on performance. In addition, the activities are novel, often fun and invigorating—providing opportunities to experiment with new behaviors and skills in a safe environment which encourages risk taking of all kinds. Through participation in the multi-dimensional learning activities, individuals are provided with an acceptable medium for personal testing, and, as a result, gain a more intimate view of their strengths, weaknesses, and character. Currently, there is a wealth of literature and research that substantiates the positive effect of using adventure based activities to increase participants' self-esteem, alter their locus of control, reduce asocial behavior and improve problem-solving abilities (e.g., Colan, 1986; Ewert, 1989; Luckner, 1989; Rawson & McIntosh, 1991; Smith, Roland, Havens, & Hoyt, 1992; Rudolph, 1991; Stich & Senior, 1984; Wichmann, 1991). A summary of additional benefits of adventure based learning that has been developed by Ewert (1989) is found in Table 15.

◆ **TABLE 15** ◆

Potential Benefits of Adventure Based Learning

Psychological	Sociological	Educational	Physical
Confidence	Belonging	Problem solving	Fitness
Self-concept	Compassion	Outdoor education	Skills
Self-efficacy	Respect for others	Nature awareness	Strength
Personal testing	Communication	Conservation education	Coordination
Sensation seeking	Behavior feedback	Improved academics	Exercise
Well-being	Friendship	Value clarification	Balance

❖ WHY IS ADVENTURE BASED LEARNING EFFECTIVE?

Each of us have our own beliefs about why adventure based learning is effective. Certainly, in the discussion that follows, we will agree on several points and probably miss a few that you have thought of. But, that is all right and hopefully you will share your ideas with us, and we will add those points to the next edition of this text. The first reason, one that we all agree on, is that it is experiential—each of us learn best by being actively involved. Second, the perceived risk that often accompanies the activities and the social environment impel people into a state of readi-

ness for learning. The excitement and emotional nature of the experience focuses people's attention on the tasks at hand. Consequently, people remember what they have learned and experienced. Third, the activities and setting tend to be atypical. The uncommon activities and problems that emerge cause each member of the group to be reliant on others. Fourth, there is a direct correlation between cause and effect. The consequence of ones' actions are easily observed (not looking at a map while hiking; leaving your raincoat at the bottom of your pack; belaying your friend who falls while traversing the high beam). And, fifth it is generalizeable. Many of the behaviors and patterns demonstrated by individuals and groups during the experience also occur in other settings. Accordingly, new learning—specific skills, personal insight, coping strategies, and social connections can be applied to other settings. A more in-depth look at each of these factors is provided in the following segment.

❖ ADVENTURE BASED LEARNING PROCESS MODEL

Drawing from the work of Walsh and Golins (n.d.), Piaget (1977), and Yalom (1975), we have attempted to develop a theoretical foundation that explains why adventure based learning is effective. We believe that by having a solid theoretical understanding of why adventure based learning works, and what the components of a successful experience are, you can explain your program to people who are not familiar with experiential learning, plan courses, and make decisions that will enable you and your students to have positive gains from your time together. In addition, while this model generally focuses on programs that are conducted in outdoor settings, those of you who operate challenge programs indoors can enhance the quality of your courses by having an understanding of this model.

The following is a brief explanation of each of the components. They are graphically depicted in Figure 15.

1. *The Individual:* People come to the structured experience with a preconception of what it is going to be like. Generally, the expectations that they have set the stage for a meaningful-learning opportunity. For some individuals, the anticipation causes a sense of internal stimulation. Others do not experience this feeling until they are immersed in the experience. This internal state that permits learning to occur is referred to as . . .

2. *Disequilibrium:* As discussed in the section entitled "Promoting Change", disequilibrium refers to an individual's awareness that a mismatch exists between old ways of thinking and new information. It is a state of internal conflict that provides motivation for an individual to make personal changes. Disequilibrium must be present for learning to occur. By involvement in an experience that is beyond one's comfort zone, individuals are forced to integrate new knowledge or reshape existent perceptions. These qualitative and quantitative changes are referred to as the processes of accommodation and assimilation. Individuals experience the state of disequilibrium by being placed in a . . .

3. *Novel Setting:* Placement in an environment that one is not familiar with helps to breakdown individual barriers. When this factor is combined with the underlying conditions of effort, trust, a constructive level of anxiety, a sense of the unknown, and a perception of risk within a . . .

4. *Cooperative Environment:* Establishing an atmosphere and method of teaching that makes use of cooperative rather than competitive learning fosters opportunities for individuals to develop group cohesiveness. This bonding is cultivated through a structure that focuses on shared goals and the provision of time for interpersonal and intrapersonal communication. This foundation exists while each individual and the group continually are presented with . . .

5. *Unique Problem-Solving Situations:* New skills and problem-solving situations are introduced to individuals in a sequence of increasing difficulty. The learning opportunities are concrete and can be solved when group members draw on their mental, emotional, and physical resources. Completion of such tasks leads to . . .

6. *Feelings of Accomplishment:* Success can lead to increased self-esteem, an increased internal locus of control, improved communication skills, and more effective problem-solving skills. The meaningfulness of these success experiences is augmented by . . .

7. *Processing the Experience:* Individuals are encouraged to plan and reflect and in some manner express their thoughts, feelings, and behaviors that they experience. Processing is essential if there is going to be . . .

8. *Generalization and Transfer:* The ultimate goal of the adventure based experience is to assist individuals in providing their own linkages, bridges, and connections to what they are learning, so that they can integrate their personal insights and desired behaviors into their lifestyle during the remainder of the experience and when they return home.

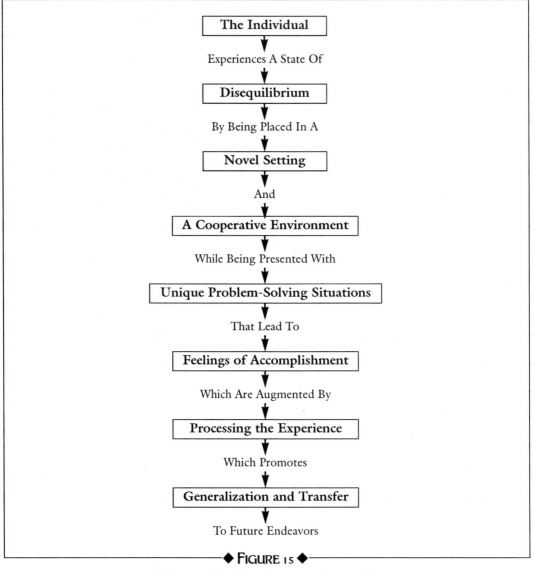

The Individual

Experiences A State Of

Disequilibrium

By Being Placed In A

Novel Setting

And

A Cooperative Environment

While Being Presented With

Unique Problem-Solving Situations

That Lead To

Feelings of Accomplishment

Which Are Augmented By

Processing the Experience

Which Promotes

Generalization and Transfer

To Future Endeavors

◆ FIGURE 15 ◆

Adventure based learning processing model

CASE STUDY

Megan and Cliff are experienced outdoor, adventure education leaders. They have been hired to do a two-week, wilderness trip with a group of students from an alternative high school. The course was arranged by the high school and contracted with the national, outdoor adventure program where Megan and Cliff work. The course occurred in the early autumn, in the mountains of Idaho as part of the school's leadership program. The group was composed of 7 males and 5 female students and one teacher from the school, who was the director of the leadership program. In general, it was a typical high school group, with participants ranging in age from 16–18, and everyone being either a junior or senior.

Prior to the start of the course, Megan and Cliff visited the school on several occasions for group meetings. At the meetings, everyone participated in some teambuilding exercises, discussed the specifics of the trip, group and personal goals, and basic requirements for equipment and supplies. The planning meetings went well and every member of the group seemed to be very excited about the upcoming experience.

The wilderness trip was demanding and positive. Because it was early fall, there were not many other travelers in the woods. The nights were clear and crisp and other than some brief rain showers, it was perfect weather. Of course, there was the usual grumbling about the weight of the packs, getting started on cold mornings, and complaints about the trail food. Nevertheless, the group bonded well, had fun, and became skilled travelers. Regularly, throughout the course, Megan and Cliff provided skills instruction, presented group problem-solving initiatives, and held processing sessions to plan, reflect, and discuss personal and group functioning as well as to create transfer from the course to their lives back at school and home.

On the evening of day 7, the group was camping near a lake that had a fire ring from previous campers. They decided to build a fire using the fire ring and then destroy the ring in the morning. While sitting around the campfire Cliff noticed that everyone was there except Chad and Carme. He casually asked "If anyone knew where Chad and Carme went." Mario commented that he thought that, "they were practicing the hypothermia drill." Most everyone laughed.

A few minutes later Chad and Carme came walking up to the fire and everyone smiled at them. Chad asked what everyone was smiling about, and Gregg told him what Mario had said. At that moment, Carme ran from the fire and headed to the woods.

Cliff and Megan looked at each other and immediately the light went on. While they had noticed Chad and Carme spending more time together as the days passed, they didn't think that it was anything more than adolescent flirting. Obviously, they had missed something. While each member of the group quietly stared at the fire, Cliff asked Angela and Stacey to go look for Carme and ask her to rejoin the group. When Carme, Angela and Stacey came back to the fire, Megan let a few minutes pass and then asked for an explanation.

Chad and Carme looked at each other while the others continued to stare at the fire. After what seemed like an eternity, Chad said that "me and Carme became attracted to each other over the last few days and one thing has kinda led to the next." They admitted that they have been having sexual intercourse the last few nights, but that it is really nothing to get worried about since they both wanted it to happen. Then Chad said to Cliff "This is no big thing, let's not blow it out of proportion. We're having a great trip. Carme and I are just having a little additional fun. If you want, Carme and I will chill out until we get home from the trip."

Megan and Cliff were uncertain about what to do or say next. This was definitely an awkward and difficult situation. In essence, what had transpired was minors, having sex, possibly unprotected sex, while on a personal-growth outdoor adventure expedition that they were leading. There were six days left on the trip, and they were approximately two days travel away from their van.

CASE STUDY INVITED RESPONSE

Jeff Nelson

What are your thoughts about how to handle this situation? The best method for handling this type of situation is to avoid it from happening. Beginning with staff training, wilderness instructors should be prepared to deal with sexuality issues between genders and between same sex attractions. Sensitivity to the desires that probably exist between most adolescents, and clear boundaries between what is and is not acceptable, are paramount. Simply drawing a line and saying "no" will not necessarily alleviate the problem.

What suggestions do you have for avoiding situations such as this? Starting from the first night, it should be clearly stated that the development of relationships, whether sexual or mutually exclusive, are not acceptable. Instructors should acknowledge with the students that they understand that the feelings or desires probably will be there, and that they are normal, but that the expedition is not an appropriate place to act on those feelings. Instructors should explain why such development is not appropriate (as they might miss out on learning from others, it may be unsafe for travel, others might feel left out, etc.), so it does not seem as if some arbitrary rule is being placed upon them. Finally, instructors should attempt to create a safe environment where students can discuss sexuality issues if they desire to do so. Often having an avenue to state internal feelings will alleviate the desire to act on those feelings; recognizing that often the opposite is true.

Instructors should also create a structure within the management of the group that prohibits the opportunities for the adolescents to "break the rules." Males and females should sleep in separate tents or tarps, preferably with the instructors in between. At no time, should adolescent boys and girls be permitted to be together unsupervised. Structure can be built into chores from the beginning, so the youth know that that is the way things are going to be. If the structure is not in place from day one, instructors risk extreme power struggles and disempowerment of students by trying to impose structure midway through the course. It is much easier to ease off on the reins, then to pull them in. Additionally, instructors should not discount the possibility that same gender attractions or relationships will develop on courses, and they should be aware of any developing relationships that seem exclusive.

Any physical touching between students, or students and staff, should be allowed only with caution. Hugs and back rubs can easily lead to more promiscuous behavior, and again, the best way to avoid this from happening is to limit the opportunity from the beginning.

Instructors should explain to students that attraction is natural, and also that the feelings that could be developing are influenced by the power of the wilderness education experience, a true "call of the wild" as it were. It is natural for one who has powerful experiences happening around him or her to attribute these feelings to those with whom

261

she/he is sharing the experience. If the feelings are real, they will still be present at the end of the course. More often than not, such feelings fade as the distance from the experience fades. Instructors must give to the students the perspective that the students' age and experience most likely lack.

Sometimes, no matter how stringent the structure, students will find a way to consummate their attraction. If such a case occurs, the two certainly should not be confronted with the rest of the group present. The potential for emotional damage is very great, and should be approached delicately. The students involved should be interviewed individually away from the group, and asked directly but compassionately what happened, how often, and with who present or nearby. Instructors should point out noticed behaviors and comments from other group members, and should seek the truth. The rest of the group should be informed that whatever happened was personal, and the instructors should immediately intervene if any further "wise" comments or innuendoes occur.

Because the students are minors, parents should be notified of the situation as soon as possible. The students should be told that as minors, under the supervision of the instructors of the program, their parents must be notified of the occurrence, and the decision for the students to continue the expedition rests with the parents. The organization should offer to assist the parents in any way possible, whether allowing them to speak to their children, arranging a trip to a medical facility, or removal from the course. If the instructors discover that other students may have "witnessed" a sexual act, all parents should be notified of the behavior in case there is some trauma resulting from the exposure. Those parents also can make the decision for their child to leave the course.

Instructors should be trained and prepared to educate the two students, and the whole group, about the risks of having unprotected sex, discussing the contraction of sexually transmitted diseases as well as the possibility of teenage pregnancy. If the scene seems safe and the instructors judge this to be an appropriate time and place, they may take this powerful opportunity to have a conversation about the differences between sex and intimacy, sex in relationships, different reasons why people choose to have sex, and how sex plays a role in self-esteem and the need to be desired: the issues that make the world go around for adolescents, and then some.

With all that said, I strongly believe that relationships between two young people should never be shrouded in shame and guilt. Too often, youth are told that sex and the feelings that go with the responsibility of being sexually active are "bad" or "wrong" in some way. This only serves to set the youth up for a lifetime of conflicting feelings and behaviors that can carry into all their relationships and even in different areas of their lives. Relationships should be celebrated—Chad and Carme, Romeo and Juliet, John and Sue. End of story!

What are your top do's and don'ts for structuring and processing experiences for groups of students on outdoor adventure courses. Basic Rules for structuring youth courses:

1. Don't give students too much rope—unless you are prepared for them to hang themselves.
2. Have "suspicious" trust. Listen to conversations, observe interactions. Most adolescents will give themselves away.
3. Start with tight structure, and relax when students can handle it.
4. Assume nothing.
5. Lay down the rules, or better yet, design them with the group on the first night.

6. Be consistent and fair in following through with the established structure.
7. Expect to be challenged. Have your answers ready ahead of time.
8. Only give students a "choice" if you are prepared for either outcome of the choice.
9. Enforce the structure without emotional attachment. Make it clear that the students are choosing consequences through their actions, not yours.
10. Develop allies within the group. They will inform you of the things that are happening.
11. Make it fun for the students as well as for yourself.

Summary of response to this scenario:

1. Secure the emotional safety of the scene. Including debriefing with individuals and the group separate from Chad and Carme. Create a learning environment if possible.
2. Make a plan to evacuate and notify the parents of Chad and Carme as well as the rest of the student's parents. (An important institutional public relations move.)
3. Let Chad and Carme and their respective parents decide what they would like to do next. Including visits to a medical facility and the decision to stay on or leave the course.
4. If the parents ask for advice from the staff, it appears that Chad and Carme are handling the situation maturely and will cease the "exclusivity", the recommendation of the instructors would be to allow (encourage) them to complete the course.
5. The final aspect that would be hard to predict would the role the "teacher" who is the leader of the high school leadership-program would play in the decision-making and the debriefing with the students. Experience tells me that this person is "a student" in most ways. The physical and emotional safety of these students are the instructors responsibility.

CASE STUDY INVITED RESPONSE

Christian Bisson, M.Ed.

*"Love is a canvas furnished by
nature and embroidered by
imagination."*

—*Voltaire*

What are your thoughts about how to handle this situation? Romantic relationships are bound to occur during any extended, wilderness experience. However, what would be considered an ordinary event in our society becomes a different situation when it happens in the context of an adventure course. When the situation involves a relationship between two students, two instructors, or a student and an instructor; newly born, romantic relationships always create waves in a group. "Newly born" means that the relationship emerges during the course which is different from a relationship exiting prior to the course. I make this distinction because from personal experiences, I have noticed that preexisting relationships, involving consenting adults, are often more mature and less distracting for the group. But, when I deal with a fresh romance, I always step in, regardless of the age of the participants.

In the case of Carme and Chad, I see three good reasons to address their developing relationship. These reasons carry different levels of responsibility that I will refer as: legal, ethical, and moral.

Legal Responsibility—In this situation my actions would be swift because it involves two minors. Instructing teenagers under 18 years of age brings a totally new dimension to a love affair. This dimension is of a legal nature and to borrow the appropriate jargon, "we say that we, as the instructors, are in loco parentis"—which means that we are "in the position or place of a parent" during the entire adventure experience. In this case, from the beginning to the end of the expedition. This assumption of "legal parenthood," implies that we are responsible for everything our students' experience, and this includes any extracurricular activity. For example, in this particular scenario, the instructor teams and the school teacher would be perceived as legally accountable for Chad and Carme's romantic affair. Therefore, from a strictly legal point of view, I would not allow or encourage this relationship to exist during the course. My actions here do not mean that I consider love or intimacy, at a mature age, inappropriate; but simply that I would embrace the most conservative position in an effort to respect the potentially orthodox beliefs of the parents.

Ethical Responsibility—The legal aspect is not the only reason why such a situation should be avoided. I believe that "newly born", romantic relationships have a strong potential to isolate the people involved from the rest of the group. As an outdoor adventure educator, it is in the best interest of the group to avoid any situation that can create a sub-group. When a sub-group exists, the social dynamics among the other participants is inevitably affected. Ethically speaking, I should never forget that it is my foremost responsibility to create a safe, learning environment for all students. The romantic relationship between Carme and Chad will and has already affected the learning environment. For example, alluding to the "hypothermia drill" had an obvious harmful reaction on Carme. Under these conditions, slowing down or even idling the relationship might be the only viable solution.

Moral Responsibility—Finally, the third reason for intervening in this scenario has to do with health concerns. Unprotected intercourse is simply unacceptable from a moral point of view. Unwanted pregnancy and sexually transmitted diseases are already too prevalent in our society. In this particular situation, I doubt that condoms were mentioned on the personal equipment list. Once again, abstinence seems to be the only solution.

Personally, I would handle the situation a little bit differently then as described in the scenario. First, I would discuss the matter with my co-instructor and the school teacher. I believe it is crucial that the leadership team agree upon the decisions and actions to take regarding such a situation. Secondly, I would have a conference with Chad and Carme alone to avoid potential embarrassment in front of the group, as well as to express a caring attitude toward their romance. The objective of this conference would be to make them reflect on the potential consequences (i.e., legal, ethical, and moral) attached to their relationship. Hopefully, we will come to the same conclusions and agree that it would be in everyone's best interest to postpone their romance until the end of the course. I believe that there is no need, at this point, to remove them from the course.

While I am talking with Carme and Chad, I would expect my co-instructor to process the issue with the rest of the group and their

teacher. I would hope that the group would agree that we should respect Chad and Carme's mutual affection, and that we should be happy for them and explain to the group that in respect for us and the goals of this experience, Carme and Chad will "chill out" their courtship. From there, I would ask Carme and Chad if they want to share and explain their decision to the rest of the group. If they are comfortable with this idea, we will use this opportunity as a spring board to talk about relationships, sex, love, and group dynamics. Eventually, we would close the issue and go on with the course. Naturally, I would stay more alert about other potential romances.

What suggestions do you have for avoiding situations such as this? To avoid this kind of situation, especially when dealing with co-ed teenager groups, I would discuss this issue prior to leaving on the trip making sure that we all share a common understanding about intimate relationships during a school expedition. I believe that such a precaution would help avoid these delicate situations. It would certainly give us more leverage if a romantic affair arises.

What are your top do's and don'ts for structuring and processing experiences for groups of students on outdoor adventure courses.

Do's

1. I try to speak little and to listen a lot.
2. I like to use the Market Feeling Cards when I want to address emotional issues.
3. I use the exercise "blind survey" to establish a baseline between the participants. A blind survey is accomplished by asking everyone to close their eyes, myself included, and then to raise their

hands if they agree with a statement. For example, I would say: I receive put downs because I deserve them. Then, I ask everyone to stand still and to slowly open their eyes. If everyone has their hands down, which is the most common situation, we discuss their thoughts about why all our hands were down. Do we have something in common? I believe that the blind survey promotes genuine introspection. Keeping your eyes closed while answering a personal question creates a neutral socio-environment. No one is influenced by her or his peers.

4. I like to ask my students to create metaphors to explain a specific event or experience. I believe that it helps them conceptualize how they perceive the experience.

Don'ts

1. I don't like to use single gender examples. For instance, I would not say: When a climber reaches the top of a mountain, he feels . . . Instead, I take the time to say he or she feels . . .

2. I don't like to force someone to talk. If a person feels uncomfortable to express his or her ideas in front of the group, I let it be. However, I will try to follow up in a one-on-one dialogue.

3. I don't allow aggressive or destructive comments to occur among students. If it does occur, I try to address it immediately and present it as a communication issue.

SECTION 2

ADOLESCENTS
GUIDING PRACTICES

❖

"You can preserve the curiosity, drive, and undefeatable spirit of children by one simple means; kindle the joy of exploration and adventure during adolescence and the devotion to skills demanding patience and care."

—*Kurt Hahn*

The transitional time period of adolescence is discussed in this section. We begin with a brief overview of adolescence—highlighting some of the changes and challenges that occur as well as pointing out some of the risk factors that confront teenagers attempting to navigate their way into their adult years. A list of suggestions for working with "youth at risk groups" is included, and we end with an interesting piece by Lee Gillis, who provides us with theoretical information as well as practical recommendations for planning adventure programs for groups of adolescents.

❖ ADOLESCENCE—AN OVERVIEW

Adolescence is the general term used to describe the changes that occur in the passage from childhood to adulthood. During adolescence, young people are required to deal with multiple changes and challenges. These changes and challenges are developmental—cognitive, affective, behavioral, and biological as well as cultural. Examples of developmental milestones that generally occur during adolescence include: (a) coping with physical development and emerging sexuality, (b) refining interpersonal skills, (c) becoming emotionally and behaviorally autonomous, (d) resolving identity issues, (e) acquiring a set of values, and (f) obtaining education and training for adult work-roles.

Cultural factors that affect the development of adolescents are numerous and varied. For the purpose of this brief discussion, we are going to highlight and comment on a few prominent variables—the family, the peer network, the media and pop culture, the school and the neigh-

267

borhood. How each of these factors interact to promote or hinder the quality of life for an adolescent can only be determined on an individual basis.

The composition and the stability of the family substantially influences adolescents' development. Today, divorce occurs in approximately 50 percent of marriages. Economic pressures generally require both spouses to work long hours and often to relocate (up to 20 percent of the population moves every year). The traditional configuration of the male as the primary provider and the female working in the home fits only 11 percent of today's households. Time-crunched parents, even in intact, two income families have limited time to spend with their children. In general, parents spend 40 percent less time with their children than they did 30 years ago, and 2 million children under 13 have no adult supervision before or after school (Taffel, 1996). Furthermore, the family's informal, support systems—the extended family, neighborhood ties, Parent Teacher Associations (PTAs), church and community organizations—that reinforced family life have gradually dissipated.

Given less adult interaction and supervision, peer groups and the media-driven, pop culture fill the lives of many adolescents. Peer groups can be positive or negative depending on their interests and actions. Of concern though is the fact that the risk of harmful choices is particularly high today because adolescents' exposure to potentially dangerous behaviors have increased. Although many adolescents make wise decisions, some develop lifestyles involving violence, drug abuse, or engage in unprotected, sexual intercourse, putting them at risk for serious long-term problems (Elliott, 1993). Simultaneously, the technology explosion has blasted into homes causing the average high school graduate to spend 15,000 hours of his or her life in front of the TV, compared with only 11,000 hours spent in school (Taffel, 1996).

With regard to neighborhoods and schools, mothers and fathers are less likely to know the parents of their children's friends than in years past. Likewise, significantly fewer adults participate in neighborhood or school sponsored activities because of custody arrangements, unforgiving work schedules and/or an energy deficit for extracurricular activities. Schools, in general, are likely to be very large, centralized-learning institutions, sometimes, located away from where the students actually live. Far too often than we want to admit, teachers and parents are at odds with each other. Many teachers feel overworked and unappreciated. Teachers often complain that parents are not interested in their child's education, and that parents are too busy to monitor what goes on at home or in school. At the same time, parents are likely to complain about teachers claiming that they are either too strict or too lenient; give too little or too much work; give too few or too many tests; they don't really take an interest in their child; or, they teach material that is not really important. This shifting of blame between home and school only adds to the confusion that exists in the lives of many adolescents.

As adolescents grow toward autonomy and adulthood, they are expected by themselves and others to move away from the adult-directed activities of childhood toward the emotional autonomy, responsibility, and self-direction that are characteristic of adulthood. This increased freedom entails growth, yet also presents significant risks. For each individual, the choices that are made during the junior high school and high school years in self-discipline, social relationships, sexual behavior, academic commitment, and work-career-family planning may influence the course of their future, life development.

Given the connection between adolescent development and future well-being, it is important for each of us who work with this population to understand some of the primary factors that currently affect adolescents and to be sensitive to the pressures that accompany this period of transition. At the same time, we need to realize that early adolescence is an essential window of opportunity for intervention. Interventions implemented at this turning  point of life may prevent detrimental choices and redirect young people so that they develop healthy lifestyles with enduring benefits (Carnegie Council on Adolescent Development, 1989).

❖ SUGGESTIONS FOR WORKING WITH YOUTH AT RISK GROUPS

Many experiential education/therapy programs work with youth at risk groups. The following are some suggestions for structuring learning/therapeutic opportunities that have been adapted from the work of Ewert (1989) and Larsen and Mitchell (1992).

1. Do not try to build your own personal, support system from students.
2. Pace yourself.
3. Care without "bleeding."
4. Do not make presumptions about what individuals know, understand, or retain.
5. Keep activities practical and sequential.
6. Model as well as verbally explain what you want students to do.
7. Try to model the interpersonal behaviors that you want students to use.
8. Avoid being judgmental.
9. Let people know what to expect from the experience in terms of activities and requirements.
10. Keep in mind that discomfort is a difficult concept for many adolescents to deal with responsibly.
11. Let the participants know what is expected of them in terms of acceptable behaviors, communication patterns, and interaction with others.
12. Look for the real messages behind individual's behavior.
13. Maintain an awareness that many adolescents live "in" and "for" the moment.
14. When a disruptive behavior interrupts the processes of the group, employ a stop-action approach.
15. Try to consistently use positive feedback to describe strengths and increments of growth for individuals, as well as for positive group behaviors.
16. Attempt to identify strengths that typically go unattended and unnoticed.
17. Promote an atmosphere in which the group members give one another feedback about one another's strengths and progress.

❖ PLANNING ADVENTURE PROGRAMS FOR ADOLESCENTS ───────────────

H.L. "Lee" Gillis, Ph.D.

Adolescents are the "life blood" of adventure programming. Youth programs using initiatives, ropes courses, short expeditions, and residential camping have been a major artery feeding the adventure field for over 30 years. Such programs have provided experiences as avenues for the development of character, as alternatives to incarceration, and as experiential-therapeutic modalities. Many adventure leaders have learned and honed facilitation skills while working with adolescent populations.

As a result, many facilitators feel as though they don't have much to learn about working with this population—they already *know* what to do. If all adolescent groups were similar, this feeling might have validity. It is our experience that adolescent groups differ on aspects of understanding and motivation in ways that significantly impact the theory and practice of adventure programming. A brief explanation is offered of how theory is viewed—highlighted by two examples of work accomplished with adolescents or observed by staff working at Project Adventure's Covington, Georgia facility.

Taking a chapter from *Islands of Healing,* (Schoel, Prouty, & Radcliffe, 1988) one general way of viewing any group, and adolescent groups in particular, is to examine their abilities in the **Affective,** or feeling domain, the **Behavioral** or 'doing' domain and the **Cognitive,** or 'thinking' domain. Whether done using formal or informal initial assessment instruments or with some combination of adventure activities, the **A-B-C**'s of assessment are valuable aids in understanding in a general way how to work with adolescents.

For example, prior knowledge about students labeled as 'gifted' might lead the facilitator to wonder how well this group can handle a cognitive activity. The leader might also listen for how these adolescents use simile or metaphor when they are reviewing their experiences. *"What was this activity most like in your life"* is a simple way to hear if the adolescent group can make leaps with their language into more abstract and cognitively-complex levels of understanding. Such listening on the leader's part is much more respectful of the group and helps the leader theoretically "match" subsequent introductions to the group's ability to understand. Metaphoric understanding can be built upon by the leader who assesses the group for their ability to comprehend such abstract thinking instead of just assuming this group will just "get it" because they are labeled as being "bright."

A leader might also be interested in how well this same group might use affective, feeling words in their descriptions of experience. The leader might assess the group's affective level directly with an activity such as a blindfold square or blindfolded line-up designed to frustrate them. Frustration and thus some measure of feeling can be achieved by manipulating the time limit or using some physical restraint such as a blindfold. Where I have personally made mistakes and observed others make mistakes with this type of group is to be so focused on the **B**(ehavior) of having fun as they were attempting warm-ups that the leader missed the seriousness the group brought to the experience. I have had more success with this type of group when I have 'matched' their 'serious' attitude with a challenging activity and then led them into more fun and feeling experiences.

The theoretical goal is somewhat simple to state and more difficult to do: Balance the **A-B-** and **C** in the group—over time. I would like to have the 'gifted group' become as effective in their **A**(ffect) and **B**(ehavior) as they may be with their **C**(ognitive) abilities once my time with them is complete. At a minimum, I'd like to stimulate their thinking, feeling, and performing with the activities and discussions we've experience together. A combination of well-matched activities with appropriate processing techniques can go a long way towards achieving this goal.

Theoretically, the leader is advised to play to the strength of the adolescent group—once this strength can be assessed. Strengths may be hypothesized from prior knowledge of the group, or they might simply be tested out as hypotheses in an initial warm-up, game, or initiative session. Hypothesizing questions from an understanding of the context from which different adolescent groups come from, and then testing out the hypotheses during novel, adventure activities comes from a theoretical conceptualization of the first four letters of Gass & Gillis' (1995b) assessment acronym "CHANGES". The CHANGES acronym is explained briefly in Michael Gass' contribution to this practice section. The key to working effectively with adolescents is to understand their strengths (or their solutions) and match activities that require them to utilize their strengths to create more solutions (Gass, & Gillis 1995a).

As much as the 'gifted' students might have a high degree of *understanding* of adventure activities and be *motivated* to participate in adventure experiences, adolescents labeled as 'difficult' or 'at-risk' may be less likely to understand *why* they are performing the activity, and less likely to participate willingly. Many of these adolescents are involved in adventure programming as an alternative to being incarcerated or as part of some mandated treatment program. When hypothesizing the strengths of this population, from our experience, a match might occur if the focus is on 'doing', or their actual **B**(ehavior) during an activity.

In the alternative to incarceration and treatment programs conducted at Project Adventure's Covington, Georgia office under the names of Challenge, Choices, and Legacy, experience has shown repeatedly that utilizing the behavioral strengths the group brings with them is a much more successful strategy than focusing on their problems. Staff make initial mistakes with this population by not assessing the concrete nature of the adolescent's initial understanding about the educational or therapeutic value of adventure activities. Staff begin to frontload activities with metaphors or similes when such language is not only counterproductive but not really understood by the adolescents. By focusing groups on 'just doing' the activity, perhaps a matching of strengths can occur and the remaining **A**(ffective) and **C**(ognitive) domains can be understood through processing techniques described in this text that relate to the group's **B**(ehavior).

The activity "Whale Watch" (Rohnke & Butler, 1995) is a good example of matching the behavioral strengths of a group. It follows the Nike™ philosophy: 'just do it'. Ask the group to *find their balance* on the 8′×13′ wooden platform that resembles a large teeter totter since it has a 6′ fulcrum in it's middle and can raise or fall 1′ depending on how the group's weight is distributed. In doing this activity the leader can assess how well the group can understand directions, treat each other with some modicum of respect, as well as observe how motivated they are to accomplish a task and have some fun. The task itself is appealing enough to let the adolescents bounce around (and bounce each other off) initially. Yet, the idea of balancing the group eventually becomes more appealing and challenging than just bouncing. From this activity, a leader can observe early in a group, individual group roles such as who in the group is a "gatekeeper", who is constantly wanting to have fun at the expense of others, and generally identify who in the group has some motivation to attempt and accomplish the task. The processing of this experience allows the leader to ascertain how well the group can understand the concept of 'balance'—either very concretely as a way of achieving the goal of the activity, or abstractly (and metaphorically) as it relates to how well they, as a group, can assess a way to pull together and work as one. The leader can then move from an understanding of the group's behavior to an understanding of their cognitive strengths and utilize this information to help gain access to their ability to express feelings.

The examples from such dissimilar adolescent groups as those labeled "gifted" and those who have been "adjudicated" point to some general do's and don'ts for practitioners that are listed below:

Do's	Don'ts
Assess the group as to their thinking, feeling, and doing capacity.	Assume you 'know' what activities to do with all adolescent groups.
Initially play to the strengths of the group with your activities.	Assume the group can automatically understand metaphorical introductions.
Match activities to the groups' strengths	Use 'canned' programs that treat all adolescent groups the same
Keep as a goal the balance of affect, behavior, and cognitive in an overall holistic program.	Force groups into 'insightful' debriefs where you, as facilitator' tell the group what they have learned or 'pull' from groups what the leader wishes to hear

❖ SUMMARY

The future holds much promise for work with adolescents. By assessing the strength of activities to highlight **A**ffective, **B**ehavioral, and **C**ognitive structures, group leaders who work with this population might begin to understand better how to match activities to group strengths. Leaders are challenged to not abandon tried and true processing techniques that help assess the groups' ability to understand what happened during an adventure experience. Leaders also are encouraged not to limit themselves only to a verbal means of processing experiences, but to stay open to nonverbal expressions of understanding that might help motivate students. All of this may warm the hearts of leaders who have a passion for working with all types of youth.

SECTION 3

FAMILIES
GUIDING PRACTICES

❖

Families are the focus of this section. We begin with a contribution by Suzanne Rudolph entitled "Families on the Ropes: Programming with Families." This is followed by a case study with some specific questions and responses from Michael Gass and Jackie Gerstein.

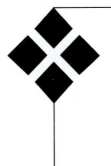

FAMILIES ON THE ROPES: PROGRAMMING WITH FAMILIES

Suzanne Rudolph, Ed.D.

Historically, adventure-based programs have provided services to groups of individuals with diverse backgrounds. Practitioners in the field have begun to recognize the limitations inherent in working with people, particularly adolescents, in isolation from their community of family and friends. According to Bandoroff (1994), the unchanged home environment is likely to make it difficult for adolescents to generalize the changes made during the experience. Although participants may leave the adventure-based experience ready to initiate changes in their lives, they may find themselves returning to the social, emotional and physical environment associated with home that does not support change. Consequently, many participants are likely to fall back into old behavioral patterns.

In recent years, there has been an increase in interest in the use of adventure-based programming as an intervention for families (Bandoroff & Scherer, 1994; Gass, 1993; Gerstien, 1994). Embracing a family-focused approach to intervention involves not only looking at the individual's influence on his/her behavior, but also it involves understanding the context, and/or multiple systems in which the behavior occurs.

According to Becvar and Becvar (1988), one of the major contributions the field of family therapy has made to the behavioral sciences is the introduction of a systemic perspective. Rather than focusing on individuals and their behavior in isolation, we look at the relationships among family members to understand how each interacts with and influences the others. In other words, difficulties tend to stem from problematic interactions between people. It is more useful to look at *what* is "going on" in an effort to describe relationships and patterns of interaction, than to focus on *why* it is happening. The focus of intervention is on the current interactions taking place among family members, and sometimes between these individuals and other social systems.

❖ GUIDING ASSUMPTIONS FOR WORKING WITH FAMILIES

Adventure-based programs are frequently used as a brief intervention or as an adjunct to other forms of therapy. The popularity of using a short-program format among program providers has been documented by Gass and Mcphee (1990). The following assumptions about people, problems, behavior and change offers program facilitators a lens for viewing families. They have been adapted from Walter and Peller (1992) Selekman (1993), and Wiener-Davis (1992), leaders in the field of brief-interactional therapy.

1. *Change is inevitable.* "Think of a mobile, constantly in motion, the various parts change in relation to other parts. No matter how we try to keep a mobile still, the slightest air currents set it in motion" (Shatz, Zimmerman & Watson, 1994, p.13). When a family member leaves, becomes ill, accepts a new job, etc., the entire family shifts. Roles and responsibilities are likely to change. Given that change in the family system is inevitable due to naturally occurring events, we can help families investigate and focus on positive changes. Your expectancy of change will have an influence on participants' behavior. Think in terms of co-creating positive self-fullfillng prophecies with families. It is more helpful to think about when change will occur—versus if it will happen at all. When talking to families about their goals, use presuppositional language such as when or will versus if or would. For example, *"When* you are getting along better, what *will* you be doing differently?"

2. *Only a small change is necessary.* All parts of a family's system are interconnected in such a way that small changes in one part of the system can ripple into changes in other parts of the system. Small changes can lead to bigger changes over time. Help family members focus on and express the small changes that they want versus what they don't want. Some families may generate a laundry list of problems. You can help the family establish small goals by asking them what they want to change first. The following criteria for establishing well-defined goals have been adapted from Walter and Peller (1992).

    a. Encourage family members to state their goals in a positive form rather than state the absence of something (e.g., less arguing). Ask family members what they want to see happening instead. For example, "So what do you want to be doing instead of arguing?"

    b. Use action-based language. It is easier to observe and track goal achievement if goals are stated in a process form in either a present or future tense. One way to know that a goal is being stated in a process form is to use verbs with "-ing" endings. For example, "I will be *listening* to what my wife has to say in a manner that helps her feel understood."

c. Be as specific as possible. Elicit a video description of how things will look differently when their chief concern is resolved. A video description should contain elements of who, what, when, where, and how. For example, one way to elicit a video description is to use a few hypothetical questions: "Lets imagine that this experience is helpful to you and your family;" " How will we know?;" "Specifically, what will you be doing differently?" "What will your family be doing differently?"

d. Make sure it's within the family member's control. Make sure that the goal you set is not contingent on something or someone else changing first.

e. The family is the expert. Focus on the goals that family members state that they want to achieve versus focusing on what you think the family *should* be working on. It's important to remember that families are the experts on what they want to work on and see changed. If they recognize other issues and choose not to focus on them at this time, respect their choice. One way to help remember what the family members stated as goals is to write down what they say they want in their *own* words.

3. *Families have the strengths and resources to change.* All families have the strengths and resources that are both known and unknown to them. Family members can have difficulty accessing these resources when they have a problem-saturated description of interaction. It's important to keep in mind that most family members do want to make positive changes; they just aren't sure how to go about it. Past successes can serve as a model for future success.

4. *If it works, don't fix it.* Encourage family members to notice what's working in their relationships with each other, compliment it, and encourage more of it! As facilitators, it is important to know when to *stay out of the way* and refrain from suggesting something different out of a desire to be helpful. Instead, we can use cheerleading to help families amplify and make distinctions between patterns of behavior that family members want to see continue to happen, and those that they want to change. Selekman (1993) describes cheerleading as giving family members high fives, handshakes, compliments, and getting family members to respond to questions such as "How did you get that to happen?"; "How did you do that?" (p.131).

5. *If it doesn't work do something different.* Frequently, problematic patterns of interaction continue because family members' attempts to solve the problem inadvertently maintains the problem. Often, the same solution is applied with greater and greater intensity. The key to solving a problem lies in doing something slightly different.

6. *There are always exceptions to the problem.* Family members can become stuck in their perception of what the solution should look like and fail to notice what's different about the times when the problem is not occurring, or when something different is happening. Exceptions to the problem pattern can offer clues to solutions. When families start to identify exceptions, problems don't seem as overwhelming as they thought. For example, a statement such as "We fight all the time," becomes "We get along better when we really take the time to listen to each other's perspective." The adventure-based exercises offer families a context in which to identify exceptions, and it gives families a blue print for behaviors and attitudes that they can practice in an effort to make their relationships more satisfying and strengthen their family.

❖ WHAT WE CAN LEARN FROM PARTICIPANTS AND STAFF

One of the first documented adventure-based programs for families was "The Family Challenge", founded in 1987 by Cynthia Clapp and Benjamin Moore. The program offered families from the greater Boston area a five session multi-family group model which combined the use of structured, skills-training exercises, adventure-based initiative activities, and facilitative discussions designed to encourage reflection and the exploration of family strengths. One year follow-up interview data was collected from 12 respondents from four single parent families and The Family Challenge program director. It is not the intent here to provide a detailed description of this study, but rather to offer a discussion of several themes that emerged from interviews with the respondents as they relate to critical issues in programming with families.

Discovering new possibilities for the family. When families feel distress, the tendency is to ignore what is going well in the family and instead, the attention shifts to what needs to be fixed. Family members then begin to watch for the problem situation to happen (Schatz, Zimmerman & Watson, 1994). Unfortunately, focusing on undesirable patterns of behavior can lead to a negative description of family life. One of the strengths of adventure-based programs is that participating families are given the opportunity to interact in novel ways. By actively engaging in behaviors that are unique, creating unique outcomes, the families can be provided with an opportunity to create experiences that contradict what typically is a problem pattern for the family. For example, one parent who participated in the adventure-based program stated, "I was able to see strengths in them [my children] that I didn't know existed. It was a wonderful experience to know that we could work together, and communicate and have fun doing it." Program facilitators can encourage family members to entertain the meaning of the unique outcomes as

they relate to their ongoing life together as a family. When processing adventure-based exercises with families, reflexive questioning can be used to facilitate the families' internalization of their sense of agency or influence over the problem-pattern of interaction. For more information on this type of questioning, see the section entitled "Co-Creating New Stories." By punctuating positive patterns of interaction through processing, family members may discover resources and capabilities that have previously gone unrecognized, and they may discover abilities in areas that can have a lasting impact on their family.

The children have good ideas. One of the more significant discoveries for some of the parents was the realization that their children also had good ideas. The adventure-based exercises called on family members to work cooperatively, leaving behind family roles and allowing for new opportunities for role flexibility. Making the most of the family's resources involved giving family members the opportunity to use the competencies they had. Facilitators can encourage parents to catch their children behaving in a positive way. Parents can be given the task of observing strengths in their children and processing the experience can include time to compliment their children. This will reinforce and promote the behaviors that they want to encourage and maintain both during and after the adventure-based experience.

Improved communication. DeVault and Strong (1986) recognized that communication is "the bedrock of family success" (p. 5). Participation in an emotionally-charged, adventure-based experience where vulnerabilities are shared and risks are taken may enhance communication and promote family intimacy (Mason, 1987). Making an effort to truly listen to family members and clarify what's being said is essential in negotiating challenges. Seven of the respondents made reference to positive changes in communication in their family.

Covey (1995) stresses the importance of improving communication as a way to strengthen relationships in the family. When families are under stress, there is a tendency to communicate efficiently which is not always effective. During the adventure-based experience, family members can be encouraged to slow down and really take the time to understand and affirm each other's point of view. One way to structure this is to have family members restate what they heard another family member say to his or her satisfaction—prior to making their point.

A new perspective on interdependence. Positive interdependence is an essential component of small groups, organizations and families. It is associated with working together to maximize mutual benefits, promote sharing of resources, celebrate joint successes and develop shared responsibility (Johnson & Johnson, 1987). Family members have the ability to function as a significant source of positive support for each other (Rueveni, 1985). For example one parent described discovering the support her children are capable of providing by stating:

> *I realized that, boy, these kids are really capable. They are really capable and I don't have to do for them. . . . I always thought I have to do, I have to do, I have to do, and [I would] never ask them for any help. When I saw them out there and what they were very capable of doing, I realized that I don't have to do this all the time. . . . I can say to June, I need you to do this and she's very capable of doing it, and so is Joe, and so is Sara.*

This parent also noted that after her experience in the program, she has been able to delegate responsibilities to her children through the sharing of household chores.

The benefits of working with similar families. Numerous benefits of working in a multi-family group were described by program participants. Among them were the recognition of commonalties in concern, support and bonding through the sharing of an emotionally-charged experience, and the opportunity to see themselves through a mirror image by watching other families in action. Several factors should be considered when grouping families together. Practitioners should consider family strengths, weaknesses and experiences, and group the families in such a way that they can maximize the potential for mutual aid. On an individual level, you should consider both the parental and the child subgroup, and look at what the members of each of these subgroups could offer each other. Grouping the families together with a similar constellation and common concerns provides a foundation for bonding upon which participants can build. It can enhance the family members' comfort level with each other and the program, and gives them the opportunity to discover that they are not alone with their problems.

Enactment of family difficulties. Adventure-based experiences demand high levels of participant engagement. The common history and intensity that families bring to the experience, coupled with the engaging nature of program events, can lead to enactment (Ewert, 1989). Families are likely to project a representation of typical behavioral patterns onto an activity. As a result, families may struggle more to complete an activity when working alone versus when working with other families in a multi-family group. You can use the exercises as an assessment tool to gather data about the way the family responds to stressful yet challenging tasks. When working with families experiencing multiple problems, the amount of information collected can be overwhelming. Program facilitators should focus on and remember what the family had identified as their chief concern/goal for the experience, and use this target information to structure program activities.

Meeting participant needs by structuring the experience. Adventure-based programs can assist families in identifying and setting specific goals, translating those goals into differences in behavior and providing families with an opportunity to actively change their behavioral patterns by engaging them in experiential exercises. The exercises offer a context for empowering families to do something different by altering typical patterns of interaction. A number of program participants commented on the way the program activities were tailored. When asked what he liked most about the program, one adolescent stated, "The way it was designed for us to all work together. They knew ahead of time what we needed to work on and they designed it around it." Tailoring the experience seems to have an empowering effect on the families and individual members as they discover capabilities in assuming different roles in the family, and they discover their own potential as a family team.

Processing. One of the difficulties in processing the experience with families stems from the difference in attention spans of the participants. There can be a wide range in the age of participants. Frequently, young children are more interested in the fun and activity part of the experience than the sitting and discussion part of the program. One parent who recognized this in her children stated, "To be frank with you, the kids didn't like that part [of the program]; they didn't like to sit and talk and discuss things." Developing creative ways to involve young family members and hold their attention during processing sessions can be an added challenge for program facilitators. You can take your cue to change your style of processing or bring closure to a processing session from the children. Once the childrens' attention is lost, consider moving on to the next activity.

Safety. Ewert (1989) stressed the importance of altering program components to enhance safety and program quality when working with special populations. He stated that while it is important to encourage participants to use their abilities to their fullest, it is equally important for staff to ensure that it occurs within a safe and reasonable structure. When working with families, this assessment process becomes more complex due to the variation in age, abilities, and roles of family members.

An important factor to consider when working with families is the physical capabilities of the people in the group, and how to help family members be accommodating. There are likely to be times during the program when the children want to do things that the parents can't do, and, in a similar vein, there are times when the parents want to do things, but the children can not. You can encourage parents to look at how they can be involved in an activity without physically participating. For example, The Family Challenge program director stated, "So your kids want to run and play tag, and you don't want to run and play tag. How can you still be a part of the game with them?" She continued, "If you can or you don't want to do this particular thing [this activity] how can you be a part of this activity but not put yourself in jeopardy? How can you still play the game but not get hurt?"

Another issue raised in working with parents and children is that some parents may be hesitant to let their children see them being vulnerable and may attempt to minimize what they are experiencing. For example, a significant incident occurred when one parent had "a terrible fall" and dislocated her shoulder. She was trying to hold herself while using a rope with a knot in the bottom as a swing to cross the area of land called the nitro pit. Although she was in significant pain when the incident happened, she chose not to let others know. She stated:

> Well, . . . when I went down, I saw this hysterical look on Michael's [her adopted son] face. Anything happens to me, I stub my toe, this child worries that I'm going to die and he's [going to] lose the only stable place he's ever lived. So, I thought, oh God, I mean I was in excruciating pain, but I thought, I knew he couldn't handle it, and I figured, as an adult, I can control this. You know I'll be all right. I'll be all right . . . then, by the evening, we got home and it was the pits and it got progressively worse. . . . I minimized it to Michael. I . . . did this martyr thing, where you grin and bear it and go through it.

Staffing. Recent evidence indicates that one of the central features of an effective adventure-based program is the staff. According to Wagner et al. (1991), the facilitator does make a significant difference to the long-term success of the program. Gillis and Gass (1991) raised the issue of training by stating that "therapists using adventure experiences or specific adventure techniques should realize that they need competency in two fields" (p. 18). Gillis and Gass cautioned adventure-based program providers against adding therapeutic components to their program by incorporating therapy jargon into their style of program delivery. In an earlier article, Gillis and Bonney (1986) presented the same caution to therapists against the danger of adding adventure-based practices to one's repertoire of therapeutic techniques without sufficient training and experience in using this type of intervention.

Program Products. Program products provide families with a symbolic way to remember the positive feelings associated with their adventure-based experience. All of the families had saved the materials they received from the program. All of the families hung the collages they developed on the wall, and three of the families pulled out the pictures that they received during the program. One parent stated, "We have the pictures. We have the collage we made up; that is very important to us." Furthermore, all of the families saved the video that they received during the program. Although it was not explicitly stated, the participants spoke with a tremendous amount of pride as they conveyed their story. Somehow they had accomplished something meaningful.

❖ Guiding Practices for Adventure-Based Program Providers _____

Based on interviews with program participants and a review of the literature, the following recommendations are made.

1. Families bring their history, intensity, and structure to the adventure-based experience which increases the potential for the enactment of family difficulties. Establish ground rules to ensure a climate of safety.
2. Respond to the emerging needs of the families and individual family members when processing the experience.
3. Respect the differences in attention spans associated with working with diverse-age participants, and plan for this difference when structuring the processing sessions.
4. Develop creative strategies, such as drawing, story telling, and journaling, to maintain the children's attention, and actively involve them in processing sessions.
5. Set aside time for parents to process and discuss issues apart from their children during the program.
6. Use a multi-session, program format when the experience is a stand-alone intervention to allow sufficient time for families to work through the phase of enactment of family difficulties to the phase of intervention as family members become empowered to actively do something different.
7. Plan follow-up sessions to assist families in consolidating change by reinforcing the gains they have made.
8. Require that facilitators have training in both family-therapy practices and adventure-based techniques.
9. Respect the difference in physical abilities of family members and the potential for parents to minimize their vulnerabilities or discomfort in front of their children. Facilitate discussion around alternative ways that parents can be involved in the exercises without physically putting themselves in jeopardy.
10. Use a one-to-one family-to-staff ratio when delivering experiences to allow for flexibility in addressing individual-family needs throughout the program.

◆ CASE STUDY

The local family service agency contacts you about the possibility of designing a program for their single-parent families and remarried families. One person on their staff had been on a ropes course and thought that it may be an interesting adjunct for them with some new funding they have received.

❖ QUESTIONS TO RESPOND TO ____

1. What strategies would you use to assess the needs of this group to design a program?

2. What general theories will guide you in regard to your program's design?

3. What would be an example of the ideal program for families that you'd suggest?

4. Give examples of your top experiential activities that you may use with the families and why these activities?

5. Thoughts about follow-up and evaluation.

6. Additional comments.

❖ CASE STUDY INVITED RESPONSE

Michael Gass, Ph.D.

❖ A COUPLE OF THOUGHTS BEFORE WE BEGIN! _____

Given this scenario, I feel that it is important to take note of the numerous-interacting systems involved in trying to affect the client-change process described above. Immediately evident are the individual families and their members, other interacting families in the program, the contacting family-service agency, schools, peer groups, and the "multiple layers of parenting" often involved in single parent and remarried families. I am constantly reminded how often such situations are plagued by the "iatrogenic hypothesis" phenomenon (i.e., clients are so enmeshed within multiple interactive, social service agencies that their problems have more to do with contraindicating messages from multiple "helpers" than their presenting "problems"). In my work in adventure family therapy, this phenomenon has been the greatest, limiting factor in my efforts to assist families in achieving lasting, functional change.

A second word of caution is the expectations of the social service agency; lasting, functional change is very difficult to achieve. In my work, I have found the changes produced in "dysfunctional" families in a one-day program to be short-term if not non-existent beyond the common, initial euphoria associated with adventure experiences. As professionals, I think we need to constantly remind ourselves that no family or adolescent wakes up one morning deciding that "Hey, we're going to be dysfunctional today!" Most dysfunctional patterns are well-orchestrated with valid reasons for their existence, "well protected" by several defensive layers of resistance. I have found that adventure family therapy can be of great assistance in producing profound and lasting changes within families, but from my research, I have also found that it generally takes longer than one day to produce these types of structural and strategic changes.

❖ ASSESSMENT STRATEGIES FOR PROGRAM DESIGN _____

Given these two thoughts, as well as others, the assessment strategies that I have found most helpful with such families are an interactive combination of traditional "paperwork" and the CHANGES model (Gass & Gillis, 1995a). Client assessment is a process most good facilitators do naturally. The idea behind a model like CHANGES is not to discount or replace facilitators' "natural" assessment abilities. The purpose of the CHANGES model is to enhance such abilities by making them more conscious, alerting therapists to potential "blind spots" and focusing efforts around creating a system of change that results in solutions to client issues.

The CHANGES model is organized into six interactive steps focusing on acquiring individual and systemic information for developing functional, client change. These steps include: (1) examining the client context, (2) hypothesizing about potential issues and resolutions for client issues (3) utilizing an action that is novel to determine the validity of therapist hypotheses, (4) generating information, from clients for potential interventions, (5) evaluation of initial hypotheses with appropriate revisions, and (6) the establishment of potential solutions.

I have also found that interfacing the CHANGES model with the GRABBS model (Schoel, Prouty, & Radcliffe, 1988) can be beneficial. The letters of the GRABBS acronym stand for: (1) Goals (e.g., What are the individual, family and group goals of the experience?), (2) Readiness (e.g., Do the group members feel, as well as look, physically and psychologically ready for the activity?); (3) Affect—(e.g., What is the level of feeling or affect among group members? Is it deep? Superficial?); (4) Behavior (e.g., How have group members behaved thus far toward the experience, each other, and toward the therapist?); (5) Body (e.g., Are group members treating each others' body respectfully?); and (6) Stage—(e.g., What stage of group development is the group in—beginning, middle, ending—forming, norming, storming, performing?).

For me, the CHANGES model provides more of a "macro" or systemic perspective, directing therapists toward an overall solution for client goals and functional change. The GRABBS model is especially effective on the "micro" level of the "Hypothesizing" and "Generating information, stories, and ideas" steps.

In closing, therapists also should recognize the approach one takes to assessment often determines what will be "seen." Professionals who are open to receiving continual client interpretations and understandings will probably find more information accessible for use. Professionals who are closed to one rigid and static understanding of client behavior will probably tend to see the "problem" in a certain "sameness" of perspective. Professionals are encouraged to continually learn client characteristics through an attitude of flexibility and spontaneity.

It is also important to remember that assessment should be viewed as an ongoing phenomenon, not a one-time procedure conducted prior to an intervention. Assessment processes are inextricably linked to intervention processes. In fact, feedback from interventions usually supply invaluable assessment for future interventions.

❖ GENERAL THEORIES GUIDING ME IN PROGRAM DESIGN

Several marriage and family therapy schools-of-thinking deeply influence my work. Probably, the way to describe this would be to state "that I am a solution oriented, structure-strategic marriage and family therapist", heavily influenced by the work of Milton Erickson and Milan therapists.

Theories that have influenced my thinking in adventure/experiential programming include the work of John Dewey, Paulo Friere, Thomas James, Lee Gillis, Simon Priest, Stephen Bacon, Rocky Kimball, Christian Itin, Carina Dolcino, Relly Nadler, Denise Mitten, Cindy Clapp-Lutvik & Sue Rudolph, Jackie Gerstein, and Ted Wichman. Deep thinkers whose conversations have added to my work include Andrea Parrish, Karen Hand, Jim Beer, Jim Burg, Dene Berman, Scott Bandoroff, and Jim Moore.

"Anti-theorists" who have taught me just as much include the masters of spontaneous excellence—Craig Dobkin and Karl Rohnke. Anything either of these two people have written pales in comparison to the "excellence of the moment" they provide when working with clients.

❖ EXAMPLE OF AN IDEAL PROGRAM FOR FAMILIES

One program model that I have found effective in working with this type of group is one that we use with the Family Expedition Program. The Family Expedition Program is a federally-funded program designed to foster healthy changes in families with troubled adolescents through the use of adventure family experiences. Each Family Expedition cycle is four months long, consisting of six multi-family sessions and three home visits. Five of the sessions occur on Saturdays; the sixth session is generally an overnight weekend experience at a "conference center" or rustic camp type setting. The session activities, in order of sequence, are as follows: (1) program orientation and goal setting activities, (2) rock climbing, (3) overnight experience, (4) seaside activities and initiatives, (5) challenge course and orienteering, (6) high challenge course and graduation from the program.

The home visit component of the program is an integral piece of the Family Expedition Program. Visits are opportunities to highlight learnings, reflect on and integrate experiences, and revisit family goals. Most importantly, each 90 minute home visit gives families a time and place to focus specifically on relevant issues that they may not feel like addressing in the presence of the larger, multi-family group.

While the second and third home visits are tailored around specific interventions for each family, the initial home visit spends a great deal of time focusing on assessment and screening. The goals of the initial visit are to affiliate with the family, outline the investment necessary for participation in the program, inform the family about potential change processes, introduce solution-oriented, goal setting, and to collect information for the purpose of assessment, screening, and the formu-

lation of CHANGE hypotheses that are highlighted above.

When conducting home visits, the following seven guidelines from Berg (1994) are used to help implement the CHANGES model: (1) Set the tone for a friendly, positive atmosphere; (2) Use normal, everyday, conversational language in a friendly, soft tone with neutral words and phrases; (3) Trust your own judgment and intuition with client interactions, being particularly willing to acknowledging a lack of information, and place clients as "experts" at the details of the situation; (4) Utilize yourself as a "tool" for helping clients, using common sense, observational skills, and senses, (5) Maintain a positive, hopeful view of clients and your work with them; (6) Pay attention to parents as well as children (e.g., many parents are isolated and lonely and they can become easily threatened when the therapist pays an inordinate amount of attention to the children; and (7) When parents make complaints about their children, recognize this as a clue that you need to find ways to compliment some aspect of their parenting (p. 20).

❖ EXAMPLES OF TOP EXPERIENTIAL ACTIVITIES FOR FAMILIES

Three examples of my favorite "experiential" activities with families are the Minefield (e.g., Rohnke, 1984), Trust progressions (Gillis & Gass, 1993), and Incline Log experiences (e.g., Webster, 1989). I chose these activities not only for their individual "richness" for client issues, but also because they mirror different concepts that have proven important for the clients in our work.

The "Minefield" activity has often provided a fantastic mirror for parent-child dynamics and interactions. Metaphorical issues of guidance, increasing responsibility levels, communication, and launching have offered a rich medium for change. Solution-oriented therapy approaches to functional change also are well-suited for this activity (see Gass & Gillis, 1995b for more information).

Trust activities (e.g., trust leans, circles, falls) have been enriching when I've been able to "contextualize" the meaning of "trust" within families. While quite "normal" as far as adventure activities go, trust experiences have often provided clients with an important ability to put goals like "increased levels of trust" into a more "process form" of client action (e.g., "I'm able to trust him when he . . . , I feel more trusting when I . . .). A good example illustrating this can be found in Gillis and Gass (1993).

In setting up the "Inclined Log" activity, we place as many set-ups on the belay wire as families in our multi-family groups. While only one family is actually "on" the log, at a time, all other families work toward preparing themselves to address specific issues as well as to serve as witnesses to each others' interactions. It is in these types of situations where I have seen the modeling and learning from multi-family systems reach its true potential.

❖ FOLLOW-UP

Follow-up is obviously critical for reinforcing functional changes that occur with families. The adventure therapy field has been criticized as early as the 1980's by government providers for not providing follow-up or any form of integration into the client's home life (e.g., Johnson, Bird, Little, & Beville, 1981).

One strong suggestion (as well as ethical consideration) is to insure the integration and transition of changes from adventure family therapy experiences into other therapeutic services where families may continue. While all professionals are aware that assisting clients in obtaining supportive services is appropriate and ethical behavior (e.g., AEE, 1992), I think we could do a better job of helping other professionals integrate changes from adventure experiences into other forms of therapy where clients may continue.

Another suggestion is to question the "lasting and independent" nature of adventure experiences. If an adventure experience only provides functional change during the program or in the presence of an adventure therapist, one should really question the validity of the approach. Therapists should center on the utilization of experiences that result in self-reinforcing behaviors that amplify positive-behavior changes as the family "oscillates" through its systemic family interactions. As stated at the beginning of my comments, professionals also need to consider the family's interactions with larger systemic influences once the adventure therapy experience is completed. This is no small task, but it is the appropriate and ethical one.

❖ EVALUATION IDEAS

Probably, the most often used measurement tool for evaluating adventure family therapy programs has been Hudson's Index of Family Relations. Its use in our programs has been positive and several other researchers (e.g., Jacobsen, 1992) have found it effective as a means for monitoring change. Clapp and Rudolph (1990; also in Gass, 1993) have also used the McMaster Family Assessment Device (Epstein, Baldwin, & Bishop) and the F-Copes Scale (Olsen & McCubbin, 1985) successfully.

❖ ADDITIONAL COMMENTS

Probably the biggest problem facing the use of adventure family therapy is not its ability to demonstrate treatment effectiveness, but its ability to be offered as a financially viable "package" for reimbursing agencies (e.g., insurance companies, HMO providers). Until adventure family therapy, as well as other forms of adventure therapy, are recognized as "reimbursable" by third party payers, the field will not reach its' true potential. While this is not an issue for some programs, this dynamic has led to the closure or discontinuance of a number of excellent adventure family therapy programs.

Another critical feature is the idea of training. In my opinion, the best adventure family therapy providers have been individuals who are "cross-trained," not only possessing experience and training in family therapy and adventure therapy, but also knowing how

these two approaches interact together (Gillis & Gass, 1993). For example, "traditional" family therapy techniques such as reframing, metaphoric inductions, restructuring are different (and empowered in my opinion) when interconnected with adventure experiences. The best providers seem to possess the ability to know how to access the best elements from each field to produce "synergistic gains" for clients, as well as when merging such elements may be contraindicated.

In closing, I need to state that the comments that I've presented here are limited and only present a small segment of what one needs in order to be successful in programming. Readers are encouraged to remain "vigilant" learners in their quest to support their clients.

CASE STUDY INVITED RESPONSE

Jackie Gerstein, Ed.D.

❖ GENERAL THEORIES

In addition to the basic tenets described for experiential education and counseling, Narrative Therapy and Strategic Family Therapy are the theories which guide me as I design experiential programs for families. Each will be explained briefly below.

NARRATIVE THERAPY

The authors of Narrative Therapy clearly articulate those values and beliefs that drive my approach for using experiential activities with families. Richard Simon (1994), *The Family Therapy Networker* editor, explains, "Rather than making the 'pathology-saturated' family story the centerpiece of the therapy, clinicians can make progress faster by zeroing in on clients' half-forgotten memories of courage and triumph, times when they did not allow themselves to be defined exclusively by their difficulties. These too-often ignored bits of personal history can become the foundation for new, more healing life stories (p.2)."

Shirley Riley (1994) in her book, *Integrative Approaches to Family Art Therapy,* states, "When the family begins telling their stories, imagining new endings, finding new thoughts, they are becoming creative." (p. 21). Experiential activities often create visible illustrations of the family story. Experiential-based counseling can become the bridge between the invented reality of the family and the facilitator's appreciation and understand-

ing of the family's reality. Through the experiential activities, families are provided an opportunity to act out their family stories and discover new, alternative endings to their legends (Gerstein, 1996).

STRATEGIC THERAPY

I draw from the works of Cloe Madanes' and Jay Haley's Strategic Family Therapy when I think about the specific, program design and activity selection. Some key principles from Strategic Family Therapy that can be directly applied to experiential family programming are:

- ◆ The emphasis is not on a specific method or techniques to be applied to all cases but on designing strategies to address the family's concerns.
- ◆ The goals of counseling are the identification and prevention of the repetition of unhealthy interactions or sequences, and the introduction of healthier alternatives.
- ◆ Interventions take the form of directives (or initiatives) about something the family members are to **do.** These directives (or initiatives) are designed to change the way family members relate to each other (Madanes, 1981).

In integrating and summarizing the concepts discussed above, experiential activities and their related, processing sessions are strategically selected and designed for each family's unique personality and concerns in order to: (a) identify and draw from strengths and resources, (b) assist the family members in telling their "story," (c) identify and change unhealthy, interactional sequences, and (d) help the family in discovering healthier, alternative "endings" to their story.

❖ NEEDS ASSESSMENT

The assessment process can be divided into three distinct phases: (a) the program orientation, (b) initial goal development, and (c) ongoing assessment. In all three phases, assessment is a collaborative effort—one in which the family and the facilitator work closely in program direction and design.

PROGRAM ORIENTATION

Every potential family candidate receives an orientation to clarify the purpose of the program and to determine if the program is appropriate for that family. The orientation addresses the program format, possible program goals, possible risks, why the program can be important to the family, and how the skills learned in the program can be pertinent to issues in their home environment. The orientation is designed to determine if the family's concerns can be addressed by this type of program; to determine if there is a "fit" between the family's problem area/concerns and the mission/goals of the experiential, family counseling program (Gerstein, 1996).

INITIAL GOAL DEVELOPMENT

Literature in the family development and therapy fields have reached some consensus as to those properties or characteristics that make up a healthy family. As part of goal development, family participants are presented with a short list of these characteristics and asked, as a family unit, to select one or two as goals for their program. The list includes:

◆ To assist each family member in becoming a caring, responsible member of the family unit.
◆ To develop more open and honest communication lines between the family members.
◆ To increase the family's skills in problem-solving and negotiation.
◆ To identify and build upon the family's strengths to support current, functional behaviors.
◆ To increase the family's ability to have fun with one another and enjoy one another's company.
◆ To shift from problem-centered, problem-focused perspective to one which emphasizes present and future successes.
◆ To assist the family in correcting the family hierarchical system—where parents are "in charge" of the children (Gerstein 1996).

Experiential activities and accompanying processing sessions are then strategically designed to match each family's selected goal(s.)

ONGOING ASSESSMENT

Because experiential counseling is an ongoing and evolving process, assessment is also ongoing and evolving. A family's story tends to change form as it emerges during the experiential exercises. The counselor/facilitator must always remain cognizant of what the family is "saying" and mold the experiential exercises and processing sessions around the family's emerging story.

Drawing from the theoretical information discussed earlier, I constantly ask myself the following questions:

a. Do the experiential exercises and related, processing sessions directly relate to the family's unique personality and their *current* concerns?

b. Is each family member getting an opportunity to tell *his* or *her* story?

c. Is the family identifying both healthy and unhealthy interactional sequences?

d. Are opportunities being provided for the family to draw upon and utilize their strengths and resources?

Based on the answers to these questions, the experiential exercises and related, processing sessions are continually selected, created, modified, adapted, and rejected with the facilitator's flexibility being the key to the effective use of this assessment information.

❖ AN IDEAL EXPERIENTIAL PROGRAM FOR FAMILIES

I believe two elements facilitate an ideal, experiential program for families. They are: (a) the program is community-based and easily accessible for the family, and (b) the emphasis is on relationships. A relationship is sought between the family members, and between the family members and the facilitator that is long-term, consistent, and respectful.

Families are asked to make a commitment from six months to a year. Since it is a community-based program, we would meet in a "comfortable" place for the family such as a local park or school. Field trips to an out-of-town ropes course, camp, rock climbing site, or residential facility may be planned later in the program with the family's approval.

Meeting times would be based on the family's availability with the knowledge that evenings or weekends will probably best meet the family's time constraints. Hopefully, a once a week, or twice a month, meeting-schedule can be established.

The optimal session length is two to three hours. This time frame (a) meets most family's schedules, (b) meets the developmental needs of younger children and older adults, and (c) allows enough time to introduce and process an experiential activity. The meeting location, the meeting times, and length of sessions are worked out collaboratively with the family.

Given the working principle that the facilitator/family relationship is collaborative, families should also have a say in the types of experiential activities in which they would like to participate. They can be given a menu of sorts: physical or not physical activities? cognitively challenging? fun and goofy? strong use of verbal skills? use of art activities? Because a family may be unsure about these types of activities that they enjoy or desire, the facilitator can introduce different sorts of activities, and he/she should make note of those that best match the family's interests, desires, motivations, and needs.

The facilitator's role is to elicit and take as much of what the family members present, and he/she should design the program around the family members. Family members are the experts about themselves. The facilitator is the expert in program design. I view it as the peg-in-the-hole philosophy. The goal isn't to form the family into a round peg so they can fit in the round hole (unless they explicitly state that this is their goal!). The designers, make the hole fit their shape. If the underlying mission is to address the family's unique personality and to empower them to have some direction in their life, then all opportunities should be provided for them to do so!

❖ SELECTION OF PROGRAM ACTIVITIES FOR SINGLE-PARENT AND STEPFAMILIES

The introductory scenario addresses two populations with very specific concerns and needs. Given my knowledge of the general needs of these populations and without the benefits of a needs assessment, I would select experiential activities and related, processing sessions based on the following information.

SINGLE-PARENT FAMILIES

The number of one-parent families has grown over the past two decades because of the increase in the divorce rate and the number of children being born to unwed mother. Single parents must accomplish the same tasks and functions as two-parent families. They are expected to provide both the instrumental (the protector and provider) and the expressive (the nurturer) functions. Because of this heavy burden, they often place "adult" responsibilities on children who are not developmentally ready to accept these responsibilities (Benokraitis, 1996). Adult-child boundaries are often less defined, as parents and children turn to each other to provide emotional support (Papernow, 1995).

Brook (1993) states that interventions in single-parent families should: (a) emphasize strengthening the executive function of the custodial parent, and (b) establish or strengthen the generational boundaries between parent and child(ren). Interventions are designed to support the parent as the expert and family leader. Counseling involves helping the parent return to her or his parent role, allowing the child(ren) to express themselves in a developmentally appropriate manner, and modifying parent-child communications to support both the parent and child(ren) as they establish healthier roles (Brooks, 1993).

Based on this knowledge, I often use the Family Obstacle Field (see Gerstein, 1996, p. 124) or the Mine Field Initiative with single-parent families. I structure this activity so that the parents lead her or his blindfolded child(ren) through a maze of obstacles. In this scenario, the parent is asked to provide the direction, or executive function, to the child. The child is encouraged to ask questions for clarification, but must depend on her or his parent as the knowledgeable adult. Comments from this activity have included, "It was nice to have my dad give me directions for once," and "My daughter had to put her complete trust in me. It was a good lesson for both of us." Basically, any experiential activity which allows the parent to be the expert guide for her or his child can be used to meet the intervention goals for single-parent families.

STEPFAMILIES FAMILIES

It is estimated that 33% to 44% of US children live in stepfamilies. Demographers predict that stepfamilies will be the predominant, family structure in the United States by the year 2000 (Visher & Visher, 1995.) Stepfamilies have dynamics that are unique and different from first-time families. "A stepfamily consists of one, and often two, already established parent-child 'minifamilies' whose members' attachment to each other is much stronger than the new, adult couple's. The bonds of the original parent-child unit include norms of behavior evolved over years of living together" (Papernow, 1995, P.5).

Those working with stepfamilies need to understand that the stepfamily will remain divided along the original, family-lines with agreement on rules and rituals with the most connection remaining within the biological subsystems. Based on this understanding, three major goals should be part of every stepfamily intervention: (a) learning the art of negotiation so that rule adaptations (a few rule adaptations at a time!) can be made so "both families" become more comfortable with one another, (b) acknowledging and normalizing that the preexisting parent-child alliances will remain stronger than other stepfamily alliances, and (c) providing adequate time; so that, various subsystems get intimate time together including the stepcouple, the biological parent-child, the step-child, and stepsiblings (Papernow, 1995; Visher & Visher, 1995).

An experiential exercise I use to address the first two goals is the Dumping Field (see Gerstein, 1996, p. 141) or as it is often called, Nuclear Cans. Parents are paired with their biological/original family children. The children are blindfolded and cannot speak, but they can touch the activity's props. The parents can see and speak, but cannot touch any of the props. The activity demands that the parent/child dyad work closely together, but to accomplish the task of the initiative the pairs must also work cooperatively with the other parent/child pairs. It becomes a great metaphor for the stepfamily dynamics!

The third goal, providing time for the subsystems to spend together, is accomplished through dyad activities—two person trust walks, dyad interviews, and dyad, processing sessions. During different activities, different dyads are paired together. The group activities are intermixed with dyad activities; so that, the smaller subsystems get an opportunity to spend quality and intimate time with one another.

❖ FOLLOW-UP

Follow-up techniques such as contracts, progress meetings, and adjunct services can support the family as they transfer learning from the counseling environment to their home environment (Gerstein, 1996).

CONTRACTS

Through contract development, the family members work together to set clearly defined behavioral limits. In other words, both parents and offspring work together to negotiate "house rules" along with the consequences if the rules are broken.

The contract also specifies a plan to deal with future problems; problems similar to the ones that brought the family into counseling. The contract describes those steps that the family will take to solve future problems (Gerstein, 1996).

PROGRESS MEETINGS

Progress meetings can be planned for the family to meet with the counselors and the other families participating at regular, pre-specified intervals following program termination to discuss progress on goals developed during the program. Continued "check-up" visits can occur every 4–6 weeks to monitor the progress of the change process (Gerstein, 1996).

ADJUNCT PROGRAMS

Adjunct programs may be recommended to the family groups based on their needs and problems. Problems within the family may require some additional treatment that experiential, family programming cannot provide. Family problems may be severe enough to indicate some longer-term and more intensive family therapy. If this is the case, the family is referred to an agency which would be able to provide this type of service. Self-help groups such as Alcoholics Anonymous, Ala-Teen, Alanon, or Parents Without Partners also can be recommended to assist the family with some needed, external supports (Gerstein, 1996).

❖ CONCLUSION _____

In conclusion, the New Mexico Family-to-Family Initiative clearly states what I believe should be the driving force when designing and implementing family-based experiential programs: *Families have a right to access services and resources that are flexible, are available in their community, and which reflect their expressed and unspoken needs.*

SECTION 4

COUPLES
GUIDING PRACTICES

❖

"People do not live by words alone, despite the fact that sometimes we have to eat them."

—*Adlai E. Stevenson*

This section focuses on couple relationships, which arguably is the most challenging, yet most intimate of all relationships. Some guiding practices for couples are first illuminated, then a case study is presented with a response from Dene Berman and Jennifer Davis-Berman.

Why are couple relationships so challenging for most of us? We spend the *most* time with this person dealing with the *greatest* number of variables, problems, and concerns of all our relationships. It becomes very easy to *assume* this person has our same expectations, motives, and understanding of the issues, and the same approach to take. We think he or she knows what we are thinking, and of course, he/she understands and agrees with us. Many relationships consequently are full of tension, frustrations, and an inability to get past the same place in an argument. Couples need help to get past these impasses in order to grow, change, and rekindle their acceptance of each other. Programs for couples in experiential learning are limited, yet, they can have profound affects for the couple, their family, and society in general.

We selected John Gray's (1992) *Men are from Mars, Women are from Venus,* as a reference for these guiding practices. His work demonstrates some of the basic themes of interest that are woven throughout this book: (a) Using metaphors and story as a communication tool, (b) the value of externalizing the problem, (c) our perception influences all that we "see", and (d) focusing on what is practical and useful. The metaphor or story he uses is that, once upon a time Martians and Venusians met, fell in love and had a wonderful and satisfying relationship because they accepted and respected their unique histories and ways of looking at the universe. They then came to Earth where amnesia occurred and they forgot they were from different planets (Gray, 1992). We are speaking about men and women differences, but these unique views of the world occur in same-sex relationships and sometimes a man has more Venus qualities and a woman more Mars tendencies.

One of the main values and success of this viewpoint is that the problem is externalized to men's or women's differences, rather than my husband just doesn't understand, or my wife keeps wanting more from me. This externalization creates a gap to see your mate in a new way. It's more the differences between the sexes that is causing the problems, than my significant other's personal problems. This view ". . . reveals how men and women differ in all areas of their lives. Not only do men and women communicate differently but they think, feel, perceive, react, respond, love, need, and appreciate differently. They almost seem to be from different planets, speaking different languages, and needing different nourishment" (Gray, 1992, p. 5).

❖ LIFE ON MARS

On Mars, men value power, competency, efficiency, and achievement. Their fulfillment comes through successes and accomplishments. Men are more goal-oriented than relationship-oriented. They feel good and worthwhile when they can solve a problem, accomplish a task and do it on their own. Men learn on Mars that you don't ask for help from another man because that demonstrates your weaknesses. They will just stay with the task until they get it accomplished, or at last resort, go get expert advise. Autonomy is the symbol of power, competence, and efficiency for men.

❖ LIFE ON VENUS

On Venus, women value love, communication, beauty, and relationships. Their fulfillment comes through relationships, sharing, supporting and helping one another. Relationships are more important than work or accomplishments. Personal expression of feelings is very important for Venusians. Women are more relationship-oriented than goal-oriented. Offering help or assistance is a sign or symbol of great care or concern on Venus. Most women on Venus have studied psychology or have a Master's in Counseling.

❖ COMMUNICATION PROBLEMS

◆ Men hear women talking about a problem and become "Mr. Fixit."
◆ Women offer advise to help men on small things, and the man feels that she doesn't trust his ability to solve problems when the big things occur.
◆ When communicating, the woman wants to just be heard and understood. The man is trying to understand the problem, so he can find a solution to it.
◆ Men are very logical and rational in problem-solving while women are intuitive and more perceptive of others' reactions and feelings.
◆ Women speak more in generalities and extremes because they are feeling a lot, and men take it literally and point out the inconsistencies.
◆ Men try to change women's feelings with solutions.
◆ Women try to change men's behavior with offering unsolicited advise and criticism.

Once these assumptions are understood and caught, couples have the opportunity to break through their typical stuck points in an argument. Men need to become better listeners, so women feel cared for and understood. Women need to not correct men's mistakes, so that men can feel accepted and trusted. "Men are motivated and empowered when they feel needed. Women are motivated and empowered when they feel cherished" (Gray, 1992, p. 43).

❖ DEALING WITH STRESS

When men and women are under stress, they each use a different strategy that often is not understood and tends to cause additional tension and frustration. Understanding that they are from different planets helps both see how these strategies work for each other. Under stress, women want to talk about the situation, and men want time alone to think and go to their "cave." The cave can be reading the paper, watching TV, or going to another room to work. When these differences are understood and stress occurs, men and women can negotiate their needs at the time and strive for the win-win solution. Gray (1992) describes the reasons men go to their caves and women need to talk.

Why men go to their caves

1. They need time to think about the problem and come up with a solution.
2. Men haven't learned to say "I don't know, or I don't have an answer and let me go figure it out."
3. Men may be upset or angry and need time to cool off or get better control of themselves. They don't want to say anything that will make it worse.

4. A man may need to find himself because he has been feeling too close or intimate and he needs to regulate it by getting some space. Then, he can come back feeling rejuvenated and ready for more intimacy.

Why women need to talk

1. They need to gather information or communicate what they know.
2. To explore what she wants to say. This is a process of thinking out-loud that helps crystallize her thoughts and feelings.
3. A woman feels better, more centered, and relieved if she can talk when upset.
4. A woman feels more connected and intimate with her mate and herself by sharing her feelings.

Understanding the unique perspectives that both men and women bring into the relationship can help when the amnesia sets in. The couple can stop blaming each other and instead understand their differences, then experiment with new ways of communicating and acting. The couple story can then have a new chapter, co-authored, that can be more empowering to each Martian and Venusian. John Gray has a few books and tape series that can be a great resource to help in your own relationship and in designing needed programs for couples.

CASE STUDY

What follows is a case study and the questions that we invited the contributors to respond to in their write-up.

A local, private-practice group of marriage and family therapists contacts you about the possibility of designing a program for couples. They are an innovative group willing to do the marketing for the recruitment, and they will also use their own referrals. One therapist had been on a ropes course and thought that it may be a unique offering for the couples and something that managed care could endorse.

❖ QUESTIONS

1. What strategies would you use to assess the needs of this group to design a program?

2. What general theories will guide you in regards to your program design?

3. What would be an example of the ideal program for couples that you'd suggest, and how would you integrate the therapists into the program?

4. Give examples of your top experiential activities that you may use with the couples, and why the selection of these activities?

5. Your thoughts about follow-up and evaluation.

6. Additional comments.

CASE STUDY INVITED RESPONSE

Dene Berman, Ph.D. and Jennifer Davis-Berman, Ph.D.

This is a project that we are excited about because it provides us with an opportunity to combine two interests: counseling and experiential learning, and therapy. Our starting point for planning this group is a meeting with the referring therapists. For the therapists, this will mean getting signed releases of information to talk with us about each couple's issues. Of course, it is important for us to know who the couples are and their present areas of difficulty—are they on the verge of divorce? Seeking improved communications? Wanting to regain the zest in their relationship?

Most therapists also have a treatment plan for each client, containing a brief statement of the presenting problem, diagnoses, goals to be worked on, and a time line for when these goals should be reached. Perusal of the treatment plans will give us valuable information about the type of problems that people want to work on, the severity of their problems, their level of functioning, and a target date for completion.

Before ever meeting the clients, we should have a reasonable picture of the needs and goals of the group, as well as the expectations of the therapists. Other valuable information should also be gathered in the process, in response to such questions as: What are the ages of the participants? Are there any physical limitations among them? What are our constraints in terms of the length of each session (can this occur all day, or in 2 hour blocks of time?) How many meetings are allotted for

this group? Are overnight trips possible? What is our budget?

❖ THEORETICAL PERSPECTIVE

There are two theories that we use to guide our work with couples in a group setting: system's theory and narrative therapy . We will briefly summarize each of these and mention how they might apply to this group.

Some of the principles of "systems theory" as they apply to couples include: 1) The couples relationship is a system in that it attempts to maintain stability. 2) It dampens forces that are perceived as threatening and would create disequilibrium or change. 3) Patterns of the marital relationship must be perceived to be dysfunctional before they can be willingly changed; otherwise change will be resisted. 4) Certain therapeutic situations make it easier for change to be made by couples.

"Narrative therapy" holds that each of us view our lives and relationships as part of a story. We are the central characters of our own stories and have the ability to write our own scripts. Two people are intimate to the extent that they share the same scripts, and each person is empathic to the extent that he or she understands the other's story.

For us, these two theories can be used to describe why couples come to therapy. Often, they are on parallel but distant life paths, as might occur when both partners have locked horns and are competing to determine which person's script will be dominant. Another example is when the couple is on a divergent path, getting more distant with time, as might happen when partners have withdrawn from each other and have put their energies into other activities or people.

What we are seeking is for each couple to create a common story that includes both intimacy and separateness, to see how their current stories interfere with the happiness they seek, and to find an equitable way of working toward their shared vision.

❖ PROPOSED PROGRAM

For this group of couples, we are suggesting four sessions of 3 hour blocks of time. Canoeing is envisioned as a medium for relationship building and as a metaphor for working together as a couple. We have assumed that the couples have little experience paddling together in tandem canoes, but have adequate swimming abilities to participate in the course.

This program is designed as being comprised of 4 sessions, each beginning and ending with a group-therapy session. The themes for the four meetings are: Joining, in which partners in each couple work together; Common Themes, where couple can talk about their expectations and compare them to their experiences; Becoming Authors urges couples to plan on how they want their experiences to take shape and experiment at making it happen: and Creating Future Stories, the final session, is a time to integrate and associate what was learned in previous sessions and decide how to use these skills in the future.

Joining. In Session 1, we meet with the couples and begin to talk about the format of the experience which will include both group-counseling that will include therapist, and on-the-water experience in tandem canoeing. The couples will be asked to share their "couple story" in terms of what has caused them to come to counseling, their current status, and any future aspirations together. From here, we will have couples begin to learn the basics about canoeing (gear, safety, strokes, etc.) Couples will be expected to take turns at the bow and the stern, to gain an appreciation for the differing perspectives and skills needed for both ends of the canoe. Most couples experience more than a little bit of frustration at this point in a canoe class. This session would end with a group discussion of how things went for each couple, with an emphasis on how the events of the day mirror both the fun and foibles of their marriage.

Common themes. Session 2 would begin with a group discussion of some of the common themes from the "couples stories." The couples can be prompted to use these themes to form expectations about the day's itinerary in terms of paddling. More water experiences follow, including a continuation of strokes and a refinement of abilities. A group session again follows paddling and includes a discussion of expectations versus the reality of the experience. Finally, a discussion could follow in which couples talk about the relationship skills needed for good paddling partners (e.g., trust, good communication, a common agenda) and how these skills might be applied to their marriage.

Becoming authors. The primary focus of this session is on changing the couple's story. In this regard, couples will be urged to talk about their successes and failures, canoeing, and to come up with joint plans for making this session work better for them. Couples would be urged to try out new roles that might work, thereby creating disequilibrium in their relationship and working on the "edge" of their comfort zone. The on-the-water experience would focus on honing skills and teamwork. The group discussion at the end of the session would include an assessment of how each couple perceived their relationship to have worked in terms of developing a new plan, their success in making it work, and the extent to which their goals were met.

Creating future stories. At the outset, couples will be asked to assess the extent to which they are working in a way that is consistent with the treatment goals that they set in traditional counseling, and the way in which they envisioned functioning during the last session on the water. They would be given time to again revise their stories about being a couple, and try it out in their canoes. Each couple would be encouraged to develop a canoe demonstration for the group that characterizes how as a couple they can work together. So, for example, one couple might show how they can spin their boat by using reciprocal draw strokes, while another might show how well they can coordinate smooth forward strokes. This session would end with couples talking about what they learned during these sessions and how they would apply what they have learned to their relationship at other times.

❖ EVALUATION

Nothing seems to work as well for documenting paddling skills acquisition as using videotaping. People can clearly see what worked well (and poorly) for themselves and others. They can also see how they progressed over time. Not only could videotaping segments of paddling be effective, but so could taping segments of the group counseling.

Since the goal for this group was to help the couples create new scripts for themselves, we could ask them to write down their scripts during each group session. This would coincide with the foci of each group: joining, common themes, becoming authors, and future stories.

Another option for evaluation might include evaluating themselves on the treatment plan goals they had when entering this experience. There are also standardized measures of marital relationships that might be used.

❖ CONCLUDING THOUGHTS

In this group, since both of us are therapists and canoe together, it would be necessary to have the referring therapists take part in the experiences. Thus, our emphasis might be more directed at providing for continuity between the traditional counseling setting and this experiential program. We also would be concerned about communicating with the referring therapists about the changes that we saw in each couple. This could be accomplished by writing progress notes and/or a summary for each couple.

It is not necessary to design a curriculum for the paddling part of the program. The program we envision follows the curriculum of the American Canoe Association (ACA) course, "Introduction to Paddling." There are numerous advantages to the ACA curriculum, one of which is the liability insurance that goes with it.

An important part of a program like the one we propose is enjoyment. If couples have a good time, we assume that they will feel better about their relationship, look forward to new opportunities to interact, find change and challenge to be less threatening, and incorporate what they learned into their daily living.

We chose tandem canoes because while many people refer to them as "divorce boats," it has been our experience that as couples learn how to paddle well together, they find it to be an enriching experience. Canoeing is a wonderful metaphor for taking on new adventures, sharing beauty and peace, communicating well, being in synch with each other, enjoying the simplicity of being together, and so many other things. The extent to which the facilitator draws out these metaphors will depend on one's style and the needs of the group.

ADDICTIONS
GUIDING PRACTICES

❖

This section focuses on using a ropes course as an adjunct to a hospital chemical dependency treatment program. A script for applying Edgework concepts and a real case study are presented along with special topics of Integrating the Twelve Steps of A.A. with ropes courses by Paul Suding, and Disordered Eating, Body Image and Adventure Therapy by Juli Hayes. We draw from our experience of providing one day ropes course experiences as part of an inpatient, hospital treatment program. It is our hope that this information will be helpful for practitioners working with addictions, and for those of you who are interested in integrating experiential approaches in your treatment program.

Issues that bring someone to this treatment program are varied and include: alcohol dependence, substance dependence, relationship addiction, eating disorders, sexual trauma, and depression. The program is very liberal on what they include as an addiction and treat them in the same way in their groups following a twelve steps program. Our purpose is to help the practitioner work within this structure instead of debating the merits of this kind of program. It is our belief that this is the most common approach for treatment of addictions, and the one that you likely will be asked to align with your experiential program.

❖ WHAT IS AN ADDICTION?

An addiction is psychological and in some cases physiological dependence on the use of alcohol, drugs, tobacco, and other substances. The criteria for an addiction are (1) a compulsive craving leading to persistent use, (2) a need to increase the dose to increasing tolerance, and (3) acute withdrawal, or abstinence symptoms if the substance is sharply reduced or withdrawn (Longman Dictionary of Psychology and Psychiatry, 1984).

John Bradshaw (1990) suggests that an addiction is anything you do that takes you away from dealing with the real and important things in your life. Today, the term dependence is being used in medical and psychological arenas instead of addiction. Dependence is more severe than abuse. The difference between the two is important for practitioners. Practitioners need to understand the severity of the problems and be aware of their own usage patterns. Table 16 contains information from the Diagnostic Statistical Manual IV (1994) which delineates the distinction between substance dependence and substance abuse.

We should assume that to be in a treatment program, most people are dependent on some kind of substance or behavior. Occasionally, there is a person who has been in recovery or currently is sober, and in the program because they are afraid of a relapse (DSM IV, 1994).

◆ **TABLE 16** ◆

Explanation of Substance Dependence and Substance Abuse

Substance dependence is a maladaptive pattern of substance use, leading to significant impairment or distress, as demonstrated by three or more of the following criteria, occurring at any time in the same 12 month period:

1. Tolerance is defined by:
   A. a need for markedly increased amounts of the substance to achieve intoxication or desired effect.
   B. markedly diminished effect with continued use of the same amount.
2. Withdrawal is defined by:
   A. characteristic withdrawal syndrome for the substance.
   B. the same substance is taken to relieve or avoid withdrawal symptoms.
3. The substance is often taken in larger amounts or over a longer period than was intended.
4. There is persistent desire or unsuccessful attempts to cut down or control the substance.
5. A great deal of time is spent in activities necessary to obtain, use, and recover from the substance.
6. Important social, occupational, or recreational activities are given up or reduced because of the substance use.
7. The substance use is continued despite knowledge of having a persistent or recurrent physical or psychological problem that is likely to have caused or become worse because of the substance use (DSM IV, 1994, p.181).

Substance abuse is a maladaptive pattern of substance use leading to clinically significant impairment or distress, as demonstrated by one or more of the following, occurring within a 12 month period.

1. Recurrent substance use resulting in a failure to fulfill major role obligations at work, school or home.
2. Recurrent substance use in situations in which it is physically hazardous.
3. Recurrent substance-related legal problems.
4. Continued substance use despite having persistent or recurrent social or interpersonal problems caused or have become worse because of the substance use.
5. The symptoms have never met the criteria for substance dependence.

❖ THE PROGRAM

Usually, the groups come to the ropes course on day nine of their fourteen day intensive program. This has been a scheduling decision rather than a therapeutic one, although it has worked out well. We believe that using the experiential component earlier in their program would assist in developing trust and facilitating their therapy. Having it in their second week of the program allows them to practice their new behaviors and insights before employing them at home or work. There are advantages of both placements within the treatment program, and these depend on your program's length and goals.

The patients have group therapy twice a day for approximately four hours, plus individual therapy, attend 12 step meetings, and special topic groups. One of the special programs includes a three day workshop focusing on recovering from childhood issues and wounds.

In general, the participants are very excited to get out of the hospital and spend a day out-doors in the mountains. The focus is more individual than a traditional teambuilding program. Individual risk, being aware of their behavioral patterns—control, trust, anger, avoidance issues, and asking for help are the focal points. Concerns, emotions, and sensitivities are issues on the surface for this population. It's not uncommon for the patients to have flashbacks, start crying, regress, panic, and lash-out at others during the ropes course day. This is one population where a trained therapist rather than a good facilitator is needed to help keep the day moving, and to put these occurrences into a constructive perspective. The hospital usually sends 2–3 therapists who are able to focus on individuals' needs when they arise, so the ropes course facilitator can continue to focus on the activities and the whole group.

❖ PRE-WORK

The pre-work takes place from one to four weeks before the program. This is important for three reasons:

1. We provide an introduction letter to prepare the patients for what will happen prior to the ropes course. We try to keep the therapeutic change conditions in mind in an effort to not give them too much information to either "psyche them up or out." We want to enhance these change conditions, their sense of hope, mystery, trust, perception of risk, and effort so the anxiety-level is constructive, and something meaningful can occur for themselves and others.

2. We have a health screening to identify individuals who should not participate because of health reasons. Our main concern is cardiac risk, and we have modified the Arizona Heart Associations survey. This screening device allows us to (a) talk with people who have a high score or are at cardiac risk to clarify their health patterns, (b) call their doctor if necessary to get a verbal or written clearance, (c) put them at ease, assure, and support them that they will be able to participate, and that activities are "challenge by choice", and/or (d) ask people to not attend if they are a cardiac risk.

3. To make contact with the program coordinator to know about any special circumstances, themes, or issues so facilitators are aware and informed. The result is a program that appears seamless to the patients, since we know the correct language to use. Also, we have an understanding of what they have been experiencing, so we can blend in our part of the program.

❖ BRIEFINGS AT THE COURSE SITE

The initial briefings with the therapists and the patients set the framework for the day, and they can help prevent issues and problems from arising.

1. *Briefing with the therapist(s)*
    This is an opportunity for the therapists to get to know the ropes course team and for us to know them. In the structure we are presenting the instructors and therapists are co-facilitators for the process. The following are four items that we need to address during our briefing:
    A. Hold a discussion on guidelines regarding how we want to interact. We see it as a two step process. We will lead the activity and the debrief after the experience, and we will tie in as best as possible the activity learning to their issues as we know them. Then, the therapist takes over by tying in pertinent, patient information and goes deeper into the patients' specific, treatment issues. When individuals need special attention, we want the therapists to attend to them and spend as much time as they need away from the group, and then they may reenter when the patient is ready to continue. Also, we want to let them know what role to take in regards to safety, like spotting during the blind walk, and general safety-awareness for their patients. We check-in numerous times during the day with the therapists to get their feedback, and to make adjustments in the program. "How are things going? What do you need from us? Is there anything that we need to change or do differently?" We view their feedback as vital so to make sure our part of the program fits tightly with what they want for the patients.
    B. Check on patient concerns. Who are the individuals that have specific needs or issues that we should be aware of? Where are they in their recovery process? Who needs more support and focus? What tips can they give us for working with specific patients?
    C. Give overview of the day. What are the specific activities that we are considering and why? What are the benefits and possible issues that the activity will generate? Keep in mind that they don't know the activities and nuances that one activity has over another. We are giving them a menu to choose their preferences. We will talk about time frames, what to expect during the day, and specific guidelines that they can help reinforce. For example, sometimes group members may want to smoke cigarettes, so we need to establish ground rules and specify times and places.
    D. Decide on specific events for this population. You will certainly have your agenda of activities before the group arrives, but you will need to be flexible given specific patient and therapists' concerns. Here are three considerations that we have found helpful:
        (1) **Don't do standups** (where the group starts in pairs, sitting with feet touching and hands touching and have to stand-up simultaneously, and then do this in larger groups). As much as we like this activity for quickly bringing people together, there is always a heavier person in the group, and this exercise starts the day off with a failure for that individual. This, then, may affect your credibility for getting some members of the group to do more challenging activities for the remainder of the day.
        (2) **Eating disorders/Body image issues.** You must understand the body image issues for people with eating disorders. (See the section entitled Disordered Eating,

Body Image, and Adventure Therapy for more information). How we use language to refer to one's body, talk about food, and the selection of activities can either be obstacles or ingredients for a successful day. We should refrain from stand-ups, giants ladder, and trapeze leap with this population because they involve more upper body strength which many participants don't have. They, then, incorporate this failing into a self-blame story, which we could have prevented. Meanwhile, the spider's web and trust falls bring up helpful discussions about perceptions of their body, which are not so dependent on their own physical strength.

(3) **Give trust fall options**—high and low. This is a great activity for recovery groups because it gets at the control and trust issues. We found it helpful to have a few different trust fall heights, so people of different sizes can participate.

2. *Briefing with the group*

A. After the paperwork is done and we have completed some stretching, we like to introduce the day with the Edgework talk. This talk sets the frame for the day, and it explains to the patients the "why" of what a ropes course experience has to do with their recovery program. We will present a brief outline here, and encourage you to develop your own Edgework story using this and the section on Edgework as references. We find it helpful to graphically talk about the edge and to visually demonstrate yourself walking from the inside of the circle to the outside of the circle.

◆ Have everyone in a circle and say "We want to give you a framework that we have found useful for exploring why you are here at a ropes course in the middle of your treatment program."

◆ "Let's say this circle represents the circle of comfort. Here in the middle (walk to the middle of the circle) is where I am comfortable, it's predictable and familiar, it's the known area, it's safe and secure. This is where my successes in the past lived. It feels like home, here."

◆ "Now let's imagine that outside of this circle (point outside of where people are standing) is new territory, the unexplored aspects of our lives, where our future successes live. This is the area of new growth. It holds the uncharted paths of our recovery. As we master it, it becomes part of our tamed territory. But it's dark out there, not as well lit as in the middle here. It's seems risky out there. All the "un" words live out there. Unfamiliar, unpredictable, uncomfortable, and unknown. We feel insecure out there."

◆ Now slowly walk to the edge, represented by the people standing in the circle. "Where you are represents the edge between the known and the unknown, the familiar and unfamiliar, the predictable and the unpredictable, the comfortable and the uncomfortable. What do you think my tendency is as I get closer to this edge? (Let them answer, you are looking for someone to say you want to go back to the middle. When they answer correctly, pull yourself back to the center). It is like a magnet as we get closer to the edge, we get pulled back to the center often without our awareness of how we got back here again. This could explain relapses and dysfunctional habits, as this center is the old behavior pattern or addiction that brought you to treatment."

◆ "So what happens at the edge that helped pull us back to the middle or propelled outside the circle? Many times we have a breakthrough and get out here into new territory (Move outside the circle), and we ask people "how did you have this success?" They've said "I don't know, I just did it." How then are we to learn from these retreats into the circle of comfort, so it doesn't happen all the time, and what about these successes? How can we retain the formula or the success factors, so we can replicate these journeys into new territory?"

◆ Now you will talk through the major "edge components" to increase their awareness of what happens there, "Let's put the edge under the microscope, or slow down what happens so quickly for us. (Go back into the middle of the circle and walk towards the edge and ask the following questions, eliciting quick answers from as many members of the group as you can and supplying the answers if they don't respond.)

> As I walk towards the edge will my feelings be more or less intense? (more intense)
>
> What kind of feelings will I have? (anxiety, fear, apprehension, confusion, etc.)
>
> Will my self talk or inner committee be louder or softer as I approach the edge? (louder)
>
> Will my self talk be more or less frequent as I approach the edge? (more frequent)
>
> What are some examples of what I may be telling myself at the edge? (I won't be able to do it, I'll fail and make a fool of myself, I can't, Everyone will be looking at me.)
>
> Will my physiology, my breathing, heart beating, and sweating be more frequent or less frequent, less intense or more intense? (more frequent and intense)
>
> Will my old, patterns of behavior be more likely or less likely to act up as I approach the edge? (more likely)
>
> What are some examples of outdated or old patterns? (avoidance, anger outbursts, doing everything self and not asking for help, not sharing feelings, isolating.)
>
> What kind of support may I look for to get through to the new territory? Will I be more or less likely to reach for the bottle, a joint, some other drug, food or a relationship to help me? (more likely)
>
> Will the pictures I make be ones of past failures or new potentials?"(past failures)

◆ "As you can see my feelings, thoughts, physiology, old patterns, old pictures, and means for support all get heightened and intensified as I approach the edge. Each one influences the others, and before I know it, I am back in the middle or outside in new territory without a clue of how I got there. Now, you have an idea of what happens there. Just being aware of what you are doing at the edge and changing one or two edge components can make the difference of a success or a retreat."

◆ "What do you think we may do or could do at the edge to have a breakthrough? (Ask these questions and try to elicit these answers or quickly walk through them.)

What about our breathing? (slow down, take a breath, and try to relax.)

What about our thoughts? (I can do it, just take one step at time, keep going.)

What about support? (Use higher power, my sponsor, ask for help)

What about our feelings? (Realize this too will pass, I can tolerate this, identify where it is and breathe through it, just stay with it, and it will get less intense.)

What about our patterns of behaviors? (Take a new risk, just keep moving forward slowly, do anything that is slightly different than you normally would.)

What about the pictures that you are making in your mind? (What would success look like?, How would others see you?, What other things could this success lead you to?)"

◆   "One distinction that we need to make about the "edge." Some people find it easier to be *on the edge* as we described it because it's exciting, thrilling, full of adrenaline, and harder to stay in the middle—where it is safe. In the middle, is where you recharge, take quiet time, reflect, reevaluate, plan, and take care of yourself. You need to spend time there. So, the goal is to try to expand "your edge" and at the same time, come back to the middle and recharge, so you can push the edge more later. It's like a rubber band; you can't keep it stretched without it breaking."

◆   "So for some people, their edge is really the middle because they don't go there and take it easy or say no to all the adrenaline. Instead, they live on the edge because it is more comfortable, predictable, and known for them, than the middle. How many of you does this ring true for, that your edge is really going to the middle? (Try to get a few people to comment about how it is hard to be quiet and by themselves.)

"One of our goals, today, is to have you get to your "edge", be it outside or inside, and have time to become aware of what you are doing there. What leads to your breakthroughs, and what happens when you retreat to the old patterns? We are on the practice field today, and it is all about learning and applying what you've gained so far in treatment. We'd rather have you make a mistake here and learn from it, than to do the same thing at home or work, and end up in a relapse. So, our job is to change the rules and make things challenging, so you can experience your "edges" here. We'll stop the activities a few times when it's chaotic, and, we will ask you what you are feeling or experiencing, just to put the "edge" under the microscope and reveal what you are doing."

B.   What is an area to work on today?

As mentioned previously, this population is used to talking in therapy groups, and they are very aware of their issues. As a means of continuity with their treatment, we like to ask them for a focus for the day, an area that is on their "learning edge" that would help them in their recovery. Each person states what that focus is for him/her, and we facilitate what kind of support that they will need to stay with this learning. This process works very well after the Edgework model talk, as they all have the same point of reference. In addition, the therapist can use this frame of reference for individual issues in the subsequent groups after the ropes course. Weaving the learning into the rest of the treatment program promotes the seamlessness and helps to increase the transference.

❖ ACTIVITIES FOR ADDICTION'S COURSES

The day usually goes from 9:00 A.M. to 5:00 P.M., and we traditionally complete only four activities because of the extra time spent on processing. These are the activities that we try to do in the ideal situation by combining group and individual risk taking. By doing such the quality of the experience for the participants is increased. Again, we are flexible in our planning—considering the size of the group, physical make up of the group, and the special needs and concerns from the therapists. Some sample activities include:

1. Blind Walk
2. Trolley's
3. Low Wild Woosey or Trust Fall
4. Trapeze Leap & High Wild Woosey-both activities going and rotating through.
5. Trust Circle Lean and Closing

❖ ACTIVITIES ADJUSTMENT FOR EATING DISORDERED COURSE

1. Blind Walk
2. Trolley's
3. Trust Fall
4. Trapeze Leap or Spider's Web
5. Trust Circle Lean and Closing

CASE STUDY

The purpose of this segment is to give you a real case example. Responding to this case study will help you be prepared if something similar happens on the course tht you are facilitating. This example is from an addiction's course with the hospital program.

"IT'S A LONG FALL"

One of the male patients from the treatment program, ten years earlier, fell 60 feet from a building construction site, where he worked, and broke his back and legs. He had pins in each of his thighs to hold his femur together. In his recovery process from the fall, he became addicted to morphine and other pain medications.

On the trapeze leap, he was frightened of the height, and his legs locked up. He stayed there for about ten minutes without moving and communicating minimally with the people below. Eventually, he jumped for the trapeze and was able to grab it. As he let go of the bar, he let out a loud scream. We think the free fall reactivated his accident, and he blanked out and became disassociated. When he came down, he was shaking and made no connection with anyone; he just stared at the ground.

His therapist was trying to make contact with him, by asking him questions, but he was not answering. The therapist had a touch of fear in her voice, being surprised by his lack of response to her or anyone else. Her initial fear reaction did not seem to be helpful for him. I

just kept talking to him, telling him that he is all right, and that he did well and it must have been very frightening for him. It took ten minutes before he lifted his head and made some contact with his therapist, who was seated directly in front of him.

He then walked off with his therapist, who reassured him, and she tried to connect his feelings to what had happened to him in the past. They were gone for a half-hour, and he was feeling better and reconnected when he rejoined the group. We continued with the activity putting new people through the trapeze leap. Everyone was concerned for him, but the intensity of the activity and knowing that he was in good hands with the therapist kept everyone focused on their leap or supporting others. When they walked back to observe the others, the scene quickly reactivated his state again. The therapist walked away, again, with him and he continued to process what he was experiencing.

At the end of the day, he described his experience and how falling scared him. The free fall did reactivate that fall of ten years ago. Now, he stated that he was able to work through the fright, the feeling out of control, being vulnerable, and able to rely on himself and support from others to break through to this new territory. He felt very good about doing the activity, and he was able to link the sense of powerlessness to past drug usage. Now, he had new resources to utilize in the next "edge" experience.

LEARNING'S

1. Always have a therapist or enough staff present that one person can be off working through the issues, while the other staff continues the program.
2. Continue to be calm and reassuring with the patients, even though you may feel apprehensive and nervous.

❖ DO'S AND DON'TS _____

DO'S

1. Spend plenty of time up-front helping the group feel comfortable, communicating that they are in charge, and they can always choose to abstain from activities. From our experience, this population needs more assurance. We try even in our voices to **bathe** them in nurturance and support. If this is done well, the rest of the day will go smoothly. We like the metaphor of packing a snow ball at the top of a mountain, for the course setup, and if it is packed and structured-well in the beginning, it will roll down the hill and gather more snow in a natural way, just like the course will develop effectively.
2. Spend time connecting individually and early with the clients, who appear to be scared, unsure, or negative about the experience. Your contact, individually and early in the program, can help shape and modify the rest of their experience.
3. Connect frequently with the therapist as your co-creators and co-facilitators on the course. Share your thoughts and ideas of the activities and strategies for the course with them, so they can give you specific patient information and concerns.
4. Ask the patients frequently in the processing to identify: "How is what is going on here similar to the learning you are having about yourself in treatment?" "Or, how does this tie into your recovery issues?" Let them make the connections for themselves.
5. Remain humble and curious to their learning and struggle for becoming sober or living a recovered lifestyle.
6. Tie in present fears and experiences to past ones. Where appropriate, help them to reprocess and create new, and more constructive and empowering stories.
7. Continue to trust yourself and your instincts. Have faith in people's ability to heal themselves, and get what they need from the experience.

DON'TS

1. Don't talk too much or try to interpret everyone's experience. This population is into talking about their issues, and you can easily get in the way of their processing their new learning. Ask questions versus interpreting.
2. Don't limit the processing in favor of activities. This is one population that it's okay to spend more time processing. Remember, they spend 4–5 hours a day in treatment where they are just talking.
3. Don't be afraid to appropriately share about you or your friends or family members struggle with alcohol and/ or drugs.
4. Don't talk about how you stopped your usage if you are not in a formal

recovery program like the 12 steps of Alcoholics Anonymous. To this population, you are either in recovery or not, addicted or not. If you are still abusing substances these courses are **not** the ones for you to work with. They will think you are in denial, and you will lose your credibility.

Integrating the Twelve Steps of Alcoholics Anonymous with Ropes Courses

Paul Suding

❖ HISTORY

Imagine yourself at an Alcoholics Anonymous (A.A.) or other 12 Step "Anonymous" meeting. You are sitting in your chair, and the meeting is ready to start. The words that follow will be heard by the person visiting for the first time as well as people at all levels of recovery. (In the most recent edition of *Alcoholics Anonymous* printed in 1976, it was conservatively estimated that A.A. had a membership of over 1,000,000 and 28,000 groups meeting in over 90 countries. In 1985, it was estimated that over 58,500 groups existed in 114 countries.) Almost all meetings begin like this. For someone who doesn't know, it tells a lot about A.A. in a short space. And for people in recovery, it is one more time that they will hear why they are there and what they need to do to stay in recovery. (References to alcohol, alcoholism, drinking, sober, etc. can be adapted to the pertinent addictive behavior.)

> *"Alcoholics Anonymous is a fellowship of men and women who share their experience, strength and hope with each other that they may solve their common problem and help others recover from alcoholism. The only requirement for membership is a desire to stop drinking. There are no dues or fees for A.A. membership; we are self-supporting through our own contributions. A.A. is not allied with any sect denomination, politics, organization or institution; does not wish to engage in any controversy, neither endorses nor opposes any causes. Our primary purpose is to stay sober and help other alcoholics to achieve sobriety.*

> *"The heart of our program is laid out in a portion of Chapter 5 from our Big Book,* Alcoholics Anonymous. *To those who are new, these pages may sound strange and unrelated to your specific problems. Do not be discouraged. Take what you can and file the rest for future reference."* (This is from the standard introduction reading for an A.A. meeting.)

Chapter 5—How It Works

Rarely have we seen a person fail who has thoroughly followed our path . . . Our stories disclose in a general way what we used to be like, what happened, and what we are like now. If you have decided you want what we have and are willing to go to any length to get it—then you are ready to take certain steps . . .

Here are the steps we took, which are suggested as a program:

1. *We admitted we were powerless over alcohol—that our lives had become unmanageable.*
2. *Came to believe that a Power greater than ourselves could restore us to sanity.*
3. *Made a decision to turn our will and our lives over to the care of God as we understood Him.*
4. *Made a searching and fearless moral inventory of ourselves.*
5. *Admitted to God, to ourselves, and to another human being the exact nature of our wrongs.*
6. *Were entirely ready to have God remove all these defects of character.*
7. *Humbly asked Him to remove our shortcomings.*
8. *Made a list of all persons we had harmed, and became willing to make amends to them all.*
9. *Made direct amends to such people wherever possible, except when to do so would injure them or others.*
10. *Continued to take personal inventory and when we were wrong promptly admitted it.*
11. *Sought through prayer and meditation to improve our conscious contact with God as we understood Him, praying only for the knowledge of His will for us and the power to carry that out.*
12. *Having had a spiritual awakening as the result of these steps, we tried to carry this message to alcoholics, and to practice these principles in all our affairs.*

Many of us exclaimed, 'What an order! I can't go through with it' Do not be discouraged. No one among us has been able to maintain anything like perfect adherence to these principles. We are not saints. The point is, that we are willing to grow along spiritual lines. The principles we have set down are guides to progress. We claim spiritual progress rather than spiritual perfection."

(Alcoholics Anonymous, *1976, p. 58–60*)

The above is from the introductory "readings" of an actual A.A. meeting which includes an excerpt from the Big Book, *Alcoholics Anonymous.* The fundamental elements for recovery from alcoholism and other addictions using this program are contained there. Keep in mind that the 12 Steps are only the framework and that recovery goes far beyond them. However, this population, whether early or advanced in their recovery, will have a reasonable familiarity with the 12 Steps and a activities and facilitating the processing, recognition of their depth and "sacredness." Your familiarity with them will allow you as the facilitator to draw on them as a rich and valuable resource to utilize in the ropes course and experiential program. They can serve as a basis for framing.

❖ KEY COMPONENTS OF TWELVE STEP RECOVERY

The following topics are primary components of 12 Step programs with a brief explanation of each and their potential relevance to a ropes course and adventure program. The application of these components into actual activities and processing are presented in the application section.

THE 12 STEPS

The 12 steps can be broken down into three areas in the practice of recovery:

1. Surrendering to a Higher Power. (steps 1–3)
2. Cleaning house. (steps 4–11)
3. Helping others. (step 12)

It really is a simple program, albeit not always easy. Practicing the 12 Steps has the potential to be a very deep and conscious soul searching experience. Or, it can be as practical and tedious as putting one foot in front of the other. The practice can also be explained as: 1) Take away your ego; 2) take a personal inventory; do your best to purge your defects; and 3) be of service. This has been AA's "formula for success" for over 60 years.

Participants in their early stages of recovery are working within the first three Steps, possibly starting the fourth Step. The fact that they are in a recovery program strongly suggests that they have at least taken the first half of the Step One—they admitted that they were powerless over their addiction (the exception being if they are there, knowingly or unknowingly, to satisfy someone else, which can eventually result in a relapse). If they have been honest with themselves, they can see how their addiction has negatively affected themselves and how their "lives had become unmanageable."

This brings them to Step Two, which suggests that a belief in a Higher Power might have a profound effect on their lives. Step Three proposes the affirmative choice of turning their lives over to this Higher Power. It is a process of surrender broken down into three steps.

This process for individuals in early recovery can take weeks or even months to adequately allow them to move to Step Four (their "inventory"). Even then, these first three Steps will be revisited over and over again, often many times daily, to assure the solidity of their recovery "foundation."

Even though most participants from the hospital groups, we work with, have not yet delved into the depths of Step Four, they have heard and read it (along with Steps Five and Six) many times. They know what's coming. A ropes course offers innumerable opportunities for "defects of character" to surface which participants can register for later use. Awareness of their "shortcomings" often evolves naturally, but it can be heightened prior to activities and during processing.

A recognition of the Steps, and asking where most of the participants "are" in their recovery program will be invaluable in your facilitation and processing of the activities.

Higher Power

It is clear from the onset that recovery involves a spiritual program. Yet "A.A. is not allied with any sect denomination" (*Alcoholics Anonymous,* 1976). The Big Book goes to great lengths to address this apparent dilemma. "Lack of power, that was our dilemma. We had to find a power by which we could live, and it had to be a *Power greater than ourselves.*" It suggests that the first step in this spiritual program is a mere "willingness to believe in a Power greater than ourselves" (*Alcoholics Anonymous,* 1976, p.45–46).

In a twelve and a half page chapter, the Big Book draws a logical conclusion that if you are indeed powerless over your addiction, and you want to recover, then you need a higher power than yourself, "your own conception of God." With only an open-mind to the possibility that a Higher Power exists, the "spiritual awakening" referred to in Step 12 will begin to unfold.

Sponsor

Another integral component of recovery is the sponsor/sponsee relationship. A sponsor is like a big brother/big sister or a guide to help the sponsee through recovery and especially the "working" of the steps. For instance, working steps 4, 5 and 10 suggest "admitting to . . . another human being"—this is usually a sponsor.

Sponsees are suggested to choose a sponsor who "has what you want" or has the kind of recovery that they are looking for (suggested to be of the same gender). The individuals in a sponsor/sponsee relationship can change during the course of recovery. But most people who have long-term recovery will testify that *always having a sponsor* is significant to their success.

Fellowship

The fellowship of 12 Step programs plays a similarly important, but often not as obvious role in recovery, as does the sponsor. Indirectly, it shows the newcomer that he or she is not alone, which is a common fear amongst those wanting to face their addiction. More directly, the fellowship acts as a broad support or safety net, much like the role that a sponsor might play on an individual basis. Being "a part of"—having a commonality amongst others—whether spoken or unspoken, goes a long way when traveling down the sometimes frightening and unknown path of recovery.

Relapse

Relapse Happens. Many do fall off the path of recovery, but you don't have to and certainly not everyone does. Since relapse is a reality in 12 Step recovery, fortunately "the only requirement for membership is a desire to stop" the addictive behavior. Perfection isn't. We as facilitators can address relapse in these ropes courses and adventure experiences when individuals do things without thinking or revert back to old behavior (i.e., doing things on their own and not asking for help).

In recovery, just an alertness by itself can be enough to deter relapse, but the best prevention includes a program of 1) going to meetings / being a part of the Fellowship); 2) having a sponsor; 3) actively working the Steps; and 4) rigorous honesty. Absence of any of these components can increase the chances of relapse. The integration of these elements within the adventure experience reinforces their importance to the participants.

❖ Application ─────────────────────────────────

This section presents examples of integrating the 12 Steps within a ropes course program. Our reference point is a 2 week intensive inpatient treatment program where we provide a one day ropes course. The participants come with their group therapists.

Blind Walk

Framing: When participants are paired up for this exercise, the therapists have been invited beforehand to take part in matching the individuals since they are more aware and sensitive to the dynamics of the group and personalities. After one person in each pair has his or her blindfold on and everyone has been instructed to maintain silence for the rest of the activity, we explain to the group that the blindfolded people are "newcomers" in the program, and the sighted people are their sponsors. The sponsor will be leading them to a 12 Step meeting. Along the way, they will experience some obstacles and challenges much like the path of recovery. Remind them that they will not be using their voice, and that they must rely on nonverbal communication. Ask the sponsors to consider how they, themselves, might like to be led, and to be aware if that is the best way to lead their sponsee. Also, remind them to be especially aware of any feelings, thoughts, body reactions or old patterns (i.e., edge components) that may come up during the exercise. And finally, let them know that they will be switching roles halfway through the activity.

We have them end the Blind Walk with the "All Aboard." Once there, let everyone know that they are at the meeting place, and their sponsor will guide them "into the meeting." As you say this, motion to the sighted people that they will be helping the blindfolded people up onto the platform and supporting them there. Usually there is not enough room for all the participants to get on our platform, all at once. If this is the case, remind everyone that there is always room for newcomers at the meetings. Once they are either all on the platform or supporting the blind people, let them know that they have all succeeded in making it to the meeting, and now they can take their blindfolds off and climb down.

Processing: Being the first activity of the day for us, the participants usually have been thoroughly engaged and are very enthusiastic about discussing their experience. With this in mind, your challenge as a facilitator will be to maintain their focus, give everyone the opportunity to share and to pace the processing, to stay within the allowed time frame.

These objectives can be achieved by asking the participants to share their one or two most significant awareness or learning's during the exercise. Remind them of the edge components and to possibly tie in their own "edge reactions" with their addiction and recovery. Have them share one at a time by going around the circle, but if they aren't sitting next to the person they were paired with, have the person they were paired with speak after them. Topics to focus the processing on include:

1. How much guidance did the sighted person or sponsor person give?
2. How much of their "own footwork" did the blind person do?
3. Was it easy or hard for the blind person to let go of contact and trust another or a "higher power?"
4. How was this exercise similar to your recovery experience?

TROLLEYS

Framing: As with the Blind Walk, we often ask the therapists beforehand if there is a preferred grouping of "teams" for this activity based on addictions, group therapy, etc. Since we also usually have half of each team blindfolded with voices, and the other half muted with sight, we check with the therapists to see if they have a preference for who receives these "handicaps."

The name we have chosen for this activity relates well to this population. We have dubbed it the "Sea of Relapse" named for the area that they will be traveling over. The trolleys represent their program, and as a group, they must figure-out how to use these "vehicles" for recovery. They will be going from one shore to another (each side marked by rope or webbing) representing the span of their first 30 days of recovery. As with recovery, unforeseen challenges and changes arise, and the group on each set of trolleys together will deal with these unexpected encounters. Since recovery is measured in consecutive days, if one of the participants falls into the Sea of Relapse, they must start over.

As they cross the "sea", if time or progress warrants, impose further handicaps, challenges or obstacles. For instance, if any of the team members are dominant with their voice or communication, take it away by possibly relating it to him or her not being called on at meetings to share. Another handicap is turning someone around backwards associating it with not always knowing where you're going in recovery. Also, an obstacle that we often use immediately, before they reach the "shore", is changing the "landing spot." This indicates that they might not always end-up where they first thought they would after 30 days. Use your imagination and keep in mind that it usually isn't the framing of the added challenge that is important, it is the participants' response(s) to it.

At some point during their journey, approach each group and have them take a time-out. Ask each individual, one at a time, to share in one word what they are experiencing. This is freezing the "edge moment" for many of the participants. If you make a mental note of these words, its possible to use them for discussion later.

If any of the groups are headed for failure, don't rescue them—allow them to fail. This is only the second activity of the day, and a failure can provide a constructive learning opportunity for later activities.

Processing: You can process this activity in a variety of ways. One method is to hear from one team at a time. Another way is to pose some key questions and let the whole group process the activity as more of an open discussion. Whichever way you choose, there are some issues that you can include that relate well to the initial framing of the activity.

One of the first elements of this exercise is to heighten their awareness about how the blind-folded people were included (or excluded) in "working out the program" or figuring out how to use the trolleys. Processing questions include:

1. How might this relate to the support they give to or receive from other newcomers?
2. Did the blindfolded people include or exclude themselves?
3. Whose responsibility is it to include them?
4. Did anyone have defects of character that surfaced during this activity?

    One of the principles for success in A.A. and other Twelve Step programs is that in order to keep your recovery, you must offer it to others. This important principle can be applied throughout the teamwork aspect of this activity.

5. How did the participants practice this principle in this activity?

    Another element of this activity that you can bring to their awareness is how their "program" (or use of the trolleys) was arrived at or started within the groups. Usually, if there is more than 1 group, one team sees how the others are standing on the trolleys and mirrors them. In this regard you can ask:

6. Did anyone notice if another group represented a good "program" model that might help your own group?
7. What was it about their program that you wanted?

WILD WOOSEY (LOW & HIGH)

Framing: For this population, we call this event the **Commitment Wire.** The low version adds the element of spotters to the initial description of the activity. During the explanation, we let the participants know that before they mount their respective wires, they will be choosing a primary spotter or "sponsor" from their support group or "fellowship" to help guide them on their "commitment walk." In the high version of this activity, the "sponsor" will only need to coach since there is no need for spotting.

Before the participants venture out onto the wire, ask each individual what he/she is committing to in his/her recovery. As each person walks the wire, have the sponsor coach the physical level of commitment as well as offer any suggestions for each person's success. Deep breathing can be particularly beneficial in helping people stay centered and focused, especially for the high version.

The participation of the rest of the group as spotters (for the low wire) and their encouragement to the "walkers" can be re-emphasized during the activity. This is their contribution and role to the recovery success of each person.

Processing: Debriefing this activity can take place as each pair finishes or after everyone completes the event. One of the questions to pose is

1. How committed did you feel you were and how might that affect the ability of the other person to be committed?

    For the low wire, check to see how the "sponsors" and "fellowship" may have played a role in each person's ability to be committed during their "walk."

"One day at a time" or "one step at a time" certainly comes into play with this event! Other processing questions include:

2. What did you do when you felt "shaky" and "insecure"?
3. What learning can you talk about related to your recovery from the commitment wire?
4. Who are the people in your program that you must commit to?
5. What do you need to do in your program when you are "unsure" and "shaky"?

TRAPEZE LEAP

Framing: The framing for this event can be simplified into two questions: "In recovery, what are you reaching for or jumping towards?" and "Are you ready to take this **Leap of Faith?**" However, not to be underestimated, this activity has often had the most impact of all the day's events for many participants. During the explanation of this event, ask the group to ponder the first question, and let them know that you will be asking them again individually, immediately before they jump. Remind them that it is the jump from the tree that counts—not if they catch the trapeze. In fact, they can even jump without the trapeze if they want.

Before each participant starts climbing, have them pick their ground support team—two people to anchor the ladder while they climb and two people to adjust the trapeze distance. As they climb the ladder, in the tree, or on the platform positioning themselves, continue to check in with them. Ask them how they are feeling and remind them to keep breathing. Once they are positioned to jump you can guide them through a quick visualization to enhance the association of their physical leap with their emotional, mental and/or spiritual leap. Ask them to close their eyes and visualize what it would look like if the "leap" for what they want in their recovery comes true. Keeping their eyes closed, have them visualize their feet pushing off from the tree or platform. While their eyes are still closed, invite them to share out-loud, if they want, what they are jumping for. Then have them open their eyes.

Finally, when they are ready to jump, ask them if they are ready to take this "leap of faith." When they answer, let them know that you are ready to support them.

Processing: The best processing for this event usually takes place during the activity or right after they are lowered to the ground by helping them stay centered and focused. Constantly checking in with them helps them maintain their conscious awareness of their feelings, thinking, and physiology. Once they are back on the ground, reinforce and acknowledge their "leap of faith" and congratulate them on it.

If you do a group debrief of this activity, have each individual share a few words about their experience and level of faith before and after their jump. Another, topic to offer is How does the A.A. saying "Let go and let God" apply to this activity. Processing questions include:

1. How did they experience their faith?
2. How did they quiet their "inner committee?"
3. What does this leap of faith tell them about their recovery program and themselves?

TRUST CIRCLE/CLOSING CIRCLE

Description: Prepare ahead of time a length of rope or securely attached pieces of webbing in a continuous loop or circle to adequately fit all of the participants standing side-by-side holding onto the rope or webbing. Have the entire group gather around in a circle holding the rope/webbing in front of them with both hands.

With everyone leaning outward holding onto the rope/webbing for support, the whole group will lean back and sit down as a unit. After the closing processing, everyone grasps the rope/webbing securely, positions their feet flat on the ground in front of their butts, pulls slowly and evenly on the circle, and stands-up as a unit.

Framing/Processing: While initially standing, holding the rope/webbing circle, ask the group as a whole "What can a circle represent or symbolize?" Many answers will be offered. After all have been heard, suggest that the circle can be compared to the Twelfth Step: "Having had a spiritual awakening . . . we tried to carry this message to others in recovery and to practice these principles in all our affairs."—a way of coming "full circle" in recovery. For this day, let them know that you are all coming back together here as one fellowship, one community to close the day. Then, have the group sit as a unit as described above.

Depending on time, different approaches can be used for this final processing opportunity. One of the closings that we use is to go around the circle, and have everyone share two things:

1. What was one awareness, learning or "awakening" that you experienced today that you can carry with you into recovery?
2. Name one person in the group who particularly impressed you or inspired you today?

The primary objective is for the participants to reflect back on the day and to come back together as a whole. You may want to add, subtract, enhance or simplify as you see fit, and as time may allow.

❖ CONCLUSION

The longevity and success of 12 Step programs is inferred in Step 12—"Having had a spiritual awakening as a result of these steps . . .", but it doesn't really spell out in the previous 11 steps, when or how this happens. It might take years and volumes of research and involve another field of psychology to adequately answer that question. Does it happen? It has been my experience that it does. Just ask or observe a few people who do work the steps. They've had a spiritual awakening. It does happen. One step at a time. Further evidence of this can be heard in the irony of statements made in meetings by many members who are grateful to be alcoholics. Having found recovery, they now have a way of life in the 12 Steps that "normal" people don't have. It has become an invaluable, life process for them that they wouldn't ever want to give up.

DISORDERED EATING, BODY IMAGE AND ADVENTURE THERAPY

GUIDING PRACTICES

Juli A. Hayes, R.D.

Adventure therapy is an ideal therapeutic tool for addressing body image issues in the treatment of disordered eating. The nature of this experiential learning that puts participants at their "edge" or in a vulnerable state includes:

- unknown and unfamiliar environment and activities;
- physical exertion (especially for the anorexic);
- activities where group members closely observe one another;
- dirt, sweat and lack of washing facilities;
- inability to predict what will happen next;
- having to trust or rely upon others; and
- having their bodies touched (i.e., during exercises that require spotting, blind walk, etc.)

This section will describe the many forms of disordered eating, take a look at the weight and food-preoccupied culture that breeds such disorders, and provide suggestions for aiding in the facilitation of an adventure based course for eating disordered women.

❖ WHAT IS DISORDERED EATING?

Normal Eating	Occasional Dieter	Chronic Dieter	Compulsive Exerciser	Binge-Eating Disorder	Bulimia	Anorexia Nervosa

It is useful to think of disordered eating as variations from an ideal or normal relationship with food, ranging from chronic dieting (which is seen as normal in this culture) to anorexia nervosa. If viewed on a continuum, on the far end would be "normal" or a perfectly healthy relationship with food and one's body, where a person usually eats when hungry, stops when satisfied or full, and eats what she feels like eating (although she may be aware of health guidelines and attempting to maintain a nutritious pattern of eating to maintain good health). When she isn't hungry, preparing food, or eating she usually isn't thinking about food. This person doesn't feel guilty when indulging in delicious but not so nutritious foods. She has a realistic and positive view of her body, whether or not she fits into an accepted cultural view of "ideal."

Normal Eating

Normal eating is being able to eat when you are hungry, and to continue eating until you are satisfied.

It is being able to choose foods you like and eating them until you've had enough—not just stopping because you think you should.

Normal eating is being able to use some moderate constraint on your food, but not being so restrictive that you miss out on pleasurable foods.

Normal eating is giving yourself three meals a day, or it can be choosing to munch along.

It is leaving some cookies on the plate because you know you can have some again tomorrow, or it is eating more now because they taste so wonderful.

Normal eating includes overeating at times and feeling uncomfortable. It is also under eating at times and wishing you had more.

It takes up some of your time and attention, but keeps its' place as only one important area of your life.

In short, normal eating is flexible. It varies in response to your schedule, your emotions, your hunger, and your proximity to food.

Author unknown

THE CHRONIC DIETER

Moving along the continuum, away from "normal eating" would be the occasional dieter, then the chronic dieter. The chronic dieter is starting to get into a serious pattern of "disordered eating." She is no longer fully in touch with her own signals for hunger and satiety, nor is she in touch with what would feel good in her body. She has replaced these normally inherent abilities with diet rules and regulations about what is "good" food and what is "bad" food. She eats when the diet program she currently follows tells her to eat, instead of when she is actually hungry (if she can even identify this sensation any more). She thinks about food throughout much of the day, even when she's not hungry. She typically stays on her diet until she is no longer satisfied with the rate of weight loss (as her metabolism has now possibly slowed down enough to keep her from losing weight at a satisfactory rate), or she can no longer tolerate the great sense of deprivation that accompanies most diets. She "throws in the towel" usually by bingeing on "non-diet" foods, and she vows to start a new diet before bikini season, her sister's wedding, or on New Year's Day. Unfortunately, she is quite likely to gain back all the weight she lost (and maybe more) due to the metabolic changes that low-calorie dieting causes, along with the "all or nothing" thinking that is inherent in the diet mentality.

Compulsive Exerciser

Continuing along the continuum, we see the compulsive exerciser next to the chronic dieter. Compulsive exercisers suffer from a body image that is directly related to how much they are or are not working out. They often follow a strict diet, low in fat, to help them attain their body shaping goals. He or she is compulsive about working out for "calorie burn" and/or "shaping." If they miss a workout for a day or two they may complain of feeling "fat", guilty, or out of sorts. This person often continues a workout regimen even if injured or ill. The social life of a compulsive exerciser revolves around his or her workout routine.

As we move our way up the continuum, it is apparent that the disorder affects more and more of the person's life.

Binge Eating Disorder

Binge Eating Disorder is next on the continuum. Binge Eating Disorder is similar to Bulimia in that a person binges on large amounts of food during times of emotional stress, but does not engage in vomiting, laxative abuse, or fasting to compensate for the binge. Binge eaters have a sense of lack of control during the binge episode. They often eat until uncomfortably full. They generally eat alone because of the shame associated with the disorder. Binge eaters often feel self-disgust, depressed, or very guilty after a binge. Binge eating has become a way to deal with distressing emotions.

It is a mistake to think that all "overweight" people are binge eaters or that "normal weight" people are not. Binge eaters come in all sizes, as do normal eaters.

Bulimia

Bulimia falls close to the far-end of the continuum. Bulimia is the binge-purge syndrome. People with bulimia typically binge on large amounts of food, and then they "undo" the binge by either vomiting, taking laxatives, exercising excessively, or fasting. Vomiting is the most common form of purging. A person with bulimia often started out earlier on the continuum by becoming dissatisfied with her body and dieting. The sense of deprivation that accompanied her diet became strong, and eventually she may have broken her diet and ended up bingeing on the foods that she formerly deemed forbidden. Feeling guilty and out of control after eating these foods, she decides to purge "this one time." The bingeing and purging behavior becomes more frequent, with some bulimics bingeing and purging several times a day. By this time, what started out as a way to control weight or to "have one's cake and not have it too" becomes a distinct coping mechanism for dealing with emotions such as anger, fear, loneliness, boredom, anxiety, etc. Instead of dealing directly with an uncomfortable emotion, the bulimic will binge on large amounts of forbidden food, feel guilty about the binge, and purge. The feelings of self-disgust and guilt over a binge along with continued concern over how her body looks are certainly not pleasant, but they are often more tolerable than feelings that she may have never learned to cope with effectively.

Bulimics often overestimate the size of their body and have a poor, body image, regardless of their weight and shape.

ANOREXIA NERVOSA

At the very end of the continuum is anorexia nervosa. As with bulimia, an anorexic often starts out with dieting and gradually becomes more and more restrictive. She typically has lost at least 15% of her body weight, has ceased to menstruate, and is obsessed with food, calories, weight, and often exercise. An anorexic often enjoys preparing food for others and watching them eat without herself indulging in anything but minimal fare. Pleasure in eating is replaced by guilt, anxiety and ambivalence. She often feels irritable, isolated, depressed, and has great difficulty concentrating, and she has an extreme narrowing of interests. An anorexic usually has a highly-distorted view of her body, believing it is much larger than it actually is. She has an exceptional fear of gaining weight, and she is often in denial of her problem and resistant to going into treatment because of her fear of losing control and gaining weight. Controlling her food and body have become the ways in which she can feel a sense of control in her life. Recovery often requires hospitalization. Anorexia is one of the most serious of psychiatric illnesses, with a 12–18% fatality rate.

❖ WHO HAS DISORDERED EATING?

Can you imagine a significant period of time without hearing a woman somewhere talk about needing to lose a few pounds? Research shows that most women are ashamed of their bodies. Eighty to ninety percent of American women have dieted at some time and 40–50% are dieting at any given time. Unfortunately, the shame effects even very young girls. A study conducted in California several years ago showed that 80% of 10–11 year old girls had already dieted. Another survey reported 50% of 9 year olds had dieted. It is estimated that 1% of adolescent girls develop anorexia nervosa, and another 3–5% of young women become bulimic. But, these statistics refer to the most severe clinical conditions that meet the DSM IV criteria. When considering those with some but not enough of the symptoms to fit a classic diagnosis, disordered eating has affected a much higher number of our adolescent girls (Brody, 1995). Consider this anonymous quote from a 17 year old:

> *"Let me tell you something . . . on any given day, the younger girls (13- and 14-year olds) can be found throwing up breakfast and lunch in the school washroom. It's a group thing: peer pressure, the new drug of choice. They go in groups of two to twelve, taking turns in the stalls, coaching each other through it . . . In my group of friends, we are addicted to the 'five-pound-less syndrome.' Five pounds less is always better. I must admit, I've done it all to lose weight. I've fasted for ten days strait (sic), overdosed (sic) on laxatives, exercised more*

hours than not, ate lettuce at 6 p.m. just to throw it up. I'm sick, but I keep
most of these things secret. Two of my best friends know because their (sic) sick
too. We have starving contests, see who can weigh the least next week. . . . I hate
to say it, but it is the exceptional girl who isn't anorexic or bulimic, in my school
anyways. This is normal. I am normal and my friends are normal. We're the
women of the future." (Brody, 1995, p.95)

Although men too suffer with eating disorders and body dissatisfaction, approximately 90% of those suffering from anorexia and bulimia are women. Men also report less body dissatisfaction than women. One recent poll found that boys expressed dissatisfaction with appearance at almost half the rate of girls. As adults, women are approximately three-times as likely as men to have negative thoughts about their bodies (Schneider, 1996). Part of this difference lies in the fact that as a boy reaches puberty and becomes more muscular, he looks more like the culture's male ideal. However, as a young girl matures into a women, she gets hips and normal increases in body fat. Thus, she grows further from the ideal standard set for women. The average 14-year-old girl of 5'3" weighs 110. By the age of 18 she has grown to 5'4½" and weighs 125 (League, 1993). In a culture that despises fat and idealizes thinness, it becomes increasingly difficult to maintain a positive body-image as a young woman matures.

It is obvious that movies, TV, and magazines play a significant role in shaping our values around what we deem as the current "ideal body." The cultural ideal for women has become increasingly thinner over the past several decades. The average height and weight of a model is 5'9" and 110 pounds (Schneider, 1996). She is 23% below average weight, exceeding one of the criteria for anorexia nervosa. We are increasingly bombarded by countless "perfect" images in media. Models are often surgically altered, eating disordered, and airbrushed to "perfection", and many women pressure themselves daily to at least try to look more like this "unrealistic ideal." Although eating disorders are complex problems with many causes, psychologists have long believed that media imagery is at least partly responsible for the growing rate of such problems, and they have recently been able to demonstrate this link. One study from Arizona State University showed that the more media-saturated a woman was (based on time spent reading magazines and watching TV), the greater likelihood of eating disorder symptoms. Another study showed that just looking at photos of very slim models (as opposed to looking at pictures of women of "average" size) made it more likely for women to report feelings of depression and body dissatisfaction (Wartik, 1995).

It has become increasingly more difficult for women to live up to the impossible ideals put upon them by media and advertising. Many women feel inadequate in their bodies, but the truth is that the ideal is impossible for the vast majority of women to reach. Ideally, our goal should not be to change our bodies, but to change what we see as "perfect" from the largely unattainable thin to nourished and healthy at whatever weight we are.

❖ DO'S AND DON'TS

1. Respect all physical limitations of each individual. Some participants will need to limit themselves in an activity if they are weak from malnourishment. Others, who are in good physi-

cal condition may respond positively to the activity. Make sure that each group member has been cleared by a physician to participate, and that you know the risk factors of your group ahead of time.

2. It is helpful to include women facilitators. They can be powerful role-models for participants.

3. Avoid casual (non-therapeutic) discussions about food with the participants. They often engage others in such conversations and by doing so, you only reinforces their preoccupation with food.

4. Be sure not to make derogatory comments about your own body or anyone else's when working with this group. Individuals with eating disorders are constantly comparing their bodies to everyone else's. If you make a negative comment about your own body and she sees you as thinner than herself, she will likely spend time obsessing about her own body and about what you must think of her.

5. Avoid positive comments associated with having lost weight. This reinforces the cultural standard that attractiveness is dependent on weight.

6. If a participant raises issues about feeling fat, you might want to ask her what else she is feeling, realizing that feeling "fat" is often a mask for feeling out of control, anxious, uncomfortable, etc.

7. Examine your own attitudes about weight and body image, so that you don't convey fat-prejudice or add to their desire to be thin.

8. If possible, provide a pleasant space and setting for lunch. It should not be scheduled after a particularly intense activity, unless there is a well-trained therapist who wants to process how the activity affects how participants feel about their bodies and eating. Be prepared for this to take some time to process.

9. Do not bring "diet" food and beverages. It is ideal to provide a delicious, wholesome lunch (i.e., whole grain breads, low-fat lunch meats, variety of fruits and vegetables, with spreads and yogurt-based dips) without it necessarily being "low calorie". Provide plenty of water and juices for drinking. Fruit and "healthy" cookies (i.e., whole grain, fruit sweetened, not fat-free) are appropriate desserts. Facilitators should eat with participants, and be sure not to skimp on your own lunch. Attempt to be an example of a "normal eater."

10. Do not take on the role of "food police" during meal times. It should not be your responsibility to watch what participants are or are not eating. However, if a participant is clearly not eating, an appropriate person from the treatment facility should be notified as it could affect her ability to safely participate in the afternoon activities.

11. Talk about things other than food, weight, and treatment during lunch and snack-time. Try to keep eating times comfortable and stress free.

❖ SUGGESTIONS FOR INITIATIVES

SPIDER'S WEB

The spider's web is often an interesting activity to do with this population. Each participant must find an opening in the spider's web that she thinks her body can fit through. Only one person can go through each opening. Facilitators will see body image distortion played out before their very eyes. Also, this will require participants to compare their bodies with each other's. In a therapeutic environment, this is a great opportunity to confront body image distortion and to get realistic feedback from other participants, therapists, and facilitators. Processing may need to take place during the event as well as after, so plan extra time.

TRUST CIRCLE/TRUST FALL

In the trust circle, the participants and facilitators form a circle and one person at a time steps into the middle of the circle and does a trust fall, being passed to different people in the circle. Again, this exercise will bring up body image issues. Participants will be afraid that nobody will be able to catch them, and they will be embarrassed about others discovering how heavy or light they are. This is a great exercise to bring out distortions in body image, to provide realistic and honest feedback, and to build trust among group members. The trust fall can also be used in this way. Again, sufficient time should be available for processing. It would be helpful to have a therapist present who specializes in body image issues.

TRAPEZE LEAP

The trapeze leap has been a very intense experience for the eating disordered participants we have worked with. For many, it is a great opportunity to challenge their body's to do something that they may have thought was impossible to do. It is a chance to value their body for it's strength and ability, rather than how it looks. We always give a little talk ahead of time about "challenge by choice" and encourage them to "leap" for some aspect of their recovery. Participants feel very energized and renewed by this activity.

SECTION 6

CORPORATE PROGRAMS
GUIDING PRACTICES

❖

In this section, we will focus on providing programs to the corporate or business sector. We begin with some general guiding practices for leaders who have selected this niche. Then, we have a contribution from Tom Vachet on marketing the corporate program. A case study is presented, and responses to the case study are contributed by John Ruffin and Steve Klett.

❖ EXPERIENCE BASED TRAINING AND DEVELOPMENT

We have all seen the proliferation of corporate, team-building programs over the last five years. There are currently over 500 corporate and organizational programs listed internationally in the 1996 Association of Experiential Education (AEE) directory, close to 300 of them are

DILBERT ® by Scott Adams

DILBERT reprinted by permission of United Feature Syndicate, Inc.

actively providing corporate programs. Go to any annual AEE international conference and you'll see Outward Bound instructors or adventure program leaders running around with their new brochures, saying "I am doing corporate programming these days." These individuals have evolved from climbing a rock face to climbing the corporate ladder, and from the ropes course to the board room team course. Why not? Team building and teaming are very popular in corporate training, and development and it pays better than chasing adolescents around in the woods. In *Training* (1996), an American Management Association survey of 519 senior, human-resource executives, who were asked how they can best achieve their business results indicated that training was the second highest priority. When asked what they thought crucial to their business goals, the executives stated: (1) Workers who could adapt to change, (2) more teamwork, and (3) an "ability to see the big picture." In a related story, "Are we smart enough for our jobs", Stamps (1996) stated, "Having decided that teams are the embodiment of everything good and forward-looking in the workplace, it appears companies are anxious to figure out how to make them work" (pg. 50). Even traditional corporate trainers, without an experiential background, are trying to find ways of incorporating experiential learning into their training programs.

This exciting convergence to experiential methodologies raises some provocative questions: Why the interest in experiential training? What's different about the experiential learning environment that leads to its effectiveness? Where are the opportunities to "add value" for the corporate client? How do you market in general and specifically to the corporate culture? What are they actually looking for when they call you and say "Do you do teambuilding"? We will attempt to respond to these questions in this section.

Why the interest in experiential training?
"The premise is simple—that we have all been brainwashed by the a cultural myth that learning occurs "in our heads" not in all of us, and that, until we challenge that belief, our capacities for any sort of deep learning are severely limited. . . .Our learning is "in our heads", but we don't seem to get it out," and apply it (Senge, 1996, pg. xix & xxi).

One of the reasons is that experiential training is very different from traditional training; it focuses on learning that involves the whole person and applies the learning in all aspects of being. The activities are unknown and unfamiliar to the participants; they involve simulations, outdoor challenges, and ropes course events, which create crises and chaos, similar to work. The team must project their decision-making process and group intelligence onto the experience for the team to be successful. This "practice field" allows learning to take place in a setting where cause and effect are closely linked in time. And, knowledge is generated to improve teamwork, communication, and collaborative problem solving.

What is different about the experiential learning environment that leads to its effectiveness? We have generated a dozen reasons that are unique to experiential training when contrasted to the traditional training room or classroom.

1. *Equality:* It provides a common yet novel experience, where all participants are equal in their knowledge about the tasks or projects. The "Mahogany Row" doesn't exist in this setting. One year or twenty years with the organization doesn't help in solving these unique problems.

2. *Relationships Build Quickly:* This is accomplished by the communication, collaboration, cooperation, and physical effort needed to solve these exercises successfully. Participants are in close proximity all day, and they are interacting in new ways. The end result is that they have to rely and depend on each other in clear and significant ways, which builds trust in an accelerated manner. People get to know each other more in a day, than they have over the last one to two years.

3. *Disequilibrium:* Because of the unknown and unfamiliar quality of the challenges, participants are put into a state of disequilibrium or disorder. They are stripped of their normal status, roles, and defenses. Prior experience isn't as relevant in this environment. This creates a pure, learning environment as the group has to self organize around the challenge.

4. *Projective Technique*: In organizing the instability or disequilibrium, the group projects their problem-solving skills, project management ability, and leadership style onto the experience. The experience provides a "got ya" where participants are "caught" in doing what they typically do, inspite of knowing otherwise. The learning is profound and revealing when presented in a more meaningful and relevant way than would come from an organizational assessment. This window or mirror into their process provides unlimited information or data to shape their team learning. This is one of the prime reasons experiential learning is an excellent "learning laboratory." Other methodologies don't provide such a rich, projective technique.

5. *Decreased Cycle Time:* The space between project initiation and outcomes are compressed, so consequences of organizational decisions can be examined and improved. Typically, in the corporation, there is more of a time-lag and more variables to consider, so the learning from doing is diluted and delayed.

6. *Meta Learning:* In this "learning laboratory", as the projections shed light on the managerial process, the group is asked to step back and evaluate itself. The learning is about themselves, their leadership, problem solving skills, teamwork, communication, and managing change. These are all the relevant subject matter. This time to reflect and develop lessons learned after studying themselves and their processes is usually not done with the same intensity within the organization.

7. *Chaos Management In A Safe Environment:* Teams are able to experience chaos, disorder, and changing requirements for success in a safe environment where the consequences for failure are limited. The groups develop strategies or best practices to manage the change back at the work site.

8. *Kinesthetic Imprint:* Experiential learning anchors the cognitive material. Participants have a kinesthetic imprint or whole body learning of cognitive principles because the learning is graphic as it involves physical, mental, behavioral, and even spiritual dimensions.

9. *Common Language/Story Making:* The experience provides a common language, story, and imagery that can be transferred to work. This language becomes a short cut in communicating a shared vision or "learning disability" very quickly. The intense experience is storied in a way that the participants see themselves and others in a new light. This story then becomes the catalyst for continuing the same theme in the organization.

10. *Encourage Risk Taking:* The experience allows participants to take new risks, try on new roles, and make mistakes with little costs to the organization. Risks are perceived rather than actual. Each person taking a risk vicariously pushes others to try something out of their circle of comfort. There are always individuals who shine in this environment—whose leadership ability hasn't been noticed at work.

11. *Diversity Of Strengths:* The activities include physical and mental challenges which requires the resources of the whole team. Differences become necessary strengths to solve the challenges. One person alone could not complete most of the challenges, like at work, so the interdependencies of the team are highlighted.

12. *Fun:* Experiential learning provides a fun way to learn how to become a high-performing team. Fun also helps participants learn more because they are more open to the experience, and typically become more creative.

Why is this not enough? In today's world, learning is the critical advantage that will separate the organization from their competition. The ropes course, teambuilding seminar of yesterday was a one shot event, where the need today is for a curriculum of ongoing learning. To stay ahead of the trends, we have to leave the paradigm of being a vendor of a one-day ropes course and move to becoming learning partners with the organization marrying traditional and experiential approaches. Consequently, inspite of how dynamic the experiential learning is in comparison to the classroom or training room, the one-day format is not enough.

Another reason why learning needs to be improved can be found from the systems perspective. Often, the learning or training is not embraced or reinforced back in the real world. (See the learning activities and retention strategies section for how to facilitate transfer of learning.) Many times, the training is a solution to an undefined or complex problem. It may be a band-aid doomed to fall off and reopen the existing wound. Broad and Newstrom (1992) identified the main barriers to the transference of learning. Notice how many of these are present in both traditional training classes as well as in experiential approaches from the old event paradigm. They are presented in rank order with the first being the greatest impediment:

1. Lack of reinforcement at the work site.
2. Interference from others—customers, coworkers , supervisors.
3. Nonsupportive organizational climate.
4. Training seen as impractical and irrelevant content.
5. Participants are uncomfortable with the amount of change needed to implement the learning.
6. Leaders or trainers not there as support mechanisms.

7. Training is perceived as poorly designed and delivered.
8. Pressure from the support group to resist making any significant changes.

How do we add value? The short answer is to provide better quality in what we are doing, and more services than we currently are providing. To add value means to go beyond the client or customer's expectations. This may also be an obstacle to many providers who don't have the skills or capabilities beyond the one-day event. Being honest about our strengths and weaknesses as a provider is vital for the field to maintain its high credibility and high quality programs. If we are going to continue in the business arena, we will need to always be learning and reinventing ourselves; the same message that the employees are hearing within the corporation. Below are some suggestions to add value for the corporate client:

◆ Partner-up with individuals or organizations that have diverse and complimentary skills, (i.e., traditional management consultants, business schools, leadership centers).
◆ Educate yourself to the business world with seminars, audiotapes, books, and advanced degrees.
◆ Add more traditional lectures as organizational content to integrate during the learning experience (See Leadership topics sections for specific lesson plans).
◆ Integrate survey tools and assessment instruments to provide data and feedback. How will they know that they are making the changes that you and they both hope to achieve?
◆ Use activities and strategies presented in this book to improve your processing, retention, and application of the learning.
◆ Spend time in the organization finding out what the issues really are, rather than having the client diagnose themselves, and tell you what they need. Many times they are too ingrained in the system to know what the real problems are.
◆ Provide a curriculum with follow-ups and ongoing services rather just an event.

The two responses to the case study presented later in this section are excellent examples of bringing and adding value to the client.

Corporate training principles Experience based training and development as a field is continually growing and incorporating new skills and activities. As we innovate and create how corporate America and the international marketplace are learning and growing, we must keep in mind the basic premises of working with adults which we have been discussing throughout this book (see section on Adults). The following points have been adapted from Pike's text (1989) *Creative Training Techniques Handbook:*

1. Adults are like kids in big bodies, they learn best by experience with hands-on activities.
2. It's hard to argue with your own facts. The more we get the corporations involved and use their own projections as the learning material, the more likely it is to be retained and relevant.
3. The more fun they have; the more they will learn.
4. No learning has taken place until behavior has changed. They must "walk the talk."

5. Learning has ultimately taken place only if the participant can teach others what you have taught them.

We are seeing just the start of experiential methodologies converging with traditional training. In the future, the merger will make it impossible to distinguish between ropes course facilitator and corporate trainer as they will be sharing the same bag of tricks. Our job, then, is to continue to grow, learn and synthesize what works best for the corporate client.

"The ladder of success doesn't care who climbs it."

—*Frank Tyger*

SALES AND MARKETING OF YOUR PROGRAM

Tom Vache't

❖ INTRODUCTION

You may be wondering what is the relevance of a discussion on Sales and Marketing in a book which you presumed was intended to assist you in becoming a better facilitator? I believe John and Relly considered, and I concur, that it is very appropriate to explore an area, which, although it encompasses an essential skill, is simply not considered, by most practitioners of the art of experiential education, to be pertinent. Simply put, we may not currently think of ourselves as salespersons, or even have the most basic desire to do such for that matter. Truthfully, you may feel that the whole concept of sales and salespeople is abhorrent. The fact is however, that each one of us must, to some degree, assume the role of a salesperson, in order to motivate our clients to allow us the opportunity to provide programs for them. My objective in this discussion is to help you through any reticence that you may have regarding sales and marketing, as well as offer you a few "pearls of wisdom" that you may choose to incorporate into your efforts.

As I considered what I might pass on in such a brief discussion, I began to mentally play-back the tapes of the many sales and marketing seminars that I've attended over the years, as well as the countless books on the subject that I have read. I wondered how I might distill all of this information, and then put it into a succinct and concise form that I could squeeze into just a few pages. I came to the realization that this effort was not only useless, but inappropriate. After all, you could simply buy and read the same materials, as well as attend similar seminars and training programs. What I have to offer that is of most value and also unique, which you cannot buy at the corner bookstore, are my years of personal experiences and insights as a sales and marketing professional. It will not be possible, obviously, to cover every topic or strategy. However, I will attempt to introduce to you that information which I believe may have the most impact on your efforts.

Through the years, I acknowledge, albeit at times grudgingly, having made many professional mistakes as I acquired sales and marketing experience. I reflected on each of these retrospectively, made adjustments or modifications to my technique and style, and then tried again, until I was finally successful and satisfied. The net result of these trial and error experiences has been the development of a formula which I have now duplicated, and implemented successfully

337

time and time again. I have employed it in a variety of distinctly different scenarios, in a range of industries and corporations, as well as with a diversity of clients all over the world.

❖ WHY IS MARKETING IMPORTANT?

You may be saying to yourself, rather emphatically, that you are not now a salesperson, nor did you ever have any desire to become one. The fact is that neither did I. I have no memory of any counselor in high school or college directing me to sales as a desirable career. What I discovered, as a practical matter, was that there were tremendously exciting services or products that I, or companies with which I worked for throughout the years, had to offer. It was then necessary to convince prospective clients to try these services/products. In order for this opportunity to be created, and for my clients to be induced to engage in a business relationship with me, I had to demonstrate to them that there was a benefit in their doing so. This interaction was nothing more or less than a basic, sales transaction.

I was slowly, and somewhat painfully, forced to realize that, although sales and marketing were not my primary interest or avocation, I needed to develop reasonable skills in these areas in order to enable me to do the things which I really liked best. As well, you must realize that in order to conduct the experiential education or training programs, which you love, you must first sell your client on what you have to offer. Then, throughout your relationship with the client, even in the midst of the program that he or she has engaged you to provide, you must continue to reinforce the features and benefits of what you have sold.

To be a successful salesperson or marketing professional does not really require the stereotypical, plaid sport coats, or even beltless, polyester trousers. I believe that it does require five very important and essential ingredients. These are:

- ◆ Honesty
- ◆ Integrity
- ◆ Enthusiasm
- ◆ Sincere, passionate, and communicable belief in the value of the product or service you have to offer.
- ◆ A real and genuine interest in the needs of your clients.

People do business with people whom they admire, trust, respect, and who demonstrate a concern for them and their needs. They also do business with people whom they like personally, and with whom they can share a passion. Remove any of these ingredients, and you will reduce your chances of a sale. Combine them in a meaningful fashion, and I will personally guarantee your success. First however, we must be prepared to meet our prospective client face to face.

Successful marketing lays a foundation for successful selling. Implemented correctly, it can set a positive tone, and create an atmosphere charged with interest and excitement. Performed incorrectly, it can slam the door of opportunity so hard on you that it may never be opened again. Competition in today's business world is not tolerant of mistakes. Poorly considered or inadequate marketing can be one of those errors that is immediately lethal. So how do we avoid the pitfalls, and enhance our chances of success? We do it in large part through careful planning, and the development of a rational strategy.

❖ DEVELOPING A MARKETING PLAN_____

A marketing plan is our guidebook to a successful, sales encounter. It is one of those building blocks which is essential to any business. I assume that the proper foundation laying, such as writing a comprehensive business plan, developing a coherent policy and procedure, and establishing attainable, sales goals has been accomplished. There is one other very critical element in the preparation for marketing your services; a philosophy and mission statement. Thoroughly understanding what is unique about your company, its personnel, and services is essential, and it is expressed in this document. You must know who you are, what you stand for, where you are going, and what methods you intend to use to get there. Remember, your philosophy and mission statement can, and should be, the most powerful description of what your company is about that is ever written! It becomes the benchmark that is available for reference if you ever begin to question why your business was founded. I believe this situation often occurs relative to personal, as well as professional, introspection regarding the relationship between goals and values. That, of course, is an entirely separate discussion.

In writing your marketing plan, take care to determine who your prospects are. The scatter-gun approach to sales is generally unsuccessful. Niche marketing, with some careful diversification to serve as a safety net, is a more intelligent strategy. Within the identification process, research your prospective client population. If you intend to enter into a collaborative, long-term relationship with your client, then you must understand what it is that they do, as well as how well they do it, and finally, why. If you are knowledgeable about your client and his or her business, then you can reasonably determine in advance what benefits you have to offer, and what problems you can solve. If you cannot communicate either of these two, then you will, unfortunately, have no basis for a discussion.

Marketing is about knowledge. It is also about emotion. Reflect for a moment on those national, advertising campaigns which have had the greatest impact on you. Was this the result of the information which they imparted, or because of the emotional connection you experienced? Reams of paper with words and statistics do not catch and maintain our attention. If you are sending out a marketing piece in this format, you are simply wasting our natural resources as well as your efforts. Most executive managers do not have the time to read and review a stack of paper. As an alternative, develop a simple marketing piece that communicates a strong emotion.

❖ DEVELOPING YOUR MARKETING PIECE_____

A successful marketing piece is also not necessarily expensive. It does not, as a rule, demand the talent of a graphics-design professional. It does require creativity, emotionality, and brevity, as well as an intimate understanding of your company and what it has to offer. My first pieces were done on the fly, or on the cheap, as you may say. I did the design work. I wrote all of the copy. Then, I sought help on layout and production. Do not underestimate what you are capable of doing if you just try. I have even done my own photography.

Our clearest memories are nearly always associated with emotional events in our lives. Make that emotional connection with a prospective client in the marketing piece you create, and they will not only never forget you. Also, you have laid the perfect groundwork for a face to face encounter. It lays the groundwork for a meeting because the marketing piece should always precede it.

DON'T

There are few real absolutes in this world. Although I am somewhat hesitant to state one here, I have to say that I am adamantly opposed to the concept of cold-calling on a prospective client without the benefit of an appointment. Throughout my career in executive management, I never once met with someone who did not have a scheduled appointment with me, and I could recount that most of my peers did not do so either. It was not entirely arrogance or ego that prohibited me, although I often strongly felt that it was inconsiderate of someone to think that I could just drop everything I was doing to see them. It was actually more of an issue of time management. Every day was scheduled, and if I broke my schedule everything that I had hoped to accomplish in that day would be jeopardized. On the other hand, if I scheduled an appointment with someone, it was because I had a genuine interest in what they had to offer, and I was eager for a discussion. This also means that I was very prepared to take some form of action, make a commitment or decision—that I felt was appropriate.

❖ THE APPOINTMENT

Now comes the easy part of the process. This is exactly what you had hoped for. You are now sitting in an executive boardroom, meeting with the senior vice-presidents and managers of your targeted, prospective client corporation. This is where the rubber meets the road, so to speak. You have been given the exact opportunity you hoped for. Unfortunately, if it is beginning to feel like a trip to the dentist, I understand and empathize. We all like to operate in familiar territory. Take us out of our element, and it can be an unnerving as well as an intimidating experience. The key to avoiding or moving quickly through these feelings is preparation.

It really does not matter whether your prospects are that boardroom full of corporate executives, or the teaching staff of a local community college. If you are going to be able to conduct business successfully, you must be viewed as a professional peer, who has something valuable to offer that your client does not have the resources to provide internally. An integral part of your preparation is understanding the culture of your prospective client, and then honoring it. Years ago, when I began to travel in Asia on business, I undertook to become educated about my client's countries, histories, and peoples. There were certain formalities and nuances which it was essential that I understood, even those pertaining to something as simple as the presentation or acceptance of a business card. In order to experience any success in my negotiations, I had to adapt to my client's culture, assimilate their business practices, and in doing so, show my respect.

These issues exist wherever you go. They are not limited to just foreign travel. You must show respect for your client by honoring his or her culture. If the corporate culture demands that you dress in a certain fashion, consider that you must respect this, or risk being dismissed. This is not to say that you must participate in someone else's culture in total disregard for your own feelings and values. For example, although in Japan a significant portion of business is discussed in the evening over drinks, it is acceptable to very politely decline alcoholic beverages. But, even this must be done carefully, and with consideration not to offend. In all situations you must be wise, and alert. Measure what you say, and how you say it. Business meetings are full of pitfalls and land mines. Your level of preparedness will be directly proportional to the success that you will enjoy.

Finally, when in your meeting, be yourself. Remember that your client is as much buying you, as he or she is buying your product or service. Do not attempt to take on a "persona" or an approach that is not genuine to you. Now is not the time to recreate yourself in what you believe to be the proper, sales personality. If your client perceives that you are being honest, that you are truly concerned, and that you have viable answers or solutions to problems, then you will have a strong basis for a business relationship.

❖ SUMMARY

Above all, use your opportunity in meeting with your client to demonstrate your strengths, and share your passion. Communicate the joy and satisfaction that you take in the work you do, and the benefits that are derived. Create an emotional event, and your client will be asking you to show not only how it can be sustained, but how you can assist him/her in passing it on to others. Sales and marketing can be very rewarding in its own right. It is an essential step in the process of providing your services, and it need not be distasteful or unpleasant.

Do's

1. Maintain your honesty and integrity as they are linchpins in a long-term relationship.
2. Market on an emotional level, and the details will fall in place.
3. Stay focused on providing achievable solutions for your clients.
4. Communicate the joy and passion you have for your work
5. Honor their culture.
6. Be truly interested in the needs of your clients.
7. Be yourself!

CASE STUDY

What follows is a case study, and the questions that we invited contributors to respond to in their write-up.

Zinon, Inc. has just downsized its computer-chip, manufacturing organization from 850 to 600 people. Their previous, executive staff of ten had two staff take early retirement and two were transferred within the corporation. Two new executives were added to the team, one person from within Zinon, Inc. and one person from their competition. Zinon, Inc.'s human-resource director contacted your organization because they heard that you do "teambuilding" and they are interested in having you work with their reorganized team.

❖ QUESTIONS

1. What are your initial contacts and with whom? Do you send material, interview with the HR director, try to see the decision makers on the staff? Paint a picture of your best case scenario.

2. How do you acquire information about this case? What assessments would you want to use, interview strategy, or other means of acquiring relevant data?

3. What general theories underlie your strategies? What theorists or authors do you use as your philosophical foundation? Name the book titles for us.

4. After you acquire the information, walk us through a typical intervention strategy that you might use or suggest, (i.e., meetings, lecture topics, experiential activities, follow-ups.)

5. If you do a day or days of experiential activities—which activities would you use and why? Give us your most potent, activity schedule. What would be the objective of each activity, and the experiential component as a whole?

6. How would you evaluate your program?

7. Are there any follow-up activities that you would suggest?

CASE STUDY INVITED RESPONSE

John Ruffin

❖ BACKGROUND AND INITIAL CONTACT

Zinon, Inc. is a mid-sized company that has just downsized its total workforce by 30% and experienced 40% turnover in its executive ranks. This is an organization that is very likely in "transition shock." The fact that the HR Director has contacted us for "teambuilding", versus help with the transition process, raises an initial concern about HR's, and possibly management's, sense of reality about the impact of what has just happened. It is unfortunately, typical that the notion of a quick and inexpensive solution for getting people motivated again seems to be prevalent.

There are two tendencies that are often present in a scenario such as this and we feel that it is important to be aware of and resist them as we move through the initial diagnosis. The first tendency is to believe or accept that the client accurately knows what they need in this situation, and secondly, the belief that our favorite solution, or the one we are most financially committed to, is right on-target for their problem.

Our initial contact would be with the HR Director who contacted us, but we would stress the importance of meeting with other key members of the executive team, and preferably the CEO. We also want the CEO to be involved with and committed to the plan of action, so as not to second guess the plan mid-stream. We would typically not send a lot of promotional material ahead of time

(i.e., fixed solutions in search of a problem), and only leave pertinent information following an interview.

We would respond to their request for teambuilding with the question "what are the indicators that tell you that you have this need?" Often, in a scenario such as this, the management team will respond with observations such as "people are not getting along well, seem angry, or seem withdrawn; or they should be happy that they survived the downsizing, and they're not; or they seem confused even though we've explained that things will be better now." These are generally initial indications that the organization has been through some major trauma, usually with little or no meaningful communication from the decision makers. If you ask the workforce, they will confirm this for you.

❖ DIAGNOSIS

One of the major questions we would want answered is, "why did Zinon downsize at this point, and why to this extent?" Is this a result of a reengineering effort, loss of business to the competition, shift in product lines, major advance in automation, or just a simple attempt to increase value by cutting costs? The answer to this question will help us diagnose the nature of the problems that teambuilding is projected to fix, and it will also give us the context in which to understand the comments from the workforce.

343

We can't suppose that teambuilding is the "fixall", and even if appropriate, we need to know this context in order to design the emphasis and processing of the teambuilding components. We may also want to know what has been accomplished prior to the downsizing, if anything, to deal with preparation of the organization for the event itself, and the obvious after-shock which will follow?

The downsizing experience in an organization is not unlike the family with two teenagers who has had to suddenly pack-up everything, move to another city from the only home they've known, and lost the family dog along the way. The only way to deal with the trauma is to get the family together to talk it over, allow some complaining, some crying, and get a new vision for how they will collectively meet the new environment. Any other alternative, (making believe that "they will be all right, they're big kids") is head-in-the-sand management and will lead directly to resentment and protective behavior.

We would proceed with a request to hold focus groups with employees to get their "unedited" observations on the downsized organization, as well as to conduct an organizational climate survey with a cross-section (15–20%) of the population. We would capture and summarize these findings in a report to the management team, re: "clarifying teambuilding objectives." Additionally, conducting a 360 degree survey on each member of the management team (except for the external hire) would provide significant information for structuring individual and collective development goals for the intervention. The ability to get this quality of diagnostic information up-front will have a substantial impact on the ability to develop real solutions, but it is often difficult to get approval from clients who think they know what the solution is already.

In managing the client relationship, we may need to stay with the perception of pursuing a training solution. However, our bias at this point would be to shift the focus to the emotional state of the organization, particularly non-management, to get a better sense of the real mood of the organization as a whole. (We could work with the new management team in a vacuum, yet if not approached in the context of the organization's perceptions, the results would be window-trimming only). If the response from the organization is "look, stop asking so many questions, and just give us the training", then we would think seriously about opting out of this opportunity. The other angle is to begin the process, and see if we can shift their consciousness along the way.

The information which we would have developed by this point would let us know something, however minimal, about the extent of the problem in the organization and how much we want to address. Let's assume that what we found is that the organization is basically sound at the core, meaning that they have a clear mission, a good business plan, essentially good skills at all levels. However, the management team seems uncoordinated, and they are giving unclear, operational signals, and the workforce is still in shock from the blood-loss. Also, there is a tremendous amount of pent-up emotion in all ranks.

❖ THE INTERVENTION

With this perspective, and having gained commitment from the client to proceed with a two-three day, senior-management, teambuilding session, we would begin the training part of the intervention. This is the opportunity to introduce both cognitive and experiential learning through a combination of instruments, models and the "low ropes" initiatives. We would plan to begin with the executive team and follow up with the next level of management, in a second round of training.

❖ MANAGEMENT DYNAMICS AND PERSPECTIVE _____

Zinon's turnover in the management ranks will have likely created several new dynamics in the senior team, one being the lack of comfort and predictability that they'd had with the previous team. The second would be the uncertain response to change within the new team. The third would be the need to quickly develop new lines of understanding and trust. We would use the Myers-Briggs Type Indicator (MBTI) as the key diagnostic and prescriptive instrument in this setting. The MBTI will give the new Zinon team the personal and interpersonal understanding to address most of the interaction dilemmas that they may be facing, and to build a framework for communication that will be essential as they try to lead the rest of the company through this trauma. They will also have a context in which to understand the impacts of the downsizing on individuals within the organization.

The MBTI, while a powerful instrument of change on its own, adds a multiplier to the processing of the experiential activities, in that individuals can further identify how their own preferences were influencing their behaviors within the events. We always find that this combination takes processing insights to an entirely different level. One of the other tests we would employ early in our interaction with the Zinon management team would be to assess their own recognition of the dynamics of change within the organization. Let's assume that the management team looked at the downsizing process as a largely logistical event, with a shifting of boxes on the organizational chart, and a payout to those departing. In this event, we would spend some time with a change model adapted from work of William Bridges, emphasizing that the downsizing was at least as much of a psychological event in which we need to recognize the end-ings and neutral zones—before we can hope to pursue new beginnings in the organization. This understanding can lead to a significant amount of consultation and coaching in order to work with the organization, and also this understanding is integral to how additional, experiential activities are planned and processed.

❖ EXPERIENTIAL ACTIVITIES AND PROCESSING _____

We would use the experiential initiatives, not so much as self-contained events from which to learn key lessons of trust, communication, collaboration, innovation, and the like (though those lessons are certainly present), rather as opportunities to expose the issues and get to the core of the problems or pain that they face in the organization. The exercise is the door opener, but the wandering around inside, opening the closets, and knocking down the cobwebs is where the work is needed. It is the meta-experience beyond the exercise that we find is often most important and relevant to their work relationships. This most often requires knowledge of the organization's work systems and their culture in order to be able to go after the right closets, and be somewhat credible in the process.

The activities that we would use in this situation would begin with a communications, ice-breaker exercise like the "Hog Call" (assigning animal names to participants and having them speak in animal tongues, blindfolded, to find other members of their animal team) or something similar to put everyone in a silly frame of mind and level any hierarchy that may exist. We would debrief this exercise by acknowledging the silliness and "fun of it all", but we would also ask what other issues it raised. Usually, clarity of communicating and listening are prevalent issues as is the comfort in finding a team to which you belong. While validating their experience of the exercise, we would shift attention gradually to the similarities or dissimilarities to their organizational experience of communication, and we would stay with that framework to see how willingly they will go into untouchable areas.

Our constant amazement is that the simplest of exercises, with few or no props, can elicit dramatic insights. The insight for us is that people in organizations are eager to talk about their condition, but they need a context and caring guidance to present it effectively. It's the difference between what may often sound like "water cooler whining" and a relevant discussion of issues that clearly have bottom-line impact. We have also consistently found the "low", or ground-based initiatives to be more powerful from a team-involvement perspective, than the "high" ropes.

Following the hog call type of opener, we would then use their animal teams to form discussion groups to brainstorm answers to a key question, such as, "what concerns do you have about teamwork in this organization?" Processing and capturing the answers (usually all problem areas) on a chart provides us with a compass to set up, and process the remaining experiential activities.

Following on this initial combination of cognitive and experiential learning, we would tailor the menu of activities to the needs being presented. Nothing is more unfortunate in training than to continue to pursue an agenda that is not serving the needs of the participants. Be willing to dump the planned activities in the interest of staying with a breakthrough moment. This will be particularly important if you have not been able to gather much information from the group at the start.

Among the initiatives that might follow would be trust-development activities such as the Trust Circle and Trust Walk, and depend-

ing on the physical capacity of the group, the Trust Fall. These are certainly not new events, yet depending on the set-up for each, and the observations that participants make, they can be focused on the issues at hand. The trust walk, for instance, with a few innovative elements is a wonderful opportunity for mirroring the psychological aspects of the change process.

Other activities would depend on key factors that surfaced in some of the processing. When internal competition appears, we would employ an Acid River variation with modifications targeting the competition/collaboration dilemma. Two to four teams are presented with a challenge of working, it seems, at cross purposes, and with resources that need to be usurped or shared in order to succeed. They are instructed that they have a short amount of time to plan, and that the first team across the river is the winner; and by the way, both teams have to finish before the organizational mission is accomplished.

This creates significant mental conflict for most groups who can't merge serving the organizational mission, and their own need to win. Most often, the latter prevails. It is an excellent way to enter their world of internal competition and dysfunctionality. We use selected examples from the exercise to reflect their battles over resources, recognition, budget, promotions, etc. It also can aptly raise the question of how present is their thinking about the organizational mission.

You can be sure that Zinon's downsizing will not have created a collaborative environment. Everyone will have taken on a greater degree of self-protection and preservation. As one recent participant in a corporate, team-building program explained after completing the Acid River exercise—he stated, after tricking the other team out of key resources (which could have been used collaboratively), "I was most concerned about how my people would survive this challenge, so I did what I had to." Wow, imagine what it might be like if everyone in downsized organizations started behaving this way.

Processing with that group of executives gave us the opportunity to go much deeper into organizational issues of competition, and also to explore the management behavior of that particular senior executive. Work with executive coaching and mission clarification has been the result, as it probably should be within Zinon. The obvious value of the experiential component is that these organizations may never have been able to recognize some of their needs if addressed by using a purely, cognitive approach. The experiential drama presents the consulting moment.

Additional initiatives could include the Knots or Hands-Across activity as a way of demonstrating the frustration in organizational "gridlock", particularly after a major event. Processing generally reveals that success in getting out-of-the-knot and forming a circle, and it takes everyone's input and a willingness to do what is necessary. Powerful points for a team that may be feeling stuck.

The Ball Toss initiative presents an interesting way to look at the reorganization or reengineering process. The simple event of tossing the ball across the circle followed by rethinking the way to have all participants touch the ball more quickly is just a simple entrée to the discussion of organizational process improvement and how to involve the workforce in maximizing output.

❖ EVALUATION AND FOLLOW-UP

Evaluation of this intervention would be an on-going process, principally centered around witnessing the change in language and behavior of the key senior members, as well as testing the same observations with some of the non-trained population. For the team-building activities specifically, we would use a verbal-feedback session with the participants at the end of the workshop, generally organized around the question "what are your principal learnings from this workshop, and how do you intend to act on them?" We would also give them a more detailed evaluation form for their response on specific aspects and components of the workshop, including "who else should be trained?"

Regarding follow-up activities, if we have done our homework carefully with Zinon at the outset, and we helped the senior team understand the gravity of their current situation, then they may be talking about follow-up before we've completed the initial session. We would always endeavor to structure the follow-up during the contracting stage, but frequently the client needs to be a believer first. Follow-up should certainly include: taking the principal instruments and activities to the next level or two down in the organization, and to identify the other organizational systems components which will be key in supporting this growth.

In summary, we must remember that the Zinon Corporation is facing a highly complex situation, and no quick assessment or "cookie cutter" approach will do justice to their needs. If we are able to help them recognize their needs, then we have been effective. If we are able to convince them that we are committed to their ability to lead their organization into the future, not just solve problems, then they will keep us involved in their growth over a much longer term than a teambuilding workshop.

CASE STUDY INVITED RESPONSE

Steven Klett, M.A.

The Zinon, Inc. scenario is not that unusual these days, and I get calls like this routinely. Here is an organization in flux, and I mean flux with a capital "F." There is more than enough anxiety to go around today without a crisis like these people are going through. And certain industries, integrated chip manufacturing among them, are particularly vulnerable to the changing winds of the marketplace.

❖ WHAT'S THE OPPORTUNITY HERE?

I understand that this call has something to do with "teambuilding" for the senior management group. Not a bad idea. However, my first thoughts go to the six hundred employees who have remained behind after the layoff. What is going through their minds today? I'll be surprised if they aren't experiencing what David Noer (1993), senior vice-president of training and education at the Center for Creative Leadership, Greensboro, North Carolina describes as layoff, survivor-sickness in his book *Healing the Wounds*. This sickness is characterized by fear, insecurity, frustration, resentment, sadness, guilt, betrayal and distrust, (aimed at senior management, I might add)—altogether a challenging laundry list of feelings from which to rally the troops and begin the process of getting on with life and business. I also suspect productivity is down, and it will remain so for some time at Zinon.

Several minutes into a conversation with the caller, I may conclude that nothing short of a multi-layered approach will be needed here because organizational life is so complex. If this is the case, I know from experience that senior executives, in their desire to achieve a quick solution, may lack the commitment to carry out a thoughtful and inclusiveness process. And, over the past several years, experiential programs have been increasingly placed in the "quick-fix, feel good" camp.

Nevertheless, I'm going to listen intently when I speak with the HR director (whom I'll assume, has had some sleepless nights recently because she/he has most likely been given the unpleasant task of administering the "downsizing"). This is my first opportunity to get the kind of information that helps me begin to formulate a picture of what's *really* going on here, and, *my initial assumptions could well be wrong*.

Asking the right questions is critical, and I want to take notes of the most significant bits of information I hear. Keep a record. Peter Block, author of *Flawless Consulting,* and commentator on contemporary, organizational life suggests that most consulting failures occur during the contracting phase with a client. Listen "with squinted ears" so you hear and capture significant data, something another colleague has reminded us do.

Before I come back with any recommendations, I am going to request that I am forwarded any relevant documentation that Zinon is willing to share with me. I am particularly interested in any recent, organizational climate-surveys, annual reports, company newsletters, mission statement or any other expressions of what this company is about, and how it would like to be.

Secondly, and maybe more importantly, I'll want to speak with a cross-section of stakeholders to get several perspectives on the current reality at Zinon. Depending on one's position in the organization, I may hear everything from expressions of despair to more optimistic and hopeful responses. The truth is somewhere in the middle. (Incidentally, my questions should be the same for each person, allowing some leeway for a spontaneous and candid conversation). As people are busy today (and at Zinon, 600 people are now doing the work that 850 performed the previous week), I will restrict these calls to between ½ and 1 hour.

Also, I'll be very interested in speaking with the senior-management team—particularly the CEO. After all, I am trying to develop an intervention that reinforces and "brings to life" what the leadership team in the organization values. This should be their agenda, not mine. Conversely, I am of little use if I do not push back at times and challenge their thinking.

Time permitting, I may suggest administering a reliable, assessment instrument to gauge employee perceptions of the state of the corporation or its leadership. I like the recently published Campbell Work Orientation (CWO) series David Campbell, Ph.D. has created. Taken in aggregate, the results can provide one more overlay from which to get a picture of where issues really exist.

❖ WHAT'S OUR ORIENTATION?_____

The world moves quickly today. I want to respond with both a sense of urgency and a list of quality requirements that drive my

responses to this client's requests. In being supportive, I want to try to:

a. work with them to identify their real needs and begin to search for the right approach to resolving significant organizational issues, not the least of which is rebuilding trust in this case.

b. complement them on their effort to elicit support in this regard, (and, infrequently, I may even steer them to other resources if I feel we don't have the capacity to support their needs).

c. partner with them to take advantage of their knowledge of the history and culture of the business and to allow them the opportunity to jointly develop an effective intervention with me.

Some years ago, we concluded at Peak Performance Associates that "action-learning" was not just about the wilderness, or ropes courses or 8-person rafts, but rather an approach to learning. It is now seen as the thread that is woven into the fabric of all we do—including classroom presentations and consulting.

Moreover, we now promote what we define as our "Performance Development Process", a systemic approach to facilitating complex and transformational change. Assuming a state of readiness, we encourage clients to concurrently address individual, team, and organizational development, and not to be lulled by the "quick fix."

I believe practitioners in the field of experiential learning must make a shift in their thinking, today, to continue to be relevant. While I still feel it is unequaled as a vehicle for anchoring important lessons of leadership and teamwork, it needs to be more effectively integrated with business objectives. We can continue to promote the value and power of action-learning, while at the same time recog nize its inherent limitations. We need more tools to address long-term needs. The managing partner of the consulting group, Block, Petrella, Weisbord, John Dupre, has often challenged the consultants in my firm to "get your hands dirty" by moving out of the woods after a program and into the workplace of a business client. He has encouraged us to support them fully through consulting and coaching as they grapple with real issues back at work or home. After all, it is in the application and integration of the lessons learned in the field that our work has real meaning for participants.

❖ WHAT'S OUR RESPONSE?————————

I'm going to suggest that we work with the senior-management group first. Given their critical role in leading this team through a difficult time, I want to see them recognize that they need to quickly develop steadfast and unequivocal support for each other and gain confidence in their ability to lead the organization together. And, they must be able to gain clarity on what they need to be doing to recover from the setback. They must accept that they may be "unpopular" for a time and exhibit what Professor Tom Cronin, President of Whitman College in Washington State refers to as "unwarranted optimism." I think 3–4 days at an appropriate, conference retreat is good place to start.

The first morning of the program, following introductions, we should build in an opportunity that allows each executive to express what she/he hopes to accomplish at the retreat. Then, we should devote time to putting the off-site meeting into a context. While this is an interactive process, I like to fairly quickly get outside for some applied learning exercises. There are many options available here, but I want to select challenges that demand leadership, require collective problem-solving,

use all the group's resources, and provide opportunities to develop trust in one another. I am particularly interested in exercises that emphasize "brains over brawn."

Days 2–4 might include more guided discussions, an assessment instruments to provide the executives with individual information as well as a group profile (particularly given the new team members), and some larger, more compelling exercises to highlight the meeting. While I do not suggest a ropes course to everyone, it is, nevertheless, a powerful experience for groups that are ready. Above all, I want to ensure everyone's dignity and allow people to participate at the ropes course in a way that contributes to a successful day. I particularly value some of the new course designs that allow pairs or triads of people to accomplish the events together, with team belays. Even a ropes course, often characterized as promoting individual accomplishment, should support the development of unity in the group. This is a powerful experience for groups that are ready.

We will close the meeting with a session devoted to defining next steps and gaining a commitment from each manager to fully address the need to re-build the recently compromised relationships with the employees. I also want to request a follow-up meeting to monitor progress in the team and look to designing an appropriate developmental process for all the others at Zinon, which includes employees in the re-building process. This will give this effort the greatest chance for success.

❖ HOW WILL WE MEASURE SUCCESS?————————

Certainly, the most obvious and immediate measure of success is the subjective response received at the end of the executive retreat. If the response is favorable, this is at least an indication that I have followed through on the first part of the bargain. Ideally, I have been effective in providing a catalytic experience which has given the Zinon executives a strong foundation upon which to continue building. Also, in the short term, I would like to hear that my strong recommendation to provide developmental opportunities for employees is being seriously considered. And, if the executives are committed to taking action in a new way that benefits both the company and its people, I'd say that real progress has been made.

If Zinon requests further support with their employees, one of my first orders of business is to work very closely with them to define, as best we can, which aspects of their operation can be affected by a developmental process. As a consultant, you cannot do this in isolation because you will need internal "champions" to ensure accountability. We will want to take a look at the critical issues and objectives to see how they are currently being defined and measured, respectively. Then, we would co-create an intervention which, if successful, would hopefully help employees find more effective ways of problem-solving and interacting to meet their organizational objectives.

EDUCATION
GUIDING PRACTICES

❖

"Education is not a preparation for life; education is life itself."

—*John Dewey*

As noted at the beginning of this text, experiential education means learning by planning, doing, reflecting and generalizing. Consequently, experiential educators contend that optimum learning does not occur when the teacher functions as a fountain of knowledge and the student as an empty vessel waiting to be filled. Rather, they believe that individuals are inherently active, self-regulating, intelligently acting on a perceived world rather than passively responding to the environment (Iran-Nejad, 1990; Resnick, 1987). As a result, educators who teach experientially believe in the direct and immediate experiencing of objects, people, ideas, and events in order for individuals to develop, learn concepts and form ideas. Support for experiential learning is found in the work of Brady (1989) who suggested that we learn and retain:

10 percent of what we hear.
15 percent of what we see.
20 percent of what we both see and hear.
40 percent of what we discuss.
80 percent of what we experience directly or practice doing.
90 percent of what we attempt to teach others.

Experiential educators incorporate learning activities in their instructional approaches that teach new information in the context of previous knowledge and relevancy while de-emphasizing more microscopic, step-by-step approaches to teaching (Iano, 1990). In addition, they structure learning opportunities that: (a) promote students' self-directedness and control in establishing and attaining goals; (b) encourage experimentation with real-life situations; and (c) and foster productive interactions with peers (Cranton, 1989). Specifically, experiential educators structure and support student learning and development by:

a. Planning experiences that build on the students' interests and needs;

b. Organizing environments and routines for active learning;

c. Establishing a climate for positive social interactions;

d. Encouraging students' planning, action, interaction, problem solving, and reflection;

e. Observing and interpreting students' learning, development and behavior (Hohmann & Weikart, 1995).

Examples of instructional methods and techniques for promoting active learning that have been adapted from Lee and Cafferella (1994) are found in Table 17.

Additional information, teaching techniques and procedures that you can use to help plan learning opportunities that are experience based are discussed below. They include the experiential learning continuum, thematic teaching, expeditionary learning, independent study contracts, learning journals, service learning, and supplementary, outdoor activities.

◆ TABLE 17 ◆

Instructional Methods and Techniques for Promoting Active Learning

Poster presentations: Students develop poster sessions on a given topic or issue. The sessions are presented concurrently on a prearranged date. Individuals alternately monitor their own booths to answer questions and dialogue, and attend the sessions of others.

Concept maps: Students construct a diagram that interrelates the major conceptual components of an issue or set of practices.

Reaction panel: A panel of individuals reacts to a presentation by an individual or group.

Demonstration with a return demonstration: A resource person performs an operation or a job, showing others how to do a specified task. Students are then asked to perform the task that was demonstrated.

(continued)

◆ TABLE 17 ◆

Instructional Methods and Techniques for Promoting Active Learning *continued*

Storytelling: Individuals are asked to tell stories that relate to how they feel about a particular event or experience.

People networking: Forming loosely configured groups of people who have similar experiences, interests, problems, or ideas for the purposes of giving and receiving information and providing mutual support and assistance.

Debate: Presentation of conflicting views by two people or two groups in order to clarify the arguments between them.

Group discussion: A group of people have an exchange of ideas about a specific problem or issue.

Games: Activities characterized by structured competition or cooperation to provide students with opportunities to practice specific skills and actions.

Journaling: Learners keep a reflective record that focuses on experiences relevant to the content of focus.

In-class case study: Written or oral presentation of an event, incident, or situation for a small group to analyze and solve.

Critical incidents: Students are asked to describe an important incident related to a specific aspect of their lives, which is then used as a base for analysis.

Case study research: Learners observe the implementation of particular practices in an applied setting, then systematically record and analyze the results.

Role assumption exercise: Students intentionally place themselves in situations or seek experiences that they would not normally engage in (1) to gain understanding of the life experiences of others (i.e., volunteering in a prison), or (2) to gain fresh perspectives on their own experiences (i.e., leadership retreat).

Analysis of practice: Students examine in real-world contexts how they perform certain activities or roles, or how they react to certain situations. Role playing can be used to help individuals transition from how they function currently, and how they want to function in the future.

Coaching: One-to-one learning by demonstration and practice, with immediate feedback, which usually is conducted by peers, supervisors, or experts in the field.

Mentoring: Involves an intense caring relationship in which persons with more experience work with specific learners to promote professional and personal growth. Mentors model expected behavior and values and provide support for the person with whom they are working.

Apprenticeship: Formal relationship between employer and employee through which an employee is trained for a skill or craft through practical experience under the supervision of experienced workers.

On-the-job training: A master or expert worker provides instruction to the novice while both are engaged in productive work on the job. Often used when work is complex and the worker or craft person is the best person to pass on knowledge and skills to the learner.

❖ EXPERIENTIAL LEARNING CONTINUUM

Finding ways to establish learning environments that are active and experiential can be challenging at times. A tool that you may find valuable is the experiential learning continuum (adapted from Gibbons & Hopkins, 1985). The stages of an experiential learning continuum and examples of specific activities that you may want to use with your students are found below. As you move along the continuum, the level of involvement and degree of real-life application increases.

Simulated Experiences—individuals view slides, pictures and films or role-play simulations of reality (e.g., establish a grocery store in the classroom, conduct a mock trial, role-play a job interview, choose a stock on the stock market and chart the progress).

Spectator Experiences—individuals observe the objects of study to identify specific behaviors as the basis for subsequent discussion (e.g., go to the police station, go to the stock market, go to a restaurant, go to a meat-packing business).

Exploratory Experiences—individuals are involved in open-ended real-world activities and settings where they develop an awareness of and personal questions about the subject at hand (e.g., tutor in the classroom of younger children, volunteer at a center for disabilities, interview a professional or parent, shadow a professional).

Analytical Experiences—individuals are involved in experiences that require the application of theory in real situations, and they are learning by a systematic analysis of the setting or solving problems (e.g., conduct a fund raising event for a class trip, serve on a student-advisory council to the principal, develop a cultural awareness or disability awareness day, plan and purchase a menu for a trip).

Generative Experiences—individuals learn by taking part in the creation of products, processes or relationships (e.g., develop a class newspaper, develop a learning center, write a letter to a senator to change existent legislation, develop a videotape to demonstrate appropriate, recycling procedures).

Simulated Experience	Spectator Experience	Exploratory Experience	Analytical Experience	Generative Experience

❖ THEMATIC TEACHING ⎯⎯⎯⎯⎯⎯⎯⎯⎯⎯⎯⎯⎯⎯⎯⎯⎯⎯⎯⎯⎯⎯⎯⎯⎯⎯⎯⎯⎯⎯

Thematic teaching is designed around the study of a theme or topic through active participation in a variety of activities. For example, instead of gaining information about a topic such as electricity by reading from page to page in the science text, you would teach about electricity through interrelated activities that connect the study of electricity to other academic areas. Students might be calculating the average cost of the school's electric bill for the past 6 months, setting up an experiment, demonstrating the idea of a circuit, visiting a power plant, writing to the energy commission, and reading about Thomas Edison and his experiments with electricity.

Through thematic teaching, students are able to see that learning in subject areas (e.g., reading, science, language and math) occurs throughout the day rather than only during a specific time period. In a like manner, as previously discussed, the brain searches for common patterns and connections. Thus, history, properly enlivened by relevant literature becomes a way of generating meaning out of other content. At the same time, thematic teaching is motivational because it often takes advantage of a students' special interests, natural curiosity, experiences, and cultural background. Also, inclusion of a variety of activities fosters individualization of instruction as well as opportunities to socialize and discuss the content material for real purposes. Finally, one of the keys to understanding is redundancy. By being provided with multiple opportunities to interact with content material, students are likely to increase their understanding and application of the material.

DESCRIPTION

Thematic teaching may be subject centered or interdisciplinary (integrated). Subject-centered themes concentrate on one major content area, while integrated themes incorporate the areas of math, language arts, and other content into the topic. It is possible to create either a subject-centered theme or an integrated theme for almost any topic. For example, if your study of the Virgin Islands includes only social studies objectives, it is a subject-centered theme. However, if a theme on the Virgin Islands includes objectives from other areas, such as math (requiring students to chart and compare the temperatures and rainfall of the different months of the year), reading (requiring students to read *Treasure Island*), and writing (requiring students to write reports about Carnival) it is an integrated unit.

Thematic teaching may also differ in the amount of student input. In a teacher-prepared unit, the teacher decides the topics and information to be presented. In a teacher-student prepared theme, the teacher generally selects the topic but he/she guides the students in their selection of the content and the methods used to learn the information. In a student-prepared theme, the students totally decide the topic, the approaches, and the length of time. The following steps are valuable to adhere to when creating a thematic unit: (a) select the theme or topic, (b) select the subtopics, (c) identify the general goals, (d) identify the specific objectives, (e) develop activities to meet the objectives, (f) determine how the objectives will be evaluated, and (g) compile a list of resources. The steps are not always sequential, as sometimes it is easier to identify the general goal before the subtopics, or sometimes the activities before the objectives.

DEVELOPING ACTIVITIES AND LEARNING EXPERIENCES

Ideas for activities may come from suggested experiments, curriculum guides, use of the experiential continuum, peers, students, or your own creativity and experiences. There is no limit to the number of possibilities. Possible projects may include making a movie, role-playing, writing a TV script, creative dramatics, developing a newsletter, or some formal presentation. A couple of examples include: (a) for a thematic unit on food, elementary-age students invent a new cereal and then develop an advertising campaign for the cereal. This campaign includes writing slogans, designing billboards, designing and labeling the box, and so on; (b) a thematic unit on the study and exploration of classical and modern fairy tales might culminate in having middle-school students write their own fairy tales; and (c) for a thematic unit on Mexico, high school students sign up for subtopics that interest them. In the sub-topic groups of two or three students, some members read and compile the information; some write reports or stories about the information; and others draw the charts, graphs, murals, and diagrams. The students choose their major roles, but at the same time, they participate in all of the activities. As a culminating activity, the teacher and students hold a fair and invite parents and members from other classes to visit the various booths designed by each sub-topic group. Visitors are treated to sample foods, dramatizations, reports, and visual displays concerning Mexico. During the fair, booths on food, folklore, city life, village life, history, religion, and government are presented.

❖ EXPEDITIONARY LEARNING

In expeditionary learning environments, students function as groups of learners who participate in multi-disciplinary, project-based, learning activities. These projects include in-depth studies of a single theme or topic involving intellectual, emotional, physical, and service dimensions, sustained over several weeks of study (Cousins & Rodgers, 1995). Program components that are common to expeditionary learning and that differentiate it from traditional-educational approaches include:

1. *Role of the Teacher*—The teacher's role is to facilitate learning and development by structuring experiences and by providing guidance with care, compassion and respect for students' diverse learning styles, backgrounds, and needs. Teachers scaffold student learning; similar to constructing a building where initially the scaffold is built to support the wall, but as the wall becomes more structurally complete, it supports itself and the scaffold is disassembled (Bruner, 1978). Scaffolding strategies include various types of questions, prompts, information sharing, and restatements that provide support for what students are trying to learn and accomplish.

    Collaboration and conferencing are also essential aspects of what expeditionary-learning teachers do. Teachers collaborate by structuring time for reading, writing, problem-solving, and discussion as well as informing students about additional resources, teaching essential skills, modeling their own interests and frustrations, and providing assistance in formulating ways to acquire or demonstrate growth and development. Conferencing occurs with the teacher as well as with peers. For example in the area of writing, students read their work to the teacher and to each other; they help each other edit their work, and often are asked to self-reflect on the writing to identify what they like about it as well as what they don't like about it.

2. *Schedules*—School schedules are arranged so there are large blocks of flexible time and common, teacher planning time to accommodate learning expeditions that may engage students for parts of a day, days, weeks or months.

3. *Curriculum*—The curriculum emphasizes character development as well as intellectual development and encourages self-discovery. Interdisciplinary, learning expeditions replace subject-separated classes. Learning expeditions are sustained, in-depth studies of a single theme or topic that generally take three to nine weeks to complete. The theme or topic integrates disciplines, though some themes lend themselves more to one discipline than another. Sample themes include: Bhutan, The Iditarod, Fighting for Freedom, or Rural Life. Individual and/or group projects that call for concrete products or actions which address authentic problems, situations and purposeful fieldwork are the center of each expedition. Sample projects include: interviewing local politicians to create a book about them, or planning, fundraising and building a playhouse for the Headstart program. According to Cousins (1995) a successful project:

   a. Uses skills that need to be taught.
   b. Uses the different talents and strengths of each student.
   c. Uses local resources—people, places, and organizations.
   d. Includes some mandatory and some optional components.
   e. Has a flexible schedule, so students can pursue interests.
   f. Promotes student self-assessment through use of the writing process and conferencing.
   g. Requires students to work together so knowledge is shared.
   h. Includes a forum for presenting their final work.
   i. Has an end product that is beneficial to the community.

4. *Assessment*—Real-world performance is used as the primary way to assess students' progress and achievement. Group projects are balanced with individual assignments. Individual assignments provide teachers the opportunity to obtain information on the strengths, interests, and areas of concern for each student. Work on individual projects does not mean that students work in isolation. Rather, learners can help each other by sharing information, skills, and resources while simultaneously critiquing each other's work without sacrificing their individual products.

5. *Linkages to Community and Service Organizations*—Expeditionary learning programs seek to develop working relations with community members, organizations, and service agencies. Fieldwork in the community promotes opportunities for immersion into a theme or topic, in-depth research, adventure, and service. While in the community students conduct interviews, make detailed observations, sketch, take measurements, and work with others.

6. *Staff Development*—Expeditionary learning depends upon the ongoing development and renewal of staff. The teacher's self-definition and role as a collaborative learner and curriculum designer requires continuing intellectual and personal growth in order to create learning expeditions for, and with, students.

Sample Expeditionary learning courses that have been developed and implemented by the Dubuque, Iowa Central Alternative High School are found in Table 18.

❖ INDEPENDENT STUDY CONTRACTS

As much as possible, students should have a compelling interest in exploring or mastering a subject, topic or skill. One way to help students immerse themselves into learning about some-

◆ TABLE 18 ◆

Sample Expeditionary Learning Courses

Course Title: City as School
Description: Students will discover the city as a learning place by participation on a community site four times a week for approximately 70 hours per quarter. Through the provision of service to others, students will increase their sense of self-worth, work ethic, and communication skills.

Course Title: Do Unto Others
Description: Students will study examples of intolerance in American History and will analyze why some people discriminate against others. The class will also analyze the impact of discrimination on a personal level to understand how it affects both the victims and aggressors.

Course Title: Dubuque and The Civil War
Description: This course will take an in-depth look into the causes of the Civil War, and analyze how ordinary Americans accomplished extraordinary deeds before the war began as well as on the battlefield. We will analyze articles from local Dubuque newspapers' accounts of events and people.

Course Title: Fitness
Description: Fitness is a life long journey. People who actively monitor their fitness level and work to improve it will live a longer, fuller, and happier life. A healthy person is able to experience more in life. There are several types of fitness. The major ones are cardiovascular fitness, muscular fitness, and mental fitness. All types of fitness are equally important to being a well-rounded, healthy person.

Course Title: Gear It Up
Description: In this course student will learn about the variety of uses that bicycles have throughout the world. Students will also learn to be a bicycle mechanic and develop an owner's manual for the bikes that are repaired. Bikes and manual will be donated to local elementary students. Students will also design a tri-state trail guide to be used by local bicyclists.

Course Title: Natural Reflections
Description: Natural Reflections is offered to develop an increased awareness of the interconnectedness of humans with their environment, and to increase observation skills. Students will demonstrate their connectedness by sketches and by reflective writings.

Course Title: Senior Portfolio
Description: Career awareness and self-awareness—Students will be required to complete a series of personal and career exploration activities; complete a job shadowing experience, write a rough draft of a senior reflection paper, and present the career portion of their Life Plan Portfolio to a review panel.

Course Title: Sites of Dubuque
Description: Students, in small groups, will select a section of Dubuque to observe. Students will record observations on site by means of photographs, notes, sketches, and tape recordings of location sounds, as well as conduct interviews with the people who live or work there. Students will then create narrative works of art (tell the story), that reflect the information that has been collected. Students will share their narrative works and some of their research.

(continued)

◆ **TABLE 18** ◆

Sample Expeditionary Learning Courses *continued*

Course Title: This Living Planet-Bluffs and Trees
Description: Environmental Connectedness—This Living Planet is offered to develop an increased awareness of the interconnectedness of humans and this planet. Students will focus on the Central hillside, trees and especially seeds. We will plant bulbs for spring, read from Thoreau's *Faith In A Seed,* do close observations, and write reflections.

Course Title: U.F.O.s
Description: U.F.O.s have been reported for thousands of years. The students will go into an in-depth study of the U.F.O. phenomenon. They will be required to research past investigations that were conducted by the government and determine how adequately they were carried out. Students will also research some unsolved U.F.O. cases and decide for themselves what really happened. Once students have completed their unit, they will be required to write a personal letter that is either for or against continued U.F.O. research and send it to their local congressperson.

Course Title: Faces
Description: Figuring out who you are is a lifelong process. It requires looking back and discussing or rediscovering how the persons, places, and events in our lives have shaped us into who we are as individuals, and who we are as a group.

Developed by the staff of Central Alternative High School, Dubuque, Iowa. Permission for use granted by David Olson, Principal

thing is to develop an independent study contract with them. A contract is a joint agreement between a student and an educator to accomplish a specific objective. The contract may be developed for an individual student, a group of students or an entire class. The students and the teacher should discuss the topic of study, establish long and short-term goals, identify resources, and describe how the students will demonstrate what has been learned. When using contracts, it is important to schedule regular meetings to discuss progress and problems. In addition, educators need to be certain that students know where they are going, how they can reach their goal(s), and how they will be evaluated. A sample format for an independent study contract is found below.

SAMPLE CONTRACT

1.   What do you specificlly want to learn?
2.   What questions do you have regarding this topic?
3.   What specific resources can be used to help you learn about this topic?
4.   How will you demonstrate what you have learned?
5.   When will you demonstrate what you have learned?

Signed: Student   _____

              Teacher   _____

              Date   _____

❖ LEARNING JOURNALS

Learning journals stimulate critical reflection in learners and provide personal records of students' observations, impressions, feelings, thoughts, opinions, insights and evaluations of class materials and experiences. Entries are maintained in a notebook and should be submitted on a regular basis. They are returned to the students after you read each journal entry and respond, querie or just note points expressed by the student. All communication between you and studenst should remain confidential.

There are many ways to structure the use of learning journals; one approach is to use the following categories of journal entries:

1. *Diary entries* which function as an outlet for student reactions to the course or to something in their lives that is related to the course (e.g., narratives of personal experiences, statements of opinion or expressions of strong emotion);

2. *Notebook entries* which help learners to develop more reflective and critical responses to the course (e.g., summaries and critiques of activities and readings, short answers to questions, asked by you or other students, mini-reports of group discussions or special activities);

3. *Dialogue entries* which allow students to engage you in a written interaction regarding issues about which they might be uncomfortable raising in class or in a face-to-face teacher-student conference (e.g., questions that solicit your response to a particular entry, requests for another viewpoint or further information, criticisms of lessons or classroom dynamics);

4. *Integrative entries* which provide students with practice in synthesizing personal and academic knowledge (e.g, entries that use personal experiences as evidence to support or contradict concepts, or that attempt to apply these concepts to their lives outside the classroom); and

5. *Evaluative entries* which require students to undertake periodic self-assessment of their progress (e.g., reflections on and analyses of their performance in the class, shifts in attitudes or ideas, and goals for future performance).

Students are required to make at least one notebook entry (i.e., diary, notebook or dialogue) each week, an integrative entry at least every three weeks and three, evaluative entries during the semester.

❖ SERVICE LEARNING

Service learning programs emphasize the accomplishment of tasks which help fellow humans in combination with conscious, educational growth (Kendall & Associates, 1990). There are many areas, both in and out of school, and at all grade levels, where involvement in service activities can provide students with a unique and valuable part of their education. By undertaking projects that help people, students experience what it means to be important in the lives of others, and, as a result of their positive accomplishments, they improve their self perceptions (Williams, 1990). Projects such as painting the homes of elderly citizens, gleaning food for homeless people, turning vacant lots into playgrounds; cleaning rivers and streams, participating in walk-athons, washing cars to raise money for medicine, and collecting clothes and food to aid disaster victims promotes students use of social skills in order to work together. They practice decision making and problem solving, and they learn about the needs and abilities of others as they help improve the lives of people in our society. Service learning offers students the chance to discover, develop, and demonstrate skills and talents—that may not have the opportunity to surface in a school setting.

❖ SUPPLEMENTARY OUTDOOR ACTIVITIES

Decades ago, Sharp (1952) noted an illogical, educational practice when he remarked "On the way to and from school, our youth pass by and through the very things that they go into the classroom to study about" (p. 20). As we continue to seek ways to make teaching and learning more pertinent, using outdoor activities to expand what goes on in the classroom is a valuable, educational practice. Students are actively involved, and they are learning social skills, thinking skills, problem solving, and an appreciation for the environment.

Educators who use outdoor activities seek to achieve the goals and objectives of the curriculum by structuring learning experiences that use natural, community, and human resources be-

yond the traditional classroom. The activities complement content areas of the school curriculum and help students develop important life-skills through the processes of observing, classifying, describing, measuring, inferring, and predicting. Use of supplementary outdoor activities can be applied to all curriculum areas. Students can draw maps of the playground, spend a day living off the land, like the pioneers, or set up a full-size, model replica of an oil field to discover how it works. Basic concepts in math such as counting, measurement, estimation, and problem solving can be introduced, taught, and reinforced in using outdoor activities. Theories and concepts that are difficult to understand begin to have meaning—as they are used to determine tree height or the angle of the slide on a playground.

SAMPLE ACTIVITIES

The following is a sample list of activities to help you start integrating outdoor activities into your teaching. Each activity can be modified easily to meet the age and skill-level of your students.

Litter we know—Divide the class into teams. Take the class outside and collect any litter that is on the school grounds. Have the teams make and display collages of the collected litter. Discuss the potential hazards litter poses for wildlife. Ask the students to assign a numerical value to each kind of litter; the higher the number, the more dangerous it is to wildlife. Have each team figure a total score for their collage (Charles, 1985).

Energy treasure hunt—Energy is an issue of great importance. Have the class map the energy sources in the community. By using visual keys, they can identify where the sources of energy are located, and how the energy is being used.

Sharing circles.—Group development and cooperative learning are also key goals of using the outdoors. When students are involved in group activities, they must communicate with others, participate in group discussions, apply previously learned -concepts and principles during discussions. In addition, they must develop vocabulary to describe what they are discussing, keep accurate records, and interpret their own work and findings (Johns, Liske, & Evans, 1985). One activity is to build group cooperation and communication skills in a sharing circle. Students can make visual products (e.g., charts, graphs, diagrams) to use for discussion purposes, or collect some items from the activity to discuss. For example, groups of students are asked to collect three, natural items; then, they write a story using these items in their story.

100 inch hike—Give each student a magnifying glass, spool with 100″ of string, and 10 painted sticks. Select an environment that provides opportunities for exploration, such as a grassy or wooded area. The students blaze a trail on their hands and knees. They lay out the string as a trail and examine the microworld using their magnifying glass. The students can use the sticks to identify unusual findings (Hammerman et al. 1985). A discussion of what each person found can then be undertaken.

Envirolopes—Write challenges on the outside of business-sized envelopes. For example, "Find three of each of the following: different seeds, unusual leaves, textures, indications of animal presence, indications of human presence." Give each pair of students an envelope. Tell them they have 15 minutes to collect their samples, and the samples must fit in the envelope. Display the objects each team finds and discuss them (Hansen, 1990).

Counters—Collect natural objects such as pebbles, twigs, acorn caps, to be used as counters in math (Johns, Liske, & Evans, 1985).

Environmental advertisements—Advertising has a major impact on our contemporary society. Bring in some advertisements from magazines and discuss their potential impact. Some criteria to use are: (a) emotional appeal, (b) factual base, (c) values conveyed, (d) overall effect. Then, have students go out into the comunity and locate advertisements such as billboards, signs and posters. Use the same criteria to discuss the advertising found in the community, plus factors such as potential costs, aesthetics and impact on the environment (Project Learning Tree, 1989).

Dinosaur in the parking lot—Discuss the different dinosaurs. Talk about the different sizes. Divide the class into small groups and have them choose their favorite dinosaur. In a large area, such as a field or the playground have the students measure out their dinosaur. The students then mark it with colored stakes. Compare the different sizes (Johns, Liske, & Evans, 1985).

Packaging products poll—Nearly $1 of every $10 that we spend for food and beverages pays for the packaging of products. Many of the products that we buy come in unnecessary extra boxes and containers. Ask students to go to the market and compare how products are packaged. Have them identify those products that come in extra, unnecessary containers. As a follow-up, they can write letters of concern to the companies that make a practice of wasteful packaging.

Interview a spider—Divide the students into groups of two. Have each pair choose an animal which can be easily observed (i.e., spider, squirrel, worm) and write a list of questions to "ask" the animal. Have the teams go outside and observe the animal—to answer the questions. The questions which can not be answered by observation should be researched. Each team uses their notes to write a newspaper article about their animal (Western Regional Environmental Education Council,1986).

Urban nature search—All environments have some characteristic life forms. In an efffort to help students identify some of these commonalities, you can give them a questionnaire that will guide their observations. Sample questions to give students include: (a) Describe and sketch three plants that you find on or near a building, which direction are they facing? (b) Describe and sketch the kinds of wildlife (animals and insects) that you see, what are their food sources? water sources? shelter? (Western Regional Environmental Education Council,1986).

❖ SUMMARY

In many classrooms, teachers "cover" lots of vocabulary, facts, dates, names and rules. Unfortunately, students often forget much of what has been covered because they never really understood or saw the purpose of what they were learning. Rather than covering material and slogging through the facts, we can help students better understand and see utility in learning by *actively* involving them in the learning process. Active learning helps prepare students to be self-directed, lifelong learners-an ability they will need in a society where individuals change jobs numerous times in their working years and have extended, leisure-time after retirement.

In this section, we have presented a variety of information regarding experiential approaches, techniques, and activities for you to consider using in your educational setting. The common thread that unites each subsection is the premise that multiple complex and concrete experiences are essential in order for personally meaningful learning and development to occur. As a result, our primary focus as educators should be on expanding the quantity

and quality of approaches that learners are exposed to the content and context. This is accomplished when (a) we arrange experiences in which learners are in touch directly with the realities of the subject matter; and (b) we immerse learners in complex, interactive experiences while involving them in practical projects, social interactions, appropriate physical movement, and creative enterprises.

"Through direct experiences with nature, people, objects, things, places, and by actually 'learning by doing' there is scientific evidence that the learning process is faster, and what is learned is retained longer; and there is a greater appreciation and understanding for the things that are learned firsthand."

—*L.B. Sharp*

SECTION 8

ADULTS
GUIDING PRACTICES

❖

"Almost any adult can learn anything they want to, given time persistence, and assistance."

—*A.B. Knox*

In contrast to generations past, we no longer can assume that a fixed body of knowledge, once mastered, will serve us for life. The pace and demands of our current society make lifelong learning and continuous, personal growth major, societal issues. As a result, increasing numbers of adults are involved in some form of personal and/or professional renewal.

The objective of facilitating learning with adults is to help them see themselves as proactive, initiating individuals engaged in a continuous re-creation of their personal relationships, work worlds, and social circumstances (Brookfield, 1986). In this section, we provide (a) a summary of the literature on adult learning principles, (b) specific suggestions for planning and implementing experiential learning opportunities with adults, (c) a segment, written by Dennis Nord, on a career-counseling course that uses an experiential component, and (d) a case study with a group of adults accompanied by responses to the case study by Bill Quinn and Jim Stiehl.

❖ ADULT LEARNING PRINCIPLES

The following is a summary of the major principles and practices of adult learning. The information draws from the work of Brookfield, (1986), Cafferella (1994), Cranton, (1989), and Cross (1979).

1. Adults have the capacity and are eager to learn new information and skills. At the same time, ongoing conceptual and technological changes mandate continuous, educational processes for survival.

2. Adults prefer to be actively involved in the learning process rather than passive recipients of knowledge. In addition, they want the opportunity to be supportive of each other in the learning process.

3. Adults have a rich background of knowledge and experience. They tend to learn best when this experience is acknowledged, and when new information builds on their past knowledge and experience.

4. Adults come to a learning situations with their own personal goals and objectives. These goals and objectives may or may not be the same as those that underlie the learning situation.

5. Adults are more receptive to the learning process in situations that are both physically and psychologically comfortable.

6. Adults are motivated to learn based on a combination of complex internal and external forces. We need to understand the nature of those forces, and how they interact to inhibit and/or encourage adult learning.

7. Adults learn best when they feel the need to learn, and when they have a sense of responsibility for what, why, and how they learn. Defining goals for oneself and developing the ability to take the initiative to achieve those goals are essential skills for personal and professional success.

8. Adults tend to be pragmatic in their learning. They are unlikely to willingly engage in learning unless the content is meaningful to them. They are motivated to learn if they participate actively in the learning process, and if they can apply their learning to present situations. Adults should be guided in analyzing real-world contexts and creating alternative and appropriate ways to test their new knowledge in real world situations.

9. All adults have preferred styles of learning, and these differ. Instruction, materials and assignments should take into consideration adults' diverse styles, as you approach tasks of varying complexity.

10. What, how and where adults learn is affected by the many roles they play as adults (for example, worker, parent, partner, friend, spouse), their gender, their ethnicity, and their social class.

11. Adults learn both in independent, self-reliant modes and in interdependent, connected, and collaborative ways.

12. Much of what adults learn tends to have an affect on others (for example, on work colleagues and family).

❖ SUGGESTIONS FOR WORKING WITH ADULTS

Adults participating in experiential education and therapy programs will vary significantly. A thorough assessment of needs and goals is very important for planning, implementation, and transfer. Some suggestions for working with adults that have been adapted from Ewert (1989) include:

BEFORE THE PROGRAM

1. Acquire a signed activity-specific, medical clearance.
2. Explain the experience to avoid misconceptions or false expectations.
3. Share stories about successful past participants; some individuals may have questions and/or be hesitant due to personal inability or inadequacies.
4. Hire mature, knowledgable, and personable staff who can deal successfully with a variety of people.
5. Plan ways for participants to synthesize their experiences during and after the experience.

IMPLEMENTING THE PROGRAM

6. Determine individual and group expectations and fears; strive to make them manageable.
7. Novel experiences and activities often cause awareness and common sense gaps. Be prepared for safety problems which may result.
8. Staff should try to be supportive, straight-forward, and fun-loving.

AFTER THE PROGRAM

9. Structure opportunities for individuals and groups to synthesize their experiences.
10. Link the experience with everyday living. These links can provide meaning and give function to the experience.
11. Solicit feedback from participants to refine similar experiences for future groups.

CAREER DEVELOPMENT AND EXPERIENTIAL EDUCATION

Dennis Nord, Ph.D.

SELF-EFFICACY THEORY OF CAREER DEVELOPMENT AND EXPERIENTIAL EDUCATION

Adventure experiences are effective at getting us to consider—what are our values in life? Afterwards, reflection is more useful in developing perspective and priority. In fact, the high, perceived risk in a controlled situation that helps participants reconsider their values, their limits, and their willingness to take risks fits directly into the self-efficacy theory for career development. When I discovered how well self-efficacy fits adventure experiential education, it seemed natural to apply the concepts to a career program that we have evolved over several years.

The concept of self-efficacy is simply believing that you can do what is required to get what you want. The key in the description is believing. In this case, it is believing that you can get a job doing something meaningful to you. Or, believing you can complete the education required to be eligible. Too many people know what they want, but do not believe they can get it. Others, have little idea of what they want, an issue they skirt due to their fear. Why, they ask, should I bother with what I want when the market is poor, and I will just have to take whatever comes up anyway? A major breakthrough in the career process comes when people decide that it is more rewarding to work on meaningful goals than doing what they mindlessly bump-into. With the help of adventure experiential education, we are in a position to stimulate their career self-efficacy.

The four sources of self-efficacy (Bandura, 1977, 1986) stated in descending order of potency are (1) Performance accomplishment, (2) Vicarious reinforcement, (3) Verbal persuasion, and (4) Emotional arousal. The most effective source, performance accomplishment, means doing something challenging "well." This is exactly what is happening in our career-adventure retreat, participants are faced with challenges and learn to overcome them. Vicarious reinforcement is also present in the form of watching people like themselves, classmates, accomplish tasks ahead of them. If a peer can achieve success in an adventure initiative, then likely others will think themselves capable and attempt risks that they might easily avoid on their own. Verbal persuasion is present in the lecture material and probably more effectively by peers with each other. The encouragement is infectious and much more personal than what an instructor is likely to do for a particular student. Emotional arousal means having the whole physiological system "turned up", and this too is present during the adventure initiatives, especially the more challenging ones. Adventure experiential education seems designed especially to enhance self-efficacy! By crafting specific, career metaphors for the activities involved, the experiences that students have are tailored to career issues.

OVERVIEW OF THE COURSE

A two day, overnight retreat is used for career development with college students as a part of their requirement for completing a career class. The retreat has been used now with over 350 students over seven, different quarters with groups as large as 83 students. Students attend two lectures, the retreat, and nine, discussion group sessions with 15 or fewer class members. The purpose of the class is to assist college students in their career development. Homework assignments are mostly experiential, requiring students to meet career incumbents and learn from experiences about their own interests, values and skills.

TWO METAPHORICAL EXAMPLES FOR CAREER WORK

The high wall initiative is a smooth wooden barrier approximately fifteen feet high with no purchases for hand or foot. A team of 12 to 15 participants is instructed in the "rules" of the initiative in the context of career issues, which follow:

> *Instructions* We have all met the wall before. This is the wall that represents all the barriers between you and what you want in your career. This is the barrier where you face yourself and realize that you can't do this alone (if you think up a way to do this with props, they will be eliminated any way). This time you have to get help, and you will have to give help. There is not another way over. Unless you choose a very low risk career goal, the same will be true in your career.

Following the wall initiative the students are engaged in a discussion relating their experience to their career process. Here are some sample questions that might be used to move the discussion along:

> *Processing* What perception did you have of the wall when you first saw it? How did you get over the wall? What are the walls you have been fearing regarding your career? What does this say about you and the tasks ahead of you to get a career? Who are the people who have helped you get as far in life as you have?

The students' experience with the wall begins with a sense of incredulity. Standing next to the wall, most are impressed with the size of the task set before them. Getting the first person over is a major team accomplishment, followed by elation. The personal experience of struggling while supporting others and the special effort involved in surmounting the wall elicit a wide range of emotions. Concerns about responsibility, wondering if they are strong enough, doubt about whether they can do their part and keep their teammates safe are evoked. The realization that it must be possible to climb the wall challenges their intellect to consider new strategies and daring possibilities often results in chaotic discussion of what might be done. Fear of failure, of looking stupid or even getting hurt are other concerns that arise in the act. The success of getting the entire team over the wall brings this experience into focus as a team-effort and an individual experience. The metaphor is described again in the context of what this means for the career barriers not yet faced. Stretching the imagination facilitates the next step in the career process by bringing the barrier and the risk into perspective.

A spider's web is constructed to human size using cord strung between trees.

Instructions: The team is presented with a brief list of 8 career titles. They are told each person must chose one career title and more than one person can be in each career. Not all careers listed must have students in them. Each person must enter the next phase of life by passing through the hole in the web that has their career title on it. When there are two or more people in a career, they must pass through the web together. They are then told, "The web is guarded by the "Dean of Spiders" who would prefer that you remain a student forever to glean even more dollars from you. Your only chance is to work quickly and carefully to insure that you release your entire team into the post-graduate world of work. Any one caught by Dean Spider (the facilitator) will have to enroll in an additional quarter of course work and return to the student side to try again. The way one is caught is to touch the web that will awaken the old dozing dean. Once across, the "alumni" will be allowed to help the current students in their efforts to graduate."

Much communication is required to arrive at solutions that work in both initiatives. Rules are often changed by the facilitators to increase (and sometimes to decrease) the two, major factors involved: challenge and support always with an eye towards safety.

Processing the spider's web: What expectations did you have for yourself? What was your reaction as you saw where your appropriate career hole appeared in the web? How were you tempted to change? As a helper, what did you experience? When you got to the other side, did you still want to help those you left behind? This is like the alumni who volunteer to talk with students about their career experiences. In this exercise you had to touch other people and be touched by them. Did you have concerns about that aspect of the exercise? Did you feel safe sexually as well as physically? What does this mean to you?

The processing of each initiative involves a discussion of the nature of the challenge, the experience, team work, safety concerns, perceived risks, and the metaphor and the meaning that the participants can apply to their career. We explore the group dynamic and the range of feelings participants experience in the midst of the task. At times, processing will take place midway through a task.

OUTCOME DATA

Following this process, the retreat students are asked to reflect on their experience and then write-up a report on the impact of the retreat on themselves and their career thoughts. A qualitative analysis of these descriptions completed by Nord, Connor, Roberts, Solberg, and Scheck,

(1994) indicates that students are positively changed in their view of what is possible in their careers. Sample statements from student reports include:

- ◆ I was overcome with a feeling that I could do anything!
- ◆ I clarified some of my needs and goals.
- ◆ I leaned new skills and ideas (about careers).
- ◆ I felt things I never thought about before and reacted in ways that touched me.

We have collected data on the Career Search Efficacy Scale (Nord, et. al., 1994). Three of four subscales show significant differences following the career retreat and discussion sessions when compared to a random control group. Specifically, they increased self-efficacy on job search, interviewing, and personal career exploration. The results suggest that the participants are better equipped for pursuing satisfying and successful careers after the intervention.

Data on the *Career Possible Selves* (CPE) was collected from two quarters of the retreat (Duerlinger, 1996). Students made significantly more career choices from the CPE following the retreat, suggesting they increased their span of career options than they normally would have considered. We also documented increased discussion-group cohesiveness using the Team Development Indicator (TDI). We found that 5 of the 10 items of the TDI were significantly increased during the two days of the retreat. Those areas of significant increase were (1) understanding and committing to goals, (2) high standards for themselves and the team's performance, (3) looking to each other for help on resolving challenges, recognition, (4) reward of team efforts, and (5) encouraging and appreciating feedback. This additional empirical data confirms that students become very highly involved in encouraging each other during the retreat. The teaching assistants for the class confirmed this in one recent quarter when the retreat was not possible. At the end of the quarter, the teaching assistants concluded that the interaction in the discussion groups was much less effective. Groups were less trusting and the students were more resistant to experiential homework.

FUTURE APPLICATIONS

As we continue to refine the retreat, we look for means of making the retreat as powerful and easily accessible to as many students as possible. We find this a highly effective method for starting students on their career path. Our discussion groups are more productive as they make use of the group cohesiveness developed during the retreat and the knowledge of career concepts and information that all the students share. The increased career self-efficacy provides motivation and confidence in researching career opportunities. Teaching assistants with little prior experience in career development can be used effectively in the discussion groups following the retreat knowing that the major direction and concepts are set.

We have used a similar model for job search with college students in one-day workshops and with mid-life career changers during a weekend retreat. Our next target group is high school students planning for their futures.

The faculty at a rural, elementary school decided to spend a day on a ropes course with the purpose of "bonding." One teacher, a male 2nd grade educator arranged and scheduled the event for the beginning of the school year. He contacted the local university program who owned and facilitated "Team Building Ropes Course Experiences" and arranged for use of the course and instructors to facilitate the experience. Many of the 30 teachers and administration were very nervous about the anticipated experience. Throughout the summer, several of them drove to the ropes course to look through the fence at the course mentally trying to prepare for the beginning of the school year group challenge.

The scheduled day of the event arrived and individuals met at the ropes course. They received a safety briefing and divided into six teams with five people on a team. Everyone completed the lower elements such as the spider's web, the wall, and walking across a low-swinging beam. There was a general feeling of great success.

After completing the lower elements, the instructors decided that it was time to eat lunch without providing any time to formally debrief the morning's events. People got together in small groups eating their lunches that they brought from home while looking up at the high elements. They began talking about the ensuing challenge, speculating about who would try and be able to complete the various elements.

After lunch, the instructors introduced climbing harnesses to the large group. People put on the harnesses, helping each other make the appropriate adjustments. The body language indicated that some people were very anxious while others were not. Some folks walked around giving hugs, smiles and the thumbs-up sign while others began to get quiet and retreat.

Two high element stations were used—the high tension traverse which required individuals to balance and walk across it while being clipped in from above, and a high climbing wall which was belayed from below. People were divided into two groups and assigned to go to either of the two events. It was at this point that group cohesion began to splinter. Three subgroups emerged: (1) the active participants, (2) the inactive, uninvolved group, and (3) the group who was happy to provide support for others, but they did not want to participate. For example, one teacher, Kay, who is very athletic choose to do nothing. She sat with some other teachers who sulked, stared and whispered to each other. Another teacher, Barb, who is generally a very outspoken person at school, took a camera out of her purse and began taking pictures of those on the high elements, laughing and cheering, yet she never attempted any of the high elements.

Others saw the need for support and motivation and began walking around to the inactive people trying to encourage them by saying things such as "I will spot you.", "I will go with you.", or "I will climb the one next to you." The inactive individuals simply stated "No, I don't want to." After several negative responses, the people who were trying to encourage involvement became discouraged and joined the group of people who chose to participate.

Several of the teachers, who were very scared, climbed the wall, while others cheered them on. Others traversed the high wire with support from some of the folks from the ground. Many others chose not to climb the wall or traverse the wire or did not get the opportunity because there was line of people waiting for each element to be free.

At the end of the day, 30 minutes was set aside for debriefing. The lead instructor brought the entire group together in a large circle. He sat everyone down and asked "How did you feel about today." No one responded so he turned to one teacher and said "What is your name again?" She responded, "Tina." "Tina, you seemed very excited throughout the day. What are your reflections about today?" As Tina prepared to answer, she became very aware of her three friends who were looking at her. While Tina had a wonderful day, she was certain that her friends, Kay, Sandy and Madeline, who sat on the side talking amongst themselves, and who did not get involved in the high elements were angry. As a result, they hated the experience. Tina felt awkward and torn about how to respond. So, she tried to come up with an answer that would not be threatening to those who did not participate in the afternoon activities, and simultaneously she allowed herself to express

her own personal growth that occurred during the day. Tina talked about how hard it was for her. How she appreciated the fact that people were willing to wait for her. This gave her confidence to complete the high traverse, and it also allowed her to overcome her fear and climb the wall afterwards. After she spoke, there was a long silence. The instructor called on a few other people who were active throughout the day. They made statements similar to Tina's; however, the majority of people did not respond. The instructors thanked everyone for coming, packed up the equipment and headed home. The faculty from the elementary school dispersed as well—now more split and less harmonious than when they arrived early that morning.

The next day, the teachers and staff had a meeting. People talked about how the day on the ropes course had backfired. There was no bonding. People were angry. In fact, throughout the entire school year, the staff was split between those who participated on the high elements and those who did not. The negative feelings caused a separation in the teachers' lounge when people ate lunch and on the playground during recess duty. It also carried over to philosophical beliefs about the importance of risk taking in educational settings. In the year and a half that has passed since the team building ropes course experience, Tina noted that whenever she comes in contact with Kay, Sandy and Madeline—she becomes anxious. In reflection of the day, Tina said "I feel bad for the people who did not attempt the high course; yet I also feel bad for myself and others who did attempt it."

CASE STUDY INVITED RESPONSE

Bill Quinn, Ph.D.

What is your assessment of what happened? It appears that little if any discussion between the university and the school group concerning goals and expectations took place before the teachers attended. This contributed to a day where the ropes course instructors had insufficient knowledge of the group or individual issues, and, therefore they offered a packaged type of "standard" day. There was no up front attempt to match activities and reflective sessions with the existing dynamics within the participant group, nor were the participants included in a discussion about what was expected of them.

The opportunity to discuss the morning activities was not taken. This only compounded the problem in ineffective communication all around. The instructors seemed to be mentally absent, only concerned with doing the activities.

The final debrief was mishandled from the instant it began. "How do you feel" is probably a poor choice even in a highly open and honest group, let alone a group that has splintered and has not worked well, all afternoon.

Evidently there was no one who could organize and facilitate a group discussion back at the school the next day either. Bad feelings were only left to fester.

How could you have prevented this from happening? The first thing that I would have done was to gain a clear understanding from school administrators and teachers as to what they wished to accomplish from the session. I

would have visited the school and spoken to a few representatives of the faculty and administration. I would have written a letter to all participants describing in general the types of activities and anticipated outcomes, and what my expectations of the participants would be.

At the beginning of the day, I would have led a discussion about individual goals and expectations to see what the group really had in mind, and if previous conceptions of what was understood between the school and the university were accurate. I would present the attitude that no one was being forced to participate, and that each person has a choice. Also, the facilitators and other participants will honor whatever choice was exercised.

If there came a time during the day that participants were losing interest, "splintering" or developing negative attitudes, I would stop the activities and "back up" a bit. By backing up, I mean to reexamine what has already transpired and try to correct the present and/or escalating problems. Doing these programs in a proper, sequential order is crucial. Trying to match the difficulty of the exercise to the ability and readiness of a group or individual to handle and overcome the problem is a key element of proper, teambuilding activities. I would examine the sequence, try to decide if it has accelerated too fast, and try to regroup and realign the sequence of activities to match more closely what is occurring within the group. With the group in this case study, it seems that poor communication at the beginning became worse as the day progressed. I would have attempted to reopen and reestablish effective communication lines. This reexamining process should involve all the facilitators, and quite possibly the participants, as well.

The final debrief was a disaster, and if everything previously mentioned had been done, the stage for a disaster would not have been set. Furthermore, I never start a debrief with such an invasive and personal question as "How do you feel," nor would I have been so callous all day as to not remember someone's name—then casually say "what was your name again?" This is not the way to approach a person when asking a question that is seeking an answer of depth and feeling. I rarely put a participant on the spot during a debrief unless I know the person well, or if I am convinced that that is the most appropriate question to ask at the time. Even then, I would hesitate or not proceed at all if I did not believe the group had built up the support, trust, and respect necessary to handle directly pointed and important personal questions.

Finally, a time for a follow-up discussion back at the school would be appropriate. This should be led by the person in charge from the university or by someone with suitable skills at the school.

In the debrief, at the end of the day, what strategies and interventions could the instructors have undertaken to increase the positive impact of the experience? I would first reflect upon the afternoon section of the day by asking questions such as: What effect did the high events have upon you? Did you feel afraid at anytime, and how did you respond to that emotion? How did you see others respond to the challenge presented? I would try to involve everyone by posing the question, telling everyone a brief response is expected (this however relates to clearly-communicated expectations, and the idea of personal choice) giving everyone a moment to think. Then, I would proceed around the circle of participants until everyone has had the opportunity to speak.

I would debrief the entire day in a similar fashion, but the lead question would involve a revisiting of the goals as previously stated by the individual participants. The question would be: did you meet your personal goals, and would you please give a specific example of how they were or were not met? Each person would be asked to respond, but not necessarily in order.

Sometimes I may ask participants to go off in pairs and try to creatively describe how something that happened during the day could be metaphorically construed as similar to what happens in your professional life. When we reassemble, these metaphors are presented and discussed.

I always ask at the end of the discussion period if anyone has anything else they would like to say to anyone else or to the entire group. At this point, I usually do something to bring closure to the day, either high-five, back slaps all around, or handshake circles or lets have a drink?

CASE STUDY INVITED RESPONSE

Jim Stiehl, Ph.D.

What is your assessment of what happened?
In general, the facilitator did not successfully structure situations so that they would encourage a positive reaction from the participants. With minimal questioning and analysis of events prior to the lunch break, a serious downward spiral of events occurred. To me, this downward spiral arose chiefly from unacknowledged anxieties that had been building among several participants in anticipation of the ropes experience.

How could you have prevented this from happening? The unfortunate, downward spiral of events might have been minimized, if not eliminated altogether, at several junctures. First, the purpose was vague (i.e., "bonding"), with no concrete, preplanned goals. As a consequence, even if future difficulties had been anticipated by the facilitator, s/he could not have reiterated initial objectives. Crucial to assisting a group in becoming a cohesive, effective team are (1) goal setting (with clear explanations of challenges and objectives), and (2) a clear contract (i.e., framework of agreements) with the group to accept the challenges, one of which might have been "if I become uncomfortable, it is my responsibility to let the group know." Opening questions might have included: "What do you want to gain from today's experiences?"; "What do you perceive might be difficult for you today?"; "What types of support would you like from other group members?"

Second, there was neither immediate feedback nor discussion of feelings. An effective facilitator helps group members discuss their own feelings and their feelings toward one another as an outcome of the activity. Before proceeding to the next activity, they often are encouraged to summarize their learning about themselves, the team, and how this learning can be applied to future events. Failure to do so prevents the development of an open, highly-energized group. In this case, bringing forth the right questions or comments before lunch might have precluded participants from speculating among themselves in small groups, with little guidance or common understandings. I might have asked, for example, "What are some feelings that you experienced this morning?"; What feelings are difficult to express?"; "What feelings did you notice others expressing, both verbally and nonverbally?"; "Do you have any concerns about this afternoon's events?"; "What changes need to be made in order to approach this afternoon's challenges successfully?" To the group's misfortune, however, any good that might have occurred prior to lunch was likely to have been negated by the ensuing haphazard conversations.

Finally, a typical policy on ropes courses is the concept "challenge by choice." This concept allows participants a chance to try potentially difficult or frightening challenges in an atmosphere of support and caring. Also, it allows participants to back off, knowing that opportunities for future attempts will be available. Participants in this scenario, however, were assigned to only one of two high elements, thereby, affording them no choice of challenge, nor much opportunity to repeat an attempt. Indeed, they were guaranteed an opportunity to perform under the watchful gaze of at least 15 other adults. Performance pressures and self-doubts can become magnified under such conditions.

In the debrief, at the end of the day, what strategies and interventions could the instructors have undertaken to increase the positive impact of the experience? Generally, the facilitator was not fully aware of the group's anxieties and needs. In order to salvage the day, rather than focusing on "successful" experiences, the facilitator might have respected the diversity of participants by including questions about "what did not work so well." Unfortunately, the facilitator did little to demonstrate his or her sense of the emotional state of the participants. In fact, I suspect that several members of the group perceived the facilitator as someone who had less than a deep sense of caring about them and their group. This was exemplified when the facilitator put Tina on the spot. She immediately was asked a difficult, abstract question, "How did you feel today?" While having had a wonderful day, she felt awkward about expressing her true feelings in front of friends who obviously hated the experience. Not only was Tina placed in an awkward position, but her friends' more negative feelings were neither valued nor respected in the process.

Nonetheless, if individuals' concerns were explored openly, then any emerging conflicts and criticisms might have been used to the group's advantage in the future. In other words, an effective debrief could have pointed out how today's experiences might best be used in making future decisions (i.e., learning from the experience is of greater consequence than the nature of the experience, positive or negative). I might have asked questions such as: "What did you learn about yourself and the group today?"; "What worked for and against you today?"; "How did differences in the group prove to be a strength/hindrance?"; "In what specific ways will you apply what you have learned from today's experience?" And again, had there been initial goal setting, a useful question might have been: "What goals were you able to meet? Not meet?"

SECTION 9

INDIVIDUALS WITH DISABILITIES
GUIDING PRACTICES

❖

In this section, we begin with a brief discussion of the potential, negative impact that can occur when we label people—specifically, individuals with disabilities. This is followed by a short summary of some important legislation related to people with disabilities that may be valuable for you to be familiar with. Specific questions that you can use to gather appropriate, assessment information from individuals with disabilities for planning purposes are included. Some general guidelines for working with individuals with disabilities, examples of useful adaptations, and a brief explanation of task analysis are provided. Finally, a case study that focuses on a group of students with behavior problems is presented along with a response to the case study by John Guarrine.

❖ THE LIMITATIONS OF LABELS

A great deal has been written about the similarities among people with regard to their needs, interests, and aspirations. Clearly, people are more similar than they are different. However, when discussing the educational and therapeutic needs of individuals with disabilities, the tendency has been to focus on the differences. In a like manner, there has been a tendency to group individuals with similar disabilities (e.g., deaf, learning disabled, blind). The primary reason for this has been the practice of grouping individuals for the purposes of instruction and the need to establish eligibility criteria to receive special education services. But, these practices have created a problem. All too often, people use labels such as the "mentally retarded kid", or the "crippled guy", or the "emotionally disturbed girl" to refer to individuals, rather than calling them Cliff, Roberto, or Meg, like other people are referred to.

While professionals are required to use terminology that facilitates communication, and the federal and state governments rely on definitions as part of an eligibility criteria for special education services, these terms should not be intended to label people. All people are at a disadvantage when the terms become labels to identify them. This point has been substantiated by numerous research studies documenting the negative consequences of applying labels to individuals. Therefore, as you work with diverse individuals, try to be sensitive to the power of language and the impact of labels on people. Use appropriate terms and do not use labels in a manner that is harmful to individuals with disabilities.

The following are two lists of terms—one list contains terminology that has strong negative connotations because the terms focus on what a person cannot do. The second list contains terms that reflect a more positive attitude by focusing on each individual as a person, first. This list has been adapted from The Ability Center, (1988).

Avoid	*Use*
handicapped	person with a disability
cripple	individual with a disability
victim	person with multiple sclerosis (MS)
spastic	person with cerebral palsy (CP)
patient (except in hospital), invalid	person who had polio
stricken with "_____"	person who has muscular dystrophy
crazy, manic, insane	person with an emotional disability
retard, idiot, imbecile, feeble-minded	person with an intellectual disability
birth defect, inflicted	caused by "_____"
afflicted	born with "_____"
wheelchair bound	wheelchair user
blind	visually impaired
deaf and dumb, deaf-mute	deaf
normal, regular person	nondisabled

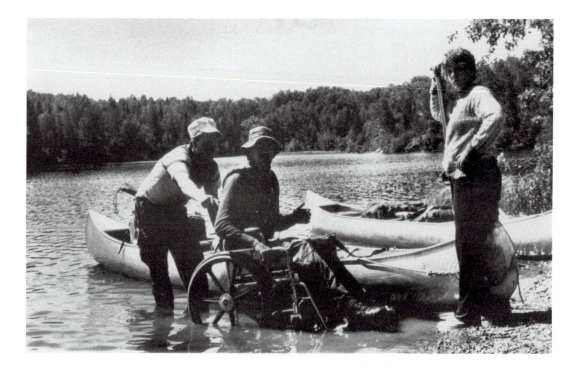

❖ LEGISLATION

Several, important legislative actions have been passed that have a direct impact on experiential educators, trainers and therapists. It is beyond the scope of this text to go into detail about all the appropriate legislation. However, we will touch on a few laws that you should be knowledgeable of.

Public Law 93-112—In 1973, Congress passed the Vocational Rehabilitation Act, which serves as a civil rights law for individuals with disabilities. Section 504 of this legislation forbids discrimination against individuals with disabilities in education, employment, housing, and access to

public programs and facilities, and requires institutions to make architectural modifications that increase the physical accessibility of their buildings. Section 504 also provides all individuals with a right to have access to the regular, education curriculum, extracurricular activities in their local schools, and instructional and curriculum adaptations.

Public Law 101-476—The Individuals with Disabilities Education Act (IDEA) of 1990 was originally titled the Education of the Handicapped Act Amendments of 1990. It was renamed, emphasizing use of the word disabilities, in place of handicaps. It reaffirmed the earlier goals of (a) free, appropriate public education, including special education and related services, (b) guarantees of individuals' rights and the rights of their parents, (c) assistance to the states to carry out these basic goals, and (d) establishing a means to assess and ensure the effectiveness of the efforts of the schools in meeting these basic goals.

Public Law 101-336—The Americans with Disabilities Act of 1990 (ADA) is the most significant, disability legislation ever passed. It gives civil rights protection to individuals with disabilities similar to those provided to individuals on the basis of race, sex, national origin, age and religion. In summary (a) it protects against discrimination in employment, (b) it requires that employers provide specialized equipment needed by workers with disabilities, and to modify facilities in order to make them accessible to individuals with disabilities, (c) it requires various modifications in public buildings to make them more accessible, (d) it requires at least some provision for accessibility on public transit, and (e) it includes various provisions to make telecommunication more accessible. Its provisions extend to such entities as restaurants, hotels, theaters, retail stores, libraries, parks and museums. Private clubs and religious organizations are exempt from ADA's requirements for public accommodations.

❖ ASSESSMENT

As indicated earlier in this text, assessment is an essential component of providing quality programs for individuals and groups. This is equally true for planning programs for individuals with disabilities. Also, noted above, is the limitation of using labels—this is also true for assessment and planning purposes. For example, two people may write on their application that they are physically disabled. While this may be true, this is extremely limited information for you to use when planning structured experiences. One of those individuals may have full range of movement while the other individual has a spinal cord injury (C-4), has considerably less motor control, uses a motorized wheelchair which he operates himself with a mouthstick. Same label, yet substantially different motor abilities.

Noting the limitations of labels and the need to gather accurate information for planning programs, we need to acquire specific data from individuals so that we can try to anticipate their needs. The following is a list of questions that have been adapted from Schlein, McAvoy, Lais, and Rynders (1993) that you may want to consider using to help assess individuals' needs and to ensure safe, quality educational and/or therapeutic experiences.

1. Do you have a disability?
2. Can you walk without assistance?
3. Do you use a wheelchair?
4. Do you have problems with balance?
5. Do you have a hearing loss?
6. Do you have a visual impairment?
7. Do you have problems with pressure sores?
8. Do you need assistance with eating?
9. Do you need assistance with toileting?
10. Have you had any blackouts or seizures in the last two years?
11. Do you have any dietary restrictions?
12. Are you taking any medications?
13. Are you currently under the care of a medical specialist?
14. Who is completing the form?

❖ GENERAL GUIDELINES FOR WORKING WITH INDIVIDUALS WITH DISABILITIES

It is beyond the scope or purpose of this section to provide in-depth information about working with individuals with disabilities. As noted in the beginning of this section, individuals with disabilities are as similar in their needs, interests, and aspirations as you and me. Likewise, they are equally as different as you and I are. Each individual brings with him or her a different personality, diverse life experiences, as well as different abilities and support systems. It is almost impossible for any professional to be knowledgeable of all the characteristics and implications of working with individuals with different disabilities. Consult with other professionals, references, and agencies to increase your ability to appropriately meet the needs of persons with disabilities.

The following is a list of very general points to consider when working with individuals with disabilities. Again, the caveat is that each suggestion will not apply to all individuals and all disabilities. Many of these suggestions draw from the work of Havens (1992).

1. Ask people with a disability what adaptations, special equipment, or teaching procedure works best for them.

2. As much as possible, allow individuals with disabilities to do what nondisabled peers do; promote risk-taking and don't overprotect.

3. Ensure effective communication with persons who are disabled by providing interpreters, large print, and Braille.

4. Hire persons with disabilities to work in your program.

5. Hire consultants to assist with modifying activities and services for persons with different abilities (e.g., physical therapists, occupational therapists, therapeutic recreation specialist).

6. Provide training for staff which focuses on successfully including persons with disabilities in activities and experiences.

7. Develop program manuals that include information about activity-modification procedures, facilitation strategies, and safety requirements to ensure effective participation by persons who are disabled.

8. Openly discuss uncertainties on when and how to assist an individual.

9. Present materials and/or activities in a hands-on, manipulatable manner rather than in an abstract format.

10. Let participants know what you expect of them and how much assistance you will provide.

11. When sequencing activities allow extra time during transition phases. Make sure individuals understand the directions for each activity and have an opportunity to express ideas, fears, and concerns.

12. Make sure that there is adequate time for each activity and structured experience in order to avoid additional pressure.

13. Model appropriate behavior and refrain from words or actions you do not wish to have participants imitate.

14. Reinforce appropriate behavior.

15. Vary the format of instruction using group instruction, hands on learning, independent practice and discussion.

16. Balance individual needs with group requirements.

17. Assume—until proven otherwise—that persons with unintelligible speech understand at a higher-level than their expression indicates.

18. Invite a person who has a disability to review your program and facility.

19. Ask a professional, who represents persons with disabilities and is knowledgeable about the Uniform Accessibility Standards (UFAS), to assist you.

In addition, the information found in Table 19, which was developed by the United Cerebral Palsy Association, Inc, (1992) provides some valuable communication tips for interacting with people with disabilities.

◆ TABLE 19 ◆

Ten Commandments for Communicating with People with Disabilities

1. Speak directly to a person who is deaf rather than through a companion or sign language interpreter who may be present.

2. Offer to shake hands when introduced. People with limited hand use or an artificial limb can usually shake hands, and offering the left hand is an acceptable greeting.

3. Always identify yourself and others who may be with you when meeting someone with visual impairment. When conversing in a group, remember to identify the person to whom you are speaking.

4. If you offer assistance, wait until the offer is accepted. Then, listen or ask for instructions.

5. Treat adults as adults. Address people who have disabilities by their first names only when extending the same familiarity to all others. Never patronize people in wheelchairs by patting them on the head or shoulder.

6. Do not lean against or hang on someone's wheelchair. Bear in mind that people with disabilities treat their chairs as extensions of their bodies.

7. Listen attentively when talking with people who have difficulty speaking and wait for them to finish. If necessary, ask short questions that require short answers, a nod or shake of the head. Never pretend to understand if you are having difficulty doing so. Instead, repeat what you have understood and allow the person to respond.

8. Place yourself at eye-level when speaking with someone in a wheelchair or on crutches.

9. Tap a person who is deaf or hard of hearing on the shoulder or wave your hand to get his or her attention. Look directly at the person and speak clearly, slowly and expressively to establish if the person can read your lips. If so, try to face the light source and keep your hands, cigarettes, and food away from your mouth when speaking.

10. Relax, Don't be embarrassed if you happen to use common expressions such as "See you later," of "Did you hear about this?" that seem to relate to a person's disability.

❖ ADAPTATIONS

Relatively few disabilities prohibit people from participating in an experience, providing careful attention is given to developing adaptations that help bridge the gap between their needs and the demands of the activity or environment. Schlein, McAvoy, Lais, and Rynders (1993) suggests that adaptations can be categorized into five basic types:

1. *Material adaptations*—use a large tire tube to sled rather than a conventional sled; use a large plastic pail instead of a small dish to gather seeds.

2. *Procedural and rule adaptations*—role play situations that may occur on a structured experience prior to the experience; to gather pond samples, work from a dock rather than the end of a pond, and have everyone wear lifejackets.

3. *Skill sequence adaptations*—use a "buddy" to make a transfer on a bus prior to undertaking the experience independently; before a snowshoe hike in the woods, put on the snowshoes indoors.

4. *Environmental modifications*—use a FM (frequency modulated) system with a hard of hearing student; plan to travel on walking paths that are hard surfaced rather than gravel surfaces.

5. *Lead-up activities*—practice interviewing someone in school prior to interviewing a person from the community; learn to sit in and paddle a canoe in a swimming pool before canoeing in a lake.

❖ USE OF TASK ANALYSIS

Task analysis is the process of dividing tasks into smaller steps. The steps then become separate objectives. Many skilled-experiential educators routinely use this approach without thinking of it as task analysis. Task analysis may help you identify (a) what steps are necessary to accomplish the targeted task, (b) where individuals are having difficulty with a task, (c) what should be taught next, and (d) what adaptations may assist individuals with task accomplishment.

Frank (1973) outlines four steps in task analysis:

a. clearly state the long-term goal,
b. identify the subskills of the terminal behavior and sequence them from simple to complex,
c. informally assess to see which subskills the individual already can perform, and
d. start teaching in sequential order, beginning with the easiest subskill which the individual has not yet mastered.

CASE STUDY–STUDENTS WITH BEHAVIOR DISORDERS

Ken and Leah are co-leaders for an adventure program at an outdoor-education center. They are responsible for recruiting, planning, instructing, and facilitating groups on the climbing wall, low-elements challenge course, and the high-elements ropes course. In addition, they coordinate 2–7 day trips that include an array of experiences, such as hiking, camping, rock climbing, caving, snowshoeing, cross-country skiing, service activities, and canoeing.

One of the frequent clients at the center is a local Board of Cooperative Education Unit (BOCES) that provide services for students with behavioral disorders. Twice a year, students from the BOCES come to the center to participate on the challenge course. The goals of the program are to: (1) increase communication skills, (2) increase problem-solving ability, (3) develop alternative strategies for dealing with anxiety, and, (4) cultivate trust in themselves and their peers.

On a clear September day, Ken and Leah were working with a group of 10 students with behavioral disorders, ranging in age from 13 to 17 from BOCES. It was the first time that they have worked with this specific group of students. They were at the center for a short-course experience (2 days, 1 night). Previous to the students' arrival, Ken and Leah worked with the teachers to develop the goals for the program, the activities, a brief outline of the sequence of activities, and some summary material explaining the "challenge by choice" option.

Accordingly, Ken and Leah carefully informed the group about safety requirements for spotting and belaying each other, the value of working together as a team, as well as challenging them to make the most of their time at the center.

After a short session of stretching, the instructors began the day's events—which included: a sequence of trust activities, initiative problems, challenge-course tasks, and debriefing sessions. The initial trust sequence procedures went fairly well. Group members paired off for individual trust drops, and then they worked with the whole group as they played "willow in the wind."

The next activity in the sequence was the "trust fall." Ken and Leah brought the group over to the 3-foot high post that is used for the "trust falls." Leah described the task, carefully highlighting all safety considerations and giving explicit instructions about falling and catching. Then she asked, "Who wants to go first? Gina, a 14 year old, female, said "I'll go, I might as well get it over with." Immediately, Gregg yells out "no way she goes first, we don't have enough people to catch her and that big butt of hers."

Ken and Leah were both surprised and uncertain about what to do. They wondered if they should avoid confrontation and simply say "comments like that are not acceptable while you are here at the center", or sit the group down and discuss behavior expectations for the experience. They could ignore the statement and suggest that the person who seems to be a leader in the group go first, or they could have Gina go first and show them how to safely catch a heavy person. They worried that if they took too much time to have a discussion that they would turn the group off to the entire experience. They worried about the schedule that they developed and feared that if the discussion lasted too long that they would never be able to complete the team-challenge course. They wondered if it would be best to skip the trust fall activity and begin some initiative problems. And they worried, if they didn't take charge now—would they have a course that became a two-day nightmare?

CASE STUDY INVITED RESPONSE

John Guarrine, M.Ed.

What are your thoughts about how to handle this situation? My thoughts/comments regarding this scenario are based on the assumption that there are some staff (teachers, aids, therapists, etc.) who know the students within the group throughout the experience at the outdoor-education center. This is, I believe critical. It is next to impossible to know the most productive response without knowing and hopefully having a rapport with the students. Knowing your group and accurately assessing their abilities is essential for effective facilitation of a team-course experience. It is much more of a challenge to facilitate a group that consistently behaves outside what is considered the norm (by the facilitator). It most likely will take longer to assess the group and establish a rapport with them. Thus, if you can access someone who does know the students (their staff), their input could be invaluable.

I suspect that Gregg's comment is typical of his behavior in the class room. If the team course is to be a metaphor for the "real world," in this case the class room, then this comment could relate nicely to the goals of the program, namely: 1. increase (productive) communication skills, 2. develop (appropriate) strategies for dealing with anxiety, and 3. cultivate trust in self and peers. Thus, the comment *should* be dealt with.

How—depends on what Gregg's intent was, and the effect it had on the rest of the group. It could be an attention-seeking behavior, or Gregg's way of dealing with his own anxiety, or maybe it is his way of communicating his genuine lack of trust in both himself and the group. It may be something totally different, without knowing Gregg, one can only guess. It is also important to observe the effect it had on Gina and the rest of the group. Gina and the rest of the class may be used to Gregg and his comments and just ignore him. I doubt it though, usually students like Gregg know how to push people's buttons and get pretty effective at it. So did Gina retaliate back? Did the rest of the class join in, or do they come to her defense (this could be a good indication of the pecking-order in the class)? Again, how the class responds will most likely be typical of their classroom behavior. To facilitate effectively it is important to take all of the above into consideration and then respond. To respond without knowing the individuals in your group would be like a physician prescribing a treatment without diagnosing the problem first.

I would think that when Gregg made this remark the staff from BOCES would have dealt with Gregg in a manner consistent with their behavior-management program back at school. A natural consequence of this may be that the group gets turned-off, or they will not complete the challenge course. Maybe Gregg is given the option to participate appropriately in this activity or to sit this one out. I suspect that this will be nothing new for this group, and it could provide for a worthwhile debrief. One point that should be discussed is how their behavior keeps them from actually doing what they want to do.

In any case, if I felt that the staff from BOCES was competent, I would communicate with them. Depending on clues from the staff and my rapport with the group, at this point I might give my feedback to Gregg and the rest of the group. I have found that with groups of students with behavioral disorders that a very direct and honest approach devoid of any sarcasm can work wonders.

Once, I had an idea of what was going on with the group and I had the go-ahead from the BOCES staff, I would support them and their behavior-management model. For example, if from my observation of the group and a brief dialogue with the staff, I felt that Gregg was expressing his anxiety regarding catching Gina; I would actively and empathetically listen to Gregg. Making sure that he knew that I heard what he was attempting to express and that his feelings might be very legitimate. Once, he knew that he was heard, and he believes that his concerns will be taken seriously (this is where rapport is so important), we might be able to coach him in a more effective/appropriate way to communicate his feelings. Depending on the response of the group including Gina's, I would involve them as much as possible, all the time modeling effective empathetic/active listening skills.

As with any group, you run the risk of "over processing" the occurrence. Groups with behavior disorders tend to tolerate processing much less than their peers, so I would make sure to monitor their interest and keep the discussion going only as long as it was being productive.

The least of my concerns would be trying to complete the schedule developed for the team-challenge course. At best, the schedule should only be a "guide." It is the mark of an effective facilitator to be flexible and focus on the groups' needs, not the schedule.

By working in tandem with their staff, it will provide a united front, and it should allow me to "take charge" in the most effective way which is to stay consistent with the behavior management model that they are used to.

What suggestions do you have for avoiding situations such as this?

Pre-visit

1. When I met with the teachers to discuss their goals, I would discuss with them the social/emotional levels of their students and then share with them the specifics of the activities that I was considering. I would also ask them for feedback on the proposed sequence and if they could foresee any problems, or suggest any modifications.

2. I would also ask what type of behavio-management program that they had, and if they were planning to continue using it at our center. I would spell out what I expected of them regarding their controlling class behavior, and what they could expect from me.

3. If possible, I would also like to visit the class to observe and maybe do some initiatives to help start establishing rapport. If appropriate, I would ask them "what are their goals and expectations for the experience?"

At the challenge course

1. I would include more activities in the trust sequence (i.e., triad trust catches, lofting and or trust carries).

2. I might have them do low level activities that involved having them lift each other (i.e., the spider web or electric fence). Another activity that I have successfully used to lead up to the Trust Fall is the Wobbly Woozy.

3. I would start with modifications of the activities that would ensure their success. Acting-out behaviors can be a way of dealing with anxiety. So, whatever I can do to reduce their stress, will be helpful. Also, all students—

but especially those with behavior disorders—need all of the successes that they can get.

What are your 6 do's and 6 don'ts for structuring and processing experiences for groups of students with behavior disorders or groups of youth at risk?

Six Do's:

1. Talk to them in an open and honest, age appropriate manner Use "I-messages" and listening skills.
2. Get the group involved in an activity quickly.
3. Be positive. Encourage and praise all positive behavior.
4. Make use of natural and logical consequences.
5. Be consistent. Do what you say you are going to do.
6. Ensure their success by modifying the initiatives to be easier than what you think they can handle. If you are

going to error, error on the side of making it too easy rather than too hard. It is always easier to go back and make the initiative harder. This sends a much more positive message than having to make it easier because you over-estimated their ability.

Six Don'ts:

1. Don't talk down to the students or use sarcasm.
2. Don't take what they say or do personally.
3. Don't compromise your safety procedures.
4. Avoid power struggles.
5. Don't worry about how many activities the group accomplishes.
6. Don't forget to utilize the visiting, school staff. They are your best resource for knowing how the group functions, and what is the most appropriate way to respond to them.

SECTION 10

SPIRITUALITY
THE SPIRIT OF NATURE

Wendy Webb, M.A.

❖

> *"All those who love nature, she loves in return and will richly reward, not perhaps with the good things as they are commonly called, but with the best things of this world—not with money and titles, horses and carriages, but with bright and happy thoughts, contentment and peace of mind."*
>
> —*John Lubbock*

How great are the advantages of solitude! How sublime is the silence of nature's ever-active energies! There is something in the very name of wilderness, which charms the ear, and soothes the spirit of man. There is religion in it (Evan as cited in Nash, 1967, p. 44).

There is an unmistakable stirring that occurs as one steps out onto an untouched snowfall, strolls through a forest of freshly fallen leaves, or listens to the rhythmic pulse of the ocean. An awakening transpires; an awakening of the senses as well as a deeper awakening that alters one's interiors.

The wilderness setting can quiet an overzealous mind, or enliven the creative flow of a psyche entrapped in a stagnated state. Mother Nature can evoke fear, peace, restlessness, and curiosity. She can settle, free-up, or disrupt our emotional state that may have otherwise remained fixed in a pattern of coping with the routines of one's life.

It is here in nature, removed from the reminders of human influence and social pressures, that one's inner-most thoughts and feelings tend to rise to the surface. There is a vulnerability that develops as one leaves behind the urbanized distractions and lays focus on the natural landscapes from which all life flourishes.

Nature often produces an interior shift that seems mysterious, yet undeniable. As Greenway (1995) suggested upon reflection of the wilderness experience: "It is also obvious, to me at least, that I am attempting to explore an experience of such depth and complexity that the terms 'ineffable' or 'spiritual' are appropriate" (as cited in Roszak, Gomes, & Kanner, p. 128). It is here, in relationship to nature, that I have come to know, more deeply, my meaning of the word "spirituality."

❖ WHAT IS SPIRITUALITY?

"Spirituality" is a word that begets connection, a being part of something greater than one-self. "'Spiritual' refers to the experience of being related-to or in-touch with an 'other' that transcends one's individual sense of self and gives meaning to one's life at a deeper than intellectual level" (Schroeder, 1990, p. 25). A person's spiritual beliefs can reside within an organized religious doctrine or group belief, or it can upsurge from an interior source. One may believe in a universal God, many gods and goddesses, or a higher power that may reside within or outside of oneself. It is a faith in which one can trust, receive support and guidance, and find solace. There may be a belief in a universal plan of which one is a part, or a simple reliance upon a power greater than oneself.

❖ MOTHER NATURE

Many cultures throughout the world continue to honor their connection to the Earth in relationship to their spiritual beliefs. Mother Nature has remained the foundation of spiritual philosophies throughout the world (McLuhan, 1994). The Japanese consider their mountains sacred and their gardens pathways of the soul. The essential foundation of the Aboriginal perspective rests on the intertwining energies of humans, animals, and the Earth that they share. Most Native American philosophies and spiritual beliefs focus on their connection to the land.

Many in our culture, however, have lost touch with the natural landscapes within and without. All too often, people become entangled in an inner-war that arises from the discrepancy between who they truly are, and the image that society has projected upon them. As Alan Watts (1958) so aptly stated, "Distorting premises can be abandoned only by those who go down to the roots of their thinking and find out what they are" (Watts, p. xii). I believe that if one can take the time to remove oneself from the confusion of industrialization, there is a natural pull towards the interior self, a connection to the environment, and a vulnerability that allows for a re-alignment to the "real self." I believe that it is within this place of truth that one can begin to hear one's own inner-voice, the spiritual soul that resides within.

A spiritual focus often arises during the processing stage of an adventure activity. Perhaps, it is through the expansiveness of the wilderness setting that the ego's voice is quieted. Individuals are suddenly reminded that they are not the center of the universe, but instead they are a part of something much larger. Simultaneously, there is a vulnerability of being at the mercy of the unpredictable forces of nature, and it is in these moments that one can reside in fear or give into the comfort of believing in a higher power.

As there are multitudes of spiritual practices and principles, it is important that facilitators be open, accepting, and non-judgmental in responding to each participant's beliefs. There are, perhaps, as many avenues to spirituality as there are people with spiritual beliefs. The use of a more generic term such as "Higher Power" tends to be accepted by most.

There is often a focus on spirituality with participants in recovery. A belief in a higher power has proven to facilitate the recovery process. With participants wishing to bring in a spiritual focus, a ropes course or outdoor program provides an opportune setting to emphasize spirituality. As a facilitator, one can use metaphors and focus the processing of activities to accentuate spiritual concepts.

❖ SPIRITUAL METAPHORS

Trust fall sequences lend well to spiritual metaphors such as "being in the hands of others" and "trusting that something is there that you can't see." The Trapeze Leap can easily be renamed "The Leap of Faith." This can be an opportunity to truly connect with a higher power, and process what this experience was like for each person. The Blind Walk has patterns that emerge which resemble resistance to trust in a Higher Power. Questions regarding "the grasp" of their higher power can elicit a learning conversation.

❖ CREATING A SPIRITUALITY FOCUS

Perhaps, more important than a metaphoric connection, the facilitator must uphold an attitude of acceptance, and an ear tuned towards the subtle insinuations that often accompany talk of spirituality. There may be resistance to talk about something so illusive. The intangible qualities of spirituality can create a vulnerability, an awkwardness, as one tries to communicate this experience or feeling. Creating a safe and accepting environment, while maintaining an understanding of this difficulty, may be the allowance needed to facilitate the expression of spirituality.

I believe that as facilitators, we must recognize that, in the connection to the natural environment, there is often a shift in one's interiors, a quieting of the ego, that allows for a clarity where the voice of the deeper-self can be heard. It is here that one may, more easily, be able to connect to one's uniqueness and one's inclusiveness. It is here that people can, perhaps, more easily wade through the imposed restrictions and influences that have molded their lives, and they can begin to come in touch with a deeper meaning to which they are called. "With this connection between human consciousness and the natural world reestablished, people will feel compelled to make the journey back to the source in nature that inspires their work and teaches what contribution is asked in return" (Aizenstat as cited in Roszak, Gomes, & Kanenr, 1995, p. 98).

As facilitators or therapists in a wilderness setting, we are given the opportunity to support the deeper-voices as they emerge. The deeper-voice may be difficult to express as spirituality does not seem to reside within intellectual understanding. It is often within the ineffable, however, that transformation takes place. It may also be upon the witnessing of this heartfelt occurrence that new meaning may arise. As we are able to support the spiritual evolution of the client before us, we may be supporting the least visible, yet the most transformational experience that occurs.

In processing the adventure-based experience, we owe it to ourselves and the individuals that come before us to acknowledge and appreciate the profound effect that nature has on the individuals we work with. Nature has the ability to alter one's perspective on both conscious and unconscious levels. There may be a planned emphasis on spirituality, or it may simply emerge unsolicited. In any event, acceptance, encouragement, and appreciation of what is often unexplainable is required.

Adventure-based programs afford us the opportunity to utilize nature as a profound source of inspiration. Let us honor this resource. Let us have the courage to open ourselves to support and nurture the divine as it emerges within our presence. For each individual, this may mean something different. Let us trust in our ability to uphold and recognize what may not appear as rational, yet may be sacred beyond our understanding.

❖ QUESTIONS WITH A SPIRITUAL FOCUS

1. How do you think that your higher power influenced you during your last activity?
2. In what way is your spiritual connection affected by this setting?
3. How can we, as a group, better support your link to your higher power?
4. At what times did you feel spiritually connected, and at what times did you feel out-of-touch with your spirituality?
5. How did losing touch with your spirituality influence your connection to the group and your involvement in the activity?
6. What would help you to maintain your faith throughout the next activity?
7. How was your approach to this activity similar to your approach to spirituality?
8. Were there certain aspects of this activity that you had faith in from the beginning, and if so, what did that feel like?
9. Were there certain aspects of this activity in which you lacked faith, and if so, what did that feel like?
10. What could you have done to help yourself through the times in which you lacked faith?

CROSS CULTURAL ISSUES
GUIDING PRACTICES

Richard Jenkins, M.A.

❖

It has been stated that all interactions are multicultural in nature. When facilitating experiential learning, it is important to be aware of cultural and ethnic backgrounds in order to provide an optimal learning environment. Both facilitator and participants bring to the experience values, attitudes, behaviors and assumptions that have been reinforced by a set of interactions within a specific group.

Culture can be described as the sum of an individual's values, beliefs, patterns of thinking, behavioral standards, esthetic standards, language patterns and styles of communication. Culture is also a set of learned behaviors shared by and transmitted by members of a particular group.

Cross cultural involvement provides a structure to foster understanding, acceptance, and constructive relations among people of many different cultures. Ideally, it encourages people to experience different cultures as a source of learning.

❖ WHY IS IT IMPORTANT TO BE AWARE OF CROSS CULTURAL ISSUES?

The United States is experiencing tremendous shifts in its ethnic, demographic patterns. Recent U.S. Census Bureau data indicates that by the turn of the twenty-first century, people of color will experience a substantial rate of growth while the rate of birth among whites will decline significantly. The U.S. is also experiencing a tremendous influx of immigrants. This combined phenomena brings new, world views and different experiences into a group process.

With the rise in the number of ethnic minorities and new arrivals, this country will become increasingly pluralistic. Daily, we experience greater diversity in the composition of our work forces, schools, private institutions, and places of worship. With this diversity, there are greater challenges.

Well-intentioned leaders can sometimes be misunderstood by participants who are culturally different from the facilitator because of limited awareness of cross-cultural issues. As a result of this misunderstanding, it is not uncommon for some participants to become hostile, decrease their interactions, or withdraw from the group. It is important for the facilitator to search for innovative strategies, techniques, and different experiences directed at non-majority participation.

Now and increasingly in the future, leaders are more likely to work in cross-cultural settings. It is important for these facilitators to include exercises for people to more effectively live, work and interact in pluralistic settings.

❖ GENERAL THOUGHTS FOR DEALING WITH DIVERSITY

There is an inherent danger in working with multicultural groups when the leader assumes that all people from a specific group are the same, and only one methodological approach is universally applicable to each group setting.

Cultural differences are real and should be addressed in experiential exercises. People within our field must endeavor to be more inclusive in developing their experiential activities. Facilitators need to be prepared to confront issues of racism and oppression as they arise and affect the goals or the interactions of the group. The leader should provide a structure and setting where individuals can address sensitive issues.

It is important to address the issue of terminology used to refer to individual members of a group. The name(s) that people choose to describe themselves and their heritage or group is important to these individuals. Further, whatever term people choose to refer to themselves should

be respected. It is important to note that in any given setting; a group of people may want to be referred to by a particular term. This term does not necessary transfer to the next group of people who have a similar ethnic or cultural backgrounds. Helpful advice for concerned facilitators is to listen carefully to how individuals refer to themselves and other members of their group. Sometimes, these terms emerge during experiential exercises, and at other time these terms occur during an informal setting, such as, during breaks. If, after a certain time, no reference is made which will give a to clue to what an individual considers an appropriate term, a thoughtful, respectful question may be asked. Facilitators who are themselves a member of a group being discussed may elect to share their preference of terms with the group.

❖ DO'S AND DON'TS

Here are some general DO'S and DON'T'S without regard to specific groups or populations, that can be helpful in being sensitive to cross cultural issues.

Do's

1. Create a safe atmosphere for the welfare of the participants and a common concern of participants and facilitators, alike. It is very important for facilitators to raise self-esteem among participants.
2. Refer to individuals as individuals and not as members of their racial or ethnic group.
3. Be aware of "cultural taboos" for the major ethnic groups.
4. Learn more about the dominate patterns of an ethnic group through reading and asking privately what is appropriate or inappropriate behavior.
5. Define the structure of the group and the types of experiences that they can expect to encounter. Then check their comfort level with these experiences.
6. Respect individual and group differences.
7. When communicating cross-culturally test what you are saying with the listener.

Don'ts

1. Never refer to an individual by his or her racial group.
2. Refrain from asking individuals "what do members of his or her group think about this situation?"
3. Never tell ethnic jokes.
4. Don't compare one individual's behavior to another member of his or her ethnic group.
5. Be aware of "touching" issues with specific, cultural groups.
6. Never assume that individuals have similar, cultural experience to that of the facilitator.

Efforts to be politically correct and sensitive to various populations can sometimes backfire. One term can work well with a particular group while that expression can be offensive to others within the group. An example of this follows: referring to a political activist, who may be a bicul-tural or multicultural individual as a "Chicano or a Chicana" is an appropriate way to a refer to them. To others, those terms may be offensive. "Hispanic" is a term relating to people, speech, or culture of Spain and/or the people of Spanish-speaking countries in the Americas. This term is often used by government institutions, the media, health care, and behavioral scientists. Similarly, the term "Latino or Latina" is sometimes a general label that refers to individuals from Central and South America.

❖ SUMMARY

When working with groups, it is important to be aware of the composition of the audience with whom you are working with and their cultural issues. There are no universal truths or formulas to respond to gender and cultural diversity within group settings. All interactions are cross cultural or multicultural in nature. Both facilitator and participants bring to the relationship, values, attitudes, behaviors and assumptions that have been reinforced. A skilled facilitator is able to view each person within a group as a unique individual, while, at the same time, takes into consideration his or her unique experiences and cultural heritage.

P ◆ A ◆ R ◆ T   VI

CURRENT AND FUTURE PERSPECTIVES

Invited Response—*Karl Rohnke*
Invited Response—*John Huie, Ph.D.*
Closing Comments

A prudent person profits from personal experience, a wise one from the experience of others.

—*Joseph Collins*

In this section, we have an opportunity to see the field of experiential education through the eyes of two, seasoned practitioners. Together, they have accumulated more than 60 years of experiential education wisdom. Their perspectives are full of passion, commitment, and dedication to the field. Keep in mind that the first Outward Bound School in the United States was started in Colorado in 1962, so our field is only thirty five years old. Throughout much of this history, Karl Rohnke and John Huie have been leading the way. Aside from both being jokesters and veterans of many Outward Bound and other experiential programs, their stories tell of where the field has come from since it's inception and their concerns for the future. We asked them to respond to some questions. First, we will hear from Karl and then John's response follows.

CURRENT AND FUTURE PERSPECTIVES: INVITED RESPONSE

Karl Rohnke

HOW HAVE YOU SEEN THE FIELD GROW OVER YOUR 30+ YEARS?

Thirty years ago I was employed as an outdoor education, trail teacher for The Long Beach California Unified School District. I resided at the mountain site to which the 6th grade students were bused each Monday. It was my weekly responsibility to lead basic biology walks, emphasizing the importance of ecology and conservation. I've often wished I could have spent those hours on the trail knowing what I know now about adventure education. I'd have been considerably more effective as a teacher and facilitator if I had known about the usefulness of games, initiative problems, trust activities, and the functionality of fun.

Thirty years ago, the "field" of adventure education was unknown to me and the teachers with whom I worked. The curriculum emphasis was entirely upon "outdoor education" and how the five-day, outdoor experience related to what had been learned indoors (classroom) via text books and indoor experiments. Communication, cooperation, commitment, trust, team building, self-awareness—lip service only. Hiking to Kodak Moment areas to "discover" the teachable moment, then droning on about soil profiles, water cycles and the web of life, made up the daily lesson plans.

WHAT AREAS HAVE YOU LIKED IN THIS GROWTH AND FOR WHAT REASONS?

Adventure education existed thirty years ago, but it certainly wasn't mainstream. I think Project Adventure (PA) had as much to do with increasing the profile of teaching-through-adventure as any other individual or organization. PA originally (1971) took the best gleanings from Outward Bound and condensed them to fit a 50-minute high school class schedule. When the students balked at the marginally painful demands, rather than applying the ". . . and not to yield" catch phrase of Outward Bound, the early staff at PA established the Challenge By Choice approach out of necessity and found that students responded with alacrity to the opportunity of being able to challenge themselves, rather than having to perform to an established standard.

- ◆ I like being able to play with the students toward reaching jointly, set goals.
- ◆ I like making fun a functional and regular part of the curriculum (and life) rather than finding fun and play relegated to an extracurricular add-on, a reward, ". . . if you're good and achieve your goals."

401

- ◆ I like seeing physically-deprived students cheer and applaud themselves and their teammates for having just ". . . set a new world's record" at something that's only as important as the moment.
- ◆ I like seeing twenty-year, tenured teachers change their approach, their demeanor and their lives as the result of becoming more adventurous themselves.

WHAT AREAS DO YOU HAVE CONCERNS ABOUT AND WHY?

One of my concerns is that this societies' concern for safety has become insidious. It seems that whenever someone (committee) sets a safety standard, someone else (another committee?) feels obligated to escalate the standard. Years ago, I asked a graduate class, "Can something be too safe?", hoping that they would recognize that you can go too far in applying safety concerns and systems. But no one wanted to answer in the affirmative for fear that they might be thought of as not being safe enough.

It's widely recognized that a single belay works well. Wouldn't it be a better idea to have two ropes, in case something happens to the first one? And, shouldn't we apply a third rope, "just to be sure?"

One of the things that makes the field of adventure education so attractive is that there are literally hundreds of different activities to choose from—to the extent that an entire semester's content could vary from day to day. If you find a particular activity that you and your students really enjoy, the quickest way to kill enthusiasm for that activity is to pursue it, perfect it, keep serious score, establish traditional rules, require certain shoes to play, and hand out trophies for participating. The strength of an adventure program depends upon the diversity of the approach and the content.

I'm concerned about the amount of time "adventure" employees spend in front of the PC tube. I understand that adventure is where you find it, but . . . rather than the scrapes and dings resulting from adventurous mishaps, eye strain and carpal tunnel syndrome are the buzz word maladies of many adventure employees.

WHAT IS YOUR IDEAL VIEW OF THE FIELD FOR THE NEXT 30 YEARS?

I don't think I have one, but I'm hoping that a classic, adventure curriculum never develops. It's well known that as soon as you know exactly what you're doing, creativity ceases to exist.

WHAT DO WE NEED TO FOCUS ON IN THE FUTURE?

I keep four words close at hand for those times when I get programmatically lost. These four simple concepts represent what I hope makes up the large part of an adventure program, thirty years from now.

- ◆ Communication—Talking and listening
- ◆ Cooperation—Working together to overcome an obstacle and making something happen.
- ◆ Trust—Physical and emotional trust; without which the above two will never happen.

◆ Fun—Gotta have it! No matter how significant your subject is, if there's no fun or enjoyment in your message, students will not gladly return for more of what you have to offer.

Until people begin to take their fun and play seriously; i.e., using fun and play as part of their working vocabulary, not much is going to happen in the wide-world of adventure that isn't already part of what ails us. Someone once asked me, "How come you get to have all the fun?" My response was, "Because—I work at it."

CURRENT AND FUTURE PERSPECTIVES: INVITED RESPONSE

John Huie, Ph.D.

HOW HAVE YOU SEEN THE FIELD GROW OVER YOUR 30+ YEARS?

The field of experiential education has changed dramatically over the last four decades. The sheer growth and proliferation of schools, programs, adventure courses, ropes courses, publications, and curriculum guides is in itself the most obvious change in the field. At the North Carolina Outward Bound, for example, we graduated about 400 people in 1977 (nearly all were youths under 18). Today, the school graduates over 4000 students from its four, base locations plus mobile courses overseas, and there are countless variations in course types, lengths, and populations served. This phenomenal growth has in many cases turned small and simple outdoor programs into complex business enterprises with a full-range of marketing, fundraising, management, and business issues. Growth, expansion, proliferation, and complexity are the words most descriptive of the field in the past, four decades.

Because of the proliferation of programs, tens of thousands of people of all ages and walks-of-life can taste the rewards of experiential education. Leaders in the movement such as NOLS, Outward Bound, and Project Adventure can see on the landscape today the full blossoming of seeds planted by many creative pioneers. I can remember 20 years ago when there were no more than 200 outdoor adventure programs in the country. Today the number is surely in the thousands.

WHAT AREAS DO YOU HAVE CONCERNS ABOUT AND WHY?

- ◆ Safety is more important than ever, and it must always remain the highest priority. Vigilance, high-quality staff training, and professional review systems are critical. The larger the movement becomes, the more challenging it is to insure the highest safety standards. The same is true, of course, for program quality.
- ◆ Service as a component of adventure programs is in jeopardy, and in many programs it has already been crowded out. As course length shrinks, the service theme is often reduced to superficial projects like picking up litter on the trail. Wouldn't it be wonderful if today's adventure leaders called for a national conference to generate a renewal of the service ethic in adventure education?

◆ The business complexity of many large, adventure programs, today, often threatens the beautiful simplicity of the student experience. We read Thoreau's words on simplicity at our course openings, then rush to a three-hour marketing meeting at the office. Some of us are more insecure without our computers than we are without a seat harness on belay! We often live in two worlds, and we have difficulty staying focused on the field where the real action is. Sometimes, this puts program quality and authenticity in jeopardy. Program delivery in the field has to be liberated from the dominant, corporate culture back at headquarters. Many of our schools and programs have become very complex, business enterprises—a result of long years of success and growth. Certainly, a major challenge for the profession now is to retain the naturalness, authenticity, simplicity, and rugged character of adventure programming. Down-home friendliness, plain language, unpretentiousness: these are qualities to cherish for adventure programs who want to offer a contrast to the crazy, over-worked, slick, impersonal culture—that we have all around us most of the time.

Adventure programs in the future need to get even more serious about environmental ethics and responsibility to teach environmental sensitivity in courses. Despite our best intentions over the years, we have—in many subtle ways—fostered the mentality that underlies our environmental problems. Conquering nature, bagging peaks, westernizing the vision quest. . . . we have to move even further away from all this, we have to work steadily to give up our arrogance towards nature.

WHAT DO WE NEED TO FOCUS ON IN THE FUTURE?

To find the right balance between stress/challenge and environmental sensitivity in short, intense adventure programs is a real challenge. It has to be addressed very intelligently. Our focus must move all the way from ego-centric to eco-centric, and we have a long way to go.

In the long run, I think we have to acknowledge that the core values of adventure programs: self-esteem, respect for others, and compassion, will take on meaning only in the larger context of reverence and respect for the Earth itself. If we're seeking a mission for the 21st century, the Earth is talking to us. However, as we go about it in adventure programs, we have to make time to create the space for teaching and learning how to live in deep-harmony with the Earth.

CLOSING COMMENTS

"Our answer, must consist, not in talk and meditation, but in right action and in right conduct. Life ultimately means taking responsibility to find the right answer to its problems and to fulfill the tasks which it constantly sets for each individual."

—*Viktor E. Frankl*

Experiential education, training and therapy are exciting fields to be part of. At the same time, learning to be an effective instructor, trainer and/or facilitator is an on-going formidable task. We are required to establish safe, yet challenging, learning environments while simultaneously offering individuals and groups the best of our knowledge, skills, and judgment. Consequently, each of us have a responsibility to develop a variety of tools that can be used to encourage the growth of individuals and groups.

In this text, we provided information that is both theoretical and practical in nature. Our goal was to offer you a foundation of resources from which you can draw-on to refine or expand your processing skills. We know that the

skills necessary to process the experience are complex and at times difficult to implement. We suggest that processing is an artful science, with training required in scientific skills such as observation of events and behavior, decision making, and refined communicative/interactive skills, such as active listening and giving feedback. Simultaneously, it is a form of art, whereby we cannot follow a planned recipe. What worked with one group may not work with another group. As a result, we need to be flexible and trust our knowledge, skills, and intuition. We need to be able to recognize what is happening in the group or with a specific individual and take the risk to ask a question, do an activity, or make a statement that feels right at that moment.

As a trainer, facilitator, instructor, you play an essential role in the lives of the individuals with whom you interact. We encourage you to set personal goals and seek to increase your knowledge and improve your ability to promote learning. If you approach the development of skills for effectively processing the experience in a manner similar to the way that you learn to master the skills to become a seasoned sailor, paddler, mountaineer, trainer, counselor, teacher, or skier, then, you and course participants will grow and benefit from your ability to design and deliver quality learning experiences.

APPENDIX I

REFERENCES AND SUGGESTED READING

Adams, S. (1996). *The Dilbert Principle*. NY: Harper-Collins

Andersen, T. (1991). (Ed.) *The reflective team: Dialogues and dialogues about the dialogues*. New York: W.W. Norton & Company.

Anderson, R.H., & Snyder, K.J. (1989). Team training: Who makes a good team trainer and what should a training team do. *Training & Development Journal, 2,* 58–61.

Argyris, C. (1993). *Knowledge for action*. San Francisco, CA: Jossey-Bass.

Association for Experiential Education (1992). *Ethical guidelines for the Therapeutic Adventure Professional Group*. Boulder, CO: Association for Experiential Education.

Association for Experiential Education Board of Directors. (1995). AEE definition of Experiential Education. *The AEE Horizon, 15,* 1,21.

Bacon, S (1983). *The conscious use of metaphor in Outward Bound*. Denver, CO: Colorado Outward Bound School.

Bagby, S.A., & Chavarria, L.S. (1980). Important issues in outdoor education ERIC/Cress Mini Review. *Outdoor adventure education and juvenile delinquents*. (ERIC Document Reproduction Service No. ED 191 639).

Bandoroff, S., & Scherer, D. (1994). Wilderness Family Therapy: An innovative treatment approach for problem youth. *Journal of Child and Family Studies 3*(2), 175–191.

Bandura, A. (1977). Self-efficacy: Toward a unifying theory of behavioral change. *Psychological Review, 84,* 191–215.

Bandura, A. (1986). *Social foundations of thought and action: A social cognitive theory*. Englewood Cliffs: Prentice-Hall.

Bateson, G. (1979). *Mind and nature: A necessary unity*. New York: Dutton.

Becvar B. & Becvar, R. (1988). *Family therapy a systemic intergration*. Boston, MA: Allyn and Bacon, Inc.

Berg, I.K. (1994). *Family based services: A solution focused approach*. New York: Norton.

Beyer, B.K. (1987). *Practical strategies for the teaching of thinking*. Boston, MA: Allyn and Bacon.

Bisson, C. & Luckner, J. (1996). Fun in learning: The pedagogical role of fun in adventure education. *Journal of Experiential Education, 19* (2), 107–112.

Block, P. (1987). *The empowered manager*. San Fransisco, CA: Jossey-Bass.

Block, P. (1981). *Flawless consulting: A guide to getting your expertise used*. San Diego: University Associates.

Bohm, D. (1965). *The special theory of relativity*. New York: W. A. Beajamiz

Bolton, R. (1979). *People skills*. New York: Simon & Schuster.

Brady, M. (1989). *What's worth teaching? Selecting, organizing, and integrating knowledge*. Albany: State University of New York Press.

Bradshaw, J. (1990). *Homecoming*. New York: Bantam Books.

Broad, L., & Newstrom, W. (1992). *Transfer of training*. Reading, MA: Addison Wesley Publishing Company, Inc.

Bridges, W. (1991). *Managing transitions: Making the most of change*. Reading, MA: Addison-Wesley.

Bridges, W. (1991). *Job Shift: How to prosper in a workplace without jobs*. Reading, MA: Addison-Wesley.

Brody, L. (Nov., 1995) "Are We Losing Our Girls?", *Shape*, p.95

Brookfield, S.D. (1986). *Understanding and facilitating adult learning*. San Francisco: Jossey-Bass Publishers

Brookfield, S. (1996). Experiential pedagogy: Grounding teaching in students' learning. *Journal of Experiential Education, 19*(2), 62–68.

Bruner, J. (1985). Narrative and paradigmatic modes of thought. In E. Eisner (Ed). *Learning and teaching the ways of knowing* (84th yearbook of the National Society for the Study of Education, pp. 97–115). Chicago: University of Chicago Press.

Buchholz, S., & Roth, T. (1987). *Creating the high-performance team*. New York: John Wiley & Sons, Inc.

Buchholz, S., & Woodward, H. (1987). *After-Shock: Helping people through corporate change*. NY: Wiley & Sons.

Caffarella, R.S. (1994). *Planning programs for adult learners: A practical guide for educators, trainers, and staff developers*. San Francisco: Jossey-Bass Publishers.

Caine, R.H. & Caine, G. (1994). *Making connections: Teaching and the human brain*. Menlo Park, CA: Addison-Wesley Publishing Company.

Campbell, D. (1994). *Campbell organization survey*. Minneapolis: National Computer Systems, Inc.

Chafe, W. (1990). Some things that narrative tells us about the mind. In B.K. Britton & A.D. Pellegrini (Eds). *Narrative thought and narrative language*. (pp. 79–98). Hillsdale, NJ: Erlbaum.

Clapp, C. & Rudolph, S. (1990). Adventure therapy with families: The family challenge program. In R. Flor (Ed.). *Proceedings manual for the 18th Annual Conference for the Association for Experiential Education*. (pp. 71–75). Boulder, CO: Association for Experiential Education.

Cohen, E. (1991) *Caution: Faulty thinking can be harmful to your happiness*. Florida: Trace-Wilco Publishers.

Coleman, J.S. (1976). Differences between experiential and classroom learning. In M.T. Keeton and Associates (Eds.). *Experiential learning* (pp49–61). San Francisco: Jossey-Bass.

Colorado Outward Bound School. (1992). *Instructor's manual*. Denver: Author

Combs, G. & Freedman, J. (1990). *Symbol, story and ceremony: Using metaphor in individual and family therapy*. New York: W.W. Norton and Company

Copper, R. K. (1988). *Health and fitness excellence*. Wilmington, MA: Houghton Mittlin Publishers.

Corey, M.S., & Corey, G. (1987). *Groups: Process and practice*. Belmont, CA: Brooks/Cole Publishing Co.

Cousins, E. (1995). Expeditionary learning in the classroom: One teacher's view. In E. Cousins, & M. Rodgers (Eds.). *Fieldwork: An expeditionary learning Outward Bound Reader, Volume 1*. (pp. 12–19). Dubuque, Iowa: Kendall/Hunt Publishing Company.

Cousins, E. & Rodgers, M. (Eds.). (1995). *Fieldwork: An expeditionary learning Outward Bound Reader, Volume 1*. Dubuque, Iowa: Kendall/Hunt Publishing Company.

Covey, S. (Speaker). (1995). *The seven habits of highly effective families*. (Cassette Recording). Provo, Utah: Covey Leadership Center, Inc.

Covey, S.R. (1990). *Principle-centered leadership*. New York: Simon and Schuster, Inc.

Covey, S.R., Merrill, A.R.,& Merrill, R.R., (1994) *First things first*. New York: Simon and Schuster, Inc.

Covey, S.R. (1989). *The seven habits of highly effective people*. New York: Simon and Shuster, Inc.

Cranton, P. (1989). *Planning instruction for adult learners*. Toronto: Wall and Thompson.

Crockett, L.J. & Crouter, A.C. (Eds.). (1995). *Pathways through adolescence: Individual development in relation to social contexts*. Mahway, NJ: Lawrence Erlbaum Associates, Publishers.

Cross, P. (1979). Adult learners: Characteristics, needs, and interests. In R.E. Peterson, (Ed.). *Lifelong learning in America*. San Francisco: Jossey-Bass.

Culbert S. A. (1996). *Mind-set management: The heart of leadership*. New York: Oxford University Press.

Davis, M., Eshlelman, E., McKay, M. (1982) *The relaxation and stress reduction book*. Oakland, CA.: New Harbinger Publications.

Davis-Berman, & Berman, D.S. (1994). *Wilderness therapy: Foundations, theory & research.* Dubuque, Iowa: Kendall/Hunt Publishing Company.

DeLay, R. (1996). Forming knowledge: Constructivist learning and experiential learning. *Journal of Experiential Education, 19*(2), 76–81.

Deming, E.W. (1986). *Out of crisis.* Cambridge, MA: Center for Advanced Engineering.

de Shazer, S. (1988). *Clues: Investigating solutions in brief therapy.* New York: W.W. Norton and Company.

de Shazer, S. (1991). *Putting difference to work.* New York: W.W. Norton and Company.

Devault, C., & Strong, B. (1986). Successful families: What makes them work? *Family Relations, 4*(4), 4–8.

Dewey, J. (1938). *Experience & education.* New York: Collier Books.

Doll, W.E., Jr. (1989). Complexity in the classroom. *Educational Leadership, 4*(1), 65–70.

Dozier, Jr., R. W. (1992). *Codes of evolution: The synaptic language revealing the secrets of matter, life, and thought.* New York: Crown Publishers.

Drake, S. (1993). *Planning integrated curriculum: The call to adventure.* Alexandria, VA: Association for Supervision and Curriculum Development.

Duerlinger, J. (1996) *Career Possible Selves and the Conscious use of a Metaphor in an Adventure Retreat.* Masters Thesis. Loyola University, Chicago, IL

Efran, J. S., Lukens, M.D., & Lukens, R. J. (1990). *Language, structure, and change: Framework of meaning in psychotherapy.* New York: W.W. Norton and Company.

Eitington, J.E. (1989). *The winning trainer (2nd ed.).* Houston: Gulf Publishing Company.

Ellmo, W. & Graser, J. (1994). *Adapted adventure activities: A rehabilitation model for adventure programming and group initiatives.* Dubuque, Iowa: Kendall/Hunt Publishing Company.

Epstein, N., Baldwin, L., & Bishop, D. (1983). The MacMaster family assessment device. *Journal of Marital and Family Therapy, 9* (2), 171–180.

Epston, D. (1989). *Collected papers.* Adelaide, South Australia: Dulwich Centre Publications.

Ewert, A.W. (1989). *Outdoor adventure pursuits: Foundations, models, and theories.* Columbus, OH: Publishing Horizons, Inc.

Fosnot, C.T. (1989). *Enquiring teachers, enquiring learners: A constructivist approach for teaching.* New York: Teachers College Press.

Freedman, J., & Combs, G. (1996). *Narrative therapy.* New York: W.W. Norton & Company, Inc.

Freedman, R. (1988) *Body love: Learning to like our looks and ourselves,* New York: Harper and Row

French, J. (1992). Putting principles into practice: Implementing foxfire in elementary school. *The Journal of Experiential Education, 15*(2), 30–35.

Friend, M. & Cook, L. (1992). *Interactions: Collaboration skills for school professionals.* White Plains, NY: Longman Publishing Group.

Fritz, R. (1991). *Creating.* New York: Fawcett Columbine.

Gaetano, R.J., Grout, J. & Klassen'Landis, M. (1991). *Please talk with me: A guide to teen-adult dialogue.* Dubuque, Iowa: Kendall/Hunt Publishing Company.

Gardner, H. (1993). *Multiple intelligences: The theory in practice.* New York: Basic Books.

Garvin, D.A. (1993). Building a learning organization. *Harvard Business Review* (July–August), 78–91.

Garvin, D. A. (1996) *Putting the learning organization to work.* Boston: Harvard Business School Publishing.

Gass, M. (1985). Programming the transfer of learning in adventure education. *The Journal of Experiential Education, 8*(3), 18–24.

Gass, M. A. (1991). Enhancing metaphor development in adventure therapy programs. *The Journal of Experiential Education, 14*(2), 6–13.

Gass, M.A. (1993a). The evolution of processing adventure therapy experiences. In Gass, M.A. (Ed.). *Adventure therapy: Therapeutic applications of adventure programming.* (pp. 219–229). Dubuque, Iowa: Kendall/Hunt Publishing Company.

Gass, M.A. (1993b). Enhancing metaphor development in adventure therapy programs. In Gass, M.A. (Ed.). *Adventure therapy: Therapeutic applications of adventure programming.* (pp. 245–258). Dubuque, Iowa: Kendall/Hunt Publishing Company.

Gass, M.A. (1993). (Ed.). *Adventure Therapy: Therapeutic applications of adventure program-*

ming. Dubuque, IA: Kendall Hunt Publishing Company.

Gass, M.A. (1995). *Book of metaphors: A descriptive presentation of metaphors for adventure activities—Volume II.* Dubuque, IA: Kendall Hunt Publishing Company.

Gass, M. & Gillis, H.L. (1995a). CHANGES: An assessment model using adventure experiences. *Journal of Experiential Education, 18*(1), 34–40.

Gass, M. & Gillis, H.L. (1995b). Focusing on the solution rather than the "problem": empowering client change in adventure experiences. *Journal of Experiential Education, 18*(2), 63–69.

Gass, M. A., & McPhee, P. J. (1990). Emerging for recovery: A descriptive analysis of adventure therapy for substance abusers. *The Journal of Experiential Education, 13*(2), 29–35.

Gerstein, J.S. (1996). *Experiential family counseling: A practitioner's guide to orientation, warm-ups, and family building initiatives.* Dubuque, IA: Kendall Hunt Publishing Company.

Gerstein, J. S. (1990). *Northern Illinois University Corporate Adventure Handbook.* DeKalb, IL: Northern Illinois University College of Continuing Education.

Gibbons, M. & Hopkins, D. (1985). How experiential is your experience-based program? In R. Kraft & M. Sakofs (Eds.). *The theory of experiential education* (2nd edition). (pp. 135–140). Boulder, CO: Association of Experiential Education.

Gilbert, T. (1978). *Human competence: Engineering worthy performace.* NY: McGraw Hill.

Gillis, H.L., & Bonney, W. (1986). Group counseling with couples or families: Adding adventure activities. *Journal for Specialists in Group Work, 11,* 213–220.

Gillis, H.L. & Gass, M. (1993). Bringing adventure into marriage and family therapy: An innovative experiential approach. *Journal of Marital and Family Therapy, 19*(3), 275–286.

Gillis, H. L., & Gass, M. A. (1991). *An overview of adventure experiences used in marriage and family therapy.* Unpublished manuscript.

Glasser, W. (1986). *Control theory in the classroom.* New York: Harper & Row Publishers.

Glendinning, C. (1994). *"My name is Chellis & I'm in recovery from western civilization."* Boston, MA: Shambhala.

Goleman, D. (1995). *Emotional intelligence.* New York: Bantam Books.

Goddard, N. (1984). *Wilderness therapy: Piercing the heart with the mountain.* Unpublished Masters Thesis, Pacifica Graduate Institute, Carpenteria, CA.

Gottman, J., Notarius, C., Gonso, J., & Markman, H. (1976). *A couple's guide to communication.* Champaign, IL: Research Press.

Hackney, H. & Corimier, S. (1994). *Counseling strategies and interventions.* (4th edition). Boston: Allyn and Bacon.

Hagberg, J. & Leider, R. (1988). *The inventurers: Excursions in life and career renewal* (3rd edition). Reading, MA: Addison-Wesley Publishing Company.

Haley, J. (1976.) *Problem-solving therapy.* New York: Harper Torchbooks.

Hammel, H. (1986). How to design a debriefing session. *The Journal of Experiential Education, 9*(3), 20–25.

Hammerman, D. & Hammerman, W. (1973). *Outdoor education: A book of readings.* Minnesota: Burgess Publishing Co.

Hammerman, D.R., Hammerman, W.M., & Hammerman, E.L. (1985). *Teaching in the outdoors.* Danville: Interstate Printers and Publishers Inc.

Hansen, K. (1990). "Hands-on habitat." *Learning, 18*(7), 38–41.

Harmin, M. (1994). *Inspiring active learning: A handbook for teachers.* Alexandria, VA: Association for Supervision and Curriculum Development.

Harper, A., & Harper, B. (1992). *Skill-building for self-directed team members.* New York: MW Corporation.

Harper, A., & Harper, B. (1994). *Team barriers.* New York: MW Corporation.

Harrington-Mackin, D. (1994). *The team building tool kit: Tips, tactics, and rules for effective workplace teams.* New York: American Management Association.

Hart, L. (1983). *Human brain, human learning.* New York: Longman.

Havens, M.D. (1992). *Bridges to accessibility.* Hamilton, MA: Project Adventure, Inc.

Henderson, K.A., Bedini, L.A., & Bialeschki, D. (1993). Feminism and the client therapist relationship: Implications for therapeutic recreation. *Therapeutic Recreation Journal, 27*(1), 33–43.

Hendricks, G., & Ludeman, K. (1996). *The corporate mystic.* New York: Bantam.

Hendricks, W. (1991). *Leadership series: How to manage conflict.* Shawnee Mission, Kansas: National Press Publications.

Hirschman, J., & Munter, C. (1995) *When women stop hating their bodies,* New York: Fawcett Columbine

Hohmann, M & Weikart, D. P. (1995). *Educating young children.* Ypsilanti, Michigan: High/Scope Press.

Hornyak, L., & Baker, E. (1989) *Experiential therapies for eating disorders,* New York: Gilford Press

Horwood, B (Ed.) (1995). *Experience and the curriculum.* Dubuque, Iowa: Kendall/Hunt Publishing Company.

Hunt, J. (1986). *Ethical issues in Experiential Education.* Boulder, CO: Association of Experiential Education.

Hussmann, T. (1984). The use of high elements in adventure activities. *The Bradford Papers Annual, 5,* 25–30.

Iran-Nejad, A. (1990). Active and dynamic self-regulation of learning processes. *Review of Educational Research, 60,* 573–602.

Jackson, L. & Cafarella, R.S. (Eds.) (1994). *Experiential learning: A new approach.* San Francisco: Jossey-Bass Publishers.

Jacobsen, J. (1992). *Family strengths: Effects of participation in an experiential/adventure-based program for clinically presenting families.* Masters thesis, University of Texas at Arlington. (University Microfilms No. AAC 1351730).

James. T. (1980) *Can the mountains speak for themselves?* Unpublished manuscript. Colorado Outward Bound School.

Johns, F., Liske, K., & Evans, A. (1985). *Education goes outdoors.* Berkley, CA: Addison Wesley

Johnson, G.; Bird, T.; Little, J. W.; Beville, S. (Center for Action Research, Inc.). (1981). *Delinquency prevention: Theories and strategies.* U. S. Department of Justice: Office of Juvenile Delinquency Prevention.

Johnson, D. W., & Johnson, F. P. (1987). *Joining together.* Englewood Cliffs, NJ: Prentice-Hall, Inc.

Johnston, W.B., & Packer, A.H. (1987). *Workforce 2000: Work and workers for the 21st century.* Indianapolis, IN: Hudson Institute.

Jordan, D. (1987). Processing the initiative course experience. *The Bradford Papers Annual, II,* 73–78.

Kalisch. K.R. (1979). *The role of the instructor in the Outward Bound process.* Three Lakes, Wisconsin: Author

Kano, S. (1985). *Making peace with food,* Boston: Amity

Katzenbach, Jon., & Smith, D. (1993). *The wisdom Of teams.* Boston, MA: Harvard Business School Press.

Kayser, T. (1994). *Building team power: How to unleash the collaborative genius of work teams.* Burr Ridge, IL: Irwin.

Kazdin, A.E. (1977). Assessing the clinical or applied importance of behavior change through social validation. *Behavior Modification, 1,* 427–452.

Kelley, M.P. (1993). The therapeutic potential of outdoor adventure: A review, with a focus on adults with mental illness. *Therapeutic Recreation Journal, 27*(2), 110–125.

Kendall, J.C. & Associates (1990). Combining service and learning: A resource book for community and public service Vol 1. Raliegh, NC: National Society for Internships and Experiential Education.

Kendall, J.C. & Associates (1990). Combining service and learning: A resource book for community and public service Vol 2. Raliegh, NC: National Society for Internships and Experiential Education.

Kjol, R., & Weber, J. (1990). The 4th fire: Adventure-based counseling with juvenile sex offenders. *The Journal of Experiential Education, 13*(3), 18–22.

Knapp. C. E. (1984). Designing processing questions to meet specific objectives. *Journal of Experiential Education, 7*(2), 47–49.

Knapp. C. E. (1985). The science and art of processing outdoor experiences. *The Outdoor Communicator, 16*(1), 13–17.

Knapp, C.E. (1990). Processing the Adventure Experience. In J.C. Miles, & S. Priest (Eds.). *Adventure education* (pp. 189–197). State College, PA: Venture Publishing, Inc.

Knapp, C.E. (1993). Designing processing questions to meet specific objectives. In Gass, M.A. (Ed.). (1993). *Adventure therapy: Therapeutic applications of adventure programming.* (pp. 239–244). Dubuque, Iowa: Kendall/Hunt Publishing Company.

Kolb, D.A. (1984). *Experiential learning: Experience as the source of learning and development.* Englewood Cliffs, NJ: Prentice-Hall, Inc.

Kotter, J. P. (1996). *Leading change.* Boston: Harvard Business School Press.

Kouzes, J.M. & Posner, B.Z. (1987) *The leadership challenge: How to get extraordinary things done in organizations.* San Francisco: Jossey-Bass

Koziey, P.W. (1987) Experiencing mutality. *Journal of Experiential Education.* 10(3), 20–22.

Kraft, R.J. (1990). Experiential learning. In J.C. Miles, & S. Priest (Eds.). *Adventure education* (pp. 176–183). State College, PA: Venture Publishing, Inc.

Kraft, R.J., & Kielsmeier, J. (Eds.). (1995). *Experiential learning in schools and higher education.* Dubuque, Iowa: Kendall/Hunt Publishing Company.

Larson, C., & LaFasto, F. (1989). *Team work.* Newbury Park: Sage Publications.

League, L. (9/20/93) "How Thin Is Too Thin?", *People*

Lee, P. & Cafarella, R.S. (1994). Methods and techniques for engaging learners in experiential learning activities. In L. Jackson & R.S. Cafarella (Eds.) (1994). *Experiential learning: A new approach* (pp. 43–54). San Francisco: Jossey-Bass Publishers.

Leider, R. J. (1995). *Repacking your bags: Lighten your load for the rest of your life.* San Francisco: Berrett-Koehler Publishers.

Lewin, K. (1951). *Field theory in social science.* New York: Harper and Row.

Luckner, J. (1989). Effects of participation in an outdoor adventure education course on the self-concept of hearing-impaired individuals. *American Annals of the Deaf, 134*(1), 45–49.

Madanes, C. (1981.) *Strategic family therapy.* San Francisco: Jossey-Bass.

Mallory, C. (1991). *Leadership series: Team-building.* Shawnee Mission, KA: National Press Publications.

Martik, N. (Apr.,1995) "Can Media Images Trigger Eating Disorders?", *American Health*

Mason, M. J. (1987). Wilderness family therapy: Experiential dimensions. *Contemporay Family Therapy, 9*(1–2), 90–105.

Masterson, J. (1988). *The search for the real self.* New York: The Free Press.

McGough, D.J. (1989). *Cispus ropes course specific safety guidelines.* Randle, WA: Cispus Learning Center.

McLuhan, T.C. (1994). *The way of the earth.* New York: Simon & Schuster.

Meyers, C. & Jones, T.B. (1993). *Promoting active learning: Strategies for the college classroom.* San Francisco: Jossey-Bass Publishers.

Miles, J.C. & Priest, S. (Eds.) (1990). *Adventure education.* State College, PA: Venture Publishing, Inc.

Mitten, D. Building the group: Using personal afirming to create healthy group process. *The Journal of Experiential Education, 18 (2)*, 82–90.

Nadler, G. & Hibino, S. (1990). *Breakthrough thinking: Why we must change the way we solve problems, and the seven principles to achieve this.* Rocklin, CA: Prima Publishing and Communication.

Nadler, G., Hibino, S., & Farrell, J. (1995). *Creative solution finding.* Rocklin, CA: Prima Publishing & Communications.

Nadler, R. S. (1980) *Outward Bound and Confluent Education: A demonstration project emphasizing affective learning,* Santa Barbara: University of California, Master's Thesis. (Eric Document Reproduction Service No. ED014254).

Nadler, R.S. & Luckner, J.L. (1992). *Processing the adventure experience: Theyory and practice.* Dubuque, Iowa: Kendall/Hunt Publishing Company.

Nash, R. (1967). *Wilderness and the American mind.* New Haven, CT: Yale University Press.

Noer, D. (1993). *Healng the wounds.* San Francisco: Jossey-Bass.

Nord, D., Connor, D., Roberts, S., Solberg, V. & Scheck, M. (1994). *Career Metaphor in an Adventure Retreat: Effects on Career Self-Efficacy.* Presented at the 22nd International Conference of the Association for Experiential Education at Austin, TX, AEE Conference Proceedings, 98–102.

Okun, B.F. (1992). *Effective helping: Interviewing and counseling techniques* 4th edition. Pacific Grove: CA: Brooks/Cole Publishing Company

Olson, D. & McCubbin, H. (1995). *Family inventories: Inventories used in a national survey of families across the life cycle.* St. Paul, MN: University of Minnesota Family Social Science.

Olson, D.R. (1990). Thinking and narrative. In B.K. Britton & A.D. Pellegrini (Eds). *Narrative thought and narrative language.* (pp. 99–112). Hillsdale, NJ: Erlbaum.

Ormrod, J.E. (1990). *Human learning: Theories, principles, and educational applications.* Columbus: Merrill Publishing Company.

Paris, S. G., & Byrnes, J.P. (1989). The constructivist approach to self-regulation and learning in the classroom. In B. Zimmerman & D. Schunk (Eds.), *Self-regulated learning and academic achievement: Theory, research, and practice* (pp. 169–200). New York: Springer-Verlag.

Paul, J., & Paul, M. (1988). *From conflict to caring.* Minneapolis, MN: CompCare Publishers.

Polkinghorne, D.E. (1988). *Narrative knowing and the human sciences.* Albany, NY: SUNY Press.

Poplin, M.S., (1988). Holistic/Constructivist principles of the teaching/learning process: Implications for the field of learning disabilities. *Journal of Learning Disabilities, 21*(7). 401–416.

Priest. S. (1988-89). A model of G.I.F.T. : A model of group initiative facilitation training. *The Outdoor Communicator, 18,* 8–13.

Project Learning Tree. (1989). *Activity Guide 7–12.* Washington, DC: The American Forest Council.

Proudman, B. (1992). Experiential education as emotionally-engaged learning. *The Journal of Experiential Education, 15*(2), 19–23.

Pugach, M.C. & Johnson, L.J. (1995). *Collaborative practitioners collaborative schools.* Denver: Love Publishing Company.

Quinsland. L.K., & Van Ginkel. A. (1984). How to process experience. *The Journal of Experiential Education, 7*(2), 8–13.

Raths. J. (1987). Enhancing understanding through debriefing. *Educational Leadership, 45*(2), 24–27.

Rawson, H.E., & McIntosh, D. (1991). The effects of therapeutic camping on the self-esteem of children with severe behavior disorders. *Therapeutic Recreation Journal, 25*(4), 41–49.

Real, T. (1990). The therapeutic use of self in constructionist/systemic therapy. *Family Process, 29,* 255–272.

Reddy, B. (1994). *Intervention skills.* San Diego, CA: Pfeiffer & Company.

Rees, F. (1991). *How to lead work teams: Facilitation skills.* San Diego, CA: Pfeiffer & Company.

Resnick, L.B. (1987). Constructing knowledge in school. In L.S. Liben (Ed.), *Development and learning: Conflict of congruence?* (pp. 19–50). Hillsdale, NJ: Lawrence Erlbaum.

Riley, S. (1994) *Integrative approaches to family art therapy.* Chicago: Magnolia Press.

Robbins, A. (1996). Interview with Deepak Chopra in *Powertalk: Strategies for lifelong success.*

Rohnke, K. (1984). *Silver bullets.* Dubuque, IA: Kendall-Hunt Publishing Company.

Rohnke, K. (1996). *Funn stuff: Volume 1.* Dubuque, Iowa: Kendall/Hunt Publishing Company.

Rohnke, K. & Butler, S. (1995). *Quicksilver: Adventure games, initiative problems, trust activities and a guide to effective leadership.* Dubuque, Iowa: Kendall/Hunt Publishing Company.

Roland. C. (1981). *The transfer of an outdoor managerial training program to the work place.* Unpublished Doctoral Dissertation, Boston University.

Roland, C.C., Summers, S., Friedman, M.J., Barton, G.M. & McCarthy, J. (1987). Creation of an experiential challenge program. *Therapeutic Recreation Journal, 20*(2), 54–63.

Rose, C. (1985). *Accelerated learning.* New York: Doubleday

Rose, S. (1989). *The conscious brain.* New York: Paragon House.

Rosenthal, N. (1995, December 21). Experiencing happiness. *The Denver Post,* D-3.

Rosenthal, N. (1995, December 28). A hard look at happiness. *The Denver Post,* D-3.

Roszak, T. (1992). *The voice of the earth: An exploration of ecopsychology.* New York: Simon & Schuster.

Roszak, T., Gomes, M. E., & Kanner, A. D. (1995). *Ecopsychology.* San Francisco, CA: Sierra Club Books.

Rubin, J.Z. (1989). Some wise and mistaken assumptions about conflict and negotiation. *Journal of Social Issues,* 45, 195–209.

Rudolph, S. & Luckner, J. (1986). Outward Bound and the disabled: A personalized perspective. *Palaestra: The Forum of Sport, Physical Education and Recreation for the Disabled,* 3(1), 47–50.

Rueveni, U. (1985). The family as a social support group now and in 2001. *The Journal of Specialists in Group Work,* 10(2), 88–91.

Rummler, G., & Brache, A. (1990). *Improving performance: How to manage the white space on the organizational chart.* SF: Jossey-Bass.

Sakofs, M. & Armstrong, G.P. (1996). *Into the classroom: The Outward Bound approach to teaching and learning.* Dubuque, Iowa: Kendall/Hunt Publishing Company.

Sarbin, T. (1986). The narrative as a root metaphor for psychology. In T.R. Sarbin (Ed.), *Narrative psychology: The storied nature of human conduct.* (pp. 3–21). New York: Praeger.

Schatz, M., Zimmerman, T. & Watson, C. (1994). *Solution Parenting: Looking for small changes in parenting fostered children and youth.* The Colorado Department of Social Services Grant No. STFC93-0230.

Schleien, S.J., McAvoy, L.H., Lais, G.J., & Rynders, J.E. (1993). *Integrated outdoor education and adventure programs.* Champaign, IL: Sagamore, Publishing.

Schneider, K. (6/3/96) "Mission Impossible", *People*

Schoel, J.; Prouty, D.; & Radcliffe, P. (1988). *Islands of healing: A guide to adventure based counseling.* Dubuque, IA: Kendall-Hunt Publishing Company.

Scholes, R. (1982). *Semiotics and interpretation.* New Haven, CT: Yale University Press.

Scholtes, P. (1988). *The team handbook.* Madison, WI: Joiner Associates Inc.

Schroeder, H. W. (1990). *The spiritual aspect of nature: A perspective from depth psychology.* In: Proceedings, EDRA 21: 1990 April 6–9; Urbana-Champaign, IL. Oklahoma City: Environmental Design Research Association.

Schwartz, R.M. (1994). *The skilled facilitator: Practical wisdom for developing effective groups.* San Francisco: Jossey-Bass Publishers.

Scissons, E.H. (1993). *Counseling for results: Principles and practices of helping.* Pacific Grove: CA: Brooks/Cole Publishing Company

Selekman, M. (1993). *Pathways to change.* New York: The Gilford Press.

Seligman, M. (1993). *Learned helplessness.* London, England: Oxford University Press.

Senge, P. (1990). *The fifth discipline: The art & practice of the learning organization.* New York: Doubleday.

Senge, P., Roberts, C., Ross, R.B., Smith, B.J., & Kleiner, A. (1994). *The fifth discipline fieldbook:* New York: Doubleday.

Siegel, M., Brisman, J. & Weinshel, M. (1988). *Surviving and eating disorder: Strategies for families and friends.* New York: Harper and Row

Sharp, L.B. (1952). What is outdoor education? *Journal of Educational Sociology,* 71, 19–22.

Simon, R. (Ed.) (November/December, 1994.) Psychotherapy's third wave? The promise of narrative. *The Family Therapy Networker.*

Smith, T.E. (1986). Alternative methodologies for processing the adventure experience. *The Bradford Papers Annual,* 1, 29–38.

Smith, T.E. (1993). Alternative methodologies for processing the adventure experience. In Gass, M.A. (Ed.). *Adventure therapy: Therapeutic applications of adventure programming.* (pp. 283–297). Dubuque, Iowa: Kendall/Hunt Publishing Company.

Smith, T.E. (1994). *Incidents in challenge education: A guide to leadership development.* Dubuque, Iowa: Kendall/Hunt Publishing Company.

Smith, T.E., Roland, C.C., Havens, M.D., & Hoyt, J.A. (1992). *The theory and practice of challenge education.* Dubuque, Iowa: Kendall/Hunt Publishing Company.

Snyder, G. (1990). *The practice of the wild.* San Francisco: North Point Press.

Stamps, D. (1996). "Are We Smart Enough For Our Jobs" in *Training : The human side of business.* Mineapolis, MN. Lakewood Publications.

Stich, T.F. & Senior, N. (1984). Adventure therapy: An innovative treatment for psychiatric patients. *New Directions for Mental Health Services,* 21(3), 103–108.

Stremba. R. (1989). Reflection: A process to learn about self through outdoor adventure. *The Journal of Experiential Education,* 12 (2), 19–26.

Sweeney, L.B. & Meadows, D. (1995). *The systems thinking playbook*. Framingham, MA: Authors.

Taffel, R. (1996). The second family. *The Family Therapy Networker 20*(3), 36–45.

The Ability Center (1988). *Focus on abilities: A guide to including persons with disabilities in community recreation programs*. Sylvania, OH: Author.

Thoughts on success. (1995). Chicago, IL: Triumph Books with Forbes Inc.

Tracy, B. (1993). *Action strategies for personal achievement*. Niles, Illinois: Nightingale-Conect Corporation

Training: The human side of business. (1990). Minneapolis, MN: Lakewood Publications.

Triumph Books. (1995). *Thoughts on success*. Chicago, IL: Author

Tubesing, N. & Tubesing, D. (1983) *Structured exercises in stress management, Volumes One and Two*. Duluth MN: Whole Person Press.

United Cerebral Palsy Association, Inc. (1992, June, 7). "Ten Commandments for Communicating with people with Disabilities," *The New York Times*, C18.

Voyageur Outward Bound School. (1994). *Instructor handbook*. Minneapolis: Author.

Wagner, R.J., Baldwin, T.T., & Roland, C.C. (1991). Outdoor training: Revolution or fad? *Training and Development Journal, 45*(3), 51–56.

Walter. G. A., & Marks. S. E. (1981). *Experiential Learning and Change: Theory Design and Practice*. New York: John Wiley and Sons.

Walter, J. L. & Peller, J. E. (1992). *Becoming solution-focused in brief therapy*. New York: Brunner/Mazel Publishers.

Wardman, K. (1994). *Reflections on creating learning organizations*. Cambridge, MA: Pegasus Communications, Inc.

Watts, A. W. (1958). *Nature, man and woman*. New York: Vintage Books.

Webster, S. (1989). *Ropes course safety manual: An instructor's guide to initiatives, and low and high elements*. Dubuque, IA: Kendall-Hunt Publishing Company.

Weil, S.W. & McGill, I. (Eds.). (1989). *Making sense of experiential learning: Diversity in theory and practice*. Philadelphia: Society for Research into Higher Education & Open University Press.

Weiner-Davis (1992). *Divorce Busting*. New York: Summit Books.

Weinstein, M. & Goodman, J. (1980). *Playfair: Everybody's guide to noncompetitive play*. San Luis Obispo, CA: Impact Publishers.

Western Regional Environmental Education Council. (1986). *Project WILD*. Boulder, CO: Authors

Wheatley, M. J. (1992). *Leadership and the new science: Learning about organization from an orderly universe*. San Francisco: Barret-Roehler Publishers.

White, M. (1989). *Selected Papers*. Adelaide, South Australia: Dulwich Centre Publications.

White, M. (1992). Family therapy training and supervision in world of experience and narrative, In D. Epston and M. White (Eds.). *Experience, contradiction, narrative, and imagination*, South Australia: Dulwiche Centre Publications.

White, M., & Epston, D. (1990.) *Narrative means to therapeutic ends*. New York: W.W. Norton and Company.

Wichmann, T. (1991). Of wilderness and circles: Evaluating a therapeutic model for wilderness adventure programs. *Journal of Experiential Education, 14*(2), 43–48.

Wick, C., & Le`on, L. (1993). *The learning edge*. New York: McGraw-Hill, Inc.

Wilson, P. (1992). *The leadership series: Change, coping with tomorrow Today*. Shawnee Mission, KA: National Press Publications.

Witman, J.P. (1993). Characteristics of adventure programs valued by adolescents in treatment. *Therapeutic Recreation Journal, 27*(1), 44–50.

Wolf, N. (1991) *The beauty myth*, New York: William Morrow & Co.

Wood. R., & Scott. A. (1989). The gentle art of feedback. *Personnel Management, 4*, 48–51.

Zenger, J., Musselwhite, E., Hurson, K., & Perrin, Craige. (1994). *Leading teams: Mastering the new roles*. Burr Ridge, IL: Irwin.

Zinker, J. (1977). *Creative process in Gestalt therapy*. New York: Vintage Books.

APPENDIX **II**

REPRODUCIBLE TRANSPARENCIES

❖

1. Processing for generalization and transfer   (Figure 4 in text)
2. Edgework: breaking through limits to new growth   (Figure 6 in text)
3. Growth   (Figure 7 in text)
4. Putting edge under the microscope   (Figure 8 in text)
5. Surface feelings and deep affect   (Figure 9 in text)
6. Levels of processing   (Figure 10 in text)
7. Sample of sentence completion exercises   (Table 8 in text)
8. Ladder of inference   (Figure 13 in text)
9. Inference styles   (Table 10 in text)
10. Ladder of inference applications   (Figure 14 in text)
11. Obstacles to solution finding   (Table 11 in text)
12. Seven principles of breakthrough thinking   (Table 12 in text)
13. Adventure-based learning process   (Figure 15 in text)

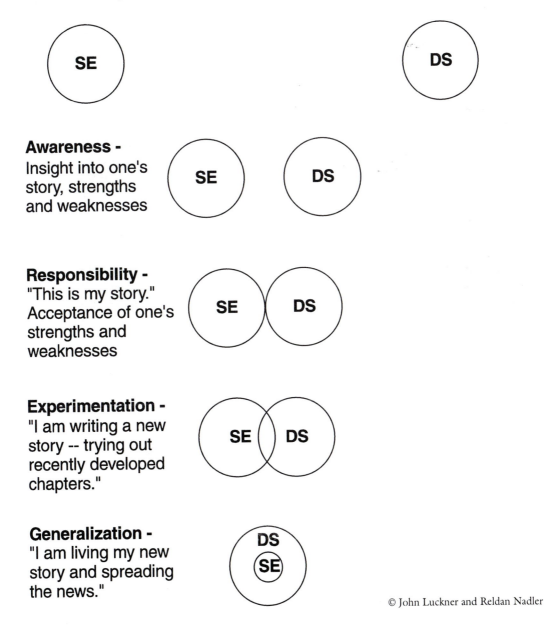

Structured Experience (SE)

Different Settings (DS)

SE

DS

Awareness -
Insight into one's
story, strengths
and weaknesses

SE   DS

Responsibility -
"This is my story."
Acceptance of one's
strengths and
weaknesses

SE DS

Experimentation -
"I am writing a new
story -- trying out
recently developed
chapters."

SE DS

Generalization -
"I am living my new
story and spreading
the news."

DS
SE

© John Luckner and Reldan Nadler

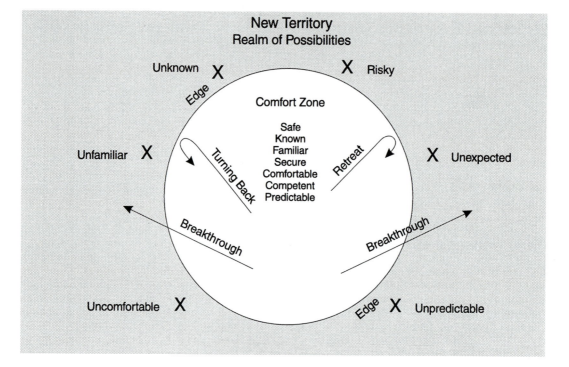

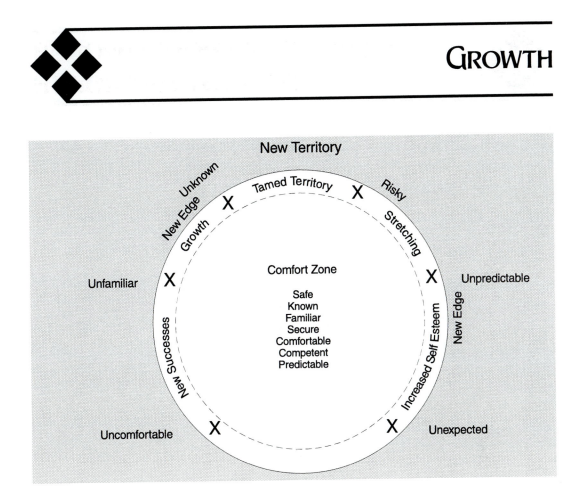

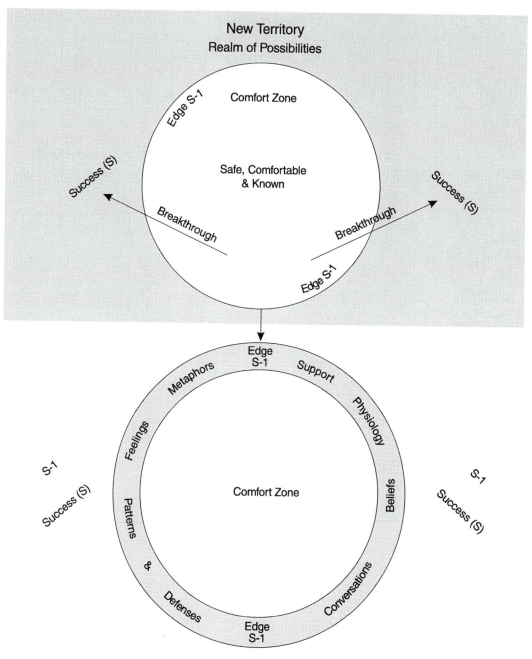

Surface Feelings and Deep Affect

Surface Feelings ·Worry ·Anxiety ·Depression ·Anger ·Good ·Guilt ·Frustration ·Pride

Middle Layer ·Resentment ·Shame ·Betrayal

Deep Affect ·Loneliness ·Grief ·Content-ment ·Hurt ·Fear ·Love ·Embarrass-ment ·Helpless ·Sadness ·Horror
Carefree-ness Rejected Happiness Inadequate
Used Joy Vulnerable

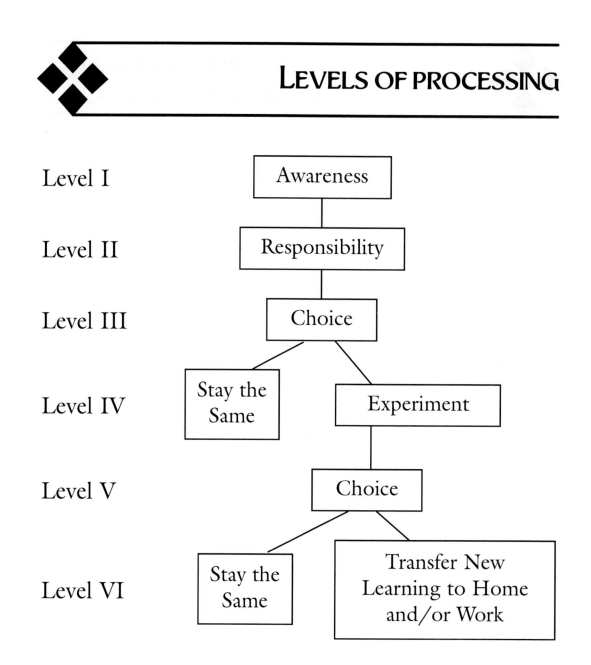

Level I — Awareness

Level II — Responsibility

Level III — Choice

Level IV — Stay the Same / Experiment

Level V — Choice

Level VI — Stay the Same / Transfer New Learning to Home and/or Work

© John Luckner and Reldan Nadler

SAMPLE OF SENTENCE COMPLETION EXERCISES

Today I am

A wish of mine is to

My friends are

Something I worry about

Three turning points in my life have been

Love is

In five years I

The biggest thing that gets in the way of doing the things that I want to do/be is

I get upset when

When I don't like people I

The hardest thing for me to do is

I am happy when

The main, overriding concern at this stage of my life is

My hero/heroine is

I feel important when

Life is

During my life, the goals I am going to accomplish are

During this experience I want to

By the end of this experience, I hope to

Something I wish I could do better is

I find these things easy to do

I find these things difficult to do

Some qualities that I like about myself are

Some qualities that I want to improve about myself are

A decision I'll have to face is

Something I wish people would understand about me is

Other people see me as

The ways I'll sabotage this learning are

Some ways that I can prevent myself from discounting this experience are

GOAL: To make **visible** your thinking
to others as you go up the ladder.

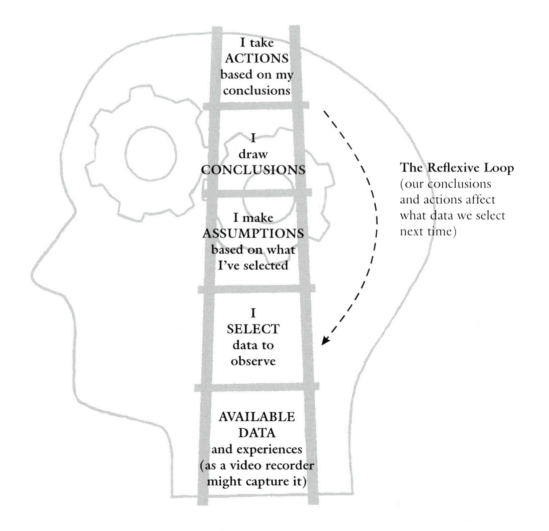

I take
ACTIONS
based on my
conclusions

I
draw
CONCLUSIONS

I make
ASSUMPTIONS
based on what
I've selected

I
SELECT
data to
observe

**AVAILABLE
DATA**
and experiences
(as a video recorder
might capture it)

The Reflexive Loop
(our conclusions
and actions affect
what data we select
next time)

From *The Fifth Discipline Fieldbook* by Peter Senge Charlotte Roberts et al. Copyright © 1994 by Peter M. Senge, Art Kleiner, Charlotte Roberts, Richard B. Ross and Bryan J. Smith. Used by permission of Doubleday, a division of Bantam Doubleday Dell Publishing Group, Inc.

LADDER OF INFERENCE APPLICATIONS

Below are some examples of sentences and sentence stubs
that will help you walk up or down the ladder.

As a Listener:

I hear your actions.
What are they based on?
How did you arrive at these plans?

Tell me what conclusion you are
drawing. . . .
Could it be possible that. . . .

Tell me what your assumptions
are. . . .
I'm curious, tell me more. . . .
Is that the only way to look at it?

What piece are you looking at?
I see you're focusing on. . . .
What is standing out to you from the
data?

Give me all the facts. . . .
What are all the findings?

As a Speaker:

ACTIONS

Therefore, this is my plan. . . .
These are steps I am taking. . . .

CONCLUSIONS

It's obvious to me. . . .
Therefore, I feel. . . .
As a result. . . .// To summarize
Here we go again. . . .

ASSUMPTIONS

So, I'm assuming. . . .
Here's what I attribute. . . .
The next step for me is. . . .

**SELECTED
DATA**

I am focusing on this piece. . . .
Here's what I see happening. . . .
Here's what I'm selecting.
This stands out to me. . . .

**AVAILABLE
DATA**

Here are all the facts. . . .
Here are all the findings. . . .

Pay attention to intentions // Make your thinking visible

INFERENCE STYLES

Each of the following inferences quickly move you up the ladder by distorting, omitting, and altering the data and by falling in assumption ruts when you make conclusions. They happen automatically, and, therefore they are invisible to you or to anyone else.

1. **Half truths:** You state some parts of the situation and leave out other parts, so there is a false understanding of the actual case. Your assumptions and conclusions are stacked in your favor.

2. **Magnification (catastrophizing) and minimization.** You exaggerate risks or percentages, anticipate disaster; you overplay your mistakes or the importance of someone else's achievements; or you erroneously shrink your positive attributes or another person's imperfections until they appear insignificant.

3. **Overgeneralization.** You make a sweeping assumption based on only a shred of evidence, a single negative event becomes a never-ending pattern of defeat. Use of strong emotional words like "always, never, every time, everyone, totally" are used to distort the frequency of events and data.

4. **Oversimplifying:** You make complex situations out to be simpler than they really are. Ignoring the complexity, other's involvement, and how the decision will be made over time can lead to a weak conclusion. Words like, "all that is necessary," " in a nut shell," or "the only thing" are signals you are oversimplifying.

5. **Mind reading:** Without checking to find out the truth, you assume that you know precisely what and why other people are thinking, feeling, and acting the way they do. You quickly leap to negative interpretations of statements and situations even though you usually lack the facts to support your conclusion.

6. **Fortune telling:** Here you jump to conclusions by anticipating a future event will turn out badly, and you act as if this is a predetermined fact, without ever questioning or analyzing the validity.

INFERENCE STYLES

7. **Ignoring the past:** When you predict something you are going to do without ever considering if this has ever been accomplished or happened in the past. The past yields valuable information for future capabilities and decision making.

8. **Insisting on the past:** While ignoring the past can result in poor conclusions about the future, you can also misuse information about the past and not give the new endeavor any hope for occurring. Just because something has happened in the past does not mean that it *MUST* continue in the future. By insisting that the future must be like the past new opportunities can be lost.

9. **Being right:** You *need* to always prove that your statements and actions are correct. You are quick to launch into defensive rationalizations whenever your "rightness" appears questionable, and you distort data and make assumptions just to defend your ego.

10. **Change illusion:** Your happiness and success depend on other people changing their bad habits and "bad" comes from your perspective of reality. You mistakenly believe that they will make these changes if you keep pressuring them enough and then you finally will have more happiness. Their changing is *your* responsibility.

11. **Control illusion:** You either feel externally controlled; therefore, you are always victimized by other people and circumstances. You blame them for your conclusions and actions. Or, you may feel internally controlled, which leaves you always believing that you are the cause or blame for everyone else's unhappiness.

12. **Disqualifying the positive.** You reject positive experiences on the grounds that they somehow "don't count" when compared with the endless list of problems or negatives experiences in your life.

13. **Either or thinking.** There is no middle ground, things are either good or they are bad. Either you perform perfectly or you are a total failure. Many possible choices are eliminated with this kind of thinking.

14. **Emotional reasoning:** You automatically assume that your self-evaluations are accurate and therefore, reflect reality. If you feel incompetent and unattractive, then you must *be* incompetent and unattractive.

15. **Fallacy of the Whole:** This occurs when you assume that because a part of something is a certain way, then, the whole thing must be that same way. There may be some similarity, but to think that it *must* be totally so is a mistake.

16. **Fallacy of the Part:** This is the opposite of the above fallacy. It is to suppose that what's true for the whole *must* be true for ech and every part.

17. **Fairness illusion:** You think you know exactly what is fair in all situations, but you feel victimized when other people often don't agree with you. You make assumptions based on your own set of fairness or principles.

18. **Labeling and mislabeling:** This is an extreme version of over generalization. When things don't go right or you become irritated with others, you emotionally assign a label to: yourself ("I'm a loser"; "I'm an idiot"), another person ("He's a quitter."; "She's a cheater."), or situations. These are based on select events, yet inferred on your or others' whole personhood.

19. **Ultimate reward illusion:** You talk and act as if monumental, daily sacrifices and self-denial are what will ultimately bring you great rewards. You feel resentful when others don't notice what you are doing or the rewards don't seem to come to you.

20. **Vague terms:** This is when you use terms that don't have clear meanings. Terms have many different meanings, so it's difficult to follow you up the ladder. For example, "my boss is not normal." Or "she's in her own little world."

21. **Misuse of authority:** This occurs when you think that a person is an authority in one area and infer that they are an authority in a different area.

22. **Jumping on the Bandwagon:** When you decide because others are doing something, that it's permissible for you to do the same. As mentioned in the mental model section, many people do things without much thinking, so it is a mistake to do something just because others are doing it.